Chasing the Santa Fe Ring

Chasing the
Santa Fe Ring

POWER AND PRIVILEGE IN
TERRITORIAL NEW MEXICO

David L. Caffey

UNIVERSITY OF NEW MEXICO PRESS • ALBUQUERQUE

© 2014 by the University of New Mexico Press
All rights reserved. Published 2014
Printed in the United States of America
19 18 17 16 15 14   1 2 3 4 5 6

Library of Congress Cataloging-in-Publication Data

Caffey, David L., 1947–
Chasing the Santa Fe Ring : power and privilege in territorial New Mexico / David L. Caffey.
pages cm
Includes bibliographical references and index.
ISBN 978-0-8263-5442-6 (cloth : alkaline paper) — ISBN 978-0-8263-5443-3 (electronic)
1. New Mexico—Politics and government—1848–1950. 2. New Mexico—Economic con-
ditions—19th century. 3. Land grants—New Mexico—History—19th century. 4. Land
speculation—New Mexico—History—19th century. 5. Power (Social sciences)—New Mexico—
History—19th century. 6. Political corruption—New Mexico—History—19th century.
7. Societies—New Mexico—Santa Fe—History—19th century. 8. Political culture—
New Mexico—Santa Fe—History—19th century. 9. Businessmen—New Mexico—
Santa Fe—History—19th century. 10. Politicians—New Mexico—Santa Fe—History—
19th century. I. Title.
F801.C27 2014
978.9'04—dc23
2013035997

COVER AND INTERIOR BOOK DESIGN: Catherine Leonardo
Composed in 10.25/13.5 Minion Pro Regular
Display type is Matchwood Bold WF Regular

CONTENTS

ILLUSTRATIONS

PREFACE

The Santa Fe Ring has long been something of a black hole in the history of territorial New Mexico. In 1878, a writer for the *Denver Daily Tribune* referred to the Ring as a matter "about which pretty much everybody has heard a good deal more than they have seen." It is still the case that, while allusions to the Ring are plentiful in territorial histories, specifics have been sorely lacking, and volunteers for the job of finding and cataloging them have been few.

I now understand the evident reluctance of historians to tackle this subject, having spent the better part of a decade studying documentary references to the Ring and its alleged participants, with the intent of writing something that might contribute to a better understanding. The Santa Fe Ring turns out to be a slippery topic, fraught with controversy from the first appearance of the phrase in the territorial press. The notion comes with an abundance of opinions but a dearth of facts. Descendants of presumed Ring members are more numerous than ever. Some still reside in New Mexico. Among them are public-spirited and generous individuals, whose contributions have enriched the state and their communities. The family of Thomas Benton Catron, the leading figure in most accounts of the Ring, comes to mind.

Among the friends that I encounter in archival repositories and historical meetings, nearly everyone has been surprised and interested that I was working on this subject. One of them, a former state historian, smiles slightly and says, "You've got a real hot potato there." Another, doubtful about the whole matter, advises me never to use the phrase *Santa Fe Ring*, unless preceded by the modifying adjective *alleged*. Still another helpful colleague insists that the nefarious deeds of the Ring are indeed common knowledge and urges me to hang 'em high. All such expressions of encouragement, personal opinion, and cautionary advice are appreciated, but I am not optimistic about the prospect of satisfying the varied expectations of these and other readers. I hope that the effort will at least encourage further attempts to better comprehend this important but still murky episode in New Mexico's history. This study should at least provide some grist for discussion and debate. The intent has not been to prosecute or defend those who have been identified with activities of the alleged Ring, but to explore what the designation has signified to contemporaries and later observers.

The work would not have been possible without the help of librarians and archivists who have gone out of their way to locate materials and facilitate access. With gratitude, I acknowledge assistance received from these institutions and organizations: New Mexico State Records Center and Archives, Santa Fe; Palace of the Governors Photo Archives, Santa Fe; New Mexico State Library, Santa Fe; Fray Angélico Chávez History Library, Santa Fe; Center for Southwest Research, University of New Mexico Libraries, Albuquerque; Rio Grande Historical Collections, New Mexico State University, Las Cruces; Eastern New Mexico University General Library, Portales, New Mexico; Clovis Community College Library, Clovis, New Mexico; University of Utah Special Collections, Salt Lake City; Utah State Historical Society, Salt Lake City; Old Mill Museum, Cimarron, New Mexico; U.S. National Archives and Records Administration, Washington, D.C.; Library of Congress, Washington, D.C.; Special Collections, Georgetown University Libraries, Washington, D.C.; Henry E. Huntington Library, San Marino, California; Bancroft Library, University of California, Berkeley; West Virginia Collection, West Virginia University, Morgantown; Haley Memorial Library and History Center, Midland, Texas; Kansas State Historical Society, Topeka; Indiana Historical Society, Indianapolis; New York Historical Society Library, New York; and Wisconsin Historical Society, Madison.

I am also grateful for gifts of research material—transcriptions of the reports of Frank Warner Angel on the troubles in Lincoln County from E. Donald Kaye, and Victor Westphall's unpublished manuscript on the American Valley murders from Walter Westphall. John Porter Bloom kindly permitted the use of his unpublished paper on the Santa Fe Ring and historical treatments of the Ring, and he offered a useful perspective in the formative stages of the work. The voluminous and highly informative works of Ralph Emerson Twitchell and Victor Westphall were resources of special value relative to my subject. These and other chroniclers who have "gone before" are acknowledged with deepest gratitude.

Malcolm Ebright read chapter 6, "The Business of Land," on New Mexico land grants and related Ring activity, and provided thoughtful and well-informed suggestions for that chapter. Robert Torrez reviewed portions including chapter 9, "A Territory or a State?" and provided helpful comments. Richard Melzer read the entire manuscript and offered suggestions that helped improve the narrative and make the material more accurate and readable. Suggestions relative to use of Spanish-language newspapers came from Gabriel Meléndez, David V. Holtby, and Beth Silbergleit. These contributions are very much appreciated. Judgments, interpretations, and factual errors remain my sole responsibility.

At least two important topics addressed in this study, the Lincoln County War and the history of Spanish and Mexican land grants in New Mexico, have received concentrated attention and are the subjects of substantial bodies of research. In discussing the activities of presumed Santa Fe Ring figures with respect to these subjects, I have relied heavily on secondary sources reflecting the work of respected scholars and writers. I am, again, responsible for judgments concerning interpretation and appropriate use of such materials.

Thanks to John Byram, Clark Whitehorn, and all the helpful people at the University of New Mexico Press, and to Jill Root, whose thoughtful editing improved the book. Thanks to Mary Caffey for her love and support through several years of research and writing, obsession with people and events of centuries past, and occasional periods of distracted living.

David L. Caffey

INTRODUCTION

What Do You Know of Its Existence?

In the autumn of 1875, the peace of New Mexico's northern mountains was shattered by the assassination of a young preacher who dared to challenge the prevailing social and political order. Then a series of vengeful murders took more lives and threatened to throw the region into a state of anarchy. These events further inflamed a bitter conflict between residents of Colfax County and a powerful combination or "territorial ring" that appeared bent on dominating the region for the benefit of its members. So insistent was the hue and cry against officials accused of complicity in this and other equally disturbing affairs, that the federal government dispatched an investigator to New Mexico to determine the facts and recommend corrective action. In the course of his inquiry, the investigator, Frank Warner Angel, interviewed a local attorney who was among the complainants. Having elicited the witness's account of circumstances leading to the disorders, Angel fixed his attention on a curious remark. "You have spoken of a 'Ring,'" he noted. "What do you know of its existence?"[1]

More than a century has passed since Angel's investigation, but the question remains pertinent. Across the intervening decades, virtually every historian of the territorial period of New Mexico history, a time extending from shortly after the American Occupation to statehood, has acknowledged the extraordinary influence of the Santa Fe Ring, a combination allegedly based in the capital, but maintaining useful alliances throughout the territory. According to the widely accepted narrative, those entering into this unholy union—chiefly attorneys, businessmen, and territorial officials—acted in concert to exercise control over political and commercial affairs of the territory, to the detriment of other citizens.

Land speculation was said to be the central activity of the Santa Fe Ring, but cattle, railroads, government contracts, mining, and other enterprises also provided opportunities for profitable collaboration. Corruption was assumed. One territorial paper described the Ring as "a systemized organization of rascality."[2] Another said the combination prospered "by adhering strictly to the policy of advancing individual interests at the expense of the general welfare."[3] Nearly all contemporary students of western territorial history would agree with the gist of the latter assessment, and many would go along with the first.

The notion of the Ring as an "organization" is more doubtful. No indication of formal structure has surfaced, neither the kinds of legal and official documents likely to be shunned by underground organizations—such as articles of incorporation, bylaws, membership rolls, and meeting minutes—nor much else indicating an organization with established routines, roles, and lines of authority. The Ring is more commonly described as "loose-knit," "shadowy," and "vague."

In the absence of much factual evidence of the Ring's existence, size, or shape, it is interesting to find normally disciplined scholars tossing off references to the Santa Fe Ring as if its motives and actions were common knowledge. Researchers conditioned to check facts and document propositions feel remarkably free to attribute nefarious deeds to the Ring, leaving their assertions to stand without visible means of support. Such treatment at the hands of critics in the newspaper press in the 1870s and 1880s led those accused to complain that the Ring was blamed for anything and everything that was wrong with the world, including "the low price of wool and the failure of crops."[4] More recently, a dearth of serious examination has allowed descendants of men pilloried as Ring members to say with some justification, "Just show me the evidence."

Historian Victor Westphall was something of a skeptic concerning usual characterizations of the Santa Fe Ring. He noted that the term "probably excites the romantic imagination of more people than any other words in New Mexico history."[5] Yet, said Westphall, "The appellation is little understood, and to the popular fancy brings imaginings of a sinister organization with members dedicated to the unqualified promotion of their own selfish interests." It is the purpose of this book to move beyond the romantic moniker, with its connotations of conspiracy, deception, and fraud, to examine specifics underlying the judgments of early critics of the Ring and later students of western territorial history. Through examination of relationships and events, archival materials, published accounts, and opinions, this work offers a response to Frank Angel's question concerning the Santa Fe Ring: What do we know of its existence? The intention is to probe not only what can be known of the Ring's existence, but of its composition, its activities, its influence, its duration, and its impact as a force in territorial commerce and politics.

Some confounding circumstances are immediately apparent. First, the Santa Fe Ring is essentially a construct articulated by adversaries to describe an observed pattern of relationships and activities; it is not a tangible entity. Second, the enduring impression of the Ring is likewise a creation of persons antagonistic or indifferent to its presumed membership. The connotation—a disparaging one—is widely but not universally accepted by historians. Men accused of Ring involvement have generally denied that such a combination existed. Third, persons involved in the kinds of conspiratorial activity ascribed to the Santa Fe Ring seldom leave a paper trail. Facts concerning the nature and deeds of the Ring are scant, making inference an essential tool of research and the rhetoric of the Ring's enemies a prime source of documentary evidence.

This work proceeds as a history of people and events, and of the construct created to confer meaning on an observed pattern of relationships and activities. The study involves examination of evidence—documentary, testimonial, and circumstantial. Correspondence, administrative records and reports, legislative proceedings, court documents, and judicial findings are valued sources. Hearsay, opinion, political rhetoric, and newspaper bickering are considered admissible, but are presented as such and taken for what they are. Many of the judgments expressed by the author are at least partly subjective, and should be viewed in that light.

Scholars have identified more than one "Santa Fe Ring," including groups that were active before and after the span of time contemplated in this study. These are alluded to in the course of the narrative. The term *Santa Fe Ring*, however, is most closely associated with the combination acknowledged to have been led by Stephen Benton Elkins and Thomas Benton Catron, and that alliance is the focus of this inquiry. The time frame identified for the study, 1865 to 1912, corresponds with the active life of the combination, dating roughly from the arrival of Elkins and Catron in the mid-1860s and lasting until New Mexico's attainment of statehood in 1912. The most active phase of Ring visibility and influence occurred between 1872 and 1884, after which persistent fractures in the Republican Party diluted the combination's political power.

Readers may be struck by the notable absence of women in this narrative. In territorial times, women doubtless were among the victims of legal and political chicanery, but in view of the prevailing expectations with respect to gender roles, it is hardly surprising that no woman was identified as a Ring member in any of the sources consulted. At least three women had the temerity to speak up in opposition to presumed Ring members and activities, and one helped curb the power of the combination, at least temporarily. In the early days of the Ring's emergence as a force in the territory, Mary Elizabeth Tibbles McPherson, a visitor to Colfax County, was persistent and vociferous in alerting Washington authorities to charges of public corruption in New Mexico, including the presence of an active and predatory territorial ring.[6] Her complaints helped bring about an investigation that resulted in the removal of a governor, Samuel Axtell, and other officials. Susan McSween later attempted, with little success, to gain legal redress for grievances in connection with the Lincoln County War, including the burning of her home in Lincoln and the killing of her husband, Alexander McSween. The pursuit put her in direct opposition to Ring figures and their interests in Lincoln County.[7] In 1894, Juliana Chavez of Santa Fe spoke out in a published denunciation of Thomas Catron, whom she believed to be at least partly responsible for the murder of her son, Francisco Chavez, the late sheriff of Santa Fe County.[8]

A note on usage in this book is in order. With reference to Spanish-language names and expressions, the intent has been to use standard or preferred practices in the application of accent marks. This is somewhat problematic, in that there is considerable inconsistency in documentary materials, especially with respect to proper names. Accent marks are used or not used in keeping with the evident preference of the named individual, or are consistent with common usage. The word *Ring* is capitalized as a short form of reference to the Santa Fe Ring.

The Santa Fe Ring has fascinated students of New Mexico history for decades, even as particulars remain elusive. A century has elapsed since New Mexico attained the statehood that men of the old Ring sought. In the meantime, partisan rhetoric has not waned, nor has official corruption been eradicated, but neither has any combination since 1900 achieved the sustained influence or notoriety of the men known to their nineteenth-century adversaries as the Santa Fe Ring. This intriguing topic, so frequently invoked, so seldom examined in any depth, recalls the words of a frontier editor. Inviting discussion of a dispute involving one of the territory's more controversial judges, he advised readers, "Let us have fair play, at all events, and 'see how the old thing works.'"[9]

CHAPTER ONE

THE GILDED AGE, EAST AND WEST

S amuel Langhorne Clemens and Charles Dudley Warner did not invent the syndrome of values and aspirations that characterized the period between the Civil War and the turn of the century, but in a satiric novel of contemporary society, they gave it a name: *The Gilded Age*. In truth, the postwar boom in industrial development, speculation, and large living was not all that far along when the book was published in 1873, but Clemens—Mark Twain—and Warner had seen enough to portray some of its more egregious features. Creating a caricature in words, they drew attention to the unbridled pursuit of wealth, an increasing penchant for speculation, the ostentation of the newly rich, and the discovery of "Beautiful credit!" as a foundation of modern society.[1] Historians of post–Civil War America have been faulted for too great a reliance on the cynical view expressed in the novel, but there can be little doubt that the authors had identified some signal characteristics of the period.

Enterprise and Exploitation

Fueled by the second Industrial Revolution and continuing waves of immigration, the postwar period saw unprecedented growth in population and manufacturing. In the industrial Northeast, and then in the Midwest, cities mushroomed. In the 1860 census, the ten largest U.S. cities had a combined population of fewer than three million. By the end of the century, New York alone had more than 3.4 million residents, and the total for the largest ten had grown more than three times. The proportion of urban residents doubled from 20 percent to 40 percent, while rural residents declined from 80 percent of the population to 60 percent and falling.[2] During the same period, demand for fuels soared. The American steel industry was born, and by the early 1900s it had grown to strapping proportions, leading all other producers in the world. Manufacturing also grew rapidly, increasing fourfold between 1870 and 1900.[3] With all of their problems and possibilities, the nation's industrial cities grew up, attracting waves of immigrants, along with many of the rural poor who chose the city over a hazardous and uncertain journey to the frontier West.

With growth in population and productivity came corresponding expansion of wealth and income. By one estimate national wealth, the sum of tangible assets to which a dollar value could reasonably be assigned—just over $16 billion in 1860—had grown to more than $88 billion by 1900.[4] Estimates of national and personal income showed similar gains.

Boats of all sizes rose with the tide of increasing income and wealth, but they did not rise at the same rate, and many who were struggling lost their boats. Spectacular fortunes were made by some, and less spectacular but still substantial fortunes were made by thousands of others. The emergence of an economy in which manufacturers could produce inexpensive goods for national and international markets created opportunities all along the chain of production—in mineral extraction and production of steel and other basic materials, in manufacturing and transportation, and in finance. The achievements and wealth of men like John D. Rockefeller, Andrew Carnegie, and Cornelius Vanderbilt are the stuff of legend, and they helped put a human face on the phenomenon by which men of ordinary means amassed incalculable fortunes. Opulent homes and lifestyles provided visual evidence of fabulous wealth and prestige, inspiring ambition in some, envy or scorn in others.

The rapid economic growth of the Gilded Age was made possible by advances in technology and transportation, but companies and capitalists also benefited from a favorable regulatory climate and a tax system that supported accumulation of personal wealth. Congress was slow to react to complaints concerning monopolistic practices, and its members were equally reluctant to assume a more active role in management of the economy. Official Washington took its time in addressing the grievances of an increasingly vital and vocal labor force. Urban problems festered for decades in the absence of any significant response on the part of the government. Moreover, the U.S. Supreme Court, during the interval between the Civil War and the new Progressive Era, maintained a posture that was notably friendly to business, rendering key decisions that deflected threats to corporate power.

The rise of corporations holding unprecedented sway over markets and labor created new opportunities for their chiefs to exploit and manipulate on a grand scale. Government, in its reluctance to regulate economic activity, provided a flimsy line of defense. Prevailing conditions invited abuse in the form of official corruption and corporate exploitation of workers and consumers. Some incidents, like the Star Route mail fraud of the early 1880s, rose to the level of public scandal. More common were allegations of graft, price gouging, and monopolistic practices that benefited managers, owners, and not infrequently government officials at the expense of the public.

For some, the government's laissez-faire attitude with respect to internal economic matters amounted to a license for the rich and powerful to run roughshod over the weak in society and to steal from the public coffers. These conditions facilitated the emergence of a new class of robber barons, derided for gains believed by many to be ill gotten and undeserved. In the view of one student of the period, "The unscrupulous capitalist was a product of his age, and he measured his success by his power and control. No one taxed his wealth. No one told him how to run his business. No one protected his labor force."[5] As *gilded* connotes a gleaming but fragile exterior concealing something base underneath, the ostentation of the privileged concealed, and was often supported by, the misery of the poor and the corruption of those whose pursuit of wealth was unrestrained by ethical or humanitarian considerations.

For many other aspiring entrepreneurs, investors, and professionals, for whom personal ambition was constrained by civic spirit and respect for law, the values of the age normalized and justified the notion of economic progress as the signal activity of society and pointed to affluence as the accepted measure of success.

To be sure, the boom in business growth and the increases in wealth, income, and corruption that characterized the Gilded Age did not last forever, nor was the upward trend in economic expansion unbroken. The Panic of 1873, brought on by abandonment of silver as a standard for U.S. currency and the failure of one of the nation's largest investment bankers, J. Cooke and Company of Philadelphia, threw the country into a long and painful depression. A monetary crisis in 1893 resulted in hundreds of bank failures, thousands of corporate bankruptcies, and widespread unemployment.

The Pendleton Civil Service Reform Act of 1883 left much to be desired as an antidote to the spoils system, but it foreshadowed more substantive reforms to come. Likewise, the Interstate Commerce Act, passed in 1887 for the major purpose of regulating railroad rates, fell under the spell of big business and failed to achieve all that reformers had hoped. The Sherman Antitrust Act, adopted in 1890 to curb monopolistic practices, instead preceded a period of unprecedented growth in trusts and monopolies. Eventually the reality of reform would catch up to the intent, as organized labor and muckraking journalists helped hasten the end of a commitment to laissez-faire that precluded any meaningful regulation of business. While it lasted, however, the Gilded Age offered enterprising capitalists unparalleled opportunity to accumulate wealth at the expense of workers, customers, and the public.

Across the Wide Missouri

The expanse of territory now comprising the lower forty-eight states had been acquired by the United States prior to the Civil War. The national map had undergone few changes since the 1803 acquisition of the Louisiana Purchase, but within the space of nine years, the country fulfilled the aspirations of those who advocated expansion to the Pacific as its Manifest Destiny. This was accomplished through the annexation of Texas (1845); a treaty with Britain giving the United States possession of the Oregon country (1846); the Mexican Cession, including a vast portion of the modern American Southwest (1848); and the Gadsden Purchase, a smaller tract needed for a southern transcontinental railroad route (1853).

The conventional understanding of Manifest Destiny emphasizes national ambition and economic expansion, but it should not surprise that an expansion the magnitude of the Mexican Cession comes with unintended, unanticipated consequences. In addition to an Indian population that was small but impossible to ignore, the United States gained a population of new citizens who spoke Spanish and lived under different systems of law and governance. These characteristics, regarded by many of the English-speaking newcomers as marks of an inferior culture, were the same ones that speculators and other opportunists exploited. For Hispanic New Mexicans, Manifest Destiny meant colonization of a homeland they had known as northern Mexico, followed by a long struggle for property and dignity, and the emergence of a distinctive Mexican American people.[6]

If the Gilded Age was a time of exploitation and development, the western territories offered much to exploit and develop. Agricultural lands, grazing lands, timber, and minerals were available in abundance, and cheap if you didn't count the hazard and effort involved in acquiring them and delivering goods to market. The Confederate surrender at Appomattox freed hundreds of thousands of men in the prime of life, many of whom had little to lose in abandoning their old homes and everything to gain by trying their luck out West.

The importance of postwar railroad construction to the development of the western United States can hardly be overstated. By the turn of the century, five transcontinental lines had been built, revolutionizing ease of access throughout the West.[7] Writing about a narrow-gauge spur between the fictional New Mexico town of Saragossa and nearby Ridgepole, Eugene Manlove Rhodes remarked in *West Is West* that exports of the track-end hamlet were "cattle, sheep, wool, hides, horses and ore," while imports from the wider world included "food, playing cards and school ma'ams."[8] On a grander scale, the transcontinental railroads facilitated a similar exchange, transporting natural resources and range-fed livestock to the industrial East, while bringing throngs of settlers and supplying them with an ever-increasing array of manufactured goods.

The prospect of increased settlement and increased productivity attracted speculators, both individual and corporate, who hoped to acquire large tracts of cheap land and reap quick and generous returns. Working hand in glove with the speculators were the local boosters, who advertised promises of prosperity to all who would come to establish ranches, farms, or businesses and contribute to the growth of new towns and territories. A brochure produced by the Maxwell Land Grant Company was typical of promotional materials calculated to attract settlers. Having invested in ditch systems intended to increase the value of its lands, the company promised abundant crops, ready markets, and reasonable costs for fuel and materials, and proclaimed, "This section has the healthiest and most beautiful climatic conditions that can be found in any portion of the United States or the world." An illustration, likely created by an artist who had never seen the area, depicted three men in a boat, afloat on a vast and peaceful lake.[9]

The work of winning the West was not quite finished, as much of the territory coveted by white settlers was inhabited by Native Americans, many of whom resisted the assault on their homeland. Thus a military presence was required for the protection of advancing railroad builders, miners, merchants, and settlers. The presence of hostile Indians was widely viewed as an intolerable hazard and an impediment to progress—a virtue beyond question in the Gilded Age—and the public incurred significant expense in the deployment of troops to remote outposts for the purpose of protecting the aggressors. These conditions created still more opportunities for commercial ventures, since the soldiers and forts had to be supplied with beef, grain, and other necessities, as did Indians who were compelled to become reservation dwellers and wards of the American government. These needs were generally supplied through contracts with enterprising, sometimes unscrupulous ranchers and merchants.

New Mexico offered an additional attraction—an abundance of land grants awarded by the Spanish and Mexican governments prior to the American Occupation. These were protected under a protocol adopted in connection with the ratification of the Treaty of Guadalupe Hidalgo, but many grants were shrouded in ambiguity as to size and ownership, and their creation under alien legal systems rendered them confusing to American courts and judges. The nature of these claims requiring confirmation by the American government invited exploitation of native people, many of whom lacked fluency in English or familiarity with the American legal system. These grants provided opportunities for speculators and for attorneys whose services were needed to secure confirmation. Some grants may eventually have been confirmed as intended, in accordance with the Spanish and Mexican laws under which they were made, but a failure of the U.S. government to competently administer the confirmation process also resulted in erroneous and damaging legal interpretations, as well as instances of deliberate fraud and abuse.

The newcomers were interested in acquiring land, mining claims, livestock, and virtually anything of immediate or potential value. In the words of one observer, "Whether the Westerner was an agrarian, a capitalist, or community promoter, speculation was his way of life."[10]

The Machine

After the Civil War, migration from Europe and rural America to the cities of the East and Midwest accelerated, and massive social and economic change gave rise to a syndrome of urban problems that would become all too familiar. Concentrated in cities and cut off from the sustenance of the land, emerging classes of urban poor and working-class people needed food, housing, employment, transportation, work, and education. When times were good and jobs were plentiful, they managed. When business was bad and work was scarce, they struggled. Municipal governments were ill prepared to deal with the diverse needs of the masses, but a new structure emerged to meet the mutual interests of those who craved power and those who had none. The urban political machine offered an informal but often efficient structure through which individual needs could be addressed.[11] In turn, those who were dependent on the machine for employment and other needs provided a reliable political base that kept the boss and his minions in office. On the street, the machine was personified by a ward heeler—a functionary who had access to influence and who could help his constituents land a job, get medical aid for a sick child, ply the judicial system for leniency, or put food on the table in hard times. The machine was equally capable of denying services and otherwise punishing those who were disloyal to the cause.

Nineteenth-century urban political organizations fulfilled some functions of the modern social welfare state and took the place of government agencies that had not been created or thought of. The machine could be benevolent or ruthless. Many of them operated as businesses, providing services to their political dependents while ensuring a steady flow of revenues to the proprietor and his associates. The revenues generally came from corrupt practices, including but not limited to fraudulent contracts, graft, nepotism, padding of bills and payrolls, election fraud, court fixing, and creative accounting. Under this model, politics could be made to pay well, but the enterprise was not without risks. Political bosses were sometimes toppled by adversaries or prosecutorial do-gooders, and some did hard time for their crimes.

The most notorious political machine of the Gilded Age was the Democratic powerhouse known as "Tammany Hall," for the headquarters of a powerful New York political organization with roots in the eighteenth century.[12] At its center was the Tweed Ring, led by William M. "Boss" Tweed—a group that attracted sufficient attention to merit treatment in Clemens and Warner's satiric novel. Perhaps because of the attention afforded by the New York press and the highly publicized prosecutions of its leaders, the major figures and their roles and relationships have been more clearly delineated than they might have been elsewhere than New York. The heyday of the Tweed Ring was relatively brief, beginning soon after the Civil War and ending in 1871 with the exposure of its activities and the prosecution of its principal members. But what a heyday it was. The Ring's résumé included election fraud, bribery, embezzlement, and large-scale graft on a host of public projects. Its revenues were estimated in the hundreds of millions.

The Ring itself comprised a cozy and complementary foursome consisting of Tweed, whose political power far exceeded that of his official position as a member of the Board of Supervisors, and the city's chamberlain or

Figure 1 Tammany Hall, New York, ca. 1914. Tammany was symbolic of machine
politics in New York, as dominated by powerful Democrats including
William M. "Boss" Tweed in the post–Civil War era. Photo by Irving Underhill.
Library of Congress, No. LC-USZ62-101734.

financial officer, mayor, and controller. Other public officials and political
functionaries contributed to the cause and were rewarded accordingly.[13]
Tweed's accomplishments in aggregating political power by means both formal and informal have assured him a measure of historical immortality, and
by some he is credited with visionary political acumen in nurturing the loyalty of his constituents through advocacy of their interests in labor and land-
lord issues, and in marshaling other assistance foreshadowing modern social
welfare programs. But Tweed's personal fortunes came crashing down with
his arrest and conviction on corruption charges. He died in the city's Ludlow
Street Jail in 1878, at the age of fifty-five, but the phenomenon of the urban
political machine continued in New York and elsewhere, an invention ap-
pealing to some for its efficiency in organizing and administering municipal

services, and to others for its potential as a vehicle for profitable collaboration and personal financial gain.

The Machine in the Garden

In a book published in 1964 and reprinted many times since, Leo Marx considered the impact of technology on "the pastoral ideal" in America.[14] Marx's analysis was innovative, or at least unusual, in his extensive use of literary works to support a historical analysis of the change wrought on society by the introduction of modern technology. In Marx's metaphor, the "machine" implies technology in a broad sense, and the "garden" is the rural or pastoral landscape, including values commonly associated with agrarian societies.

The iconic symbol for technological invasion of the "garden" is the railroad locomotive, a machine that embodied power sufficient to transform landscapes and societies. The ominous and unsettling response aroused by the sudden intrusion and relentless advance of the machine, shattering the tranquility of the rural landscape, was duly noted by Nathaniel Hawthorne and Ralph Waldo Emerson, and by a good many others since. If the machine produced trepidation in some, its possibilities stirred anticipation in the Gilded Age men who understood its capacity for turning the raw resources of a near-wilderness continent into practical, personal wealth. Both responses were evident in the southwestern U.S. territories of the late 1870s, where traditional societies had much to lose and eager Euro-Americans had just as much to gain.

In New Mexico, the railroad had been long anticipated, but its arrival was delayed by the Panic of 1873. By early 1873, rails had reached the southern Colorado town of Pueblo, but not until the last days of 1878 were tracks laid across Raton Pass into the Territory of New Mexico. By this time, many Euro-Americans had made their way to New Mexico in anticipation of the arrival of the railroad and the immediate increase in business opportunities that the event would bring. Among these early arrivals was a young attorney, Frank Springer, who came from Iowa at the behest of his college friend William R. Morley, a railroad locating engineer who spent the downtime occasioned by the Panic managing the Maxwell Land Grant and Railway Company. The progress of the railroad was a matter of intense interest when Springer arrived at Cimarron in 1873, but with the collapse of the financial markets, it was soon apparent that the wait would be more than momentary. The arrival of the railroad did not fail to produce the expected flurry of commercial activity. Anticipation and trepidation were evident when, in April 1881, Springer told an Iowa friend, "The development of this country which I have expected and waited for, is now at hand. . . . It brings a new element, a new class of men, and the situation necessarily calls for a man's best ability, and all his energy, industry and pluck."[15] The machine had arrived.

The political machine had also arrived, in some cases following and in some cases anticipating the arrival of the railroad. The western territories were particularly inviting to the structures and methods of machine politics. While displaying many of the trappings of American democracy—a nominal division of powers and a bicameral elected legislature, for example—the territorial administrative system also incorporated essential features of colonial administration, a fact not lost on attentive students of territorial history and politics. One of the first scholars to acknowledge this was Clarence Carter, who in 1948 published his interpretation in an article titled "Colonialism in [the] Continental United States." From the federal perspective, the system functioned as intended, imposing democratic structures on territories made up of diverse cultural groups, preparing and vetting them for eventual statehood. "As a system for expansion, which had as an ultimate goal the full integration of newly settled regions into the national political structure," observed Kenneth N. Owens, "the American territorial system was a successful innovation in colonial government."[16]

The system may have been successful by some measures, but a model of administrative efficiency it was not. The isolation of western territories, the relatively low prestige of territorial offices, their routine use as prizes of patronage, and the low salaries for officials all combined to render territorial governments somewhat unruly and subject to a variety of ills. In the view of Earl S. Pomeroy, "Easy and dilatory administration from Washington thus gave rise to a claim of independent prerogative," in which governors sometimes saw themselves as autonomous agents of official power, independent of federal direction or oversight.[17]

Among other consequences of its deficiencies, the prevailing system of administration invited corruption and opportunism on the part of newcomers. In the absence of oversight by capable, honest, and attentive federal officials, ambitious local residents could and did exploit the political nature of territorial appointments, the cultural chasm between conquered and conquering peoples, and the geographic isolation of the western territories from Washington.

As the informal power structures found in western territories frequently resembled those observed in the eastern cities, parallels were drawn in popular usage. The term *ring* had come into general use, usually as an epithet reserved for one's political enemies. It became so popular in the political lexicon of the day that in 1875 alone, the *New York Sun* had occasion to refer to the Pennsylvania Ring, the Canal Ring, the Chrome Steel Ring, the Washington Ring, the Whiskey Ring, the Bond Ring, the Crescent City Ring, the Brooklyn Ring, the Charleston Ring, the Packard Ring, the St. Louis Ring, and a half dozen others—in addition to the Santa Fe Ring. In the territories the expression was applied to combinations of men who contrived to manipulate federal appointments, control the voting behavior of the local electorate, and otherwise secure political power and economic advantage for themselves. Such organisms were found in Colorado, Arizona, and Utah—three territories with which New Mexico had much in common. Wyoming was beset for a time by the Cheyenne Ring, while the Dakotas were worked by a combination known to local detractors as the Yankton Ring.

The Denver Ring and the Tucson Ring

The Denver Ring was an indefinite organism with multiple business interests, defined largely by its political rivals. Jerome B. Chaffee, investor, speculator, and political force in Colorado, was an acknowledged leader of the Denver Ring, along with John Evans, a native of Ohio and a physician who was appointed governor by President Lincoln in 1862. Evans's complicity in the Sand Creek Massacre led to his ouster as governor in 1865, but he continued promoting railroad construction and other enterprises in Colorado. Chaffee and Evans were prominent Republicans. By the early 1870s, newspapers favoring the Democrats had begun referring to the two and their associates, including banker and railroad promoter David Moffatt, as the "Denver Ring," the "Denver Crowd," or the "railroad ring."[18]

Among other things, the Denver Ring was accused of applying a bait-and-switch maneuver to the people of Clear Creek County in 1872, working voters for $200,000 in bonds for their proposed Denver, Georgetown and Utah Railway, then changing the location of the proposed route to the detriment of many who had voted for the proposal.[19] In 1874, the *Denver Mirror* reported on the findings of three hopeful agrarians who ventured south to the drainage of the Rio Grande and the San Luis Valley in search of land available for homestead or preemption. What the travelers found was that all

Figure 2 A territorial delegate and later
United States senator from Colorado,
Jerome Bunty Chaffee was heavily
involved in activities widely associated
with the "Denver Ring" and New
Mexico's Santa Fe Ring. Photo ca. 1876.
Brady-Handy Collection, Library of
Congress, No. LC-DIG-cwpbh-05095.

desirable tracts, including those affording access to water, had been gobbled
up by an agent for the Denver Ring—more than 6,000 acres.[20] The acreage
involved may have been considerably in excess of that reported by the *Mirror*,
for in October 1875, the *Colorado Daily Chieftain* of Pueblo reported that the
ring, supported by a corrupt federal marshal, "took up twenty-three sections
of homestead lands, through fictitious names being used in the entries." The
lands so acquired reportedly had been conveyed to D. H. Moffatt and
Company, and the matter was then under investigation by a federal agent.[21]
Whatever the facts in these cases of alleged double-dealing, fraud, and official corruption, they fed the popular notion that powerful men were hard at
work appropriating public resources for private gain.

   Better documented are the efforts of Chaffee and Evans to secure
Colorado's admission to the Union. Both had staked out large political prizes
for themselves in the event of success. In the view of Howard Roberts Lamar,
"The cause, and Chaffee's own considerable political talents, combined to
make him virtual boss of the territory from 1870 to 1876," when Colorado
attained statehood and Chaffee realized his ambition of becoming one of the
state's first United States senators.[22]

   The Tucson Ring was a force in the Territory of Arizona from the early
1870s until the mid-1880s. It was similar to other Gilded Age political ma-
chines of the West in its indefinite character and composition, and in the
principal objectives of its leaders in wielding power and making money, but

the scope of its activities was narrow compared to that of combinations in other territories. The Tucson Ring was known primarily for its exploitation of Arizona's Apache Indian population and of the military garrisons maintained for the purpose of protecting the territory's non-Indian residents. Leading lights in this combination were merchants who profited from contracts for the supply of goods to reservations and military posts, along with the federal officials who shared in their schemes. Odie B. Faulk, a vocal critic of the Tucson Ring, notes that dishonest merchants routinely entered into agreements with Indian agents "to furnish substandard rations at standard prices, splitting the profits." But, according to Faulk, this was not the worst of it: "Sometimes, with the aid of a reservation agent, they furnished no rations at all and pocketed the money."[23]

Arizona's Apaches were caught in a tragic struggle between corrupt commercial interests and the occasional Indian agent or military commander who understood their plight and could formulate and advocate sound policy. Seldom did honor triumph over the profit motive. Vincent Colyer, secretary of the Board of Indian Commissioners, was committed to a peace policy and believed that the Apaches would take up a pastoral existence and become self-sufficient, given the chance to do so. They were not given the chance, however, for in 1875, a new directive was issued, calling for transfer of diverse, often incompatible bands of Indians from tracts scattered over the southern two-thirds of the territory to a smaller number of reservations on which they would be concentrated. Sympathetic observers, including the eminently capable George Crook, saw the fine hand of the Tucson Ring in the new policy. With Indians at Camp Verde clearing land, building irrigation works, and giving evidence of intent to produce food and perhaps attain self-sufficiency, the merchants saw a threat. According to Jay J. Wagoner, "The selfish reasoning of the 'Tucson Ring' was that contractors couldn't make enormous amounts of money selling supplies to the agencies if the Indians supported themselves."[24]

Crook was among a handful of "humanitarian generals" who advocated and attempted to implement Indian policies that were progressive and just, often against long odds and the zealous opposition of men who profited from paternalistic and oppressive policies.[25] The chronicler of Crook's Arizona exploits, John Gregory Bourke, drew a parallel between the famous Tweed Ring and the lesser-known Tucson Ring, repeating a New York alderman's explanation of the ring's objectives: "The 'boys' are in it for the stuff." The Arizona men were in it for "the stuff" too, as Bourke explained: "The 'Tucson

Ring' was determined that no Apache should be put to the embarrassment of working for his own living; once let the Apaches become self-supporting, and what would become of 'the boys'?"[26]

Worse yet, the Tucson Ring was accused of cultivating public hatred of the Apaches and fomenting violent conflict for the sole purpose of maintaining a large and profitable military presence in the territory. Among other things, it was charged that ring agents incited the Indians to flight or rebellion, plying them with quantities of whiskey and, in one instance, spreading the rumor that the Chiricahua leader Geronimo would be hanged if he surrendered to U.S. troops.[27] The conflict was sustained until Geronimo surrendered in September 1886, and a military presence, with its cornucopia of military supply contracts, was assured. As there were benevolent generals in the Southwest, there were also conscientious Indian agents like John Clum, who introduced self-government to the Apaches of Arizona, but such altruistic efforts were easily negated by officials whose interests lay elsewhere.

Opportunity and Opportunists

Following a series of territorial acquisitions, ratification of the Treaty of Guadalupe Hidalgo, and the end of the Civil War, a set of conditions that were common throughout the West produced common opportunities in most of the western territories. With expansion came the potential for acquisition of land, exploitation of natural resources, pursuit of new business enterprises, and speculation—all in a region in which rapid growth was expected.

Newcomers from the states enjoyed distinct advantages with respect to law and commerce. They were familiar with American systems of law and government and fluent in the English language, in which most official business was conducted. Many were well educated and experienced in business; an inordinate number were attorneys, and others took up the profession after they arrived. Immigrants of the professional class were generally ambitious and enjoyed varying degrees of affinity with the new territorial governments and their politically appointed officials—often working to influence political appointments and befriend new appointees.

The construction of railroads to and through the western territories created opportunities for colonization and settlement, and for trade beyond the immediate region. With the application of moderate amounts of ingenuity, capital, and in some cases legal and political chicanery, the new territories could be made to function as colonies, subjugating a ready-made underclass and yielding wealth to a privileged few.

Recognizing opportunities available in the West, speculators, entrepreneurs, professional men, and home-seeking settlers migrated to the territories. Many of these were second- and third-generation pioneers, and some were fortune seekers. Tradition holds that some were fleeing legal difficulties in the states they had come from. A large contingent of war veterans, many of them introduced to New Mexico through their service with General James Carleton's California Column, stayed to try their luck at business, ranching, and politics. Among those who settled in southern New Mexico were William Logan Rynerson, Emil Fritz, George Peppin, Richard Hudson, and Albert Jennings Fountain, all of whom assumed active roles in political and business affairs of the territory.

Howard Lamar has observed that "the Santa Fe Ring in New Mexico, the Evans-Chaffee machine in Colorado, the Mormon hierarchy in Utah, and the Safford-McCormick federal ring in Arizona all played economic and political roles that were strikingly similar."[28] All benefited from the relative isolation of the western territories, and from territorial administrations that were steeped in the politics of patronage and prone to corruption. Though the specific nature of their economic interests varied, such alliances were typically drawn to new economic opportunities, including fulfillment of supply contracts for Indian reservations and military posts, construction of railroads, and, especially in New Mexico, acquisition of land grants.

The successful combination tended to be a "flexible and open-ended frontier oligarchy" rather than a closed corporation monogamously affiliated with a single political party. It could incorporate new actors of varied political and ethnic persuasions, depending on the situation and the opportunity. Its object was economic and political control. Principals in the ruling coalition formed alliances—political and sometimes financial—with key territorial officials, including the governor, the territorial secretary, the chief justice, and, especially in New Mexico, the surveyor general. A strong newspaper was a common and desirable accessory, useful in cultivating public opinion that favored or at least tolerated the dominance of the elite. The *Arizona Miner* and the *Arizona Citizen* did the bidding of the territorial ring in Arizona.[29] In Santa Fe, the *New Mexican* performed this function. The territorial rings had their detractors, but there were also grudging admirers, for whom the combination's ability to attract capital and secure favorable attention in Washington more than made up for its heavy-handed methods.

The visionary Americans who attained dominance in New Mexico may have learned some rudimentary lessons from their associates in adjacent territories, but by the time they were done, they had far exceeded the reputations of the combinations in Arizona, Colorado, and Utah. Reasons for the extraordinary notoriety and durability of the Santa Fe Ring may be complicated, but they would include the diversity of economic activities in which its principals were engaged, and the strength and stability of its leadership over a period of several decades. Born of ambition and nurtured on opportunities found in a frontier society in which they held clear advantages, the leaders of the territorial ring provided an essential if informal structure for cooperation among ambitious newcomers and similarly inclined native residents who sought power and fortune in the borderlands of the new American Southwest.

CHAPTER TWO

A RING IS FORMED

"The word 'ring' conjures up images of Tammany Hall—of an efficiently oiled political machine dispensing favors, extorting bribes, and swiftly punishing honesty and other treachery," wrote Joel Jacobsen, who did not see any such structure or efficiency in the Santa Fe Ring. Said Jacobsen, "The Ring is best understood as an informal confederation of businessmen/politicians swapping favors and telling no tales."[1] His notion is consistent with those of most other students of New Mexico's territorial period and is reinforced by the gradual and organic nature of the Ring's emergence—a process nearer to cloud formation than to corporate organization.

The presence of a territorial political ring was established in the public consciousness, and especially in the minds of its adversaries, over a period of several years in the post–Civil War era, but its roots were deeper. G. Emlen Hall notes the presence of an "early Santa Fe land grant ring" that operated in the 1850s and 1860s, predating the Santa Fe Ring of Elkins and Catron.[2] One of the principals was Donaciano Vigil, a political official and military officer under the Mexican regime, and the second civil governor following the American Occupation.[3] Among others pursuing wealth through acquisition and confirmation of land-grant interests during this period were several American-born lawyers, including Joab Houghton, John S. Watts, and Merrill Ashurst, all of whom held territorial and federal offices. According to Victor Westphall, an even earlier iteration of the Ring was discernible in a group known as the American Party. Participants including Charles Bent, Charles Beaubien, Luis Lee, and Ceran St. Vrain combined forces to pursue large grants of land from the Mexican government.[4] After the Occupation, the potential for manipulation of land claims was enhanced by the adoption of an inefficient title confirmation process that invited corruption.

The most active and visible phase of alleged Ring domination in territorial affairs occurred between 1872 and 1884. By the time the Colfax County

War erupted in 1875, the combination based in Santa Fe had been identified as the source of assorted scams and self-serving legislative feats. The involvement of persons commonly identified with the Ring in the contentious and highly publicized troubles in Colfax and Lincoln counties served to fix, in the minds of many residents, a distinct impression of the Santa Fe Ring as a menace to the territory.

While kindred spirits were found among the native New Mexican population, the combination known as the Santa Fe Ring originated as a confederation of ambitious newcomers. During the years of its active life, more than seventy-five men were named by aggrieved parties or members of rival political factions as members of the Ring. Most of them were named on the basis of involvement in the context of a brief or limited business activity, or an apparent political connection with more prominent Ring figures.

A smaller number of men were regularly associated in business and political activity over an extended period, in some cases for decades. What these men had in common—what most of them had in abundance—was an unswerving commitment to the values of the Gilded Age. They believed in economic progress as the signal virtue of civilized society and in wealth as the accepted object of personal effort. They were competitive by nature—obsessively, in some instances—and they were looking for opportunity. By 1869, most of those who would form the core of the Ring were present in the territory.

Men from Missouri

Human geographers sometimes refer to "channelized migration," a tendency for groups of individuals from one locale to migrate to a common destination on the basis of shared history and culture, economic interests, existing relationships, or some other affinity. Something of this nature occurred with respect to the formation of the territorial ring in New Mexico.

The trail from western Missouri to Santa Fe was well worn long before Stephen Elkins and Thomas Catron arrived in the territory. The Santa Fe Trail, dating from 1821, remained the major commercial route linking New Mexico and the United States until the early 1880s, when it was supplanted by the railroad.[5] Doubtless the trail beckoned travelers from the western Missouri region from which at least four western emigrant trails diverged. Trails led away to the West and Southwest from several points on the Missouri River, including the village of Westport, where Elkins grew up. Catron's family lived in nearby Lexington. Elkins, Catron, and William Breeden attended the Masonic College at Lexington, Missouri, in the mid-1850s, probably enrolling in its preparatory division. They likely met there.[6] Some contemporary critics of territorial affairs gave Breeden equal billing with Elkins and Catron as leaders of the Ring, and for good reason. While Elkins and Catron were more visible figures in business and elective politics, Breeden held the office of attorney general for some fifteen years and provided invaluable service as the longtime chair of the territorial Republican Party.

Elkins and Catron were also classmates at the University of Missouri, graduating in 1860. While in residence at Columbia, Catron may also have known Henry L. Waldo, who attended for part of one year. The Elkins and Waldo families were already well acquainted as neighbors in Jackson County, Missouri. Elkins and Catron had no sooner graduated when the sectional clash over slavery erupted in war. In deeply divided Missouri, Elkins gravitated to the Union cause and was commissioned as a captain in the Enrolled Missouri Militia. Catron enlisted as a second lieutenant in the Missouri State Guard on the side of the Confederacy.

Elkins petitioned for an early discharge and in July 1863 was discharged from the militia. According to Elkins biographer Oscar Doane Lambert, bitter divisions persuaded Elkins that he must leave the area. He had seen countless immigrants depart to seek better lives in the West, and he meant to do the same. Elkins joined a wagon train bound for the new territory of Arizona, but upon reaching Albuquerque, he was persuaded by friends to settle in New Mexico. He proceeded south to the town of Mesilla. By the end of the year, 1863, he had been admitted to the practice of law and had been elected to represent Doña Ana County in the legislature.[7] He soon won appointment as district attorney for the Third Judicial District, and thereafter his ascent in business and politics was rapid. In 1865, Elkins followed the advice of Judge Kirby Benedict, who had told him, "Go up to Santa Fe, which is a place of more importance than Mesilla and settle down."[8] In rapid succession, he was appointed attorney general and then U.S. attorney for New Mexico. His election as New Mexico's territorial delegate to Congress in 1873 marked the beginning of a longer migration to centers of business and political activity in the East and to the national stage in politics.

Elkins's relocation to Santa Fe coincided with Catron's arrival in New Mexico. When Elkins brought his new bride, the former Sarah Jacobs, from Missouri in June 1866, Catron also came, hauling his grubstake—two wagons loaded with flour that he reportedly sold for $10,000.[9] From Judge

Figure 3 San Francisco Street at Santa Fe Plaza, looking east toward La Parroquia, later the site of the St. Francis Cathedral. Photo by Nicholas Brown, ca. 1870. Palace of the Governors Photo Archives (NMHM/DCA), No. 70437.

Benedict, Catron learned much about the people, history, traditions, and laws of New Mexico.[10] He soon had a working knowledge of Spanish and had been appointed to the post held earlier by Elkins, district attorney for the Third Judicial District. He headed south to Mesilla, and in the fall of 1868 was elected to represent Doña Ana County in the legislative council. When illness forced Merrill Ashurst to vacate the office of attorney general in 1869, Catron was appointed to that office and thereafter made Santa Fe his home. Elkins and Catron later formed a law partnership that lasted from 1874 until Elkins's departure from the territory in 1876. Sarah Elkins died in October 1872, leaving her husband a widower with two young daughters.

In 1863, Henry Waldo had left Missouri for California, where he eventually took up the study of law. Waldo maintained correspondence with Elkins in New Mexico, and when Elkins won election as territorial delegate to Congress in 1873, Waldo moved to Santa Fe and assumed responsibility for Elkins's law practice during sessions of Congress.[11] He later became active in public life, serving brief terms as chief justice and attorney general.

By 1873, Elkins, Catron, Breeden, and Waldo were living in Santa Fe. All served in the position of attorney general of the territory between 1867 and 1889, one of the four holding the office almost continuously throughout this period. In their varied roles, the men from Missouri had ample opportunity to be of mutual assistance. Without reference to questions of favoritism or corruption in the discharge of their public duties, it can be said that the decisions and actions of one usually reinforced the interests of the others.

Connections

Three others who, by reputation, became associated with the late nineteenth-century Santa Fe Ring typify the backgrounds of men who were identified with the Ring over its life of several decades. One came from the West and another from the East. The third was a native New Mexican and a member of a distinguished family of the Rio Abajo, south of Albuquerque.

William Logan Rynerson was a member of General James H. Carleton's California Column, a volunteer force that marched east to New Mexico to oppose the Confederate army in 1862. He was one among more than three hundred Union soldiers who chose to remain in the territory at the war's end.[12] A native of Kentucky, Rynerson had gone west to the goldfields in 1852. When the war broke out, he enlisted in Company C, First California Infantry, and marched overland to southern New Mexico to oppose Confederate forces. Their mission fulfilled, Rynerson mustered out in 1866 with the brevet rank of lieutenant colonel. He retained his military title in civilian life and settled in southern New Mexico, where he married into a Hispanic family and busied himself in mining, ranching, and other business ventures.[13] He learned enough law to gain admission to the territorial bar and became

involved in local politics. Rynerson became a respected citizen of the territory, but he did not shrink from partisan activity, nor from a spirited defense
of his positions, including, on at least one occasion, a resort to violence.

A lanky man with a long beard, Rynerson was known to admirers as the
"Tall Sycamore of the Rio Grande." A member of the Masonic Lodge,
Rynerson was instrumental in establishing the Aztec Lodge at Las Cruces,
serving three terms as Master.[14] He was elected to the legislative council in
1867 as its only non-Hispanic member.

An appointment to the office of district attorney for the Third Judicial
District in 1876 positioned Rynerson for involvement in the turmoil that
would rock Lincoln County and all of New Mexico. His role in the conflict
known as the Lincoln County War reinforced Rynerson's reputation as a
Ring man, though he later became an outspoken opponent of the Ring.
Darlis A. Miller points out that Rynerson consistently denied accusations
that he was a member of the Santa Fe Ring, but notes that "various links between Rynerson and members of the Ring warrant his inclusion at least
within the rear guard."[15] He was one of a small number of veterans of the
California Column—Emil Fritz and Richard Hudson were others—who appeared to have at least some degree of affiliation with the Ring in Doña Ana,
Lincoln, and Grant counties.

Other men came to the territory on account of patronage political appointments and were welcomed into the fellowship of the Ring. Governors
and surveyors general were desirable allies for men who wished to get things
done, as were judges. Born in 1812 in New York, Joseph Palen was sixteen
years older than Rynerson and nearly thirty years older than Elkins, Catron,
and Breeden. His death in December 1875 cut short his involvement in affairs
in New Mexico, but during his six-and-one-half-year tenure as chief justice
of the territorial supreme court and judge of the First Judicial District, he was
conspicuous in complaints of Ring corruption.

Postmaster at Hudson, New York, when appointed to the bench in 1869,
Palen had also practiced law for many years.[16] He harbored political ambitions and at least twice had pursued elective office. A Whig in "a hopelessly
democratic district," he was not successful, but he fared better as a Republican
in New Mexico, winning a seat on the National Republican Executive
Committee.[17] Ralph Emerson Twitchell reports that "Judge Palen counted
among his closest friends Messrs. Elkins, Catron, Breeden and Waldo, members of the bar of his court."[18]

Critics of the Ring saw a connection between Elkins and Catron as attorneys, and Palen as judge, that went beyond friendship and involved favoritism on the judge's part, and possible collusion. It was charged that Elkins and Catron had matters so arranged that they were virtually assured of success in Palen's court. Hezekiah S. Johnson, also known as Blue Dick, was also appointed to the territorial supreme court in 1869 and was regarded by some as a junior partner to Palen. When he voted with Palen, as he often did, the two constituted a helpful majority of the three-member court.[19] Political enemies of Palen and the Ring did not succeed in removing or neutralizing Palen, but it wasn't for lack of effort. In fairness, Palen was well regarded by many contemporaries, and some historians have rejected as unfair the criticisms directed at him.

José Francisco Chaves, a capable military and political leader and a native New Mexican, was a sometime confederate of the Ring. He provided critical leadership in the legislature and in elections, but he was also a political maverick whose independent power base allowed him to oppose the Catron faction when it suited him to do so.

Whatever his allegiance, Chaves was a force in territorial politics for more than forty years, beginning with his election to the legislative assembly in 1858. He was three times elected territorial delegate, serving from 1865 to 1870. He served for a time as district attorney for the Second Judicial District, presided over the constitutional convention of 1889, and was appointed territorial superintendent of instruction. Chaves's value to the Ring was most apparent in the legislature, where he was a council member from 1875 until his death in 1904 and chair of the council eight times. During the Democratic administration of Edmund G. Ross, he frustrated the governor no end, orchestrating a closely controlled caucus system that thwarted all attempts at reform.[20] From the administration of Samuel Axtell to that of Miguel A. Otero, few bills passed without his concurrence. Such was his influence that, before the territorial Republican Party was organized, the conservative faction in New Mexico was known as the Chaves Party.[21]

On several occasions during his long political career, Chaves was accused of fixing the vote in Valencia County. Concerning his support for Tranquilino Luna, the Ring's candidate for territorial delegate in 1880, *Thirty-Four*, a paper favoring Democrats, remarked, "J. Francisco Chavez [Chaves] has returned to the flesh pots and will vote his sheep for Luna."[22] The charge was made in a more serious vein following the 1882 election, when

Figure 4 José Francisco Chaves was New Mexico's delegate to Congress from 1865 to 1870 and led a political faction later organized as the territorial Republican Party. Photo ca. 1865. Brady-Handy Collection, Library of Congress, No. LC-DIG-cwpbh-00624.

Francisco Manzanares, the Democrat, challenged Luna, the declared winner, claiming that the vote had been manipulated. Manzanares, who won seven of twelve counties, some by large margins, pointed to Valencia County, which had been reported for Luna by the incredible margin of 4,193 to 66. Suspicion fell on Chaves when an investigation and testimony revealed the irregular addition of names to voter registration books in his handwriting.[23]

The challenge was sustained, and Manzanares was seated as delegate in place of Tranquilino Luna. Despite the charges, Chaves was never indicted, and he remained a force in New Mexico politics over several decades.

The genesis of the Santa Fe Ring is sometimes traced to the organization of the territorial Republican Party, an event directly attributable to Breeden's influence. According to Westphall, Breeden "invited a few prominent Republicans to a conference, and the result was the formation of the Republican Association of the Territory of New Mexico. This group became a power in politics and led the movement toward organization of the Republican Party."[24] The meeting took place in January 1868, when the *Santa Fe Weekly Gazette* reported, with some derision, the appearance of a document titled "Declaration of Principles of the Union Republican Association of New Mexico."[25] By 1869, the Republicans were holding conventions and the organization had taken on the appearance of a regular party apparatus. "Thus it can be said that William Breeden was the father of the Republican Party in New Mexico," Westphall concluded.

In subsequent years, allegiances shifted and new men came to prominence in the loose confederation of power seekers and influence wielders that was the Santa Fe Ring. These men, however—men from Missouri, soldiers who stayed, federal appointees, and like-minded New Mexicans—had significant roles in the formative phase of the combination that would exert so profound an influence on territorial affairs, for good or for ill.

A Political Odor

The Santa Fe Ring was noticed, then named, as a result of events that happened over a period of several years in the late 1860s and early 1870s. The events that raised eyebrows and ire were at first isolated and incremental. But it didn't take attentive citizens and newspaper editors long to detect a pattern of familiar faces and methods. By the mid-1870s, events of a more sensational nature would draw national attention and raise awareness in the territory concerning the presence of an emergent and seemingly corrupt political elite.

Recalling controversies that he witnessed in Colfax and Lincoln counties in the 1870s, pioneer rancher George Coe ruminated, from a safe distance of over fifty years, on an effort by forces of the Maxwell Land Grant and Railway Company to push small farmers and ranchers off land they had settled in northern Colfax County. Coe could not say positively that the troubles visited on his family and others were ginned up by the Santa Fe Ring. What he knew for certain was that "the transaction had a political odor."[26]

It was this same odor that alerted other citizens to the presence of a threatening influence. Once the Santa Fe Ring had been noticed and named, the movements of presumed members were scrutinized and adversaries were quick to ascribe impure motives to their actions, and to see new manifestations of Ring deviltry.

In the fall of 1867, two notable incidents involving men whose names would come to be associated with the Ring attracted public notice. The more sensational of the two was the lethal shooting of territorial chief justice John P. Slough by William L. Rynerson on December 15 in Santa Fe. Rynerson had been seated as a member of the legislative council on the basis of a questionable ruling by territorial secretary Herman Heath, a protégé of J. Francisco Chaves and a man possessed of lofty ambitions for the Republican Party and for himself.

The chief justice had served the Union cause, leading a force of Colorado volunteers into New Mexico and achieving victory in the battle of Glorieta Pass.[27] Slough's abrasive personality had brought him into conflict with associates time and again in his military career and in politics. At this time, in the fall of 1867, the territory was enduring a particularly vile season of political unrest, including allegations of election fraud and contested elections for territorial legislative seats, as well as for New Mexico's delegate to Congress. Agitating on the Republican side was Heath, who fervently wished to see Slough replaced with a judicial appointee more amenable to his party's interests. Knowing of Slough's temper and his penchant for self-embarrassment, Heath schemed to provoke the chief justice. It did not take much. Heath orchestrated a maneuver in the legislature whereby he himself was invited to administer the oath of office to incoming legislators in preference to the chief justice, who regularly had the honor.[28] The affront was not lost on Slough.

Slough responded in predictable fashion, blaming and publicly accosting W. F. M. Arny, a former territorial secretary and Republican leader, for the slight. Slough's response, viewed as one more instance in a pattern of intemperate behavior, provided a pretext for Heath's next move. The secretary allegedly drafted resolutions of a caustic and critical nature, concluding with a call for Slough's removal. Heath requested of Rynerson that he bring the proposals before the council. Mindful of Heath's recent assistance in securing the contested council seat, Rynerson introduced the resolutions, and they were adopted.[29]

Thereafter, matters escalated rapidly. Slough and Rynerson had a heated conversation on the evening of December 14 and engaged in a public confrontation in the bar of the Exchange Hotel the following day. Both men were armed. Angry words were exchanged and neither man gave ground. Rynerson fired his revolver, mortally wounding Slough.

The *New Mexican* saw the affair as a clear-cut case of self-defense and defended Rynerson's actions. The rival *Gazette*, on the other hand, found much to admire in the judge and deemed Slough's death an unambiguous case of premeditated murder. In response to the *New Mexican*'s praise of Rynerson, the *Gazette* responded, "No cloak of this kind can cover up the fact that he killed Judge Slough; that he killed him in the Fonda; that he killed him after having deliberated over the matter from six o'clock on Saturday evening until about one o'clock the next day; that he was fully armed and prepared to kill him when he did, and as he did."[30]

Rynerson was eventually tried for the killing of Slough. His defense was conducted by Stephen B. Elkins and the former chief justice, Kirby Benedict. Presiding at the trial was Judge Perry Brocchus, whose reputation among active Democrats was that of an ambitious and partisan tool of prominent Republicans. Indeed, the judge's instructions reflected a distinct bias, including as they did a reminder to the jury regarding alleged provocations and unflattering characteristics attributed to the deceased.[31] Outraged, the *Gazette* declared that the address amounted to "a proclamation to the people that he, Perry E. Brocchus, Associate Justice, had taken charge of the case and that no harm should come to a single hair on the head of the immaculate Rynerson."[32]

If the Slough case heightened anxieties concerning the use of the territorial courts to achieve political ends, it had an even more malignant consequence in the view of the incident's leading chronicler, Gary L. Roberts, for whom Rynerson's vindication helped legitimize violence as an instrument of political will. With Slough's murder not only tolerated but sanctioned, it was not surprising to Roberts that parties to political conflict had increasingly turned to violence.[33]

The second significant event occurring in the fall of 1867 involved charges brought against William Breeden, then serving as U.S. assessor for New Mexico. Breeden was alleged to have conspired with two others to defraud Maria Rosa Herrera, a Hispanic, non-English-speaking woman, of a pension due on account of her son's death in service of the Union at the Civil War battle at Valverde. Breeden was accused of presenting a power of attorney that he knew to have been forged, thereby drawing Señora Herrera's payment from the pension agent. Whether or not Breeden benefited financially from the affair was a matter in dispute. The pension agent for New Mexico, James L. Collins, claimed that he did.

Breeden three times faced charges related to the incident.[34] In the spring of 1868, he was acquitted in the First Judicial District Court on a charge of perjury, based on accusations that he had taken a false oath in order to receive the pension funds due Herrera. Soon after, Breeden was indicted on charges that he had drawn the money "on false and fraudulent pretenses." Again he was tried and acquitted. As Slough, previously the judge for the First Judicial District, had lately met his demise at the hands of Rynerson, Perry Brocchus, judge for the Second Judicial District, presided at both trials.

Breeden was indicted again, this time on charges that he had wrongfully withheld the funds from Herrera. The case came to trial in October 1868. Though John S. Watts had been appointed to succeed Slough as chief justice and judge for the First Judicial District, he was disqualified from hearing the case, having prosecuted Breeden on the perjury charge. The case was moved to the Second Judicial District—Brocchus's court. Due to Brocchus's absence, the trial was conducted by his judicial colleague and political rival, Joab Houghton. The prosecution case was presented by Elkins, U.S. attorney for New Mexico, and Attorney General Merrill Ashurst. When Breeden was found guilty, his attorney moved for a new trial and requested an immediate hearing on the motion. Peeved, Breeden wrote to an associate, declaring, "Watts, Houghton, Collins and Elkins must all be removed."[35]

As circumstances would have it, Brocchus returned to Albuquerque on October 12, in time to be on hand for the hearing on Breeden's request for a new trial. Houghton continued to preside in the case, but Brocchus sat in on the hearing, and when Houghton failed to immediately rule on the motion for a new trial, Brocchus intervened and granted the motion, then proceeded to conduct the trial. In the view of some, the motion should have been heard in the territorial supreme court rather than in the district court in which the matter originated. A second trial normally would not have occurred in the same term in which the cause was originally tried.[36] Brocchus proceeded with the trial and again favored the jury with a lengthy recapitulation of the facts as he saw them. The result was an acquittal.

The *Santa Fe Daily New Mexican* saw the pursuit of Breeden as a political prosecution promoted by "certain Democratic influences." The paper stated that the quest had been sustained "only by those who were interested in getting him out of office."[37] The prosecution's persistence through three indictments

Figure 5 Perry E. Brocchus was a controversial federal judge in Utah in the early 1850s and again in New Mexico, where he presided over two contentious trials that raised public awareness of an emergent political combination. Special Collections, J. Willard Marriott Library, University of Utah, No. P0150n010101.

and four trials seems to lend credence to the *New Mexican*'s charge, though it is hard to see Elkins, the prosecutor in the final case, functioning as an agent for the Democrats and opposing Breeden on partisan political grounds.

To the pension agent, Breeden's acquittal made for a gross miscarriage of justice. Collins expressed himself plainly in a letter addressed to O. H. Browning, secretary of the Department of the Interior. In Collins's view, Brocchus "accomplished what he was sent from Washington City by the friends of Breeden to do." As paraphrased by Collins, Brocchus had instructed jurors "that if three rascals get together and commit forgery and perjury and thereby obtain the pension money of an ignorant old woman who does not understand a word of the English language, it is proper and right that these rascals should be allowed to keep the money, and in the opinion of the judge giving the instructions they have committed no crime or violation of the law, and should be allowed to enjoy the fruits of their swindle, and I, as Pension Agent, should pay the amount a second time, and the government or its agent lose it."[38] Whatever the merits of the charges, the Department of the Interior conducted its own review, and Breeden soon vacated the assessor's office.

The incidents involving Rynerson and Breeden revealed deep divisions between political factions—a staunch group of Democrats and an emerging

power elite aligned with the national Republican Party. Some ambitious newcomers apparently took a pragmatic approach, gravitating to the party likely
to be in power. Following the assassination of Abraham Lincoln, those living
in the territories experienced the chaos of frequent changes in administration.
Wholesale changes had occurred during the presidency of Democrat Andrew
Johnson, and again when Johnson was succeeded by a Republican, Ulysses S.
Grant. In New Mexico, smart money gravitated to the Republican Party and
was rewarded with a succession of friendly Republican administrations lasting
until 1884, when Grover Cleveland won the White House for the Democrats.

The acquittals of Rynerson and Breeden illustrate a commonplace with
respect to the political climate of the times, and concerning the men identified with the Santa Fe Ring. Serious charges rarely had fatal consequences for
the political ambitions of the accused. In the rough-and-tumble world of
territorial politics, exposure to such accusations was an occupational hazard.
A successful defense might require judicial intervention of the kind alleged
in the Rynerson and Breeden cases, but the charges at issue could be, and
frequently were, passed off as baseless accusations arising from political motivation. The damage to one's reputation was usually slight.

The setback suffered by Breeden was of short duration. When President
Grant appointed Joseph Palen territorial chief justice in April 1869, Breeden,
who had assumed leadership of the emerging territorial Republican organization, gained employment as his clerk and continued on his upward trajec-
tory as a man of power in the territory.

Law to Order

Prior to 1870, the territory had no tax law to support local improvements or
to pay certain operating expenses. The federal government paid the salaries
of federal officials, but many other expenses, including compensation of jurors, were paid for with warrants backed by the full faith and credit of the
territory. The trouble was that there was little faith in the credit of the territory, and the warrants quickly depreciated, bringing less than a quarter of
their face value on the open market. They became useful primarily for payment of fines and license fees. Persons owing such obligations bought the
warrants at deep discounts and paid them back to the government that had
issued them, "thus, revenues for the territory consisted of twenty-five cent
territorial warrants paid to the territory at dollar face value."[39]

Following the disastrous administration of Governor Robert B. Mitchell and the election of Ulysses S. Grant as president in 1868, William A. Pile was appointed governor in early 1869.[40] Pile was not a genius, but he didn't have to be in order to see that the territory's finances were in a colossal mess. As the legislative session approached in the fall of 1869, Pile proposed that the territory's debt—approximately $60,000—be funded through a ten-year bond to be paid for by "some system of equal and just taxation." The *Santa Fe Daily New Mexican* endorsed the plan, and when the legislature convened in mid-December, Rynerson introduced such a measure in the territorial council.[41] The legislature responded, levying a tax on real and personal property, and funding territorial warrants issued prior to May 1, 1870, through the issuance of bonds bearing 10 percent interest.[42]

The *New Mexican* praised the legislature, but suspicious minds discerned an opportunistic motive on the part of an increasingly powerful and ambitious clique. Detractors noted that much of the benefit of the legislature's action would accrue to speculators who had purchased large quantities of the territorial warrants at greatly reduced values, then had pushed for the bonds and the tax to support them. The accusation persisted in political debate for years, if not decades. In 1871, the *Borderer,* a shrill critic of the Ring, aired the issue, bemoaning the results of four years of Ring rule. Said the paper, "The Governor frankly acknowledges that four years ago there was a balance in the Territorial treasury after paying all debts. Now we owe $74,000! What have we to show for it? Schools, roads, buildings? None of these things, nor any benefit to the people. But Elkins, Catron, et al., who paid poor jurors 20 and 25 per cent. for their hard earned pay, draw 10 per cent. on the bonds, or in reality, about 40 per cent. on their original investment."[43]

In 1873, the *Republican Review* acknowledged the persistent criticism and published a rebuttal that confirmed essential elements of the charges while defending Elkins and other bond holders. According to the article, the bonds funded $60,000 in debt attributable to the warrants. Elkins, the paper reported, owned $11,000 worth of bonds "obtained in exchange for warrants bought at a low price," plus another $5,000 from purchases made after passage of the tax law. Catron held $12,000 in bonds. The Spiegelberg and Staab families were identified as owning another $7,500 in the new bonds. The article characterized Elkins's involvement as an act of "true statesmanship," but the piece also confirmed that persons who became known as Ring members owned half or more of the entire issue.[44]

The controversy was on the mind of territorial editor Simeon H. Newman when he wrote to the *New York Sun* in July 1875 to complain about misdeeds of the Ring. Newman brought forth a litany of grievances. Declared the writer, "New Mexico's first and only tax law has now been in operation four years, and there is not one public building or improvement of any kind which can be pointed to as a benefit derived therefrom. Almost the whole of the moneys collected goes into the pockets of the Ring."[45]

Don Miguel Otero, father of future territorial governor Miguel A. Otero, was still making political hay of the matter in 1880, when he stood as a candidate for territorial delegate. He related the episode to a gathering of Democrats in Silver City, telling them that members of the Ring had bought up the old warrants at a quarter of face value, "and by bribery, forced a bill through the Legislature, funding this debt and fixing ten percent as the rate of interest which it should bear, and imposing heavy taxes on the people, in order to render the investment secure."[46]

In his missive to the *Sun*, Newman also described the "Omnibus Law," an act providing for the punishment of "all crimes for which there is no statute provision." According to Newman, this law gave the chief justice—Judge Palen—the power to determine whether an action already committed constituted a crime. Newman noted that the new law had already proven remarkably useful in stifling a free press. "Under this code," he wrote, "such editors as have dared to use their influence in the cause of honesty and against the Ring have been arrested and imprisoned or excessive bail required of them, and on charges of libel they have been tried and convicted, and fined or sentenced to imprisonment for simply publishing facts notoriously true."[47] Faced with such a possibility, Newman stated, the editor was generally inclined to abandon his crusade for reform, or else find an entirely new line of work.

Friends of the Court

The emerging political force in Santa Fe attracted the attention of citizens in Colfax County, where William R. Morley and Frank Springer, officials of the Maxwell Land Grant and Railway Company, became leaders of the resistance. Morley's suspicions had been aroused by an 1871 incident involving the murder of John Glass, a vocal critic of Dr. Robert Longwill, the local probate judge and a presumed Ring man. Local hearsay led Morley to conclude that Glass had been killed at the behest of Longwill, who apparently enjoyed the sympathetic counsel of Stephen Elkins. Morley's impression was reinforced in a conversation concerning troubles on the Maxwell grant when Longwill stated "that he had the juries fixed and could indict and convict who he damned pleased, and that the right way to run a country was to get somebody to shoot the sons-of-bitches who opposed you."[48]

It was one thing to find a political faction working its will in the legislative body and influencing the appointment and removal of territorial officials. It was quite another to find that the courts were also subject to manipulation for the benefit of a privileged few, but that was part of the emerging pattern that increasingly persuaded wary citizens that they were being had in Santa Fe, in Washington, and in the remote counties in which many of them lived.

Between 1868 and 1873, Elkins, Catron, Breeden, and Palen were involved in a case that some saw as a prime example of Ring mischief. As retold by the *Las Vegas Optic*, "It was the open boast of Elkins and Catron that they had made a bargain with Judge Palen by which it was impossible for any other attorney to conduct a case successfully before him. They took all the cases they could on 'spec,' and the understanding was Judge Palen shared in the division of the plunder."[49] In this case, Elkins represented the widow of Nat Webb, a merchant who did business in El Paso while two partners ran a similar operation at Fort Union. On behalf of Webb's widow, Elkins sued requesting an official determination of funds owed from the partnership. In so doing, he overstated Webb's interest in the firm. William Breeden was appointed as master in chancery and charged with examining the books and determining an equitable distribution of the assets.

Claiming—perhaps believing—Webb to have been an equal partner in the Fort Union and El Paso operations, Elkins presented an inflated estimate of funds due the estate. Breeden supported the claim, and when the matter was appealed to the territorial supreme court, Palen and colleagues upheld Breeden's finding. When the case was carried to the U.S. Supreme Court, however, it was overturned upon discovery of numerous errors in the New Mexico decisions, not the least of which had to do with Webb's ownership stake in the Fort Union business—found to be one-eighth, rather than the one-third claimed by Elkins.[50] The *Optic* stated that Palen, Catron, and Elkins were to have divided $37,000 from the judgment, with the remaining $60,000 paid to Webb's estate. The *Optic* did not offer substantial proof, but the charges likely impressed readers who were ready to believe such a report.

Figure 6 As chair of the territorial
Republican Central Committee and as
attorney general, William Breeden was a
power in New Mexico from the late 1860s
to the mid-1880s. Photo ca. 1880. Palace of
the Governors Photo Archives (NMHM/
DCA), No. 7019.

Word of the case may have helped motivate an effort undertaken in the
legislature to move Palen from the First Judicial District to the Third Judicial
District, in southern New Mexico. The northern district was more populous,
covering seven counties. The Third District took in only three, but entailed
significantly more travel—much of it over remote and forbidding terrain.[51]
Displeasure with Palen was such that a majority in both houses saw fit to go
along with the plan. The move was intended to negate Palen's influence in the
north and to break up an unholy alliance with certain attorneys, but supporters may also have hoped that the legislation would inspire the judge to consider an early resignation. It was taken up by the legislature in December 1871.

The *Borderer* was severe in its denunciation, characterizing Palen as "a
political wire puller whose place is in the caucus room, not on the bench."[52]
But the *Colorado Daily Chieftain* came to Palen's aid, rejecting charges of
partisanship and asserting that "no other Judge in New Mexico ever exhibited the legal ability of Judge Palen, and it must be further admitted that he
has a good reputation with the bench and bar generally."[53]

A governor's veto quashed the legislation, but the incident spawned one
of the more sensational accusations made against principals of the emerging
political elite. In an affidavit published in the *Borderer* and reprinted in the
Las Vegas Weekly Mail, August Kirchner, a Santa Fe butcher and sometime
federal contractor, charged that Elkins and Catron had attempted to engage

him in an effort to bribe legislators in order to secure their votes against the reassignment of Palen. Kirchner recounted conversations with both men. In one exchange, Elkins allegedly prophesied that Kirchner would be the defendant in a lawsuit brought by Samuel Ellison in Palen's court—but that if Kirchner could persuade legislators to vote against the bill, he would surely win the suit. Catron allegedly told of buying the votes of two representatives and asked Kirchner to pay $250 each to two other legislators to secure their votes. Funds would be drawn at a bank on Catron's order. Kirchner also quoted Catron as saying that "if Judge Palen is removed from the 1st District, himself (the said Thomas B. Catron) and S. B. Elkins would be ruined."[54]

When the allegations became public, Catron and Elkins collected affidavits refuting the charges and attempting to impeach Kirchner's credibility as a witness. In his capacity as attorney general, Catron reportedly brought indictments against Kirchner and others for libel. Threatened with prosecution, Kirchner gave a second affidavit in which he recanted the charges made in the first.[55] This defused the matter, but the episode generated suspicions on the part of those who had begun to smell something rotten in the Territory of New Mexico.

Charges of Election Fraud

Stephen Benton Elkins was twice elected territorial delegate to Congress in the 1870s. The office of delegate was the highest position that could be conferred by a territorial electorate and was highly prized, even though there were virtually no powers of office.[56] The delegate sat with the House of Representatives and could take part in debate, but did not vote. The office was still an attractive one, however, because it provided a platform from which an effective politician could influence federal legislation and appointments to federal offices in the territory. In Elkins's first term, 1873–1874, much energy was exerted in an ill-fated bid for statehood—an effort that, if successful, might have won him a seat in the United States Senate representing New Mexico. But that was not to be. In his four years as delegate, the recently widowed Elkins likely spent as much time and effort pursuing personal agendas as he did representing New Mexico. At the end of his second term, Elkins chose to live in the East, locating first in New York and then in West Virginia. The major accomplishment of Elkins's tenure as delegate may have been the winning of Hallie Davis's hand in marriage. She was the daughter of West Virginia senator H. G. Davis, and the union apparently was a happy one, in a family sense and in terms of Elkins's continued rise to prominence in business and politics.

In the view of his political opponents, the election victories leading to Elkins's two terms as territorial delegate were not strictly aboveboard. Charges of fraud were raised both times and followed Elkins throughout his political career. In a deposition given in 1877, John Taylor, a resident of San Miguel County, stated that he was "credibly informed" of instances of whole-sale coercion of voters during the fall campaign of 1873. According to Taylor, "During the first candidacy of Stephen B. Elkins for Representative in the U.S. Congress from this territory, many persons in San Miguel and Mora Counties were arrested, charged with illegal trading with the Comanche Tribe of Indians." Taylor testified that those charged were placed under bonds. When they appeared for trial, they were released upon payment of fees to the prosecuting attorney and a pledge to vote for Elkins as territorial delegate.[57] At this time, William Breeden was attorney general and Catron was U.S. attorney for New Mexico.

An account published in the *New York Sun* detailed other schemes to secure votes for Elkins. The paper accused Catron of commencing some six hundred prosecutions for illegal settlement on Indian lands. The cases were continued until after the election, and somehow the word was passed that a vote for Elkins would clear the name of the accused. Said the *Sun*, "Nobody was convicted, but there are people who say that the United States Attorney received $20 from the Government for each of these prosecutions, making the refreshing sum of $12,000, besides the pleasure of helping his friend to 600 votes."[58] Elkins and Catron were also accused of coercing votes through the filing of false charges against citizens for cattle thieving and by using their influence to threaten the interests of land-grant claimants. All such charges relied on hearsay, but they resonated with citizens who were conditioned to view the emerging political machine with suspicion.

Accusations of official corruption also surfaced when Elkins stood for reelection in 1875. The most detailed charges came from Frank Springer of Cimarron, an outspoken foe of the Ring. Robert Longwill, a physician by profession, was on the ballot in Colfax County as a candidate for reelection as probate judge, while Melvin Mills was running for a seat on the territorial council. Springer's interest was somewhat personal, as he had run unsuccessfully against Mills. Longwill and Mills were presumed by many to be local agents of the Ring in Colfax County.

Springer later recalled an incident from the fall campaign of 1875 that revealed apparent election fraud and illustrated the extent to which, in his mind, Elkins, Catron, Longwill, and Mills were cooperating to control political matters in Colfax County. Springer's story began with the killing of two soldiers from Fort Union by Francisco Griego in an apparent saloon brawl at the St. James Hotel in Cimarron in June 1875. Griego had fled following the incident, but later gave himself up to authorities. He was taken before the justice of the peace, a clerk in Mills's law office, and was formally charged. Bail was set at $1,000, "this action of the justice being taken after an hour's recess and a consultation with Longwill and Mills."[59]

When the fall political campaign began, Springer noted that Griego and a friend, Cipriano Lara, were working for the election of Mills and Longwill. Aware that he had heretofore supported the other ticket, Springer had occasion to ask Lara why he had changed his political allegiance. Lara explained that, with his friend Griego in jeopardy of prosecution, he had traveled to Santa Fe to meet with Breeden and Catron, who had promised that if Lara and Griego "would use all their influence with the Mexicans" on behalf of the Elkins ticket, Griego would suffer no adverse consequences. "Whether his statement was true or not, I do not know," Springer averred, "but I observed that both Lara and Griego labored earnestly in the direction indicated, and that when the District Court came on in September, Lara was appointed interpreter for the Grand Jury, and although the most positive and abundant evidence was produced against him, Griego was discharged without being indicted for anything, nor were any further proceedings taken against him in the matter."[60] Elkins, Longwill, and Mills all won majorities in Colfax County, and Elkins was returned to Washington as the territory's delegate to Congress.

In July 1875, Samuel Beach Axtell arrived in the territory and was installed as governor, having taken less than a year in wearing out his welcome as governor of Utah.[61] President Grant could have cut him loose, but instead he transferred the beleaguered executive to New Mexico. The appointment did Axtell no favor, but the public response was mixed. Citizens of Utah were mostly glad to be rid of Axtell, but official Santa Fe welcomed him. Axtell was warmly received in the capital and in Las Vegas, where Chief Justice Palen, Attorney General Breeden, Rynerson, and Ben Stevens, district attorney for the Second Judicial District, were among the luminaries at a welcoming event.[62] Men of the Elkins-Catron combination cultivated a congenial relationship with the governor, and their solicitations were generally repaid with deference and cooperation.

By the time the aspens on the Sangre de Cristo Mountains of northern New Mexico had begun turning from summer green to brilliant yellow in the fall of 1875, alarms had been set off among those who were convinced that a select group of insiders was manipulating affairs of the territory to its own advantage. Though many of the accusations were based on hearsay magnified by partisan newspaper hysteria, the more egregious charges were permanently fixed in the minds of those who were at odds with the ruling faction and believed themselves to be its victims. There had been few repercussions thus far, but by autumn of 1875, accusations against the ruling combination had been aired in the national press.

During its formative years, the dominant faction was variously called the Santa Fe clique, the radical ring, the New Mexican ring, the Elkins ring, the Federal Ring, and simply "the ring." The *Borderer* of Las Cruces, which claimed to be the "first Democratic paper of the territory," may have been the first to use the term *Santa Fe Ring*. In 1871, the paper was complaining about the radical Republicans and airing grievances to the effect that the bar of Santa Fe had assumed the aspect of a controlling clique. By December, the term *ring* was a staple in the editorial parlance, and by February 1872, readers were seeing references to the "Santa Fe ring."[63] Once the *New York Sun* began reporting on the allegations of treachery being visited on the people of New Mexico by the "Santa Fe Ring," the name came into common usage.

When violence erupted in the mid-1870s, first in Colfax County and then in Lincoln County, opponents of the Santa Fe Ring were on alert and ready to see the controlling hand of the Ring at work, flexing its political muscle and protecting the interests of its principal masters.

CHAPTER THREE

COLFAX COUNTY AND THE MAXWELL LAND GRANT

Describing the area around Cimarron's old plaza in 1970, a local writer pointed to piles of refuse, deserted streets, abandoned buildings, and the decaying hulks of junked automobiles, and lamented a forgotten past, barely discernible in this "dirty, neglected old village."[1] The town, he believed, deserved better, for its role in more turbulent times of economic and cultural conflict in a rapidly changing American West.

The writer was recalling the decade or so preceding the arrival of the railroad in New Mexico, when Cimarron was an important place in the territory, and Colfax County a field of intense struggle. The county had attracted many immigrants from the states—settlers seeking homesteads, ranchers looking for free or cheap grazing land, proprietors, attorneys, speculators, and a lawless element that was often found in the western territories. The discovery of gold on Baldy Mountain had led to a boom in mining and the advent of new towns—Baldy Town on the mountain's eastern slope and Elizabethtown in the verdant Moreno Valley. But the initial flurry was followed by a bust of near-equal proportion, leaving few active mines by the mid-1870s. The arrival of the railroad was anticipated as the key to a new era of growth and prosperity.

Satan's Paradise

The country was beautiful—much of it rimmed with the broken skyline of the Sangre de Cristos. Baldy rose above the tree line to a height of more than 12,400 feet, affording views of mountains higher still: the Wheeler range across the valley, the Truchas Peaks to the south and west, and the hulking Spanish Peaks in southern Colorado. Stands of pine, fir, spruce, and aspen covered the mountains, safe from the lumberman's ax until rails should arrive to allow for the removal of timber in commercial quantities. Low grasslands and the mountain country supported increasing numbers of beef cattle and provided habitat for elk, mule deer, bears, mountain lions, and bighorn sheep. North and east of the mountains was a rolling prairie—monotonous to look at but eminently suitable for the raising of livestock, pending access to critical water sources. The plain was too dry for farming without irrigation, but mountain streams and the drainages of the Vermejo, the Cimarron, the Ponil, and the Rayado were sufficient to support ranching, limited cultivation, human habitation, and a healthy population of trout. Much of the land was found to conceal an immense bed of commercial-grade coal.

The country was fair to behold, but it was not Paradise. There were racial tensions among Hispanics, mostly small farmers seeking little more than a home and a living; Euro-Americans, some of whom were looking for a good deal more; and occasionally black soldiers who came west with the army to man frontier forts and protect U.S. settlers and interests. Although indigenous Utes and Jicarilla Apaches had mostly relocated to distant reservations, a small number of Apaches remained in the area. Reports of occasional raids on settlers and instances of drunken behavior on the part of a few of the Indians compromised the region's appeal to potential immigrants and investors, at least in the eyes of those who were promoting development and offering land for sale. These conditions produced tensions that persisted for two decades, sometimes giving way to violent conflict. *Cimarron* translated from the Spanish as "wild," and it was that. An author native to the area referred to the Cimarron country of the 1870s as "Satan's Paradise."[2]

By the mid-1870s, storm clouds were moving in over Colfax County. At the center of the gathering tempest were two controversies. The first was a conflict between settlers who believed themselves to have located legally on the public domain and officials of the Maxwell Land Grant and Railway Company, whose claim to a large area of northeastern New Mexico was hotly disputed. Company officials pushed settlers to pay for the land they occupied or move, and many of the settlers pushed back. Serious resistance was also evident in the Baldy mining region, where the Maxwell Company attempted to extract compensation from miners and prospectors who were convinced that they were within their rights working claims in the Moreno Valley and on Ute Creek. Riots erupted at Elizabethtown in October 1870.[3] In the spring of 1871, the *Arizona Citizen* reported "a little speck of war" in Colfax County, where an armed confrontation between miners and agents of the Maxwell Company had broken out on Ute Creek. The incident brought a visit and a stern proclamation from Governor William Pile.[4] Tempers cooled for the time being, but tension between the company and the settlers remained high.

The second controversy was fueled by the resentment that leading residents in Colfax County felt toward presumed members of the Santa Fe Ring and their local agents. These contentious relationships divided friends, business associates, and neighbors and resulted in the formation of alliances among residents sharing common interests. Some local men placed their bets on the side of the Santa Fe–based faction, but many residents of the area staunchly resisted domination by the Ring. The *Cimarron News and Press* was one of a half dozen strong editorial voices in the territory, most displaying unmistakable political allegiances. The *News and Press*, with a distinct anti-Ring bias, did not fail to address the issues of the day, nor did the rival *Santa Fe Daily New Mexican*, widely regarded as a Santa Fe Ring organ. For one writer reviewing the conflict, both sides were motivated by self-interest. The "Colfax Ring," as James Peterson calls the local alliance, "had no more interest in protecting or defending settlers' rights than did the Santa Fe coalition. The Colfax men were merely the reverse side of the same coin, and desired only to protect their own bailiwick in order to keep alien fingers out of their pie."[5]

The men of the Santa Fe Ring cared little whose bailiwick they were in. Where there was money to be made, they were apt to be in evidence, for those to whom membership was imputed were alert to opportunity and zealous in their pursuit of political power and wealth. They were attracted to land, government contracts, mining claims, timber, railroads, cattle and sheep, and indeed anything that might turn a profit, and New Mexico was their parish from one end to the other. Colfax County, extending over the northeastern corner of the territory, from the Moreno Valley to Colorado and from the spine of the Rockies east to Texas, offered these in abundance.

One of the most lucrative opportunities involved speculation in Spanish and Mexican land grants. Numerous land-grant claims were up for grabs, in the eyes of speculators, when the United States acquired New Mexico via the 1848 Treaty of Guadalupe Hidalgo. There were many prizes at stake, but the largest and grandest was the Beaubien and Miranda land grant, lately known as the Maxwell land grant. Lucien Maxwell was not, in fact, a grantee of the Spanish or Mexican government, but an enterprising frontiersman from

Illinois who had acquired the claim through his marriage to Luz Beaubien, daughter of don Carlos Beaubien, and through subsequent purchase of the interests of other heirs. The grant was confirmed by Act of Congress in 1860 without reference to its size or boundaries.

By 1869, Maxwell had decided to dispose of the grant. The following year it passed into the hands of a syndicate of British and Dutch investors organized as the Maxwell Land Grant and Railway Company. From its beginning as a corporate venture, the grant attracted the attention of speculators. Numerous individuals associated with the Ring were involved with the grant at one time or another, starting with Stephen Elkins and William Griffin of Santa Fe. Elkins and Griffin were longtime business associates, along with Thomas Catron and Dr. Robert Longwill, then a resident of Colfax County. Elkins served as an advisor to Lucien Maxwell and Griffin conducted a questionable survey preparatory to a contemplated sale of the grant.[6] Secretary of the Interior Jacob Cox detected possible chicanery and ordered the survey suspended, holding that, according to applicable Mexican law, the claim could not exceed 97,000 acres, or eleven square leagues for each of the two original grantees. Undeterred, the speculators commissioned Griffin to complete the survey, then filed it with the General Land Office. The survey defined a tract of some 2 million acres—an illegal and outrageous claim in the view of many settlers and their advocates.

The party negotiating the purchase of the grant from Lucien Maxwell was led by Jerome Chaffee of Denver, a man regarded by some as a kindred spirit and ally of the Ring.[7] Despite the adverse ruling by Secretary Cox, Chaffee and his associates continued to claim the larger parcel as the true extent of the grant and moved ahead with the transaction, turning a handsome profit when the property was conveyed to English and Dutch investors.

When the Maxwell Land Grant and Railway Company organized in 1870, presumed Ring members were much in evidence, providing an American gloss for the grant's foreign ownership and perhaps syphoning off an inordinate share of their remote asset. Governor William Pile, Surveyor General T. Rush Spencer, and former judge and territorial delegate John S. Watts were original incorporators. Among sixteen Americans listed as initial stockholders were several with reputed Ring connections, including Elkins, Griffin, Longwill, Jerome Chaffee of Colorado, and Santa Fe beef contractor William Rosenthal. Also holding shares were two men named in allusions to early manifestations of Ring activity, mainly in connection with the Maxwell

Figure 7 Frank Springer, just twenty-four years old when he joined his Iowa friend William Morley in northern New Mexico, led local resistance to the Santa Fe Ring in Colfax County. Photo by Montfort and Hill, 1887. Palace of the Governors Photo Archives (NMHM/DCA), No. 45484.

transactions: John S. Watts and Miguel A. Otero—not the future territorial governor but his influential father.[8] When the company's directors met in October 1873, Elkins, Catron, and Longwill were among those elected to the board, with Elkins serving as president.[9] Local allies included Melvin W. Mills, an attorney who represented Colfax County in the legislative assembly between 1873 and 1877, and Francisco "Pancho" Griego, a strong-arm collaborator who was counted on to elicit support among Spanish-speaking residents of the county. With this vast property at stake and the company's investors an ocean away, an exceptional opportunity was at hand.

Trouble on the Cimarron

Rising in opposition to the Ring was an unlikely coalition of dissident Maxwell Company officials, advocates for the settlers who stood to be displaced by the company, and residents who resented the interference of powerful outsiders in Colfax County affairs. Among leaders of the locals were William R. Morley, vice president of the Maxwell Company, and Iowa native Frank Springer, whom Morley had summoned to serve as the company's local attorney starting in February 1873. Explained Morley's grandson, "Morley blamed Elkins and Catron for some of the woes of the Land Grant Company and felt the Santa Fe Ring was attempting to gain control of the Grant as they controlled almost everything else in New Mexico."[10] By July 1875, the contest was on.

As principal administrator for the company, Morley had ample experience with Elkins, his nominal superior, and with Catron, who had handled much of the company's legal business prior to Springer's arrival. He also had a more personal reason for enmity toward Catron, then U.S. attorney for the territory. In the spring of 1875, Catron had charged Morley's wife with mail fraud following an incident in which Ada Morley tried to head off trouble, retrieving a letter mailed by her mother at the Cimarron post office. The mother, Mary Tibbles McPherson, was a visitor to the territory who had taken an interest in local political affairs. The letter was intended to inform official Washington of corruption on the part of its public officials in New Mexico.

Catron's insistence on prosecuting a young mother-to-be apparently traced to a perceived personal slight. According to an affidavit sworn by Asa F. Middaugh, Catron had said to him in April 1875 that "Mrs. Morley had insulted him by taking away a certain buggy at a time when said Catron wanted to use it," and that Morley had been "throwing mud at him." Catron further stated that he "had a chance to get even now, and he would be a fool if he did not take advantage of it."[11] Springer attempted to intervene on Ada Morley's behalf, but as of July 1875, Catron was still bent on securing an indictment and prosecuting Mrs. Morley. In light of more urgent and sensational developments in the fall of 1875, the case faded into an obscurity from which it never emerged. The bitterness of the matter, however, reinforced the resolve of Morley and Springer to resist efforts by Elkins and Catron to dominate local and company affairs.

Another outspoken opponent of the Ring was Reverend Franklin J. Tolby, a preacher who had arrived in early 1874 to minister to a growing population of immigrants from the states and to offer Christian faith and Methodist doctrine to residents of the territory. Tolby's interests were not entirely consonant with those of Morley and Springer. While officials of the Maxwell Company and other newcomers wanted remaining Jicarilla Apaches moved from the area, Tolby came to their aid, proposing that a reservation be established in the immediate area, out of lands claimed by the Maxwell Company. Morley, Springer, and Tolby were, however, in agreement concerning the corruption emanating from Santa Fe, and they were united in opposition to the Ring.

Tolby was characterized by his superior in the Methodist Episcopal Church, Reverend Thomas Harwood, as "a rising man, bold and fearless in the pulpit and out of it."[12] Tolby demonstrated the truth of Harwood's observation, taking stock of the local scene and addressing contentious issues and powerful personalities. Tolby and William R. Morley were widely assumed to have authored a series of articles published in the *New York Sun* in the summer of 1875, criticizing Elkins, Catron, Judge Palen, and others, accusing them of manipulating the courts and imposing their will on the territory.[13] The criticism was not well received.

According to the later recollection of Melvin Mills, Tolby associated freely with the men of the community and engaged Palen in conversation when the district court was in session. As Mills recalled, "Their conversation usually ran along pleasantly until they came up to the subject of politics and then Judge Palen and Mr. Tolby would have a fierce battle of words." According to Mills, Tolby's ideas were aligned with those of the Copperhead Democrats, while the judge was a staunch Republican—"exactly the reverse kind of man in politics."[14] Despite the palpable tension and a sense of impending confrontation, residents of Colfax County were ill prepared for an event that would galvanize allegiances and move angry partisans to further violence.

Tolby ministered to congregations at Cimarron and Elizabethtown, riding horseback over the post road that wound along the canyon of the Cimarron to the Moreno Valley and the mining camp of "E-Town." Having made his weekly visitation at Elizabethtown, Tolby departed on the morning of September 14, 1875, heading home to Cimarron. As he rode alone down the canyon, he was murdered by an assailant who shot him twice in the back. The preacher's horse was left to wander and his belongings were not disturbed. News of Tolby's death shocked the community. "Mrs. Tolby and her three children were literally crushed," Harwood recalled.[15]

Friends surmised that Tolby had been killed for political reasons and suspicion fell on the Santa Fe Ring, whose leaders had been roundly criticized by the preacher. Local supporters of presumed Ring leaders were suspected of orchestrating the killing, if not personally firing the fatal shots. Tolby's friends were eager to learn the identity of his killer and to connect the clues leading to others who might be behind the murder. Impatient with the pace of the official inquiry, Oscar P. McMains, a fellow minister, initiated an investigation, aided by friends of the deceased.

Cruz Vega, who had carried the mail from Elizabethtown to Cimarron on the day of the murder, was lured one night to a field near Cimarron, where a brutal interrogation resulted in his death. Some of the men reportedly had been drinking. McMains and fourteen others were charged in the killing of Vega.[16] The interrogation of Cruz Vega led to a second suspect, Manuel Cárdenas, who, when questioned, named Vega as Tolby's killer. According to

Cárdenas, Vega had been hired by Florencio Donoghue, the regular mail contractor at Elizabethtown; Longwill, the probate judge; and attorney Melvin Mills. All were presumed agents or friends of the Ring.

Clay Allison exacted a measure of revenge on Tolby's behalf when, on November 1, 1875, he shot and killed Francisco "Pancho" Griego in the St. James Hotel barroom, in a rumpus growing out of events surrounding the murder of Tolby and the killing of Cruz Vega. Griego had killed two soldiers from Fort Union in an altercation at the St. James only a few months before and was believed by some to have been spared serious consequences through the intervention of leading members of the Santa Fe Ring. His reputation as an agent and enforcer for the Ring had placed Griego in direct opposition to the equally volatile Allison.

The last shot in the Colfax County War may have been fired on the night of November 10, 1875, when Cárdenas was shot from ambush as he was being taken from court in Cimarron.[17] Tolby's avengers pursued the men implicated in his testimony, taking Mills and Donoghue into custody and chasing Longwill to the relative safety of Santa Fe. Ring leaders reportedly came to Longwill's rescue, prevailing on the governor to use his executive power to forestall prosecution of Longwill.[18] For want of evidence, the men were never indicted, but the sudden, violent deaths of a shrill critic—Tolby—and two men who conceivably could have revealed Ring involvement stoked the suspicions of wary citizens and caused many to view the killings of Tolby, Vega, and Cárdenas as evidence of the Ring's determination to impose its will in Colfax County. The legal and political consequences of the episode would reverberate for years to come.

Aftermath

With Colfax County in a state of excitement, Governor Samuel Axtell requested troops from Fort Union; a detachment of horse soldiers reached Cimarron on November 8. In the governor's view, this action was necessary to maintain civil order, and the *New Mexican* agreed, giving its version of events under the headline "Anarchy at Cimarron." Said the paper, "U.S. troops are on the ground and they will prevent violence and bloodshed if they have notice in time."[19] In the view of some locals, the precaution was unnecessary. According to Frank Springer, "The troops remained several days, and found nothing to do—found the people quiet and peaceable, and the law taking its course, but a very bitter and excited feeling among them on account of the murder of Tolby."[20] To Springer and others, the action again showed the inordinate power of the Ring to manipulate public officials and exert power in an unjust cause.

The struggle was not yet over, as the efforts of presumed Ring men to control affairs in Colfax County continued into 1876. In January, just as the legislative session was drawing to a close, a body dominated by presumed Ring men passed an act that enraged the dissident faction in Colfax. Citing the recent violence as grounds for its action, the legislature suspended sessions of the district court in Colfax County and attached the county to adjacent Taos County, "for judicial purposes." This meant, among other things, that citizens and attorneys at Cimarron who had business with the court now had to travel approximately sixty miles to Taos, negotiating the steep trail up and over the 9,100-foot Palo Flechado Pass, in all seasons. It also meant that juries were likely to be controlled by Pedro Sánchez of Taos, chair of the legislative council and a man widely considered the local agent for the Ring in Taos County.[21] J. Francisco Chaves, an ally of the Ring and a member of the council, moved for passage of the measure in the council. Melvin Mills, often a Ring supporter, vigorously but unsuccessfully opposed the measure in the House.

The law required that judicial matters normally heard in Colfax County be moved to Taos for at least two terms of the court. A telegram denouncing the action of the legislature and calling for its veto was sent to Governor Axtell. Frank Springer traveled to Santa Fe to plead the cause of the citizens, to no avail. Axtell signed the bill, thereby becoming a particular enemy of Springer and other Colfax County residents.

More fuel was added to the fire when the elected county sheriff of Colfax County, O. K. Chittenden, was removed by the governor in favor of Isaiah Rinehart, a man more acceptable to the Ring. Circumstances of the removal were disputed, the governor claiming that Chittenden had resigned and Chittenden claiming that he had been removed over an issue concerning the sufficiency of a required bond. To those who had little faith in territorial officials, the affair was simply indicative of the Ring's determination to manipulate Colfax County affairs and maintain control over its citizens.

Residents of Colfax had been trying for some time to induce Axtell to visit the county, talk to the people, and hear their concerns firsthand. Springer later reported that when he had called on the governor to discuss the removal of the court sessions to Taos, Axtell "spoke with extreme bitterness about the people of Colfax County, and informed me that he had visited every other county in the territory, and had intended to visit Colfax in its turn, but that now he should not do so." When urged to go to Cimarron and hear directly from the people, Axtell refused, saying that "he was fully advised about matters in that county and didn't need further information."[22]

In March, however, Axtell sent word by Benjamin Stevens that he would visit Cimarron after all, and that he wished to meet with a group of men including Morley, Springer, merchant Henry M. Porter, and Clay Allison. The men were advised that the governor would arrive by coach on the coming Saturday, and that those invited should assemble to meet the coach.

The men of Colfax found the proposal highly peculiar as well as suspicious, and they did not show for the promised audience with the governor.[23] Axtell didn't show either, and evidence later surfaced—a letter from Axtell to Ben Stevens—indicating that the meeting had been planned as a ruse for the purpose of arresting Allison. Springer and others also read into the missive a plot to murder any who might oppose an arrest of Allison. This letter, the subject of a dispute between Springer and the governor, would be a key piece of evidence leading to Axtell's removal. By all appearances, the governor was firmly in the grasp and control of the powers in Santa Fe. Axtell made no attempt to disavow the letter, but denied intent to cause the deaths of the Cimarron men.

When, in the spring of 1876, indictments were sought against McMains and others for their roles in the deaths of Tolby and Cruz Vega, the apprehensions of Colfax County residents were realized. The most influential roles in the proceeding were filled by men with close ties to the Ring. Following the death of Joseph Palen in December 1875, Henry L. Waldo had been appointed chief justice and judge for the First Judicial District. Attorney General William Breeden presented the charges to the grand jury. Pedro Sánchez reportedly selected members of the grand jury, including his father-in-law, who served as its foreman. According to the *Colorado Chieftain*, a consistent supporter of McMains, Judge Waldo ordered Breeden to sit with the grand jury during its deliberations and instructed jurors to seek his counsel in all matters.[24] The *Chieftain* further reported that "it was also publicly stated in the streets of Taos during the court that Sánchez had offered not to allow the jury to find any indictments [against those accused in the murder of Tolby] provided he was paid the sum of eight hundred dollars." To no one's surprise, those implicated in Tolby's murder were not indicted, while McMains was indicted in connection with the death of Vega. Frank Springer defended McMains, assisted by William D. Lee. This was the last time Springer and McMains would be on the same side in a dispute. They spent most of the next two decades sparring over the extent and legal status of the Maxwell land grant.

McMains was first tried in Taos. He escaped prosecution when the territory suddenly suspended its case, but there were those who were still determined to see him convicted. He was indicted a second time and tried in Mora County on a change of venue. There he was convicted of "murder in the fifth degree," but went free on a technicality. A third attempt was made to prosecute McMains in April 1878, but Judge Samuel Parks reviewed the matter and dismissed the case.[25]

On the basis of facts not disputed by the defense, it appears that McMains bore some responsibility for the chain of events that led to Vega's death. But neither he nor anyone else was ever held accountable for the wrongful death of the man who may or may not have murdered Tolby, and one must wonder whether justice was denied Cruz Vega, at least in part because of his status as a poor and otherwise unremarkable "Mexican" thought likely to be guilty of Tolby's murder. Friends and allies of Tolby continued to believe that he was a victim of Ring violence, but his murder was never conclusively solved, nor was that of Manuel Cárdenas.

In essence, the Colfax County War consisted of the assassination of Tolby and a chaotic sequence of events in which other murders were committed as acts of retribution. The conflict continued as a political war involving influential Colfax County residents on one side and the territorial legislature and governor on the other. The region remained in an intermittent state of unrest, owing mainly to the conflict between the Maxwell Company and settlers who believed that much of the land claimed by the company belonged in the public domain. If nothing else, the violent events of 1875 drew attention to the Santa Fe Ring as an acknowledged center of power and corruption, and they galvanized opposition in Colfax County and elsewhere around the territory.

The Maxwell Land Grant

The Colfax County War grew out of tensions arising in connection with the Maxwell grant and the struggle for control of lands claimed by the Maxwell Land Grant and Railway Company. The larger conflict continued for more than a decade after the outbreak of violence that plagued Colfax County in the mid-1870s. Men identified with the Ring were involved from the time Maxwell sold the property and throughout the long struggle for control of the grant.

When, in 1869–1870, a group of Colorado speculators undertook to purchase the grant and file for incorporation, they sought the assistance of the sitting governor, William Pile; the surveyor general, T. Rush Spencer; and John S. Watts, a prominent lawyer and a recent chief justice of the territorial supreme court.[26] Stephen B. Elkins profited handsomely on his work in transferring the property from Maxwell to its new owners, recalling his $10,000 fee as "the easiest money I ever earned."[27]

Pile and Spencer were elected to the board of directors for the new Maxwell Land Grant and Railway Company. Spencer had lately demonstrated his support of the company by engaging William W. Griffin to survey the grant preparatory to determining its legal boundaries. Griffin's survey was not recognized by the Department of the Interior for purposes of establishing the property's boundaries, but it helped support the purchasers' claim to lands totaling nearly two million acres.

Relationships of mutual assistance and mutual benefit were evident to historian Lawrence R. Murphy, who noted, "Like Spencer, Griffin was well paid for his cooperation; when Lucien Maxwell and his colleagues formed the First National Bank of Santa Fe, he became its only paid employee, serving as teller and bookkeeper."[28] Griffin remained a reliable political and business ally of Elkins and Catron, continuing with the bank after they purchased it from Maxwell and succeeding Elkins as president from 1884 until Griffin's death in 1889.[29]

In 1877, Henry Atkinson, another surveyor general interested in acquiring land and open to collaboration with other parties, authorized a second survey of the Maxwell grant preparatory to issuance of a U.S. government patent. He first appointed Griffin, but was overruled by J. A. Williamson, commissioner of the General Land Office, whose instructions appeared to reflect his familiarity with the situation. Atkinson was advised to retain "a capable and disinterested deputy who has no connection or business transaction referable to the interests of the owners of the Grant either in surveying for them or purchasing lands falling within the Grant."[30] Atkinson may have supposed he was complying with the literal conditions of Williamson's directive when he employed John Elkins, brother of Stephen Elkins, and Robert Marmon to conduct the survey. Stephen Elkins signed on as bondsman for the contract surveyors, guaranteeing performance of their work.[31] The appointment was criticized publicly and in subsequent litigation. John Elkins and Marmon essentially followed the lines of the Griffin survey, but deleted a tract in the vicinity of the Uña de Gato Creek and produced a survey showing the grant to encompass some 1,714,764 acres. A patent was issued in May 1879, to the consternation of settlers who stood to lose their homes if the Maxwell claim was sustained.

As New Mexico's territorial delegate to Congress, Stephen Elkins worked to obtain recognition of the grant's boundaries as advocated by the company. As such, he was acting in opposition to the interests of settlers who believed their claims to be situated on the public domain.[32] Referring to an 1874 order by Willis Drummond, then commissioner of the General Land Office, who had directed that the land be surveyed as public domain, Elkins told the company's executive officer, Morley, "I will have Drummond's order revoked beyond doubt and a bill passed by which we can adjust our title without delay." Elkins complained of money due him from the Dutch ownership, telling Morley, "I cannot afford to pay Catron and Waldo as I am unless I am paid—besides just at this time I am doing important service for the Company and you know it."[33]

Other instances of Ring collaboration in the struggle over the Maxwell grant were evident. When turmoil erupted over the Tolby assassination, Governor Samuel Axtell helpfully asked for troops from Fort Union and signed what appeared to be a Ring-inspired act of the legislature attaching Colfax County to Taos County for judicial purposes. When a weakened Maxwell Company saw its real property sold for nonpayment of taxes in December 1876, presumed Ring ally Melvin Mills represented Catron at the sheriff's sale and purchased the grant for the sum of $16,479.46, immediately conveying his interest to Catron. Dutch investors rallied to redeem the property, paying overdue taxes to avoid a total loss of their investment and holding the apparent designs of the Ring in check. Elkins and Catron failed to attain the dominance over the Maxwell land grant to which they had aspired, but it wasn't for lack of trying.

From this point forward, the Maxwell Company was essentially saved from domination by Ring forces, but the disastrous administration of Frank Remington Sherwin, 1880–1883, did not represent an improvement. Just as things had seemed to be looking up for the grant's owners, a series of lawsuits had forced the company into receivership. William T. Thornton, a future

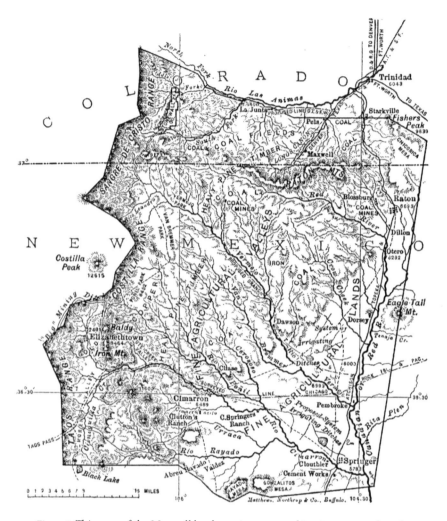

Figure 8 This map of the Maxwell land grant as surveyed in 1877 appeared on the
Maxwell Company letterhead. It shows the extent of the property as confirmed
by the U.S. Supreme Court in 1887, at 1,714,764.94 acres. Image from the CS Cattle
Company, Cimarron, NM.

territorial governor and Catron's law partner from 1877 to 1883, was appointed receiver in June 1878, but by April 1880, the property had again been
sold at auction, and a new company had been organized through an accom-
modation between the high bidder—a partnership headed by Sherwin—and
the Dutch investors who still held majority ownership. As time would reveal,

Sherwin was deeply flawed as a corporate leader, but he at least was not the Santa Fe Ring.

Colfax County and the Ring

By this time, ten years after Maxwell had sold the grant, at least twenty men named as members or agents of the Santa Fe Ring had touched the affair. This group included some of the first to be identified with Ring activity. Governor Pile, John S. Watts, and T. Rush Spencer were original incorporators of the Maxwell Company. Involved in other aspects, including disposition of judicial matters, were Elkins, Catron, Waldo, Breeden, and the late Judge Palen. The roll of alleged Ring members involved also included later and lesser lights: Henry Atkinson, William Thornton, William Rosenthal, William Griffin, U.S. Marshal John Pratt, Governor Axtell, John Elkins, Robert Longwill, and former Arkansas senator Stephen Dorsey. Of importance locally were Melvin Mills of Colfax County and Pedro Sánchez of Taos. As a leader in the legislature, J. Francisco Chaves can be credited with help in enacting legislation desired by his political allies. Some of these men had been pegged as Ring members prior to the turmoil, and others earned reputations as members or agents of the Ring as a result of their involvement in Maxwell affairs. Some like Henry Atkinson, the surveyor general, became more recognizable as associates in the Ring through other affairs.

At least one respected historian of Maxwell grant affairs identified Frank Springer as a member of the Santa Fe Ring.[34] His view in that regard was exceptional. Springer was mostly a loner who was not involved in ventures generally attributed to the Ring. He did, however, share a commitment to many of the values that animated prominent Americans in the Gilded Age— to industrial development and economic progress, and to achievement in business and accumulation of wealth as defining measures of success. Springer stood with Morley in opposing Ring efforts to dominate in Colfax County and Maxwell affairs, with Elkins and Catron particular objects of their enmity. After tensions over the affair subsided, Springer resumed friendly relations with his former enemies, involving Catron in legal work of the Maxwell Land Grant Company and taking a major role in his defense when Catron was threatened with disbarment. Springer also resumed occasional correspondence with Elkins, informing him of progress in efforts to clear the Maxwell Company's title to the grant and receiving Elkins's congratulations on a favorable U.S. Supreme Court decision in 1886.[35]

Thwarted in earlier attempts to alert federal officials to the rampant corruption in New Mexico, Mary Tibbles McPherson, the mother of Ada Morley and mother-in-law of William R. Morley, resumed her pursuit of justice in the spring of 1877. McPherson had returned to Iowa, but she stayed abreast of matters in New Mexico via letters from friends and family in Colfax County. Apprised of outrages that had followed the Tolby assassination, she meant to jar official Washington into action. To this end, she sought allies who could assist her. Her quest led to Washington and William B. Matchett. By May 1877, Matchett and McPherson had petitioned Attorney General Alphonso Taft, Secretary of the Interior Carl Schurz, and President Rutherford B. Hayes, detailing charges against the governor and other officials including U.S. Attorney Catron, Chief Justice Henry Waldo, and Associate Justice Warren Bristol. In August McPherson and Matchett submitted an expanded brief in printed form—a detailed indictment of officials said to be part of a corrupt territorial ring, complete with names of the instigators and accomplices, and particulars of the alleged misdeeds.[36]

Much of Mary McPherson's information and considerable elements of strategy came from her daughter and son-in-law, who looked on from New Mexico—eager for official attention to abuses perpetrated by the dominant political faction in Santa Fe, but apprehensive concerning McPherson's zeal and judgment. In separate letters, the Morleys expressed their support for an effort to secure removal of officials they considered inimical to local interests and urged her to focus on the goal of securing a formal investigation.[37] Apparently the appeals to Washington had the desired effect, if somewhat delayed. Following an eruption of violence in Lincoln County and further complaints about the governor from Frank Springer of Cimarron in the spring of 1878, Frank Warner Angel was dispatched to investigate. The appeals of Matchett and McPherson were among a mass of documents that Angel used to support his conclusions. Angel's investigation and report, in turn, led to Axtell's removal and Catron's resignation.

Angel's reports were filed in the fall of 1878. A decade later, after several futile iterations of company management, involving varying degrees of control by the property's English, Dutch, and American principals, a wholesale reorganization of the Maxwell Company placed its affairs in the hands of the original Colfax County faction, or what was left of it. With Frank Springer as president of the new Maxwell Land Grant Company, enjoying the support and confidence of Dutch investors, all vestiges of Santa Fe Ring control had been erased. The grant's legal status had been resolved by the U.S. Supreme Court,

Figure 9 Mary Tibbles McPherson's complaints to the White House and the Department of the Interior helped bring down Governor Samuel B. Axtell and other federal and territorial officials. Norman Cleaveland Collection, Archives and Special Collections, New Mexico State University Library, No. 250005.

and Maxwell managers could proceed with development of the grant's resources and work to recoup at least some of the property's initial value.[38]

The Grant County Secession Movement

Little noted in relation to more sensational regional conflicts occurring in the 1870s was a low-grade rebellion in Grant County, in the isolated southwestern corner of the territory. The object of the initiative was a separation of Grant County from New Mexico for the purpose of annexation to the Territory of Arizona. The secession movement did not involve charismatic or colorful individuals, nor did it result in outbreaks of violence; thus it produced no grist for dime novels and little in the way of headlines for the eastern press. While prominent Ring figures were not visibly involved in Grant County, the effort to join with Arizona was motivated by a desire to escape domination by a Ring that appeared to govern solely for its own benefit and to ignore the interests of the southern counties.

The secession movement had its genesis in the chaotic 1871–1872 session of the territorial legislature.[39] Along with the struggle over an attempt to reassign Chief Justice Palen to the Third Judicial District, there were contests over several legislative seats. The conflict resulted in the formation of two bodies, each claiming legitimacy as the House of the territorial legislative assembly. When it appeared that the Democratic Party would enjoy a rare turn at control of the legislature, forces of the Ring allegedly moved in to purchase or otherwise secure votes of key legislators and turn back the challenge to Republican primacy. In the course of events, two bills favored by the Grant County delegation fell by the wayside. One would have provided home rule for Silver City, and the other was intended to establish an improved system of public education.

Adding insult to injury, the territorial governor, Marsh Giddings, exercised his power to reapportion the legislature. In so doing, he favored the northern counties in which Ring influence was strong. At the same time, "he grouped Doña Ana, Grant, and Lincoln counties together and granted them two representatives, which was one half their previous representation." According to Grant County historian Conrad K. Naegle, "This denial of equal representation crystallized a desire in Grant County to free itself from Ring domination."[40]

For the next few years the dissatisfaction of Grant County residents with the territorial government festered. Underlying the disaffection with Santa Fe were compelling geographic, cultural, and economic factors. In its overriding concern with mining as the principal economic activity, the area had more in common with southern Arizona than with New Mexico. The region that encompassed southwestern New Mexico and southern Arizona was also beset by bands of Apache Indians, whose occasional hostilities were the cause of great concern for personal safety and a desire for a strong U.S. military presence. Silver City was closer to both the Arizona capital of Tucson and the soon-to-be-capital of Phoenix than to Santa Fe, and the Black Range provided a formidable barrier between Grant County and much of New Mexico.

The sense that the concerns of Grant County residents were not heard or heeded did not abate, but grew. At times there was talk that Doña Ana and Lincoln counties might join Grant County in a move to the territorial jurisdiction of Arizona, or in forming a new territory, but Grant finally was left to make its own case for a transfer of administration. Momentum for the idea grew in the fall of 1876, with the *Grant County Herald* announcing the "Contemplated Political Change" in an editorial on September 16. Adding to reasons previously cited, the paper alluded to a cultural divide between Grant County and the rest of New Mexico, noting that "legislation by 'American' members would be more liberal and better suited to a progressive community such as ours," and that the county's concerns would be better understood by English-speaking legislators whose economic interests were similar. Said the *Herald*, "If New Mexico should lose her richest county she can charge it to the dictatorial and corrupt spirit of a few men in Santa Fe, who have come to the conclusion that they alone are the Commonwealth, and have the right to dictate the policy of the Territory and direct her legislation in their own selfish interests."[41]

The *Daily Chieftain* of Pueblo, Colorado, characterized the rebellion as a "protest against the tyranny of the Santa Fe ring." The *Chieftain* commended the movement and noted that in its treatment of the territory's southern counties, the Ring had exhibited its "usual studied originality of rascality and fraud."[42] The cause was taken up in a public meeting on October 4, and a written declaration of intent was adopted, with causes for the action enumerated.[43] Grant County citizens overwhelmingly supported the proposal in a referendum conducted on November 7, 1876.

Support on the Arizona side was substantial but not unanimous. Governor A. P. Safford endorsed the proposal and urged the legislature to adopt a memorial petitioning Congress to act favorably on the matter. The issue provoked lively debate publicly and in the legislature, with strong opposition coming from residents of Yavapai and Mohave counties. A memorial supporting annexation passed both houses of the Arizona legislature on split votes and was signed by Governor Safford on February 8, 1877.[44]

The issue moved slowly to an anticlimactic conclusion. A resolution calling on Congress to approve the annexation of Grant County to Arizona was introduced in the House by Hiram Stevens, Arizona's territorial delegate, in October 1877. The proposal was referred to the House Committee on Territories where, as explained by Naegle, "it promptly died."[45] In Naegle's view, the effort of Grant County citizens to act in opposition to the domination of an unfriendly cabal in Santa Fe was not for naught, as the Ring-controlled legislature proved more amenable to Grant County proposals in subsequent sessions, most notably approving a home-rule charter that gave Silver City extraordinary autonomy with respect to revenue and taxation.

The Press and the Ring

Without the interest of an attentive press, nationally and in the Territory of New Mexico, the Santa Fe Ring would likely never have attained the notoriety that it did. The popular image of the Ring, in its day and later, is at least partly the result of a lively newspaper exchange between supporters and detractors. Rare was the territorial editor who was not skilled in the use of ink and newsprint to produce the rhetorical equivalent of a blunt instrument.

Party loyalties were openly displayed, and alliances with newspapers were coveted by local party organizations as essential accessories. In the 1870s and 1880s, the *Borderer* and *Thirty-Four* supported Democratic candidates and policies in the Mesilla Valley, while the *Rio Grande Republican* was true to its name. The *Grant County Herald* generally supported Democratic candidates and causes, and when the *Silver City Enterprise* appeared in 1882, it advocated for the Republicans. In Santa Fe, the *New Mexican* was a consistent supporter of the Republican Party, derided by rivals as a dedicated "Ring organ." Santa Fe papers supporting the Democratic Party, like the *Rocky Mountain Sentinel* and the *Herald*, were usually short lived. The *Las Vegas Optic* was nominally and predominantly Republican, but also a consistent opponent of the Ring.[46]

Elkins and Catron rarely acknowledged accusations concerning their involvement in an organized ring, but the *New Mexican* frequently published commentary scoffing at the criticism and denouncing the critics. William Breeden, as chair of the territorial Republican Committee, was the Ring's most vocal and visible defender. In response to Breeden's regular appearances in the *New Mexican* in defense of his political allies, the *Chieftain* of Pueblo, Colorado, derided him as "the newspaper apologist for the misdeeds of the ring."[47]

As early as the fall of 1873, Breeden had refuted charges of Ring corruption, addressing leaders of the Democratic Party who had denounced the Ring in the party's platform. During the 1876 campaign, the *New Mexican* published a long signed letter from Breeden on the same theme. The gist of his message was that the accusers should put up—produce evidence of corruption emanating from the ranks of the Republican Party—or shut up. The 1873 speech was quoted with comment in the *New Mexican* during the campaign season in 1878, and again in 1880, during Breeden's brief tenure as president of the newspaper company. Lamenting the unstinting blame heaped on the alleged Ring, the paper remarked, "Upon it was laid the burden of all the woes which the people had to bear; it was responsible for the low price of wool, disease among cattle, failures in the crops and for all careless legislation and illegal acts in the Territory."[48]

Much of the verbal sparring was inspired by little more than a determination to maintain political supremacy. In 1878, after five years of newspaper squabbling over the existence of a territorial ring and the character of its alleged members, the *Grant County Herald* could view the matter philosophically. Like it or not, the paper mused, corruption was inherent in human nature, in politics, and in conditions in Washington and in the territories. The paper's editor acknowledged the general rottenness of the system and expressed a pessimistic view of human nature, implying that, given the opportunity to govern, Democrats could be expected to turn the powers of government to serve their own selfish interests, just as their Republican rivals had done.[49]

It would be some years before Democrats would recapture the White House, allowing the *Herald*'s proposition to be tested. Meanwhile, the controversy over "ring rule" would persist and the reputation of the Santa Fe Ring would continue to grow, providing a tangible bogeyman for generations of contrary-minded newspaper editors.

CHAPTER FOUR

THE LINCOLN COUNTY WAR

Throughout the decade of the 1870s, men commonly identified with the Santa Fe Ring seemingly had fingers in every pie. Their economic interests included land, mining, ranching, railroad building, banking, wholesale and retail merchandising, and government contracts. Their involvement in these endeavors provided powerful incentives for pursuit of favorable executive, legislative, and judicial decisions in Santa Fe and in Washington. Wherever there was something of value—agricultural or grazing land, mineral deposits, water, timber, Indian agencies, and military contracts, for example—men associated with the Ring were likely to be visible. Presumed Ring principals had allies in nearly every county. They could mobilize political leaders across the territory, and in some cases judges, jurymen, and officers of the court appeared to be at the disposal of leading Ring figures. When the powers of government could be aligned to support their interests, chances for profitable outcomes were wonderfully enhanced.

The violent conflict popularly known as the Lincoln County War was the product of a time in which opportunities for financial gain were objects of serious competition. Territorial administration was weak and often corrupt, and outlying parts of the territory existed in a state approaching anarchy. Local officials and itinerating judges imposed a semblance of legal process, but a persistent tendency toward corruption often skewed the results. When push came to shove in local disputes, the forces of law and order were frequently left shorthanded with the scarce resources available to govern a vast territory characterized by extremes in geography and climate.

Popular and historical treatments of the Lincoln County War include carefully researched works by capable scholars. These writings typically portray the Lincoln County War as a conflict of competing economic interests, involving a company bent on maintaining its position and an emergent faction eager to capture a major part of the available trade in merchandising, banking, raising livestock, contracting, and other enterprises.

The dominant commercial force in Lincoln County was the enterprise of Lawrence G. Murphy and his associates, including Emil Fritz, James J. Dolan, and John H. Riley. The firm's composition changed over time, first with the death of Fritz in June 1874, then with the illness that led to Murphy's departure from Lincoln in May 1878 and his death in October of that year. The firm first known as L. G. Murphy & Company later became J. J. Dolan & Company, but local residents knew it mainly as the House of Murphy, or simply, the "House."[1] An upstart group was led by John Henry Tunstall, a brash young Englishman who was determined to break the monopoly of the "House." His principal collaborator was Alexander McSween, an attorney. All were immigrants to the United States. Murphy, Dolan, and Riley were Irish. Fritz was German-born. Tunstall was British, and McSween claimed Scottish origin but may have been born in Canada.[2] A third group, somewhat allied with Tunstall and McSween, was led by John Chisum, a Tennessee native who had established a large ranching operation on the Pecos River.

An escalation of commercial and legal disputes, intensified by personal animosities, led to one of the most violent conflicts in western American history—an episode that has spawned myriad print and cinematic works, including memoirs, documentary histories, historical novels, pulp Western magazines, B-Western movies, and more serious films. Fraught with conflicting accounts and interpretations, and embracing common dramatic elements of greed, violence, and political intrigue, the story continues to fascinate scholars, history buffs, artists and writers, and tourists. Among other consequences, the feud wrecked the hopes of both parties seeking to gain economic supremacy and left Lincoln with a reputation for violence and lawlessness. It also launched the public career of an enduring figure in western myth, in the person of William Bonney, known to some as *El Chivato* and to others as Billy the Kid.

The involvement of the Santa Fe Ring in the Lincoln County conflict was largely a result of business and political alliances that were established before the trouble began. In a deposition given in June 1878, Jimmy Dolan, a partner with Murphy since 1874, acknowledged the firm's long-standing relationship with the First National Bank of Santa Fe.[3] Founded in 1870 by Lucien Maxwell and associates, the bank had passed into the hands of a group led by Stephen Elkins and Thomas Catron, with Elkins serving as president and the two holding a majority of the stock.[4] The association of the "House" with Elkins's

Figure 10 L. G. Murphy and Company, ca. 1871: left to right, James J. Dolan, Emil
Fritz, William Martin, and Lawrence G. Murphy. They dominated mercantile
and contracting business in Lincoln County from the late 1860s to the late 1870s.
Robert N. Mullin Collection, Haley Memorial Library and History Center, No. 77.2.

bank led to involvements in the mercantile business and ranching, and formed the basis for a broader alliance.

By the mid-1870s, Elkins was New Mexico's territorial delegate to Congress and was largely occupied with interests in the eastern United States. Catron remained focused on New Mexico. He sometimes acquired property, not necessarily coveted, due to the failure of enterprises to which he had loaned money, or for which he had secured debt. It is likely that his acquisition of interests in Lincoln County was a result of the failure of the Murphy-Dolan business. As the "House" fell into debt, Catron had been a willing guarantor, advancing more than $20,000 to help the firm stay afloat. In return, he received a chattel mortgage on the assets.[5] By May 1, 1878, when the company was dissolved following a suspension of business, Catron had acquired assets including the store in Lincoln, land, hay, grain, horses, and approximately two thousand head of cattle. He had also acquired land at Roswell, then lying within the vastness of Lincoln County.

Prelude to Violence

The new year, 1878, did not promise much for residents of Lincoln County. Peaceable citizens had been enduring a period of lawlessness for some time, and tensions were on the rise. A band of outlaws known as "the boys" had been plundering the country, stealing horses and mules from the Mescalero Apaches and from area ranches in the summer and fall of 1877.[6] Jesse Evans's ruffians supplied main force for the "House" and for Jimmy Dolan, successor to L. G. Murphy. Murphy and Dolan had been accused of corruption in connection with their business with Fort Stanton and the Mescaleros, and they had been denounced for bullying small ranchers in the area. Dolan had demonstrated a willingness to use violence.

Challenging the supremacy of the "House" was the young Englishman John Tunstall, aided by McSween and an assortment of characters including Tunstall's abrasive but trusted colleague Robert Widenmann and an armed force consisting of J. G. "Doc" Scurlock, William Bonney, and other rough men known collectively as the "Regulators."

By the first weeks of 1878, links between the "House" and the dominant economic and political powers in Santa Fe had become apparent. Political alliances and business relationships determined the sympathies of the territorial ring in Lincoln County, and the actions of officials sympathetic to the Santa Fe Ring worked to their own benefit and that of the Dolan party.

Among those who had reason to fear the "House," it was widely believed that its principals exercised influence over courts that had jurisdiction in the region.[7] Alexander McSween later swore to having heard L. G. Murphy boast that "he controlled not only the courts and juries, but that he could cause the death of any person who opposed him." McSween's conclusion, reinforced by experience, was that the courts functioned as tools of the "House."[8] Through their association with Catron, Jimmy Dolan and his allies also had access to the governor, Samuel Axtell.

A pretext for action against Tunstall and McSween was found in McSween's handling of a life insurance claim on behalf of the heirs of Emil Fritz, the late business associate of Murphy and Dolan. Retained to collect $10,000 due on the policy, McSween delayed payment to the heirs for reasons he believed legally sufficient and compelling, but he stood accused of embezzlement. Doubtless Fritz's surviving brother and sister were concerned, but Dolan seems to have been an active presence in the matter, inciting their mistrust and urging them to action.

In December 1877, Dolan made use of connections to pursue what could now be called a vendetta against Tunstall and McSween. He procured an affidavit from Emilie Scholand, Fritz's sister, and used it to move his powerful associates to action. As related by Frederick Nolan, "He took it to his friend, District Attorney W. L. Rynerson, who immediately requested their mutual ally in Santa Fe, U.S. District Attorney Thomas B. Catron, to ensure that McSween did not leave the Territory before a warrant for his arrest could be sent to Las Vegas."[9] McSween had started for Las Vegas en route to St. Louis. The pretext for Dolan's interest in the matter was a debt that Fritz allegedly owed to the "House." Moreover, Dolan probably saw an opportunity to settle scores with McSween, while damaging Tunstall's initiative—perhaps fatally.

Catron obliged his Lincoln County associates, instructing the sheriff of San Miguel County to apprehend McSween and John Chisum. McSween was arrested at Las Vegas, charged with embezzlement, and transported to Mesilla, where he appeared before Warren Bristol, judge of New Mexico's Third Judicial District. Proceedings held on two days, February 2 and 4, 1878, failed to resolve the matter of McSween's culpability, but they did reveal an apparent bias on the part of Judge Bristol and District Attorney Rynerson.[10] The case was continued to April, when a grand jury would consider an indictment against McSween. Bail was set pending Rynerson's approval of bonds presented on McSween's behalf, but McSween's bonds were refused for no apparent reason other than a desire to make his situation as difficult as possible. A deputy sheriff was ordered to deliver McSween to be held in Lincoln until he could present a satisfactory bond or stand trial. A sympathetic sheriff's deputy, Adolph Barrier, escorted McSween to Lincoln, but kept him in hiding outside Lincoln rather than turn him over to a sheriff known to be on friendly terms with the "House."[11]

Evidence linking Judge Bristol to the Ring was mostly circumstantial. In January 1876, citizens of Grant County had complained of partiality in his handling of matters coming before their court.[12] Statements in his defense from Catron and Richard Hudson, a local Ring favorite, may not have been helpful in countering the popular perception that Bristol had come under the spell of the Ring.[13] Concerning the trouble in Lincoln County, Bristol expressed strong opinions from the bench and appeared to act in a manner prejudicial to McSween. When a grand jury met to review the matter, Bristol delivered a long charge to the jury, reciting and, in effect, endorsing the prosecution case against McSween.[14] It is little wonder that contemporary observers and later historians regarded Bristol as "the Ring's judge in that district."[15]

After sitting McSween for several days, Deputy Barrier returned to his home and allowed McSween to go about his business in Lincoln, still technically in the deputy's custody. McSween never succeeded in bonding out legally, thanks in part to the efforts of Dolan and Riley. Dolan's agents were said to have threatened Dr. Joseph H. Blazer with prosecution by Catron on charges of cutting timber on public lands, should he agree to post bond on McSween's behalf.[16]

As a further precaution, a writ of attachment was issued on February 7, 1878, by the district court at Mesilla, ordering the sheriff to seize assets sufficient to cover any liability on McSween's part to the extent of $8,000. This action had been requested based on an affidavit presented by Charles Fritz, brother of the deceased, charging McSween with fraud and citing an urgent need to prevent McSween's absconding with his own property and the disputed insurance money. According to Frederick Nolan, Dolan prompted Fritz's action, and Dolan and Rynerson personally provided the bond required for issuance of the writ of attachment.[17] The justification for such a writ was doubtful, and the manner of its execution further exposed the bias of the court and its officers. The seizure was to include not only McSween's property, but, based on the false premise that the men had already commenced a formal business partnership, livestock and other goods belonging to John Tunstall were to be taken as well. This wholesale attachment of goods and livestock—with no apparent effort to fairly determine the value of property seized—seemed calculated as much to ruin a competitor as to satisfy the claim of Emil Fritz's heirs and creditors.

Tunstall was under no illusions concerning the intentions of his adversaries. Shortly after his arrival in the territory, he had written to his father describing the pervasive presence of rings working military and Indian contracts, the cattle trade, land grants, and other paying businesses. Indeed, he hoped to form a ring of his own.[18] Under assault from Dolan and his powerful friends, and shaken by the attachment of his property, Tunstall bristled at a suggestion that he seek relief in the courts, expressing anger and frustration that they were controlled by the territorial ring.[19]

By 1884, William Logan Rynerson was portraying himself as an antagonist to the Santa Fe Ring, but previous actions, including those undertaken as district attorney in connection with the Lincoln County conflict, suggest that he was a strong partisan of the Ring. Most persuasive in this respect was a letter dated February 14, 1878, and addressed to "Friends Riley & Dolan," in which Rynerson said of their mutual adversaries, "It must be made hot for them all, the hotter the better; especially is this necessary, now that it has been discovered that there is no hell." Rynerson counseled firmness in dealing with Tunstall and McSween and told his friends, "I shall help you all I can for I believe there was never found a more scoundrelly set than that outfit."[20]

The letter fell into McSween's possession when, according to McSween's account, John Riley visited the McSween home on the night of February 18, 1878. Riley reportedly had been drinking and was at pains to exonerate himself with respect to an incident that was the cause of some excitement in Lincoln. The letter had been placed between the pages of a memo book left at the house by Riley—a notebook that also contained code names for several men commonly identified with the Santa Fe Ring. In the context of the day's events, the letter appeared to confer Rynerson's blessing on deeds both violent and extreme.

The cause of Riley's distress was the murder of John Tunstall at the hands of men sent to attach livestock at his ranch on the Rio Feliz earlier in the day. Exact circumstances of Tunstall's death were never discovered, but the essential facts were clear enough: members of the pursuing posse had ridden down and killed Tunstall in the hills near his home ranch. Tunstall either had or had not fired on his pursuers, depending on the version of events one chooses to believe. Some posse members indicated that Tunstall had not fired, but had been killed in cold blood.

Montague R. Leverson, a hysterical critic of Dolan and his men, saw Rynerson's letter as a clear invitation to murder and insisted that the killing was chargeable to U.S. authorities.[21] Robert Widenmann appealed to a San Francisco attorney who had extended earlier courtesies to Tunstall, telling R. Guy McClellan, "It was a cold-blooded and premeditated murder, committed in the interest of the New Mexico ring, and as the Ring controls the Courts of the Territory it is difficult to bring the murderers to justice."[22] Notwithstanding the shrill quality of these writings, there is little evidence, other than the ambiguous Rynerson letter of February 14, to indicate that anyone in an official capacity was part of a plot to kill Tunstall. It seems more likely that he was killed in the midst of a highly charged local feud by men who were no strangers to violence and who believed that they were acting in accordance with Dolan's wishes.

War for the Hell of It

In its first seven decades as a territory and then a state, New Mexico reconfigured its counties as often as states now redraw congressional districts. There were reasons for this, as advances in immigration, commercial development, and transportation influenced the distribution of people, as well as patterns of travel. In February 1878, the legislature altered the county boundaries and increased the size of Lincoln County, so that it took in nearly the entire southeastern quadrant of New Mexico, bordering Texas on the south and east, and encompassing an area of some 27,000 square miles.[23] But the county's population numbered fewer than three thousand souls, and resources for law enforcement were scarce and subject to political manipulation. Emerson Hough, who had absorbed much of the region's history and color from a brief residency in the mining town of White Oaks, characterized the setting of the Lincoln County trouble in these terms:

> Southeastern New Mexico, for twenty years after the Civil War, was without doubt, as dangerous a country as ever lay out of doors. The Pecos valley caught the first of the great west-bound Texas cattle herds at a time when the maverick industry was at its height. Old

John Chisum had perhaps sixty to eighty thousand head of cattle. It was easier to steal these cattle than to raise cows for one's self. As for refuge, there lay the central mountains of New Mexico. As for a market, there was the military post of Fort Stanton, with beef contracts for supplying the Mescalero Indian reservation. Between the market and the Pecos cow herds ran the winding valley of the Bonito, like a cleat on a vast sluiceway. It caught bad men naturally.[24]

What ensued after Tunstall's death was a series of recriminations, most of which were superficially cloaked in the garb of legal process. The day after the killing, two men loyal to Tunstall, Richard Brewer and William Bonney, swore affidavits against members of the posse that had come to the ranch to seize livestock and, as it happened, to kill Tunstall. The affidavits were taken by John B. Wilson, a justice of the peace who leaned toward the Tunstall-McSween faction. Arrest warrants were turned over to the constable, who deputized Bonney and Frederick Waite. William Brady, sheriff of Lincoln County and an ally of the "House," promptly arrested the men, holding the constable's deputies in jail. Within days, Rob Widenmann, acting in his capacity as a U.S. deputy marshal, had taken possession of the Tunstall store in Lincoln with the support of other Tunstall men, securing the arrest of Sheriff Brady and his deputy. Brady was bound over for trial at the April term of the district court, then released. Brady, in turn, arrested Widenmann and other members of his "posse" for rioting; they, too, were bound over for trial.

Based on the warrants issued by Wilson, Brewer led a posse in pursuit of the men most directly linked to Tunstall's death and captured two of them, William Morton and Frank Baker. The prisoners ended up dead, reportedly shot while attempting to escape after killing a member of the posse. To those of the "House" persuasion, the circumstances indicated something more akin to an execution.[25] In the chaotic month following the death of Tunstall, there seemingly was a near total absence of impartiality among those charged with enforcing and applying the law. Nearly everyone was on a side, or was presumed to be.

Given the chaos in Lincoln County, it is hard to blame territorial officials for attempting to intervene. They were obligated to do so, but partisanship was evident in virtually every action originating in Santa Fe or at the seat of the district court in Mesilla. For those so inclined, it was not hard to see the hand of the Ring at work. On February 24, 1878, Rynerson wired Governor Axtell, proclaiming, "Anarchy in Lincoln County. Sheriff powerless. Has been arrested on some bogus charge and property he had attached on writ from Dist. Court taken from him. Tunstall killed by sheriff's posse, resisting." Rynerson advised the governor to have Widenmann relieved as deputy U.S. marshal and to request assistance from the military to prevent further bloodshed.[26]

Governor Axtell had been the recipient of a loan from the "House" two years earlier, indicating a degree of intimacy with the Dolan faction. He was consistently responsive to the entreaties of Catron and other members of the Santa Fe power structure, causing him to be widely identified as a member or tool of the Ring. On February 25, he wrote to Colonel Edward Hatch, commanding officer for the District of New Mexico, requesting that troops be dispatched "to enforce the law and save life and property in Lincoln County," and enclosing Rynerson's telegram.[27]

On March 9, the governor visited Lincoln, where, according to Frederick Nolan, "He stayed only three hours, all of which time was spent in the company of L. G. Murphy and Jimmy Dolan."[28] As he had done earlier with respect to the troubles in Colfax County, he declined to hear from the opposing faction. Proving himself a man of action, Axtell performed "a series of official acts as extraordinary as any ever executed by a public servant in the history of New Mexico." He removed a duly appointed justice of the peace, John B. Wilson, and voided processes legally issued by him. He revoked Widenmann's appointment as U.S. deputy marshal. Axtell declared that the only legal processes to be recognized henceforth were those issued by Judge Warren Bristol and enforced under auspices of Sheriff William Brady. In Nolan's view, the critical effect of Axtell's proclamation was to "deliver all legal power into the hands of minions of the Santa Fe Ring."[29]

If the object of Axtell's involvement was to restore peace and to preserve life and property, the effort was an abject failure and may have contributed to further violence by demonstrating to McSween supporters and other anti-"House" citizens that they could not look to the law and their government for relief. Some who had been commissioned by justice of the peace Wilson to apprehend men for whom warrants had been issued were, in effect, made outlaws in consequence of Axtell's actions. Apropos of all that had occurred, the *Mesilla Valley Independent* observed on March 16, 1878, "Men are disposed to take the law into their own hands when they are forced to feel that the courts cannot be depended on to mete out even-handed

Figure 11 After a tumultuous tenure as governor of the Territory of Utah, Samuel Beach Axtell was appointed governor of New Mexico, where he became a lightning rod for the grievances of anti-Ring citizens. Research Center, Utah State Historical Society, No. 11612.

justice to its violators." Conceding that vigilante justice was "a terrible alternative," the paper concluded that "mob law is better than no law."

The death of William McCloskey, a member of the Regulator posse, and those of Morton and Baker, suspects in the killing of Tunstall, occurred the day Axtell's proclamation was issued. On April 1, Sheriff Brady and his deputy, George Hindman, were shot down in Lincoln by angry Regulators, including Billy Bonney. Three days later, the Regulators went hunting two other men of the posse that had killed Tunstall. At Blazer's Mill near the Mescalero agency, they met with one of their prey, Andrew "Buckshot" Roberts. Outgunned by the Regulators but mindful of the impromptu executions said to have been meted out to Morton and Baker, Roberts refused to surrender. He died in the gun battle that followed, but a bullet from his rifle felled Dick Brewer, leader of the Regulators. The "disorder" in Lincoln County had become a war.

As U.S. attorney for the Territory of New Mexico, Catron had official responsibilities in relation to the turbulent events of 1878, but he did not fail to attend to his personal affairs in the county at a time when the chaos threatened virtually all property interests in the region. On May 30, 1878, he wrote to Governor Axtell to report an attack on men working his livestock in the Pecos Valley. One man had been killed, and horses and mules had been run off. Based on reports from his law partner, William T. Thornton, Catron noted the presence of armed bands and complained that the sheriff—John Copeland—had deputies in the field, accompanied by posses "who are of one faction only and who take occasion at all times to kill persons and take the property of the other faction whenever they get an opportunity."[30] Citing the threat to his cattle, Catron wanted Axtell to order the outlaws disarmed and request the aid of the military to protect the citizens and keep the peace. The governor did as Catron requested, dispatching a letter to that effect to Colonel Edward Hatch. Axtell also removed Sheriff Copeland, appointing George Peppin in his place.[31]

Self-serving though his request was, it is difficult to fault Catron for seeking to protect his property and that of other citizens. More striking is the governor's willingness to accept Catron's version of events and his judgment on the sheriff, and to pass the request along to Hatch without notable modification. The incident reinforces the impression of Axtell as a tool in the hands of a powerful elite, failing to consider diverse views or gather sufficient evidence before acting.

Copeland had been legally appointed by the county commission in place of the murdered sheriff, William Brady, but Axtell, possibly with help from his clever advisors in Santa Fe, found grounds to remove him based on his failure to file a bond required of him as tax collector for the county. Axtell had used the same pretext to replace a sheriff in Colfax County. Whether or not Peppin was a more effective enforcer of the laws, he was surely a more satisfactory agent for Dolan and his Santa Fe allies. Recalling the matter some years later, George W. Coe noted, "This appointment smacked of the control of the old 'Santa Fé Ring,' and caused much comment."[32] With Peppin taking office, further polarization of the factions appeared inevitable.

The trouble in Lincoln County attracted attention in the territory nationally and, because of the Tunstall family's pursuit of redress, internationally. Territorial papers were quick to take sides. The *Independent*, edited by Albert J. Fountain and associates, was not a particular friend of the McSween faction, but in its opposition to the Ring, the paper criticized "House" partisans and the officials who supported them. The *Santa Fe Daily New Mexican* was consistently pledged to the powerful men associated with the Ring, regardless of the issue at hand. The paper jumped with both feet on a letter written by Robert Widenmann and expressed support for the actions of Rynerson, Judge Bristol, U.S. Attorney Catron, and Governor Axtell. Widenmann, according to the paper, was "a liar, a coward, and a hypocrite."[33]

Predictably, the *Cimarron News and Press* offered a more agreeable outlet for the views of McSween and Widenmann.

Both sides in the Lincoln County conflict suffered losses of life and property. The "House" fared better in the shooting war and in the territorial courts, but Tunstall's avengers had the better of the propaganda war. Derided locally and regarded by many as self-important meddlers, Robert Widenmann and Montague Leverson generated a blizzard of correspondence, launching damning broadsides against the "House" and the Ring in the territorial press and in complaints lodged with U.S. and British officials. Widenmann sent his account of events to Tunstall's family in England and to Sir Edward Thornton, the British ambassador in Washington.[34] He later plied Secretary of the Interior Carl Schurz with complaints concerning corruption in the Mescalero Indian Agency. Leverson, an attorney and an immigrant from England, wrote to Thornton and U.S. Marshal John Sherman, as well as to President Hayes and Secretary Schurz, reporting official transgressions both large and small; condemning the actions of Axtell, Rynerson, and Bristol; and urging the swift removal of Axtell and Rynerson.[35] In a March 16 epistle to the president, Leverson made broad charges against Catron, Elkins, and Surveyor General Atkinson.[36] Regarded locally as pariahs, these two alarmists gained more attention for their cause in faraway places.

Intervention and Further Bloodshed

The barrage of communications from Widenmann and Leverson put their views in broad circulation, and though the messengers were widely disparaged, their effort drew attention to the continuing turmoil in New Mexico. British ambassador Edward Thornton and Tunstall's father and uncle petitioned federal officials for an investigation. Allegations of corruption on the part of federal officials in the territory likely hastened the appointment of a special investigator. In April 1878, Frank Warner Angel of New York was appointed as federal special agent and charged with determining the circumstances of Tunstall's death and causes of the violence in Lincoln County.

By the time he arrived in New Mexico, Angel was carrying a pocketful of investigative commissions. Having learned of his appointment by the Justice Department, Carl Schurz, secretary of the Department of the Interior, wrote requesting that Angel look into accusations against the territorial governor, secretary, and surveyor general.[37] U.S. Attorney Catron also became a focus of the investigation. Angel, who reportedly carried a commission as an army inspector, was also asked to investigate charges against Frederick Godfroy, an Indian agent for the Mescalero Apaches.[38] In addition to focusing on the Tunstall murder and Lincoln County, Angel was expected to review complaints of official corruption that had been festering since the earlier disturbances in Colfax County. He stayed in New Mexico through the summer of 1878, leaving in mid-August. Though the investigation did little to resolve the controversies he was sent to examine, depositions taken from witnesses of all political stripes provided some insight into conditions in the territory and shed considerable light on the involvement of men commonly identified with the Santa Fe Ring.

If the governor and presumed Ring men appeared to have the upper hand in Lincoln County, Angel, over his approximately three-month investigative tour of New Mexico, seemed increasingly to favor McSween and anti-Ring citizens of the territory. It could not have helped the Dolan faction's cause when, in the midst of Angel's investigation, the most violent event of the Lincoln County War occurred: a conflagration that resulted in the burning of McSween's home and the killing of McSween and men loyal to him. A detachment from Fort Stanton under command of Lieutenant Colonel Nathan Augustus Monroe Dudley was present in Lincoln and gave tacit, if not actual, support to the "posse" acting under the auspices of the sheriff. A leaderless remnant of Regulators fled to the hills and, on August 5, raided the Mescalero agency, killing the agent's clerk, Morris Bernstein.

Angel's report had a severe and immediate impact in Washington. Secretary Carl Schurz moved, on September 4, 1878, to suspend Axtell, replacing him with Lew Wallace, author, noted Union general, and son of the late Indiana governor David Wallace.[39] Disapproval of the change was to be expected of the *New Mexican*, but papers not so directly vested strained to make sense of the upheaval. The *Denver Daily Tribune* reported on the criticism of Axtell and the Ring but expressed skepticism concerning the validity of charges against the deposed governor.[40]

Unresolved were questions concerning Catron's actions as U.S. attorney. Pressed to answer Angel's questions, Catron first requested additional time, then enlisted Stephen B. Elkins to plead his cause in Washington. In responding to Elkins and explaining his unwillingness to grant Catron an extension, Attorney General Charles Devens expressed his belief that the refusal was justified, "especially since he appears to have considered the matter of answering not of sufficient importance as to take precedence of his private matters."[41] Territorial secretary Ritch also tried to intercede, forwarding his testimonial on Catron's behalf.[42] Catron finally submitted responses to Angel's questions, but he requested time to obtain affidavits in his defense. Perhaps concluding that the cause was lost, he submitted a brief letter of resignation on October 10.[43]

A third casualty of Angel's investigation was the Indian agent Frederick Godfroy. Unable or unwilling to stand up to repeated abuses by Murphy, Dolan, and associates, including "borrowing" of government property for sale in their business in Lincoln, Godfroy was charged with irregularities in administration of the agency. Convinced that illegal practices had been tolerated, but with evident sympathy for Godfroy, Angel recommended that he be permitted to resign. Godfroy was suspended from office by President Hayes on August 2, 1878.[44]

Angel mostly stayed clear of references to the Ring in official reports of his investigation. The only direct reference to the Ring in four summary reports filed by Angel occurs in his report on charges against Governor Axtell, in which he refers to Pedro Sánchez of Taos as a "ringite." There are, however, allusions to the Santa Fe Ring in testimony taken by Angel, most notably in Frank Springer's deposition of August 9, 1878—a statement said to have influenced Angel's findings.[45] As references to the Ring were common in newspaper rhetoric and in the conversation of persons opposed to the powerful combination, Angel no doubt heard plenty about it. He apparently found the notion credible. In notes prepared for Lew Wallace, he identified three newspapers and several individuals as having ties to the Ring.[46]

Governor Wallace

When Lew Wallace was appointed to follow Axtell as governor, the most pressing item of business was ridding Lincoln County of its criminal element and bringing peace to a bitterly divided people. If justice could be done, so much the better. A secondary expectation, at least on the part of the territory's anti-Ring citizens, was that Wallace would suppress the Ring and bring an end to government by a corrupt ruling clique.

"In territorial histories," says Patricia Nelson Limerick, "one plot repeats. The territorial governor arrives. He is not a talented man, but he has some hopes of doing his job. He has a modest salary, less modest expenses, and some interest in his own political and economic advancement. He knows the territory's affairs are not in good order, and he would like it to be to his credit that he restored order and created a climate conducive to investment

Figure 12 Sent to quell disturbances
in Lincoln County and to curtail the
excesses of a territorial ring, Lew Wallace
found New Mexico's political structure
remarkably resistant to reform.
Palace of the Governors Photo Archives
(NMHM/DCA), No. 15295.

and prosperity."[47] The situation devolves into a struggle of competing factions to secure the executive's favor, with the losing side calling for his urgent
removal. In the end, he is likely to be both disappointed and a disappoint-
ment. With the exception of his having been a demonstrably talented man,
the profile perfectly describes Wallace's experience as governor of the
Territory of New Mexico.

Wallace came with a creditable record of service as a Union general in the
Civil War and was an accomplished working author. His abilities were unques-
tioned, but he was not happy to be in New Mexico, and he never warmed to the
region's history and culture as some political immigrants did. He had sought
a diplomatic appointment before being dispatched to the dusty Southwest, and
he continued to lobby the secretary of state for a post abroad. He hesitated in
applying himself to the Lincoln County problem, acting belatedly but deci-
sively. Concerning the challenge of reforming a corrupt political system, he
gave it a whirl, but found it an uphill job, especially for an administrator whose
heart was that of an artist rather than of a reformer.

Wallace traveled to New Mexico in the old manner, riding the rails to
the end of the line and completing the journey in a buckboard. He was
among the last gentleman travelers to reach the territory in this manner,
crossing Raton Pass only a few months ahead of the railroad. As to the buckboard, Wallace told his wife, "A deadlier instrument of torture was never
used in the days of Torquemada; had anything the equal of it been resorted

to then, there would have been few heretics."[48] Wallace spent a day in Colfax County and stopped overnight at Cimarron with Frank Springer, an implacable foe of the previous governor and a persistent enemy of the Ring. Wallace was relieved to find no apparent threat of further violence in Colfax, telling Secretary of the Interior Schurz, "Without reference to the past, there certainly appeared to be a good feeling on the part of the citizens there, and a decided disposition to keep the peace."[49]

Lincoln County was another matter, as Wallace knew. He also learned that the powers at his disposal for dealing with the turbulence were woefully inadequate. Having been in Santa Fe only a few days, he sent an urgent wire to Schurz, describing the dire circumstances in Lincoln County, enclosing reports from military officials and Judge Bristol, and requesting a presidential declaration of martial law and a stand of arms for the purpose of raising a militia.[50] He received, instead, a presidential proclamation warning offenders in Lincoln that they had better straighten up.[51] Wallace succeeded in prying some weapons out of Washington, but repeated entreaties for a declaration of martial law were unheeded.

After a scant six weeks on the job, Wallace issued a proclamation that read, "For the information of the people of the United States, and of the citizens of New Mexico in especial, the undersigned announces that the disorders prevalent in Lincoln County in said Territory have been happily brought to an end. Persons having business and property interests therein, and who are themselves peaceably disposed, may go to and from that County without hindrance or molestation."[52] A further purpose of the document was to declare a general amnesty for offenses committed between February 1, 1878, and the date of issue, November 13, 1878.

The proclamation expressly included "officers of the United States Army stationed in the County during the disorders," presumably to preclude the possibility that military officers would be made culpable for actions taken in response to the emergency. Some may have received this concession with gratitude, but it struck a nerve with the commanding officer at Fort Stanton, Colonel Dudley. In his mind, officers of the army had not acted improperly or illegally, and the intimation that they might have done so was not appreciated. Dudley demanded a court of inquiry for the purpose of clearing his name of any such implication.[53]

By this time, Wallace had experienced the formidable presence of the Santa Fe Ring. To a former comrade in arms, Colonel A. H. Markland, he wrote, "I came here, and found a 'Ring' with a hand on the throat of the

Territory. I refused to join them, and now they are proposing to fight me in the Senate."[54] Wallace's appointment as governor had not yet been confirmed. The urgent purpose of his letter was to enlist Markland's help with the confirmation fight in Washington.

Wallace was convinced that Stephen Elkins was making mischief for him in the capital. He named Elkins as the source of a lie published in the *Washington Sunday Herald*, to the effect that Wallace had been observed "standing before the bar in a saloon in the midst of a group of men who were attracting attention by their boisterous conduct."[55] The item was attributed to the *Rocky Mountain Sentinel* of Santa Fe, which refuted the report and said of the item, "Its style so closely resembles that of the Washington member of the Santa Fe ring, that we are inclined to believe its publication was effected by him." Wallace asked for Markland's earnest effort, noting that Elkins would be leading the opposition with the help of some powerful allies. Supporters of Wallace were relieved when, on December 16, word of his confirmation reached Santa Fe via a telegram sent from Stephen Dorsey to Henry Waldo and was published in the *Sentinel*.[56]

Wallace took the occasion of his amnesty proclamation and some approving words in the *Sentinel* to declare victory in his quest to pacify Lincoln County. Less than two months into his tenure—and before his confirmation—Wallace had written to the secretary of state to report his success. Having done so, he invoked the secretary's favor: "That task would seem to have been my special mission here; and as it is accomplished, do you not think me entitled to promotion? As the field in which your hand has to appear is a very wide one, with much to be done in it, I would be particularly happy if you would entrust me with some fitting part of the work."[57]

Wallace's self-appraisal was premature, to say the least, and may have been seen in that light in Washington. As a matter of fact, his real work was not behind him, but in front of him. The violence had *not* ended, and Wallace had yet to set foot in Lincoln County—a detail of which he was reminded by Huston Chapman, a Las Vegas attorney who wrote in late November 1878 to deliver a stern message. While affirming his good wishes for the governor's success, Chapman warned, "The people of Lincoln County are disquieted and tired of the neglect and indifference shown them by you, and next week they intend holding a mass meeting to give expression to their sentiment, and unless you come here before that time you may expect to be severely denounced in language more forcible than polite."[58]

Wallace did not go to Lincoln at Chapman's behest, but he went in March 1879, after Chapman's death at the hands of gun-wielding partisans of the "House." Accompanied by Colonel Edward Hatch, he arrived in Lincoln on March 6 and stayed approximately six weeks, seeming at last to come to grips with the violence. At his request, Hatch suspended Colonel Dudley, the nettlesome post commander. Wallace enlisted the assistance of the military in making civil arrests and renewed his request to President Hayes for a declaration of martial law. He saw to the arrest of Jimmy Dolan, William Campbell, Jesse Evans, and Billy Mathews for their roles in the murder of Huston Chapman, and he issued a list of some three dozen lawbreakers who were to be arrested.[59] When Evans and Campbell escaped, he offered a reward of $1,000 for their capture. He formed a company of riflemen for local protection and held parley with William Bonney in pursuit of testimony against other accused persons. The story of Wallace's assurance that the Kid should go free with a pardon in his pocket for his service in identifying Chapman's killers is part of Billy's legend, but Wallace never made good on the promise, and some have doubted that he intended to do so. In the view of Frederick Nolan, this shameless manipulation of the young outlaw "redounds less than favorably upon Wallace."[60]

Wallace left Lincoln on April 18, with mixed results to show for his effort. No one was brought to justice in the wrongful death of Chapman. The court of inquiry concerning Dudley's role in the siege of the McSween home resulted as Dudley wished, in his official exoneration. On the other hand, the district court was in session with a full slate of criminal indictments on hand, and the governor's hot pursuit of lawbreakers had caused some to leave and others to moderate their behavior. Wallace left Lincoln a more peaceful place than he had found it, but he had by no means extinguished the power of the "House" men or the public officials who supported them.

An outsider himself, Wallace relied on other outsiders for information and advice. John B. Wilson, justice of the peace from February 1877 until Governor Axtell removed him a year later, was a steady presence in Lincoln and a man Wallace could trust. Wallace's other counselor was Ira Leonard, a Las Vegas attorney who kept the governor informed via long, gossipy letters from Lincoln, where he represented Susan McSween's interests.

As the court session continued in Wallace's absence, it became apparent that the courts would be of little help in bringing violent perpetrators to justice. Leonard pegged Rynerson as "a Dolan man" and laid much of the responsibility for the Lincoln County trouble on Judge Warren Bristol, blaming the presence of violent factions on Bristol's weakness and acquiescence to the established powers.[61] Stating a widely shared construction of events, Leonard remarked that the Murphy-Dolan party, so long accustomed to dominating the region commercially, could tolerate no opposition and acted ruthlessly to eliminate threats to their supremacy. Said Leonard, "They were a part and parcel of the Santa Fe ring that has been so long an incubus on the government in this Territory." Leonard thought the public interest would be best served by Bristol's removal as judge in favor of himself—a proposition that Wallace supported, to no avail.

The belief that courts in southern New Mexico were out to protect rather than to prosecute lawbreakers was reinforced for Governor Wallace when William R. Morley, while working for the Atchison, Topeka and Santa Fe Railway in Colorado, wrote to report on his conversation with a loquacious Dolan sympathizer.[62] Morley's source was confident in the ability of Dolan's friends to obtain dismissals of their indictments in Lincoln County or on change of venue to Doña Ana, where juries could be stacked in their favor. Regarding Wallace, the source had indicated that it would be to Dolan's advantage to keep Lincoln County in a state of turmoil, so that "you will have failed in restoring order and be forced to resign." In Morley's opinion, the man appeared to be "well posted" and credible in his assertions.

Wallace continued as governor for another two years, during which conditions in Lincoln County were reduced from a rolling boil to a simmer. In addition to finishing his enduring novel *Ben Hur*, Wallace interested himself in mining prospects in the territory. Otherwise, he expressed increasing boredom and no small measure of cynicism. In March 1881, he told son Henry that he had accomplished what he wanted in New Mexico: the acquisition of "as good a mining property as there is in the Territory." Explaining himself further, Wallace told his son, "The lesson of my life is, talent and honors amount to nothing in this age and in our country *without money*."[63]

Wallace's tenure as governor coincided with the last months of the Lincoln County War and its lingering aftermath. He was rescued from his time of exile, and a long separation from his beloved wife, by virtue of an appointment as U.S. minister to Turkey. Wallace left the territory on May 30, 1881, shortly before the death of William Bonney wrote an end to the sad and sordid Lincoln County affair. When his deliverance was assured, Wallace wrote to his wife, expressing impatience for the arrival of his successor. He reflected on the years of near continual frustration, punctuated by brief moments of success, and pondered the likely fate of a new governor. Wrote Wallace, "Of course he will do just as I did, have the same ideas, make the same attempts, and with the same heartiness of effort, soon cool in zeal, then finally say, 'All right, let her drift.'"[64]

So Runs the Tide Away

Following the widely publicized clashes in Colfax and Lincoln counties, any veil of anonymity that might have shrouded the Ring's aspirations had been stripped away, and attentive citizens would henceforth view matters emanating from the elite combination based in Santa Fe with caution and with a healthy dose of skepticism.

The Lincoln County War had barely begun when the *Cimarron News and Press* noted, "Something over two years ago Colfax county passed through part of the experience which Lincoln county has lately had."[65] Based on reports of the Lincoln County affair, the paper developed an apt comparison of two disorders. Other similarities would emerge in time. Both conflicts had their origins in economic issues. The flash point in each case was the assassination of a newcomer who dared to challenge the established economic and political powers. Though distant from the capital, both counties felt the hand of the territorial ring as it moved to aid one party and suppress the other. In both instances, Governor Axtell appeared to respond in a partisan manner and at the direction of presumed Ring principals, while ignoring the grievances of large segments of the local population. In both localities, control of the courts played a critical role. As in Colfax, military forces were deployed in Lincoln County at the request of territorial officials. The assistance of the local garrison was nominally for the purpose of maintaining order, but there was also evident intent to enforce the will of Ring-related political and economic powers.

The involvement of alleged Ring members in the Lincoln County War was not indicative of a deliberate conspiracy, undertaken with premeditated malice and centrally managed by a boss or a ruling clique. Rather, the struggle proceeded as a series of reactions driven by a mulligan stew of economic interests, jealousies, grudges, and spontaneous displays of manly aggression. The involvement of men commonly identified with the Ring reflected mutual affinities, shared aims, and the capacity to marshal governmental powers in pursuit of common interests.

By the time he could conveniently extricate himself from the Territory of New Mexico, Lew Wallace had enjoyed about as much of the country as he could stand, but he was due one last humiliation at the hands of the Ring. In early 1880, it had been his duty to fill vacancies in the territorial government, among which was the office of attorney general. Candidates seeking the office included Catron, William Breeden, and Eugene A. Fiske—all Republicans, as was the governor. When Catron saw that the appointment would not be his, he withdrew from the field. Wallace appointed Fiske and encountered strong opposition.

Men identified with the Ring held what amounted to a long-term lease on the office and took offense at Wallace's impertinence in naming Fiske. Explaining his reasoning to Secretary Schurz, Wallace wrote, "Mr. Breeden is a gentleman of undoubted merit, long resident of the Territory, in politics a Republican, and a leader of the party in this region. I would have given him the appointment but that the adherents of the ring rallied unanimously to his support after Mr. Catron's withdrawal, leaving a fear in my mind that his appointment would be received throughout the Territory as a 'Ring' victory, and lose me all the results of a year or more of vigorous contest with that powerful faction."[66]

Catron helped prevent Fiske's confirmation in the council. When Wallace appointed him again following adjournment of the legislature, Catron and Henry Waldo carried their opposition to the territorial supreme court, which was presided over by Chief Justice L. Bradford Prince. Of Catron's involvement, Wallace remarked, "Mr. Catron's appearance in this case is significant of the meaning of the fight in both court and council. Well informed people here accept it, so far as he is concerned, as a last struggle of the 'Ring.'"[67]

Protracted consideration of the matter led to a decision unfavorable to the governor, and to Fiske, leaving the new governor, Lionel Sheldon, to make the appointment. Wallace and Fiske remained in touch following the former governor's departure from the territory, and in April 1882, Wallace had occasion to write from his new post in Constantinople. He touched on matters of business and personal interest and alluded to items noted in the *New Mexican*, concluding with an observation: "I also see that Breeden is at last Attorney General. So runs the tide away."[68]

Two presidents, a Republican and a Democrat, tried to curtail the corrupt influence of the Santa Fe Ring. Neither was successful. Lew Wallace was neither the first nor the last to prophesy the imminent demise of the Ring. That durable, heat-resistant combination would remain a force in territorial politics for quite some time, and when the inevitable decline came, it would be defeated not by Democrats or reformers, but by a new generation of insurgent Republicans.

CHAPTER FIVE

THE FIRM OF ELKINS AND CATRON

I n exposing allegations concerning a corrupt territorial ring in July 1875, a writer for the *New York Sun* proposed to introduce readers to "the law firm of Elkins & Catron and their co-ringmasters."[1] The reference was to a joint law practice that lasted barely two years, but a larger partnership between the two men endured for more than half a century, from at least 1859, when they entered the University of Missouri as friends and roommates, until Elkins's death in 1911. In the political lore of territorial New Mexico, the names of Stephen Benton Elkins and Thomas Benton Catron were inextricably linked to the Santa Fe Ring and to each other. Newspapers opposed to the powerful combination commonly named Elkins and Catron as its leaders. Charles Fletcher Lummis, western writer-preservationist-popularizer, disparaged "Elkins, Catron and their gang" when he crossed the continent in 1884. Three years later a frustrated Governor Edmund Gibson Ross named them "principal originators and manipulators" of a corrupt land-grant ring.[2] Historians of New Mexico's territorial period have mostly come to the same conclusion.[3]

Elkins and Catron were not only the acknowledged leaders of a powerful political and business combination. They were also two of the more intriguing and self-contradictory figures of territorial times. They shared common origins in western Missouri, ambition for political and financial success, and a consuming drive to achieve. In other respects, they were very different people. Elkins was the more dominant of the two during the decade in which both lived in New Mexico. His role in territorial affairs was less visible following his relocation to New York, Washington, and West Virginia, but given his advocacy of shared business and political interests in national centers of power, Elkins remained an indispensable ally. Catron's diverse business interests, intense partisanship, and combative personality made him a lightning rod for critics. His penchant for acquisition of property made him the cash-poor claimant of vast quantities of land—nearly all of it encumbered with debt and much of it entangled in the legal ambiguity that was typical with Spanish and Mexican land-grant claims. After Elkins's relocation to the East in 1877, Catron was looked upon by nearly everyone who believed in the existence of a controlling combination as the leader of the Santa Fe Ring.

Elkins's marriage to Hallie Davis—and into the family of Henry Gassaway Davis, a United States senator and industrialist from West Virginia—altered his life dramatically. He easily adapted to a patrician life-style and became a national political figure, aligning himself with James G. Blaine and taking leading roles in Blaine's unsuccessful attempts to attain the presidency in 1876, 1880, and 1884. Elkins later served as secretary of war in the cabinet of Benjamin Harrison and as United States senator from West Virginia from 1895 until his death. While engaged in large enterprises in coal-rich West Virginia, Elkins retained investments in New Mexico and continued to influence territorial policy and appointments through his ties in Washington. He and Catron continued to correspond and were jointly involved in business and political affairs to the end of Elkins's life.

Partners in Business

Elkins and Catron were immediately interested in opportunities presented by the wealth of land grants in New Mexico and the confusion over titles. An

Figure 13 As territorial delegate, Stephen Benton Elkins failed to win statehood for New Mexico, but he met and married the daughter of a United States senator and West Virginia industrialist. Photo ca. 1875. Barnes Photographic Collection, Georgetown University Library Special Collections Research Center.

Figure 14 In New Mexico, Thomas Benton Catron was notable for his success in politics and for acquisition of land as well as a knack for attracting controversy. Photo by Edwin L. Brand, ca. 1880. Palace of the Governors Photo Archives (NMHM/DCA), No. 56041.

earlier generation of attorneys had shown that representation of grant claimants could make for a lucrative practice, leading to rapid accumulation of land. The first property to attract Elkins's attention was the Mora land grant, awarded to seventy-six Mexican citizens under the auspices of the Mexican government in 1835 and confirmed by Congress in 1860 following the annexation of New Mexico by the United States.[4] In the late 1860s, Elkins acquired an interest in the as yet indeterminate expanse of land in return for legal services rendered. In partnership with Catron, he purchased additional interests. By November 1870, the men had acquired sixteen separate interests, jointly owned but held in Elkins's name.[5] The history of their involvement with the grant is complex. The venture yielded years of frustration and controversy and did not bring the expected return. Perhaps anticipating difficulties ahead, Elkins followed two other investors in attempting to dispose of his interest in the Mora grant in the mid-1880s, but complications extended his involvement to 1893.[6] The Catron family retained a legal interest in the grant until 1913, when it was sold by Mora County for overdue taxes.

Elkins and Catron also entered the banking business, first moving to establish a bank to compete with the First National Bank of Santa Fe, chartered to Lucien Maxwell and associates in December 1870. Presented with the chance to acquire a controlling interest in Maxwell's bank instead, they seized the opportunity. Elkins became president and remained in that capacity until 1884. Cashier William Griffin managed the bank in Elkins's frequent and prolonged absences. Catron was a member of the board, usually serving as vice chairman and briefly as chair.[7]

Elkins and Catron were jointly involved in myriad other business activities, including mining, railroads, stock raising, and buying and selling town lots. Some of these involved other presumed associates of the Santa Fe Ring. With Governor Marsh Giddings and William Griffin, they organized the Consolidated Land, Cattle Raising and Wool Growing Company. With Griffin, William Breeden, Abraham Staab, William Manderfield, and William Rosenthal, they incorporated a New Mexico division of the Missouri Valley Life Insurance Company. In later years, Elkins and Catron were jointly involved in the New Mexico Mining Company. In association with Elkins's friend Richard C. Kerens of St. Louis, they were investors in the Kansas and Texas Coal Company. Some speculations were profitable, but others, like the Mora land grant, consumed inordinate time and resources while ultimately paying little or nothing.

Steve Elkins

Sometime during his New Mexico sojourn, Stephen B. Elkins picked up the street moniker of "Smooth Steve." Chroniclers of the territorial period have delighted in using the reference, in part because it evokes essential elements of Elkins's public persona. Spoken by contemporaries, the connotation was largely but not entirely derogatory. It expressed admiration for Elkins's cool demeanor, his confident manner, and a penchant for aligning himself with men whose influence could advance his own ambitions. But "smooth" lies not far from "slick," and the phrase implied a keen sense of personal pragmatism, an ability to finesse potentially troublesome circumstances, and a willingness to skirt the truth, and possibly the law, en route to his objective. Elkins was much maligned over the years in papers favoring Democratic Party candidates and causes, but rarely if ever did he suffer practical damage to his business or political interests on this account.

Elkins and Catron were bound by a shared history and common political and financial interests, but in matters of personal style, they could hardly have been less alike. If Elkins was smooth, Catron was noticeably rumpled. Elkins's manner was calculated to soothe, but Catron was blunt and brusque, often without seeming to realize the impact of his words and demeanor. But their differences in style masked other contrasts that went to the nature of Elkins's "smooth" manner. Observed Edgar Walz, Catron's brother-in-law,

"I have often while in New Mexico heard it said that if one asked Mr. Elkins for a favor, he would shake you by the hand, smile on you, pat you on the back and ask you to come again, but he would never grant your wish; that if you asked Catron for a favor, he would bluster, take your head nearly off, but give you what you asked for if it was a reasonable request."[8]

In politics, Elkins gravitated to the national scene, where he was at ease in the company of national party leaders, in the halls of Congress, in the offices of federal executives, and among men who aspired to the presidency. For some years after leaving the territory, he continued to hold New Mexico's seat on the Republican National Committee, using the position as a platform for his advocacy of Blaine's campaigns for the presidential nomination. Catron functioned more as a whip for the Republican Party in New Mexico, urging local organizers to action, mustering support for candidates he approved, squeezing funds out of party regulars, and dispensing money and favors where needed to advance the party's goals.

Both men became wealthy, but much of Catron's wealth was in land that might or might not ever yield a profit, and much of the time he professed to be strapped for cash. For years he was continually indebted to the First National Bank of Santa Fe to the legal limit of $15,000, "and was frequently borrowing other sums with co-signers."[9] Elkins, on the other hand, did well in business and even better in marriage, and soon had a fortune in both capital and liquid assets. Elkins knew how to enjoy his wealth, spending time away from the city at a summer home in fashionable Deer Park, Maryland, and later building the comfortable and spacious Halliehurst residence in the town to which he gave his name, Elkins, West Virginia.

Following Elkins's two terms as New Mexico's territorial delegate and his relocation to the East, it would be sixteen years before he would again hold high public office. In the interim, he labored in his own business interests and those of his wife's family. By 1891, Blaine and Elkins had made peace with the notion that Blaine would not be president, and they had reconciled with Blaine's most recent Republican rival, Benjamin Harrison. Both men accepted positions in the cabinet, Blaine as secretary of state and Elkins as secretary of war.

Both Elkins and Catron were controversial in their careers in business and politics. Catron suffered severe consequences at times, including a resignation that many equated with removal as U.S. attorney for New Mexico in 1878. A defensive nature and extreme partisanship inflamed Catron's enemies and frequently exacerbated controversy. Elkins also faced criticism, but rarely suffered as a result, preferring to ignore critics where possible and to rely on the support of influential friends in deflecting charges. Several questions concerning Elkins's past could be counted on to surface whenever his name was put forward for public office.

Nearly all political men who were active after the "war of rebellion" were called upon to account for their loyalties in the conflict and the nature of their service during the war. Catron served in the army of the Confederacy without apparent distinction, but neither did his service engender controversy. Detractors later attempted to portray Elkins as a Southern sympathizer, if not in actual service of the Confederacy. Others derided him as a draft dodger. The simple facts seem to be that he served in the Enrolled Missouri Militia on the Union side for approximately one year, sought and received his discharge, and left for New Mexico in 1863, as the war continued.[10]

Elkins's departure from his home state occurred not long after the adoption of a federal conscription law in March 1863. Some critics were quick to see cause and effect in these two events. Rumors to this effect were general enough that a colleague in the legal profession felt at liberty to make a joke at Elkins's expense in open court years later. The incident allegedly occurred at a spring term of the district court in Albuquerque. Elkins's opposing counsel, W. H. Henrie, reportedly was somewhat inebriated at the time. When a powerful gust swept through the open windows of the courtroom, the attorneys scrambled to gather their papers and move out of the wind. Startled, the nearsighted judge inquired, "Gentlemen, what is the matter?" Elkins replied that the attorneys had rearranged themselves to escape the sudden draft, to which Henrie remarked, "May it please your Honor, this is not the first time the gentleman has moved to escape a draft."[11]

Questions about Elkins's activities as a speculator in Spanish and Mexican land grants, the subject of negative publicity in the eastern press, surfaced when he was a candidate for the United States Senate in 1895. Asked about his involvement in ownership and confirmation of grants in New Mexico, his standard answer, calculated to deflect the impression that he was a swindler or speculator, was that he never owned a grant to which the title was not perfect and unassailable, and that when he represented a claimant, the title in question was invariably upheld by the court.

Elkins's integrity was also questioned in connection with the Star Route scandal of the 1870s and '80s, in which lucrative contracts for mail delivery were obtained through bribery and manipulated to yield a higher return to the contractor. Elkins denied impropriety in the Star Route matter, stating that he had never had a government contract of any kind and that he had acted only in his capacity as an attorney to clients who were accused in the scandal.[12] However, a *New York Times* story on the Star Route matter named Elkins and his friend and business partner Richard Kerens as "backers" of the named contractor on two of the controversial routes.[13] Some observers thought Elkins fortunate in that the failure of an effort to convict former Arkansas Senator Stephen Dorsey likely saved Elkins the indignity of a similar prosecution.[14]

Another matter that never undid Elkins and never entirely disappeared involved his representation of James Jewett, an American investor whose South American mining concession had been abrogated by the Brazilian government. Jewett's outlandish claim for damages was widely viewed as an attempt to shake down the government of Brazil and a poor reflection on Elkins as his advocate.[15] Elkins invoked the good offices of his friend Secretary of State James G. Blaine in pressing Jewett's claim for some $50 million. Blaine was in the office less than a year, and the matter was not resolved in his tenure. The State Department had earlier declined to intervene on Jewett's behalf, and the matter was finally put to rest when another secretary of state, Thomas Bayard, declared the claim "an outrage" and declined to pursue the matter.

Elkins was normally on the receiving end of requests for political assistance by his New Mexico friends, but in the course of his campaign for election to the United States Senate by vote of the West Virginia legislature, Elkins asked friends in the territory for help in answering criticism of his land-grant activities. Accordingly, a letter attesting to Elkins's good character was sent to the *Wheeling Intelligencer* and was circulated to other West Virginia papers. Among the signatories were reliable allies including Catron, J. Francisco Chaves, Abraham Staab, and Pedro Perea.[16] Henry Waldo and L. Bradford Prince provided separate letters in support of Elkins.[17]

Despite the allegations and the negative press that they engendered, Elkins's political standing was never seriously threatened, and his career culminated in a sixteen-year tenure in the United States Senate, representing his adopted state of West Virginia. Elkins made important alliances throughout his career and used them to advantage, politically and in business. For the most part, he ignored his detractors and forged ahead, secure in his wealth, in his friendships, and in helpful party and family connections. In 1894, Elkins joined his father-in-law in establishing Davis and Elkins College in Elkins, West Virginia. The campus bordered the elegant summer homes built by both men, Henry G. Davis's Graceland and Elkins's Halliehurst. The college, offering a broad liberal arts education, may have been Elkins's finest and most enduring legacy.

Tom Catron

In April 1892, following Elkins's appointment as secretary of war, the *Las Vegas Daily Optic* commented that "Mr. T. B. Catron, who is admittedly a brainier man than Mr. S. B. Elkins, though not so politic in his ways, is a trifle envious of the success attained in public life by his former law partner and wants a touch of it himself."[18] Though a year older, Catron had been walking in Elkins's political footsteps for years. After following his Missouri compatriot to New Mexico, he emulated Elkins in making his start in the territory at Mesilla. In what amounted to an apprenticeship in legal practice and public life, each was elected to the territorial legislature representing Doña Ana County, and each was soon drawn to the territory's political center of gravity in Santa Fe. Elkins briefly served as attorney general in 1866 before moving to the office of U.S. attorney, which he held until 1871. Catron followed in these offices, serving as attorney general from 1869 to 1872 and as U.S. attorney from 1872 until his resignation in 1878. He won a term as territorial delegate to Congress in 1894 and eventually followed Elkins to the United States Senate, though not until after Elkins's death and New Mexico's attainment of statehood.

Catron was and is sometimes referred to as the "boss" of the Santa Fe Ring. He was the central if not defining figure in complaints concerning a territorial ring, but his credentials as a political boss are tenuous. As a candidate, he sustained seven defeats interspersed among ten victories, and his final attempt resulted in a defeat in his bid to retain the United States Senate seat he had barely won following New Mexico's admission as a state. Following his resignation as U.S. attorney in 1878 amid the heat of an investigation into his official conduct, Catron failed in repeated efforts to secure various appointive positions, including a second tenure as U.S. attorney and an appointment as the government's attorney for the Pueblo Indians. In 1895, he suffered the indignity of a legal proceeding that might have resulted in his disbarment for witness tampering, and the following year he was defeated when he stood for reelection to the office of territorial delegate. This defeat prompted an unfriendly paper to remark, "T. B. Catron has been buried deep in his political grave."[19] Catron had been buried before, but he also had a way of rising to torment his political enemies. Three more times he won elective office, in addition to being chosen by the state legislature in 1912 as one of New Mexico's first two United States senators.

In contrast to the more urbane and congenial Steve Elkins, Catron was decidedly rough around the edges. He was a heavy man throughout his adult life, and on multiple occasions he sought medical treatment for obesity.[20] Some observers noted a tendency on Catron's part to present a careless and rumpled appearance as to dress, particularly after the death of his wife, Julia, in 1909. According to one biographer, "His habit of wearing the same suit day after day was due in part to his custom of keeping his pockets jammed with memoranda of all kinds. These were jotted down in numerous small notebooks or on any scraps of paper that were handy when the thought occurred to him."[21] Catron's usual business attire consisted of a shirt with a black bow tie, a long black sack coat, and, when out and about, a black broad-brimmed hat.

Of considerably greater consequence was Catron's manner, described by others as abrasive, brusque, blunt, and gruff. An admirer delivering his eulogy characterized this element in his personality as "frankness" and remarked, "As the unpolished diamond reveals not its beauty, nor value within, so this great man with a more or less rugged exterior, was not always understood. His outward sternness deceived the stranger, but not those who knew him."[22] Reviewing the Catron legacy years after his death, attorney and historian William A. Keleher described Catron's personality as humorless, "permanently grim and pessimistic."[23]

For all his success in business, law, and politics, Catron seems to have been oblivious to the effect of his demeanor on others and was surprised to find himself the object of criticism. Said Keleher, "Although Catron thought little of calling people all the hard names he could think of, and on occasion treated people quite roughly, he never believed that anyone could harbor any ill will or ill feeling toward him, or resent anything that he had said to or about another person."[24] He was never more eloquent than when expressing contempt for an adversary. Approached by John Riley with a request that he use his influence to assist Richard Hudson, a Republican ally in Grant County, with a difficult business relationship, Catron expressed doubt and remarked of Hudson's nemesis, "He is a man who is absolutely without any soul. He lives on about 5 cents a day and calculates the interest on that amount as an outlay. Charley Spiess says he does not even wear any underclothes."[25]

Once a conflict had been ignited, Catron was apt to stoke the fire rather than work toward conciliation. When a client complained to Catron's law partner, John H. Knaebel, that Catron had received him in such an insulting manner that he had vowed never to visit the office again, Catron wrote to the man, not to apologize, but to explain that he may have been preoccupied. Giving his recollection of the exchange, Catron wrote, "I did not do this in an 'insulting manner' and in my opinion there was nothing to authorize you to think so, but if you did I simply say nothing of the kind was intended."[26]

Catron was judgmental by inclination and frequently acted on his grudges. He and Governor Miguel A. Otero became bitter enemies, though both were Republicans. As the end of Otero's first term as territorial governor approached, Catron wrote to Elkins to enlist his aid in ridding the territory of Otero. Among other things, Catron believed that Otero had not supported him in his pursuit of various political appointments, and he blamed Otero for creating division within the party.[27] Otero took a somewhat different view, writing some years later, "When Catron says I broke up the harmony of the Republican Party, what he really means was that I destroyed *his* power as boss of the territory."[28] Despite the objection of Catron and friends, Otero was returned to the office of governor by President William McKinley and became the longest serving of all the territorial governors, foiling Catron in that capacity from 1897 until 1906.

Catron had launched attacks on Eugene A. Fiske, appointed U.S. attorney by President Benjamin Harrison in 1889, and on Albert Bacon Fall, appointed to the territorial supreme court in 1893. He wrote in extreme terms of his future United States Senate colleague, declaring of Fall, "This is the very worst appointment that could have been made." Said Catron in a further critique of Fall's character, "He has been a member of the last two legislatures in the Territory and in both legislatures he sold himself like water."[29]

As a result of Catron's strong words and the actions that sometimes accompanied them, contemporaries learned to be cautious when dealing with him. Elkins and Catron were involved, along with three others, in an unbelievably complicated and ultimately fruitless investment in the Mora land grant. Having entered into a joint ownership arrangement, the men then had great difficulty, first in establishing what they owned in the web of overlapping boundaries and conflicting claims, and then in disposing of the property and even in parsing the terms of their agreement. In explaining to Elkins why he had appeared to favor Catron in paying on obligations owed to both men, Benjamin Butler wrote, "I looked upon Catron as a man who would cut my throat if he could, and I knew Mr. Elkins was no such man, and that I could make him whole in the matter of money."[30] Catron could be a difficult man. He doubtless paid a political price for his bluntness and, in many cases, pettiness. However, he did not accomplish all that he did during his fifty-five years in the territory and state without notable strengths and effective habits. He was a hard and persistent worker with clear priorities. He was a staunch Republican Party activist and a willing political candidate, attorney, and speculator. Perhaps most important, he was not afraid to ask for what he wanted. He asked for political appointments for himself and others. He asked for the removal of officials with whom he did not agree. He asked for money with which to pursue political ends, and he asked others to use their power and influence on his behalf. He plied presidents, cabinet secretaries and members of Congress, Republican Party bosses, local party functionaries, and business associates. He kept score and called in political favors he felt were owed him in consideration of assistance he had rendered in the past.

The loss of Catron's papers to a fire in 1888 complicates the task of assessing his role in party politics before that time, but indications are that he had long maintained close relationships with Republican activists in distant corners of the territory. By 1888, William Breeden had vacated the territorial Republican Party chairmanship. If anything, Catron's role in organizing party affairs at the grassroots level may have increased as a result of Breeden's absence. He kept up a steady correspondence with county operatives and was not above scolding valued allies. Pedro Sánchez had been regarded as a reliable friend of the Ring for a decade or more when Catron wrote to light a fire under him relative to the approaching election of 1888. In response to apparent backpeddling by Sánchez with regard to requests made of him, Catron wrote, "It is your duty to see that the Republican Party succeeds in Taos County, and I expect you to spend more than $150.00.... The party expects you to do all you can. I hope for your own sake, and your own reputation, you will see that the County is won by the Republicans."[31] In 1895, he chastised Thomas D. Burns of Rio Arriba County, telling Burns, "I see by your attempting to let politics run itself in your county you are meeting with a good deal of trouble. There is no question if you would look after your county but what you could easily carry it. Your neglect at the last election lost us the control of the legislature."[32] Not all of Catron's demands bore fruit, but some certainly did. His organization of political allies throughout the territory was likely a critical factor in his success and that of the Republican Party in local elections. Catron's influence among the territory's Hispanic residents was mixed. Robert W. Larson attributes his favorable standing among some Hispanos to his role as a *patrón*—a landowner who dispensed or withheld favors that would help meet the immediate needs of the less affluent. Larson observes that, in all three of Catron's campaigns for territorial delegate, he won most of the heavily Hispanic northern counties.[33] Doubtless Catron exerted some influence over those who were dependent on his indulgence as a landlord and mortgage holder, but he also cultivated support through his development of local contacts. As a new arrival in the territory, he had gone to some lengths to learn the Spanish language, which he used to his advantage, forming enduring alliances in counties in which Spanish-speaking people were in the majority.

Catron was a persistent obstructionist to the efforts of Governor Lew Wallace to reform the territorial government in the late 1870s, but two decades later, Wallace recalled, with grudging admiration, Catron's winning way with the Hispanic people of New Mexico, telling Eugene Fiske, "One of the curious incidents pertaining to Mr. Catron is his astonishing influence over New Mexicans. I cannot recall one instance in which he did not absolutely submerge and control all persons who came in contact with him speaking the Spanish tongue."[34]

In reality, Catron's relationship with Hispanic New Mexicans was more complicated than that, and Wallace's recollection may be, as much as anything, a reflection of the short time he spent in the territory and the lack of depth in his contact with Spanish-speaking New Mexicans. Among Hispanics who blamed the loss of family lands on Catron and his associates, his name evoked a legacy of bitterness and resentment. The Spanish-language newspaper *El Defensor del Pueblo* spoke for many of these people when, in the heat of a dispute with non-Hispanic authorities of the Catholic Church and the political and business leaders who supported them, it unloaded on Catron. The paper denounced Catron as "a perpetrator of fraudulent land claims and land grants," and further said, "it is our contention that he is the most prejudiced man politically, usurper of the liberty of New Mexicans, and boss of the inquisitorial Republican Ring that acts against our race."[35] The paper's editor, Juan José Herrera, was a labor activist who had led in organizing Las Gorras Blancas—a Hispano resistance movement active primarily in northern New Mexico.

Figure 15 Pedro Sánchez was a Republican leader in Taos County and an ally of territorial party leaders for more than twenty years. Photo by Dana B. Chase, ca. 1888. Palace of the Governors Photo Archives (NMHM/DCA), No. 11042.

Whether in or out of the legislature, Catron was intensely interested in its political composition and in the conduct of legislative business. Efforts to influence the balance of power by contesting close elections were common in Catron's day and had a place in his repertoire of political maneuvers. Just after the November election in 1894, Catron wrote Pedro Perea, the party's chief operative in Bernalillo, explaining that he was traveling to Springer because "They are attempting to count out a member of the council there, which makes it very important for me to be on hand."[36] More to the point, he gave Perea instructions concerning the canvass for three Bernalillo County precincts in which some votes were in doubt; Perea was to advocate with the commissioners—or perhaps instruct them—regarding the treatment of these returns. Following the 1896 election, Catron wrote to Pedro Sánchez, his primary political agent in Taos, who had been narrowly defeated in the race for a council seat. "I wish to advise you that I think you ought to contest," he told Sánchez, explaining that the new council would otherwise be evenly divided. "It will be the salvation of the republican party on this occasion," Catron declared.[37]

Catron was an intense competitor within the official structures of political activity and governance, but he was also something of a fixer, sometimes attempting to use influence in ways that were questionable ethically and perhaps legally. As a candidate for territorial delegate in the fall of 1892, Catron got wind of a plan of the Democrats to obtain a copy of the 1878 report of Frank Warner Angel, containing charges against Catron for alleged improper use of his office as U.S. attorney in relation to the troubles in Lincoln County. His assumption was that his enemies were looking for charges to use against him politically. Catron wrote to Elkins, asking that he see the attorney general and arrange it so that no copy of the report or related materials would be released to anyone "because they are unnecessary here."[38] Though a letter had been sent from Elkins's office advising that Catron "need have no further worry about it," Catron continued to fret about the prospect that he could be hurt by allegations in the report. Several months later, he again wrote to press his demand, in slightly expanded form. "Get Attorney General Miller to take out of the files in his office and deliver up to you that report made by Angell [sic] against me," Catron wrote. "That is a thing which they will want to use against me hereafter, simply as a piece of mud-slinging. There is no use allowing them to have it." Catron's solution was for Elkins to "get that report and destroy it."[39]

In 1892, a friend and Republican supporter, don Roman Baca, came to Catron with a tale of woe. His son had run wild when sent away to college and had entered into a hasty marriage. Back home in New Mexico, he joined the family business, but had taken his father's ready cash and squandered most of it. He had run afoul of the law while under the influence of a confidence man in El Paso and stood accused of a serious federal offense. Catron wanted to help the elder Baca extricate his son from the scrape. He wrote to J. Francisco Chaves at Los Lunas, asking that Chaves prepare a detailed written statement of facts. Then, Catron stated, "I will write a letter to Elkins and ask him to go to the attorney general and request the attorney general to direct the district attorney at El Paso to discontinue the prosecution."[40]

In the face of financial setbacks, political defeats, and endless complications in his business affairs, Catron was nothing if not resilient. His attributes of dogged determination and sometimes irrational belief in his own cause enabled Catron to endure in the highly competitive arenas of business and politics while maintaining an extremely demanding pace. He recognized this quality in himself and was proud of it. With the Panic of 1893 wrecking financial markets and personal fortunes across the country, he told Elkins, "These hard times have shut down on me as hard as they have on anybody on earth and were it not for my strong constitution, energy and determination they would carry me under; but that cannot be."[41]

An Uneasy Alliance

Some observers have asserted that Elkins and Catron were not close personally. This is a mistaken assumption. The two men were so close and familiar that, throughout their adult lives, they could express mutual grievances in strongest terms without seriously threatening the bond that they had shared through the years and across the miles. They were continually associated in business and regularly engaged in the pursuit of common political interests, and their steady correspondence never lapsed. Letters were sometimes brief and to the point; others were longer and included gossip or criticism of business and political adversaries. Some included lengthy discussion of business transactions, and some involved frank expressions of mutual resentment.

The relationship survived largely because of Elkins's conciliatory nature and willingness to overlook Catron's tendency to focus on the negative. But Elkins's patience and goodwill were occasionally tested. In 1879 Catron wrote to pour out a litany of grievances: Elkins had spoken ill of Catron to officials of the First National Bank, damaging his standing as a borrower. Given his permanent removal from the territory, Elkins should not have retained the bank presidency. Catron demanded deeds for his share of jointly owned properties, and he wanted Elkins to travel from his place of business in New York to Washington, to plead an official cause on his behalf.

Elkins's response conveyed his own sense of injury, incredulity at some of Catron's assertions, and finally, a willingness to address Catron's concerns in a practical way. Recalling exertions made to forestall Catron's dismissal as U.S. attorney, Elkins wrote, "If I had never known you before the contest I made for you and your honor, I thought that of itself was sufficient to bind you to me forever, and that nothing I might do could invoke your enmity,—but how deceived I have been."[42] Elkins denied hurting Catron with the bank, offered to help him borrow funds, and professed his own long-standing desire to resign the bank presidency. As to a settlement of jointly held properties, Elkins reminded Catron that he had provided an accounting of deeds held in his own name, but despite repeated promises, he had not received a comparable statement from Catron. "As to my going to Washington for you," Elkins wrote, "I have made a great many journeys there for you and I should go now but don't believe I could do anything with the Commissioner. Am afraid not but if you think you want me to do so I will try."

A similar frank and conflicted exchange in the fall of 1888 may have been brought on by Catron's persistent condition of financial distress. Catron was anxious for a settlement on taxes paid by each man on properties they owned jointly. His assumption was that Elkins would owe him. Catron was also aggrieved about matters concerning the Mora grant. Elkins patiently answered the complaints, requested a statement of taxes paid by Catron, and offered to be of service, "if you can suggest any way that I can help you."[43] Catron responded, "I do not propose to measure obligations with you," though that appeared to be exactly what he was doing.[44] "I prefer that we remain as friends," Catron wrote, "but that is for you to say." Elkins doubtless had weathered enough similar squalls to know that this one, too, would pass. Catron did not neglect the part of Elkins's letter in which Elkins offered to render aid. Catron asked that Elkins impress upon President Harrison the importance of appointing federal officials for New Mexico who were Republicans and current residents of the territory.

In seeking help from Elkins, Catron was not bound by ordinary limits of reasonableness. Having been elected territorial delegate to Congress in 1894, Catron saw an apparent opportunity to influence favorable action on New Mexico statehood. He wanted to be appointed chairman of the House

Committee on Territories—the committee to which statehood proposals were assigned for initial consideration. In his view, this made perfect sense. "I do not know of anyone who would be better qualified to be chairman than myself," he wrote.[45] The appointment of a nonvoting delegate, and a freshman at that, to such a position of influence would have been highly irregular. Catron knew this, but he was not dissuaded. He wrote to Elkins and Kerens to ask for their advice. Said Catron, "A man never loses anything by asking, like we do in praying for judgment in an action at law, for more than he is entitled to, and sometimes he may get it."[46]

With evident restraint, both Elkins and Kerens responded that such an appointment would be highly unlikely.[47] Having received advice contrary to his fervent wishes, Catron wrote each man a second time, arguing his position. He swept away doubts concerning precedent and the seniority of other members. Referring to Speaker Thomas Reed and his power over committee appointments, he told Elkins, "It is true I know of no precedent for it, but Mr. Reed ought to be able to make a precedent. There never was a new principle or thing brought up that did not have to come up originally without precedent."[48] Finally persuaded that his scheme to obtain the chairmanship was going nowhere, Catron still tried to influence the composition of the House committee, encouraging Representative George Perkins of Iowa to seek the chairmanship and urging the Speaker to appoint committee members who were sympathetic to New Mexico's cause.[49]

Catron did not just ask for favors. He insisted, telling Elkins in 1901 with reference to the prospect of Otero's reappointment, "Do something for us,—Do not leave us in [this] condition,—Do not allow us to continue degraded, and in want. We ask this, we hope for it, and we demand it."[50] Of E. A. Fiske's appointment to a post he had coveted, Catron told Elkins, "Fiske has been my enemy ever since he came to the Territory; he has opposed me in conventions and has always voted against me at elections; he is mean, vindictive, and dishonest." Recalling his exertions on Elkins's behalf, Catron said, "I think I have the right to ask in this matter, your active support." He pressed for a response: "Can you, and will you, do anything? Answer me immediately."[51]

The End of an Era

Catron was elected to the coveted office of territorial delegate in 1894. His single term coincided with Elkins's tenure in the Senate and provided a unique opportunity for collaboration, which the friends exercised to the advantage of their public and personal interests. Following his defeat for re-election as territorial delegate in 1896, Catron focused his energies in New Mexico, but he and Elkins continued in regular correspondence for the remainder of Elkins's life. Now balding, gray, and paunchy, far removed from their youth in prewar Missouri and their time at the University of Missouri, they retained joint business and political interests and relied on one another for assistance. They had been brothers, almost, rendering mutual aid, quarreling at times, but always against a backdrop of shared commitment and mutual loyalty. Elkins must have tired of Catron's endless appeals for assistance and his cathartic rants, but he tolerated them.

Catron routinely lobbied Elkins concerning appointments and the statehood effort, but otherwise focused his attention locally, winning election to the legislative council in 1904 and 1908, serving a term as mayor of Santa Fe beginning in 1906, and throwing himself into the final push for statehood. In 1910 he spent seven weeks in Washington lobbying, sometimes in tandem with Elkins, for passage of the New Mexico statehood bill. "Doubtless, the appearance of these two old champions of the statehood movement had its effect," Robert Larson wrote of the final effort to secure congressional approval.[52] Elkins, by this time, had served some fifteen years in the Senate and was one of its senior members. His work on behalf of the statehood bill would be one of his last official efforts, the culmination of a half century in harness with Catron.

Catron returned to New Mexico and took part in the convention called to write a new state constitution. In December he wrote to brief Elkins on its progress, noting that he hoped to go to Washington as one of the senators. But there was a more pressing matter to be addressed. Catron expressed himself with the concern of a friend, but with his characteristic bluntness: "Since receiving your letter from West Virginia during the vacation of Congress, I have seen a number of articles in the newspapers speaking of you as a very sick man." Elkins had admitted feeling a little unwell, Catron noted, "But now an article in the papers states that you are suffering from cancer of the stomach, that you can take no food, that you have become very much emaciated, and that in fact you are starving to death." With as much personal warmth as he was likely to muster, Catron told his friend, "I really hope that there is nothing in those reports; that you will soon be up and be in your seat in the Senate."[53]

Elkins died on January 4, 1911. New Mexico became the Union's forty-seventh state on January 6, 1912, and in March the legislature convened to select two United States senators. Catron's influence was by this time in its descent, and his election was not the foregone conclusion he had once anticipated. Twelve men sought the positions, and multiple ballots were required to resolve the question. In the end, Albert Bacon Fall and Catron were elected. In response to a congratulatory wire from Hallie Elkins, Catron expressed regret that he would not be serving alongside her late husband, his old classmate. "I have always desired, ever since he went to the Senate, to go there as a senator and be with him in that body," Catron wrote. "I know that he wished the same also, but fate has decided otherwise."[54]

Catron served his full term in the Senate but found himself increasingly laboring in the shadow of the younger, more energetic, and more politically astute Fall. In 1916, at age seventy-six, he sought a second term—by direct election, as mandated by the new Seventeenth Amendment to the Constitution. He was unable even to secure his party's nomination, his candidacy undermined, in part, by Fall.

Having suffered the loss of his wife in 1909 and his oldest friend and ally in 1911, Catron increasingly relied on his son Charles, his law partner beginning in 1904. In view of the personal history that Elkins and Catron shared, their mutual motivating interests, and their complementary strengths, one can imagine that Elkins's death left his aged friend with a persistent void that no other person could fill.

Admired by some, vilified by others, Elkins and Catron achieved prodigiously in business and politics in their association of some five decades. They attained notable success in the Gilded Age, east and west, in part because of the personal qualities that they had in common. They were risk takers for whom the opportunities available on the Southwest frontier outweighed any hazard or inconvenience. Each was supremely confident in his own ability and judgment, and they were resilient in the face of occasional setbacks. Elkins and Catron—Steve and Tom—were ambitious, energetic, hardworking men. Each man's potential for success was enhanced by a well-practiced capacity for suspension of ethical restraints. The ability to get things done through others played no small part in their attainments and resulted in the mix of respect and notoriety that they shared at the center of that reputed juggernaut of territorial business and politics, the Santa Fe Ring.

CHAPTER SIX

THE BUSINESS OF LAND

As a contentious struggle over the Maxwell land grant was heating up in 1882, the antigrant *Raton Guard* declared, "The curse of New Mexico is the old Spanish and Mexican land grants that are spread all over the northern and central part of the territory."[1] The problem, said the *Guard*, was in the plethora of unconfirmed grants and the difficulty of fixing their locations, boundaries, and ownership. In 1890, following litigation that upheld the claim of the Maxwell Land Grant Company but dashed the hopes of many settlers, the Maxwell Company attorney's conclusion was similar. "The question," Frank Springer said, "is not whether we are in favor of land grants or not. We all agree that the Territory would be far better off today if there had never been any."[2] The critical need, in his view, was for a process for settlement of claims that would ensure the security of land titles, so that development could proceed.

Grants of land had been awarded between 1693 and 1846 under authority of the Spanish and Mexican governments. Early grants were made, at least in part, for defensive purposes—to insulate larger, older settlements from attack by hostile Indians and to discourage incursions of foreign powers. Grants were awarded to Spanish subjects who had contributed to the conquest of New Mexico. Others were bestowed on communities, to encourage settlement in remote parts of the region. Increasingly, grants were made to friends and allies of governing officials.[3] In assuming control of lands ceded by Mexico, the United States had agreed to protect claims found to be valid under prevailing Spanish or Mexican law and any terms of conveyance.

Most land grants took the basic form of a *private* grant or a *community* grant.[4] Private grants were conferred on individuals—usually just one or two petitioners—who upon satisfying stated conditions of qualification assumed ownership of the property. These land grants were attractive to speculators because of the ease with which the titles could be conveyed to other parties.

More problematic were many community grants, under which individuals could acquire and transfer ownership of discrete plots, while the community retained ownership of common lands affording shared access to grazing, game, fuel wood, timber, and other needed resources. Common lands were intended to be held in perpetuity for the use of all residents. Variations in grant documents sometimes introduced confusion as to the intended nature of the grant, leaving critical matters to the interpretation of claimants and officials. The abundance of potential claims and the ambiguity of their legal status invited fraud and handed new authorities a puzzle of endless complexity.

If the vexatious nature of land claims was regarded as a curse in post-occupation New Mexico, it was one that came with a silver lining for speculators. Long before the American Occupation, Spanish and Mexican citizens had recognized the potential for wealth in land grants. The examples of Juan Estevan Pino and Donaciano Vigil, as examined by G. Emlen Hall, indicate that land speculation was not an American innovation. Most active in the decade of the 1820s, Pino was ahead of his time in his use of land as a negotiable asset and in the care that he took in obtaining documentary evidence of ownership. In Hall's view, Stephen Elkins, Thomas Catron, and other latter-day speculators "differed from Pino only in that they had access to wider markets and deeper pockets."[5] As an official in Mexican and U.S. regimes, Vigil advocated for his interests in land acquisition. Vigil and associates "made the bed that the more famous Santa Fe Ring then lay down in with such controversial results."[6] Americans who took to the Santa Fe Trail in pursuit of fortune and influence refined the art of transferring grant lands from the hands of native claimants to their own.

Enterprising Americans were quick to see the possibilities in the system. Colorado's first territorial governor, William Gilpin, is said to have encouraged leading residents as early as 1844 to petition for grants, including tracts larger than the legal limit of eleven square leagues per grantee, or about 48,000 acres.[7] Gilpin reportedly made his mark by obtaining title to the Sangre de Cristo grant, then trying to evict bona fide settlers so that he could sell more of the property to purchasers.[8] Before long, men who had come seeking wealth as trappers and traders "had passed beyond furs and the Santa Fe trade to that third frontier of big business: land speculation."[9]

Following the American Occupation and a commitment by the U.S. government to honor grants legally made under Spanish and Mexican authority, attorneys who spoke English and knew American law held a distinct advantage. So much the better if they knew or could learn Spanish. Such men were well represented among those who migrated to the Southwest, and nearly all of them were eager to avail themselves of opportunities to obtain wealth and property. The process for consideration of land claims provided such an opportunity, as cash-poor claimants had little choice but to pay for legal services in land. From the early years of territorial administration, attorneys, some of whom were also public officials, represented land claimants. Among them, judges Joab Houghton and John S. Watts, attorneys general Hugh Smith and Merrill Ashurst, and supreme court clerk Samuel Ellison represented at least sixty-eight claimants in confirmation proceedings.[10] Stephen Elkins, Thomas Catron, and Henry Waldo were part of a second wave of attorneys who acquired property in this manner. Charles Catron, A. B. Renehan, and other lawyers carried the practice into a new century.

The Land-Grant Conundrum

When American military and civil officials assumed control of ceded territory following the U.S.-Mexican War, they had no idea what they were getting into with respect to traditions of land tenure and of grants made under Spanish and Mexican administration. The defeated Mexican government had taken pains to ensure protection of grants awarded under Spanish and Mexican law, expressed in Article 10 of the Treaty of Guadalupe Hidalgo as it was drafted by negotiators. The United States Senate deleted this article, leaving in place a more general statement in Article 8, providing assurances that Mexican property would be "inviolably protected." In practice, the U.S. government did not provide the level of protection expected, but nonetheless accepted that it had some responsibility to review claims arising under the treaty provision and to render fair judgments as to their validity—an intention more easily stated than accomplished.

Among the confounding circumstances facing U.S. officials were missing and incomplete documentation, ambiguous and overlapping grant boundaries, confusion surrounding the types of grants that had been made, the nature of ownership rights conveyed, and the identity of owners and beneficiaries. Many grants were valid only upon satisfaction of stated conditions, such as settlement and continuous occupancy. Since the conditions had not been satisfied in all cases, not all grants were candidates for confirmation. When U.S. authorities invited submittal of claims for confirmation, they did so knowing that instances of forgery and fraud were probable.

Mistrust of the new American regime caused some claimants to avoid the process.[11] Differences in legal systems and languages also confused matters and opened the door to deliberate manipulation of claims.[12]

The response of the U.S. government to these issues was characterized by procrastination and insufficiency. Many actions of the government exacerbated problems rather than alleviated them. While U.S. control dated from the 1846 military occupation of New Mexico, no provision was made for consideration of land claims before 1854, when a surveyor general was appointed to review claims and forward recommendations to Washington. The surveyor general had neither staff nor other resources to properly investigate claims. Patronage appointments of the governor, the surveyor general, and other officials rendered the process subject to political influence.

Confirmation of claims initially was by action of Congress upon recommendation of the surveyor general, but legislators, embarrassed by some of the claims they had approved, came to realize that their understanding of such matters was inadequate to support rational decisions. By 1880, Congress seemingly had adopted a policy of ignoring claims, leaving confirmation requests unattended. The U.S. Supreme Court contributed to the confusion through a decision in *Tameling v. United States Freehold and Emigration Company* (1877), a decision resulting in confirmation of the Sangre de Cristo grant at 998,780 acres. In the court's view, Congress had awarded a grant de novo, or a new grant, and had authority to do so. Once Congress had confirmed a grant, the court held, it was not within the judges' purview to assess validity under Spanish or Mexican law.[13] This construal led to controversial rulings allowing other oversized claims to stand as valid grants.

When Democrats came to power in 1884 following an era of Republican dominance, the new president, Grover Cleveland, attempted to impose reforms on the territories. He appointed a stubbornly honest governor in Edmund G. Ross and an equally cantankerous surveyor general in George Washington Julian. The appointees made headway in curtailing the land swindlers, but in some respects, Julian's efforts magnified inequities in the treatment of claims. Julian attacked the land ring with a vengeance, rejecting or reducing claims approved by his predecessor but not yet acted upon by Congress. In Malcolm Ebright's view, Julian's zeal "led him to an overly critical questioning of many perfectly valid grants."[14] While Julian sympathized with smaller claimants, his actions were detrimental to many rural villagers who had interests in communal lands. Julian saw himself as a reformer, but to at least one observer, his decisions with respect to some valid claims made him more a "colonial bureaucrat" than a reformer.[15]

When Congress replaced the surveyor general with the Court of Private Land Claims in 1891, results were mixed. The court operated from 1891 until 1904, adjudicating claims in six western states and territories. By far the largest number of claims emanated from New Mexico. The court was conservative in its approach, and the government's attorney throughout its tenure, Matthew Givens Reynolds, assumed what some have considered an excessively adversarial posture. A leading student of the court expresses a view echoed by others: "Reynolds seemed dedicated to the defeat of as many claims as possible. If he could not defeat them, he strove to reduce the acreage confirmed as much as possible."[16]

Reynolds shortly gained the notice of Stephen B. Elkins's friend and business associate R. C. Kerens. Reynolds was a native of Missouri, as were Elkins and Catron, and Kerens lived in St. Louis. He knew Reynolds slightly and believed that Reynolds's favor could be cultivated to good advantage. In early 1892, Kerens plotted to gain Reynolds's goodwill through Catron. "I expect Catron here in about a week," Kerens wrote to Elkins from St. Louis. "He will come to form close relations with Matt G. Reynolds, U.S. Attorney for the Land Court. I will be able to do Catron a great service in this respect. It may be that he and Reynolds will also form a law partnership. If they do, we will then have no trouble hereafter in managing matters in New Mexico."[17] Reynolds and Catron did not become partners, and Reynolds proved a sturdy defender of the government's interests in the land court and an incorruptible advocate for his position.

By the time the court's business concluded, nearly three hundred New Mexico cases had been adjudicated, with approximately 70 percent of all claims rejected. According to critics, the Court of Private Land Claims was overly conservative in its approach and rejected or reduced some legal claims, inflicting injustice on claimants and communities.[18] As a remedy for excesses attributed to speculation, it was mostly irrelevant, since the most egregious abuses had occurred before the court was created. Negative effects fell disproportionally on the smaller grants and on persons sharing in claims to common lands of community grants.

The New Mexico Land Ring

Soon after President Cleveland took office in 1884, the *New York Times* called readers' attention to an egregious scandal. In the distant, sparsely populated Territory of New Mexico, citizens were said to be at the mercy of "that compact, well-organized, unscrupulous, and cruel association of Federal officials and ex-officials known as the New Mexican land ring." The Ring reportedly had its base at the land office in Santa Fe, but, said the paper, "its membership extends through every department of government and into both branches of Congress, therefore giving it an unpaid but most effective lobby." The Ring was said to control the courts and direct "bands of hired assassins," maintaining a reign of terror and dealing harshly with objectors.[19] The exposé may have overstated the danger to ordinary citizens, but it echoed the belief of people who were persuaded that a clique of crooked attorneys, speculators, and federal officials had been working overtime to enrich themselves at the expense of legitimate claimants and the public domain.

The question of Ring involvement in scandalous land dealings is not as simple as it may seem. It is clear that a goodly number of attorneys and speculators contrived to profit from grant transactions during the territorial period, whether by taking land in payment or by purchasing land for resale. But what qualifies as Ring activity? Not all speculators and attorneys were named as members of the Santa Fe Ring or the "New Mexican Land Ring," and some of those who were said to be Ring members engaged in speculation, but not in partnership with other assumed Ring members. Ring activity would seem to imply collaboration among two or more individuals who were part of the loose confederation of interests revolving around Elkins and Catron—the locus of the combination popularly known as the Santa Fe Ring.

Much of the commerce in private land claims was legitimate; some of it was tainted with subtle or blatant corruption. But transactions involving alleged Ring activity were only part of a larger problem of maladministration, corruption, and inequity in the process of adjudicating land-grant claims. In Malcolm Ebright's view, "No one individual or group of individuals is solely to blame—not Matthew Givens Reynolds, nor Thomas Catron, nor Henry Atkinson, nor even the Santa Fe Ring. They all played a part in the chicanery of land-grant adjudication, but the drama was allowed to proceed by the United States government."[20] Still, the Ring made a convenient lightning rod for criticism and drew attention to problems of land fraud and official corruption.

In the land-speculation business, it helped to have friends in high places—in the office of the surveyor general, for example, and in the offices of the governor, attorney general, and U.S. attorney, and in the territorial courts and legislative assembly. The territorial delegate could be an essential ally in Washington, as could a skilled lobbyist or a friendly senator. All of these might influence critical decisions and tip the balance in determining

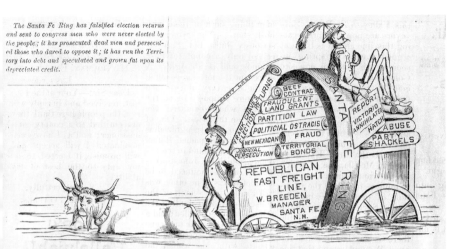

PARTY MANAGER—"*Pull up, Tranquilino, we must get the wagon out of this slough. Get up there, you lazy voter, or I'll wallop you!*"

TRANQUILINO—"*We can never pull that load through—you had better stop using that party lash and unload the wagon.*"

INDEPENDENT REPUBLICAN OX—"*This thing has gone far enough; if you don't unload the wagon I won't pull another pound, and I'll kick out of the yoke.*"

Figure 16 "Republican Fast Freight Line," cartoon in the Las Cruces newspaper *Thirty-Four*, October 20, 1880. The paper urged the defeat of supposed Ring candidates in the upcoming general election. Image from Archives and Special Collections, New Mexico State University Library.

confirmation of a grant, the size of a confirmed grant, issuance of a U.S. patent, or treatment of competing ownership rights. For a decade before the investigation by Frank Warner Angel in 1878 and the resulting shake-up in the territorial government, men associated with Elkins and Catron comprised a comfortable quorum among officeholders in New Mexico. Following a brief reform effort during the administration of Lew Wallace, a Ring-friendly climate prevailed in Santa Fe through 1884. These conditions simplified efforts to negotiate the otherwise complex business of land-grant speculation.

The Mora land grant was one in which Elkins and Catron invested jointly, beginning with Elkins's acquisition of a share of its common lands—one of the shares created through the original grant. The grant, awarded to settlers including seventy-six heads of families in 1835, was confirmed by Congress in 1860. In 1876, it was patented for 827,621 acres. According to tradition, Elkins received the claim "as payment for defending an impecunious resident charged with a crime."[21] Elkins and Catron began seeking out grantees and heirs, buying as many shares as they could. By 1870, they had accumulated at least sixteen shares. They brought in three more investors, including the surveyor general, T. Rush Spencer, who graciously approved a disputed survey upon which the size of the grant was based.[22] In order to ensure negotiability of interests, it was critical that the patent—the U.S. government's guarantee of ownership—be issued not to the Town of Mora, as the surveyor general's document specified, but to the heirs of the seventy-six original settlers, whose shares could be bought, sold, and divided. This option, it is suggested, was arranged by Elkins, who was territorial delegate at the time.[23]

From the investors' perspective, the endeavor was fraught with complications, including endless problems with the survey, disputes and succession issues among investors, resistance of residents who stood to be shorn of lands on which they relied for subsistence, and administrative and legal difficulties. In addition, speculators were not the only ones working to establish rights to the Mora grant. As painstaking research has revealed, the acreage encompassing the undivided common lands was dwindling, as other claimants, including many Hispanic residents, were able to secure *hijuelas* or deeds to parcels from the grant's internal governing authority.[24] In addition, subgrants to smaller communities contributed to a trend of privatization of ownership, such that common lands subject to partition and sale were reduced. Neither was the investing group led by Elkins and Catron the sole claimant to the common lands. Other outsiders had acquired shares, as had Mora residents who wanted to own and use the land. A suit for partition of common lands was filed, but instead of dividing the proceeds from a sale of 600,000 acres, as Clark Knowlton estimated, claimants under the partition suit may have been looking at less than 300,000 acres.[25]

By 1916, when the partition suit concluded, Spencer and Elkins were dead, and members of the Ring-led group other than Catron had sold their interests to the family of Benjamin Butler. Catron had deeded his portion to his son Charles, and it was finally sold by the county for taxes. The effort of more than forty years to treat the common lands of the Mora grant as a marketable commodity is one of the sadder episodes in New Mexico land-grant history. While the endeavor did not enrich the men of the Ring, the exertions of speculators, officials, and judges succeeded in destroying the underlying design of the Mora grant as a tract intended to supply needed resources for a self-supporting community. It is fair to ask how much of this would have been possible without the aid of a self-interested territorial delegate and a similarly motivated surveyor general.

Acquiring New Mexico Land Grants

Their ventures were not always successful, but none excelled Elkins and Catron in their zealous pursuit of land. According to Catron biographer and land-grant scholar Victor Westphall, Catron owned or held interests in no fewer than thirty-four land grants in the course of his long legal and business career. Westphall estimates that Catron held title to more than three million acres in grant lands over his lifetime.[26] Of his own exploits in the grant business, Elkins later told the *Chicago Herald*, "There were millions of acres offered for sale. The Spaniards and Mexicans who held them could do nothing with them and they were glad to sell their grants for any kind of price from 10 cents an acre and upward. I was a lawyer and I knew all about the land laws. I examined the titles of such property as I purchased, and I bought a great deal. I had at one time 600,000 acres of land and the result was that I was accused of being a land grabber and a monopolist. But the truth is, I bought every foot of land and paid for it and, though squatters and others have fought me, I have always been able to show that my titles were good."[27]

Circumstantial evidence suggests that Elkins was influential in securing patents for grants in New Mexico. In the course of his two terms as territorial delegate, Congress patented a total of seven grants. "Of these seven," Victor Westphall notes, "his business associate, T. B. Catron, was directly involved in five." Westphall concludes that Elkins also worked to influence the issuance of patents by the General Land Office, not only for the Mora grant (1876), but also for the Pablo Montoya grant (1877), for which he was the claimants' attorney, and the Tierra Amarilla grant (1881), acquired earlier by Catron.[28] In Elkins's first term as delegate, Congress repealed a law requiring that the cost of surveying a private claim be borne by or on behalf of the claimant, and that funds for the survey be paid prior to the issuance of a patent. Four New Mexico grants were awaiting survey at the time. Observed Westphall, "The fact that Stephen B. Elkins, a leading dealer in land grants, was involved in all four would appear to be more than a coincidence."[29]

Malcolm Ebright highlights two strategies used by speculators to acquire titles to grants during the surveyor general period, a time extending from 1854 until the Court of Private Land Claims was established in 1891.

These were (1) the purchase of the principal settler's interest and (2) the partition suit.[30] Both paths to ownership were used by men associated with the Santa Fe Ring. The second method, at least with respect to New Mexico, was essentially an innovation of men commonly identified as Ring members.

The principal settler, or *poblador principal*, represented a group of settlers in petitioning the Spanish or Mexican government for a grant to benefit a community. These grants typically provided for plots designated for individual ownership by each of the petitioners, along with a larger tract of common land reserved for shared use. While the names of petitioners were often included in grant documents that could be relied upon for legal purposes, it was sometimes the case that only the poblador principal was named in the documents issued by the government. This circumstance, along with the confusion resulting from a convergence of cultures, languages, and legal systems, introduced the possibility that a creative and well-connected purchaser could acquire the interest of the poblador principal and then claim to have secured the entire property.

This is what happened with respect to the Anton Chico grant, a community grant awarded to the principal settler, Manuel Rivera, in 1822, and later confirmed by Congress in 1860.[31] Henry M. Atkinson, the longest-serving surveyor general and one of the most active in pursuing holdings in private grants and public lands, took on multiple roles reflecting his official duties and personal interests. Over his eight-year tenure as surveyor general, Atkinson set a new standard for conflict of interest, participating in at least four cattle companies that relied on homestead and grant lands that could be acquired at favorable terms, possibly with the help of the surveyor general's office. Atkinson did not hesitate to issue rulings on matters in which he was an interested party.

Through his work as surveyor general, perhaps in the course of a review ordered by the General Land Office and the resulting resurvey of the Anton Chico grant, Atkinson learned of the property's potential value and determined to pursue an ownership interest. The new survey, approved by Atkinson in his official capacity, was executed by John Elkins and Robert Marmon. Meanwhile, in 1879, Atkinson began purchasing the interests of the poblador principal, Manuel Rivera, from Rivera's heirs. He did so through intermediaries who purchased the shares and then conveyed them to Atkinson. Assisting him in this way were Henry Waldo, Catron, and Charles Gildersleeve, as well as Atkinson's attorney, Louis Sulzbacher.[32] This sleight of hand obscured a clear conflict of interest, in which Atkinson, as surveyor general, was involved in passing official judgment on his claim to the Anton Chico grant.

Atkinson sought to have the patent to the Anton Chico grant issued not to the Town of Anton Chico, but in the name of Manuel Rivera and thirty-six unnamed settlers. Commissioner of the General Land Office Noah McFarland ruled that the patent should name the Town of Anton Chico as owner, but Atkinson contrived to secure a reversal of this decision, and in 1883 the patent was issued as he wished.[33] Atkinson was, by this time, in control of the interests purchased by his friends. In 1883, he deeded these to the New Mexico Land and Livestock Company. The company—Atkinson's company—laid claim to the common lands of the Anton Chico grant by virtue of purchase from Rivera's heirs, and Atkinson secured a property totaling some 383,857 acres, less deeded parcels owned by individuals of the Anton Chico community.

Most egregious were the practices by which Atkinson aided his own cause. He failed to recuse himself as presiding officer in a hearing convened for the purpose of allowing residents to plead their case for a patent that would have secured title to the common lands to the community. In ruling on the request, Atkinson seemed to contradict himself. Having favored issuance of the patent to Manuel Rivera and unnamed settlers, Atkinson now found it advantageous to rule that the names of other settlers could not be determined and that the title must, therefore, vest solely in Rivera. In 1884, Atkinson sued to quiet title to the Anton Chico grant, not including inhabited communities and other deeded or occupied tracts. To satisfy a condition that interested parties be advised of his intent, a notice was published in the *Albuquerque Journal*, in English. The village was not named in the notice. In effect, notice had been denied to the residents of Anton Chico.[34]

Atkinson died in 1886, and control of the New Mexico Land and Livestock Company fell to Catron. It was not until 1906 that the full impact of the company's claim to the common lands of Anton Chico came to light and set off an effort by the community to regain title to the grant. A lawsuit to this end culminated in 1915. The Anton Chico grant finally was recognized as a bona fide community grant with its common lands restored—less a settlement of 35,000 acres awarded to Catron and 100,000 acres conveyed to the plaintiffs' attorneys.

Another example of improper treatment of a community grant is found in the case of the Tierra Amarilla land grant. Catron is commonly pilloried for his role in depriving settlers and their descendants of their rightful interests in common lands originally designated for their use, but he was perhaps no more to blame than others who contributed to a long history of injustice, including an heir of the poblador principal, the Office of the Surveyor General, the U.S. Congress, and several U.S. courts.[35] By Malcolm Ebright's analysis, Francisco Martínez and the Office of the Surveyor General—including William Pelham and his translator and clerk, David J. Miller—led Congress to confirm the grant in 1860 as a grant to an individual, not a community or settlement grant, as seems clearly intended in documents issued by the Mexican government.

The decision of the U.S. Supreme Court in *Tameling v. United States Freehold and Emigration Company* magically transformed grants whose size exceeded limits prescribed in Mexican law. Under the Treaty of Guadalupe Hidalgo, only grants that were valid under the laws of Spain or Mexico, under which they were made, should have been confirmed, but the *Tameling* decision allowed confirmation of the capacious Sangre de Cristo and Maxwell grants. As applied to the Tierra Amarilla grant, the ruling had the effect of redefining the property as a private grant and extinguishing the legitimate and historic interests of other settlers in the common lands.[36]

The sin ascribed to Catron is essentially that of ignoring the documented rights of settlers who had received deeds recognizing legal ownership—not only of the individual allotments upon which they had established homes, fields, and gardens, but of common lands that yielded pasture, timber, firewood, and game. Despite the presence of hijuelas (deeds) that had been given to 113 named property owners, Catron bypassed these claimants by acquiring the interests of Francisco Martínez, son of the poblador principal, and by letting that action suffice to support his claim of ownership. In essence, he was treating Martínez as the sole owner of the grant.[37] Jilted settlers apparently recognized a problem with the poblador principal as early as July 1861 and appealed to the surveyor general for relief, to no avail.[38]

Victor Westphall's portrayal of Catron in a 1973 biography was largely admiring. Ten years later, Westphall was more inclined to hold Catron accountable for injustices to the heirs of the Tierra Amarilla grant. In answer to the criticism that Catron had essentially stolen the grant, Westphall replied, "He probably paid $200,000 for that land, but the question is did he pay it to the right people?"[39] Many heirs likely would have declined to sell, had they been approached. In Westphall's view, Catron had used "legal trickery" to evade or minimize his obligation to other claimants whose rights should have been protected.

Other presumed Ring members were involved in ways that proved helpful to Catron. In 1876, Surveyor General Atkinson commissioned a survey of the Tierra Amarilla grant that was criticized as an intentionally inaccurate representation of the grant's boundaries. Elkins claimed credit for his assistance in obtaining a patent issued in 1881, and former governor Samuel Axtell, removed as governor in 1878 but revived four years later as territorial chief justice, issued favorable rulings in a suit filed by Catron to quiet title to the Tierra Amarilla grant in September 1883.[40]

Catron has also been criticized in connection with the suit to quiet title, heard in the district court at Tierra Amarilla. The requirement that interested parties be given notice of a proceeding that could potentially extinguish existing claims was regularly abused, as in the case of the Anton Chico grant. Catron may have met minimum requirements in effect at the time, but his effort fell short of providing practical notice to potential claimants.[41] If he published notice in a newspaper, as the record seems to indicate, he did not do so in Rio Arriba County, which had no local paper at the time. Whatever his method, the judge found it legally sufficient, but none of the residents who presumably had interests to protect appeared in court. Accordingly, Catron was declared to be the grant's owner.[42] Present at the court session, along with Catron and Axtell, were Attorney General William Breeden and the court's clerk, C. M. Phillips, Axtell's son-in-law.

In his involvement of nearly four decades, the enterprise was moderately successful, but legal and financial complications associated with the Tierra Amarilla grant caused Catron much frustration and worry. However, the episode illustrates the extent to which alliances among Ring men could advance the interests of an individual, even when the collaborators had no immediate financial interest. In the exchange of favors likely to occur over time, all could expect to benefit.

The Partition Law

The second common stratagem identified by Ebright was the use of the partition suit to convert an undivided interest in the common lands of a community grant into cash or land that could be held in fee simple title and sold. The need for this device came about as nonresidents acquired interests in community grants. As many claimants had little cash, attorneys sometimes acquired such interests as fees for legal services. These outside owners did not intend to live on the land, and they had little use for an asset that could not easily be bought or sold. By bringing a partition suit, the owner of such an interest could force a sale of the common lands, with holders of interests receiving proportional shares of the proceeds. Ring figures made use of this device as applied to the common lands of community grants, but first they had to create it.

During the legislative session of 1875–1876, Ring influence was at its peak, and the group led by Elkins and Catron was in firm control of the assembly. A reliable ally, Samuel Axtell, was governor and William Breeden was attorney general. Elkins held the office of territorial delegate and Catron was U.S. attorney. James K. Proudfit was surveyor general, but soon to be replaced by Henry Atkinson, whose exploits as a land speculator would surpass those of his predecessors. Chief Justice Palen died as the legislative session was about to get under way and was succeeded by Henry Waldo. This was the essential cast of characters for the Santa Fe Ring of this period.

Pedro Sánchez of Taos was elected president of the council—the territorial equivalent of a state senate. Sánchez has also been identified as a local agent for the Ring, a strong Catron ally and a Taos County Republican Party leader for more than thirty years. While serving as attorney general, William Breeden was also a leading member of the territorial council, as were frequent Ring confederates J. Francisco Chaves and Benjamin Stevens.

The investigations of Frank Warner Angel would soon derail the Ring's control of offices and policies, but in January 1876, life was good and the Elkins-Catron legislative machine was in fine working order. Bills likely to invite opposition tended to be introduced late in the legislative session. The partition law was introduced in the last week, as was an act attaching Colfax County to Taos County for judicial purposes in response to recent troubles in northern New Mexico. On Tuesday morning, January 11, Breeden presented "An Act Relating to the Partition of Real Estate and for Other Purposes," designated as Council Bill 86. In the afternoon session, the bill was read for the first, second, and third times, and was passed without recorded discussion by a vote of ten yeas to three nays.[43]

The sailing was not quite so smooth in the House, where twenty-seven of twenty-nine members had Hispanic surnames and where presumed Ring influence was not as strong. Melvin Mills reported for the judiciary committee and urged passage without revision, noting "that the law in almost similar provisions exists in Colorado and other states and territories and that the working of the law has been satisfactory in its results wherever it has been in force."[44] The bill passed by a margin of thirteen to eleven. The import of the law must have been clear to its initiators, to Ring-related supporters, and to at least some opponents in the House, but there was at the time no reported discussion of the law's application to land-grant holdings and to the rights of residents holding fractional claims to common lands of community grants, though simplification of grant-related transactions must have been prominent among the "other purposes" that the sponsors intended.[45]

According to the authors of at least one official study, "The common lands of community land grants should never have been subject to a partition suit because they were not tenancies-in-common under Spanish and Mexican law; they were not private lands held by distinct co-owners."[46] Rather, the common lands had but one owner, the community to which the grant had been awarded. The practical result of a successful partition suit was that the common lands were sold rather than divided, usually to the detriment of local claimants, who lost the use of the land and received payments that did not reflect the land's true value, while speculators purchased the common lands at bargain prices.

Elkins and Catron were among the first of many attorneys and claimants to make use of the new law. In 1879, Elkins and Vicente Romero brought suit to partition the Mora land grant. As discussed earlier, the suit was not resolved for more than thirty years, and its result did not benefit Elkins or Catron. Catron also sued to partition the Domingo Fernández, or San Cristóbal, grant, in which he, Charles Gildersleeve, and others were interested. The success of that suit is also doubtful, since Catron still claimed partial ownership of the grant when he died in 1921.[47]

The results of these actions indicate the uncertainty of the partition suit as a strategy for liquidating claims. While some communities lost common lands to attorneys and other claimants in partition suits, many such occurrences came after the power of the Elkins-Catron combination declined and did not involve men identified with the old Ring. According to David Benavides, an attorney and student of partition actions, "Partitioning American-style represented the ultimate Anglo-American vindication of individual property rights: the right of a single petitioner to preserve his interest at its maximum potential value, overriding all other rights."[48]

Any assessment of the impact of a land-confirmation system that invited fraud and other abuse, by men identified with the Santa Fe Ring or by others, is mostly guesswork. In testimony provided to a congressional committee in

1975, Clark S. Knowlton stated, "Within a few years after the formation of the Santa Fe Ring the majority of the Spanish-American land grants passed into its possession." Knowlton gave as examples the claims owned by Catron, whose holdings in 1894 were said to run into the millions of acres.[49] Citing an unnamed source, Knowlton indicates that since 1854, Hispanic New Mexicans have lost "well over two million acres of private lands, 1.7 million acres of communal land, one million acres taken by the State, and vast areas acquired by the federal government." Equally important, Knowlton adds, "This land loss is still continuing on a massive scale and has already been responsible for the destruction of the traditional Spanish-American rural upper- and middle-class groupings."[50]

The Plunder of the Public Domain

As New Mexico's governor in 1883, Lionel Allen Sheldon observed that, in the hands of highly motivated speculators and corrupt territorial officials, Spanish and Mexican land grants appeared to take on "India rubber qualities," growing from modest and practical dimensions to vast estates when surveyed and presented for official recognition.[51] In 1887, a new breed of surveyor general for New Mexico, the self-righteously ornery George Washington Julian, agreed, stating that his predecessors had made a habit of approving dubious surveys and settling all questions in favor of the claimant. Said Julian, "Millions of acres of the public domain were thus appropriated to the uses of private greed." By his estimate, lands lost to the public domain totaled some four to five million acres.[52]

But land grants were not the only objects of fraudulent activity. The already diminished public domain became another target of manipulation for those eager to own land for agricultural or speculative purposes. Relatively little of the vast, arid American Southwest was suitable for cultivation, but with the rapid growth of the range-cattle industry following the Civil War, lands were sought after, and sometimes fought over, by westering cattlemen. By the early 1880s, many of the same men who found land grants an attractive proposition were organizing large cattle companies, the success of which depended on acquisition of scarce water and good grass.

Public land laws enacted with farmers in mind provided for donation, preemption, and homestead claims of 160 acres—sufficient to yield a living on good soil, with abundant rainfall or surface water for irrigation, but negligible in a semiarid region in which vast portions were suitable only for

Figure 17 As surveyor general, George Washington Julian came down on land speculators, but his view of community grants and common lands was also detrimental to smaller landholders. Brady-Handy Collection, Library of Congress, No. LC-DIG-cwpbh-04726.

grazing. Given the laws provided by Congress, stockmen adapted. They used homestead and preemption claims to secure control of water sources, which in turn gave them control over larger expanses of the public domain that were otherwise useless for agriculture. Some had claims filed in the names of their employees. Others resorted to fraud or intimidation.

Among newly organized entities attracting notice in the 1880s was the American Valley Company. The design of its incorporators was to gain control of a grazing range extending over large portions of western New Mexico. Most of the land was designated as public domain. Some parcels had been claimed by individuals under the homestead law. The company's scheme involved acquisition of desirable parcels controlling water sources. The founding principal, John P. Casey, drove cattle into the area in 1881 and established his home ranch on Largo Creek. His strategy included an eventual sale of the company to investors.[53]

The organization and management of the American Valley Company was not a project of the Santa Fe Ring, but presumed members were involved almost from the beginning. The Ring figure most prominently associated with the venture was Henry Atkinson, the surveyor general, who was considered a good man to have on the company's side because "through him they could get possession of land in the American Valley regardless of who settled it."[54] Atkinson became a partner and mingled official and personal interests in relation to matters involving the company. Catron was increasingly involved, first as Atkinson's attorney and later as an investor. Stephen Elkins was, by this time, a resident of New York with extensive connections in Washington, but he helped, putting Casey and Atkinson in touch with a potential investor, Senator John A. Logan of Illinois.[55] By the summer of 1882, Logan had traveled to inspect the property. Governor Lionel Sheldon was also helpful, approving the creation of a militia led by Casey and his partner, W. C. Moore.[56]

The enterprise is best known for the foul murders of two settlers, Alexis Grossetete and Robert Elsinger, who had filed preemption claims on lands located on the coveted range of the American Valley Company, at Gallo Spring. Casey had tried without success to buy the settlers' claims. The killings, perpetrated in May 1883 by individuals associated with Casey, climaxed a campaign of intimidation intended to drive Grossetete and Elsinger from the area.[57] The murders were reported in the national press, and the incident reverberated in the territory for years. This was the most notorious attempt by men associated with the company to gain control of the range through acquisition of lands from the public domain, but it was not the only such attempt.

In 1884, two former employees of the American Valley Company, Edward McGinty and Richard F. Mitchell, witnesses in an investigation of alleged land fraud in New Mexico, testified that false homestead entries had been filed in their names in 1883. When McGinty went to the office of the surveyor general to inquire into the matter in May 1884, perhaps at the suggestion of a federal investigator, he reported being taken into a private room where Atkinson offered him $75 to make an affidavit saying that he had never filed a homestead claim. Atkinson apparently meant to use the paper to settle a score with Casey and Moore. McGinty signed the affidavit and received the money in cash.[58] When Mitchell inquired about the claim imputed to him, Atkinson allegedly offered him $600 for a quitclaim deed to the land. According to Mitchell's statement to a federal investigator, the two men went to the office of Thomas Catron, Atkinson's attorney, and after papers were drawn up, Mitchell left with $300 and a note for the balance owed him.[59]

Daniel H. McAllister, an employee of the American Valley Company who turned state's witness in the inquiry into the murders of Grossetete and Elsinger, offered a revealing narrative of the company's practices. In June 1882, he had entered into a partnership with W. C. Moore, who intended to establish a cattle operation. McAllister implicated several associates:

At that time, it was not known that our range was to be in the American Valley, but shortly after this Mr. Moore informed me that he had formed a partnership with John P. Casey, and that General H. M. Atkinson was also in with them, thereby giving them an opportunity to get possession of land in the American Valley for a range before anyone else got in. The Atkinson referred to is the present surveyor-general of New Mexico. John P. Casey was to secure the range by causing entries to be made in the American Valley in such a manner as to obtain all the water therein. Casey did cause a large number of entries to be made, thus securing all or nearly all the water in said valley, covering an area of about forty miles square. These entries, or very many of them, were fraudulent, and I have every reason to believe that General Atkinson was fully aware of this fact.[60]

McAllister further testified that "Register Max Frost was connected with Casey and Atkinson in the location of the fraudulent entries in the American Valley," and he stated that Frost knew of their fraudulent character. Despite indictments, trials, and newspaper publicity, no one was convicted or punished for the murders or the alleged instances of land fraud.

The ensuing history of the American Valley Company was tortured, tangled, and largely futile. Catron was increasingly ensnared in its affairs, acquiring majority interest and sinking too much of his own money into the enterprise. By 1905, Elkins had a stake and Catron was enlisting Elkins's support in an attempt to wrest control from a willful and, in Catron's mind, incompetent managing partner.[61] Unable to extricate himself easily, Catron held on, acquiring the property at a foreclosure sale in 1911. Catron still held remnants of the company when he died in 1921.[62]

An epidemic of fraudulent homestead entries was evident elsewhere in the territory. In Colfax County, including portions later taken to make up the new Union County, there appeared to be wholesale manipulation of the land laws. Most of the accusations involved small operators, but scrutiny also fell on Stephen Dorsey, who, in the wake of his acquittal in the Star Route scandal, had repaired to New Mexico in search of serious money. Alone and in association with partners, he organized the Palo Blanco Cattle Company and other concerns. A mercurial streak led Dorsey to gravitate from one endeavor to another, following current enthusiasms and investing in emerging

Figure 18 Tainted by his prosecution
in the Star Route mail fraud scandal,
Stephen Wallace Dorsey sought fortune
in New Mexico land and cattle. Photo ca.
1875. Barnes Photographic Collection,
Georgetown University Library Special
Collections Research Center.

enterprises. He invested in irrigated farming in Colorado and, in 1892, established a tuberculosis sanitarium on his home ranch in New Mexico.[63]

Dorsey's friends and admirers were legion, but so were detractors. Dorsey had supreme confidence in his own integrity, but there were those who found him deficient in personal ethics. Referring to a comment attributed to President James A. Garfield, to the effect that Dorsey "had a screw loose in his moral make up," the *Boston Herald* replied that "the star router never had enough moral make up for a screw to take hold of."[64] Dorsey was active in Republican politics and, as Morris Taylor stated, he was regarded by many as "at least a peripheral member of that remarkable combination known as the Santa Fe Ring."[65] Sharon K. Lowry, a student of Dorsey's career, noted that Dorsey's association with Elkins and Catron in land speculation was sufficient to designate him as "a fully incorporated member of the ring."[66]

Dorsey first sought a base for his New Mexico cattle operation through ownership of the 600,000-acre Uña de Gato land grant. When the grant was exposed as fraudulent, he was forced to pursue other means of acquiring the land and water needed to support his stock-raising activities. According to Inspector Frank D. Hobbs of the General Land Office and Surveyor General George Julian, who had been appointed in place of the discredited Atkinson, the new strategy involved gaining control of water through an accumulation of entries made under the homestead and preemption laws—laws intended to distribute western lands to individual families that would live on their claims, develop the land, and make it productive.

In June 1884, Hobbs reported to N. C. McFarland, commissioner of the General Land Office, that he had investigated seven claims in the vicinity of Dorsey's headquarters. On paper, the entries had been "proved up," but based on the absence of improvements referred to in proof documents and of any evidence of cultivation, Hobbs believed the entries to be fraudulent. One entry had been conveyed to Dorsey, four to his neighbor J. E. Temple, and two jointly to Temple and L. K. Smith. Hobbs concluded, "An honest investigation would result in the cancellation of hundreds of fraudulent entries, and many thousand acres of land would be thrown open to entry by actual settlers."[67] He also observed that Dorsey had been fencing land on the public domain.

While in Colfax County, Hobbs learned of the alleged complicity of the *Colfax County Stockman* newspaper in abetting fraudulent entries. According to witnesses, the paper did this in concert with the Office of the U.S. Land Register in Santa Fe, printing a few copies of the notice of intent to file for final proof of homestead entries for use of claimants, but omitting the notices from papers placed in circulation. Hobbs spoke with citizens who believed that fraudulent claims were going through with the knowledge and approval of the land register, Max Frost. When local citizens were told of the need for evidence to support their allegations, Hobbs wrote, "Many told me that they dared not do it, by reason of the great influence of Frost and the 'Santa Fé ring.'"[68]

Hobbs was not gentle in his criticisms of Dorsey and others, but Surveyor General Julian took it a step farther in his provocative essay "Land-Stealing in New Mexico," published in the *North American Review* in July 1887. Of Dorsey's pursuit of the bogus Uña de Gato grant, Julian wrote, "When the forgery of the grant was demonstrated in 1879, and he thought it unsafe to rely on that title, he determined to avail himself of the Homestead and Pre-emption laws." According to Julian, "Mr. Dorsey, who was already in possession of thousands of acres of the choicest lands in the tract, at once sent out squads of henchmen, who availed themselves of the forms of the Pre-emption and Homestead laws, in acquiring pretended titles, which were conveyed to him, according to arrangements previously agreed upon."[69]

Dorsey responded with a rebuttal in the *Review*'s issue of October 1887. Much of his article was devoted to discrediting the accuser and promoting the notion that he, Dorsey, had exposed the fraud of the Uña de Gato claim. But he also criticized as inadequate the system for distribution of western lands. The regrettable error of the government, according to Dorsey, was in "dealing with the arid region, largely which is, at its best, mere grazing land, as if it was of the same character, condition, and capacity as the purely agricultural domain of the country."[70] Land without water did the farmer no good, and a tract of 160 acres, as permitted in the public land laws, could not begin to meet even minimal needs for the stockman.

When the federal investigation came to a head, Dorsey was among those indicted, but the government failed to achieve a conviction, and he suffered no penalty beyond further damage to an already tarnished reputation. By the early 1890s, Dorsey had disposed of portions of his New Mexico holdings. He moved on to Denver, then California. He died in Los Angeles in 1916.[71]

Confronting Allegations of Land Fraud

The attention of official Washington became even more intense with the 1884 election of Grover Cleveland, the first Democratic president since Andrew Johnson. In an inaugural address, the new president expressed his commitment to reform, declaring, "Care for the property of the nation and for the needs of future settlers requires that the public domain should be protected from purloining schemes and unlawful occupation."[72] In practical terms, this led to the dispatch of additional inspectors to examine reported instances of fraud in the disposition of public lands, a process well begun under the previous Republican administration.

In New Mexico, the chief whistle-blower was the former land office receiver, Elias Brevoort. As early as December 1881, he had written to the commissioner of the General Land Office, describing "a system of frauds perpetrated in making entries of lands," including donation and homestead claims. Brevoort named suspected perpetrators, including two public officials, and followed up in April 1882, naming other suspects in Colfax and San Miguel Counties.[73] Additional complaints reinforced the impression of a general epidemic of fraudulent activity. By August 1882, the Department of the Interior had opened an investigation into land fraud in New Mexico and had put an investigator on the ground—the first of at least eight agents who would take the field over the next three years. The investigation culminated in the publication of reports and testimony running to some 404 pages, submitted to the United States Senate under the short title *Titles to Lands in New Mexico*.[74] Included in the document were accusations of fraud, sworn testimony of witnesses, statements in support of the accused, and reports of the land office inspectors.

Those accused of anything from filing a false claim to illegal fencing numbered in the hundreds. Among men sometimes named as Ring figures, those implicated included Antonio Ortiz y Salazar, territorial treasurer, 1872–1880; Max Frost, register of the land office in Santa Fe, 1881–1885; William Bailhache, receiver for the land office, 1881–1885; Henry Atkinson, surveyor general for New Mexico, 1876–1884; Pedro Sánchez, Indian agent at Santa Fe, 1882–1885; and Stephen Dorsey. Catron was cited for his role in facilitating alleged illegal transactions in the American Valley matter.[75] Ortiz y Salazar was implicated in a general way in Brevoort's letter to the commissioner, but was not named in specific allegations of land fraud. Bailhache was accused of attempting to extort money and favors from Frederick Schnepple, party in a dispute over a coal-mining claim, in exchange for a favorable decision in the matter. Sánchez was said to have arranged false homestead claims, later conveyed to himself. Chief Justice Samuel Axtell was not accused of fraud, but was said to be a tool of Frost, who reportedly had said that he could injure a rival by securing an adverse decision in Axtell's court.

Individuals accused in the report argued in their own defense. Particular attention had been paid to the matter of "unlawful inclosure." Dorsey responded with a letter addressed to federal investigator R. W. Hunter, subsequently published in the *Santa Fe Weekly New Mexican*. He explained that fencing had largely ceased because it was not in the stockmen's interests and that some fencing was needed to provide for the confinement of bulls and saddle horses. Dorsey contended that existing fences did not cut off the water sources or otherwise harm the interests of other users.[76] The *New York Times* was unmoved, countering that the dire necessity that caused the stockmen to fence was "simply the necessity that certain capitalists should own great herds of cattle and make large sums of money."[77] The paper found Dorsey's reasoning hollow, stating, "The more the people of the States hear about the system of morals that justifies the stealing of public land, the better for those who are trying to execute the laws and thwart the schemes of a formidable band of jobbers. By and by the poor men of the East, each of whom would be satisfied with 160 acres, will have something to say about the men who have robbed them."

Friends of Max Frost rallied to his defense, providing statements attesting to his character and standing in the community. Among those signing a letter in support of Frost and W. H. Bailhache were presumed Ring figures, including Henry Waldo, Lionel Sheldon, William Breeden, Marshall Breeden, Samuel B. Axtell, Warren Bristol, Edward L. Bartlett, William T.

Thornton, William Manderfield, Pedro Sánchez, and William L. Rynerson.[78] Catron, L. Bradford Prince, and Henry Atkinson signed a separate letter submitted on behalf of the Bar of Santa Fe County, and John H. Riley signed a letter sent from Doña Ana County. Frost, Bailhache, Sánchez, and Atkinson offered affidavits in their own defense and in defense of others accused— chiefly Frost, since several allegations referenced collusion with Frost in manipulation of the land laws.

By Victor Westphall's count, some 641 criminal cases alleging land fraud were brought in New Mexico courts between 1871 and 1891. Only 15 of these ended in a verdict of guilty, but Westphall notes that these results do not entirely exonerate the defendants in other cases. He counts more than 300 cases in which circumstances pointed to some likelihood of guilt.[79]

Intense prosecutorial attention fell on Max Frost. In July 1886, a grand jury indicted him on fifteen charges, including official misconduct, subornation of perjury, and conspiracy. He was tried and convicted on one charge of conspiracy in February 1887. His lawyer, Henry L. Waldo, sought a new trial, which was granted. The second trial produced a verdict of not guilty. Several cases were dismissed. Frost was tried on three other charges and was again found not guilty. In February 1888, the news that eight case files had disappeared from the office of the clerk of the U.S. district court created a sensation and elicited speculation that files had been taken in order to thwart the prosecution.[80] These cases, including five naming Frost as defendant, were dismissed.

In Westphall's estimation, Max Frost "was extremely fortunate in having all the charges against him disposed of in one way or another," especially considering the evident determination of the government to see him punished.[81] Atkinson, the former surveyor general, may have been spared prosecution by his death in 1886. The long investigation and legal proceeding achieved little in the way of enforcement, but it put anyone tempted to abuse the public domain on notice that false and forged entries, illegal fencing, and collusion between public officials and claimants would not be tolerated, and that such actions would render offenders subject to prosecution.

From 1881, when the federal investigation of land fraud began, to 1891, when the Court of Private Land Claims was created, a full decade of attention was devoted to the issue of land titles and abuse of the public land laws in New Mexico. Not everyone found the exercise worth the effort. In October 1887, Stephen Dorsey was content to observe that, with some four hundred individuals indicted, the investigation had yet to produce "a grain or a shadow of truth" to show that frauds had been committed under the homestead and preemption laws.[82] The eminent New Mexico historian Ralph Emerson Twitchell, from his perspective of personal acquaintance and likely sympathy with some of the accused, characterized the investigation and subsequent prosecutions as "an assault upon titles to lands in New Mexico . . . which for violence of action and incapacity of management has never found a parallel in the history of the United States."[83]

Winners and Losers

In the course of the investigation of Max Frost and others, Franklin Jordan, a clerk in the land office, took issue with several witnesses and, in his affidavit given to a federal investigator, addressed a notion that seemed to hang over the proceeding. "The so-called 'Santa Fe Ring,'" he declared, "is composed of men who mind their own business, own property, pay taxes, obey the laws, and are bona fide citizens. Similar 'rings' exist in every town in the United States, and if they did not there would be but little protection for life or property, particularly west of the Rocky Mountains." Jordan blamed illegal entries on the long distances separating citizens from the land office, along with language differences and the low morals of the native people.[84]

In blaming the native people, who usually are cast as victims of land fraud, Jordan invoked prejudices that appeared in the reminiscences of early English-speaking travelers to the Southwest and that were used over a period of several decades by opponents of statehood. He held that abuses were to be expected "when a majority of entrymen live hundreds of miles from the land office, cannot speak the English language or read their own, live in a state of practical peonage, never hear the name of God mentioned, except as an accompaniment to the crack of a bull whip, and who would swear to a lie for a drink of whisky or commit murder for 50 cents."[85]

Jordan and his intellectual peers conveniently ignored ethical deficiencies on the part of land speculators and others who used language differences and various legal ruses to dispossess legitimate heirs, as in the histories of the Anton Chico and Tierra Amarilla grants cited earlier. Abuses persisted throughout the territorial period and beyond. In 1914, Alois B. Renehan barely escaped disbarment when Judge Herbert Raynolds gave him the benefit of a doubt. Raynolds found that, as attorney for claimants to the partitioned Juan José Lovato grant, Renehan had profited by overcharging his clients or charging them for services not rendered. Because it would have been inexplicably reckless for Renehan to risk his career in this manner, the judge reasoned that his conduct probably was "the result of a mistake rather than a deliberate fraud on the part of the respondent"—a lapse that, in the judge's mind, did not justify disbarment.[86]

The frenzied quest for land struck a nerve with many Pueblo Indian and native Hispanic New Mexicans, for whom the land was a source of spiritual as well as practical nourishment. Few issues could have exposed the gulf between the territory's Gilded Age immigrants and its native peoples more dramatically than did the differences in their orientation to land and other natural elements. The emotional impact of their experiences is expressed in art and in historical or polemical works. In the novel *Heart of Aztlan*, Rudolfo Anaya, whose understanding of place is rooted in his youth on the Llano Estacado, writes about men exiled to the barrios of Albuquerque, who remember with fondness and sadness a time when they lived close to the land, made a living from it, and took care of one another. "They told stories about the deeding of the land grants and the history behind the families who settled throughout the territory, and most important, they told in detail the aspects of the daily life of the people. And in the end they told how the government and men of power using the new law for selfish gain encroached upon the land and finally wrenched it away."[87] For their families, the land had made a home. The contrast between native peoples and speculators on this point was stark, as articulated by David Correia: "The ring saw New Mexico's land grants through a lens that brought forests into focus as marketable timber, the mountains as mineral lodes, and the vast grasslands as commercial pastures."[88]

The men identified with the Santa Fe Ring were by no means the only ones involved in manipulation of Spanish and Mexican land grants and abuse of laws regulating the distribution and use of the public domain. In numerous instances, however, presumed Ring members sought and gained access to official powers of government that could be and sometimes were exercised to the benefit of their interests. The Ring also provided a convenient object for the indignation of citizens who were convinced that there was something very wrong with official processes by which western land and water were being distributed into private hands.

CHAPTER SEVEN

A PROGRESSIVE AND
ENTERPRISING SPIRIT

I n 1891, the *Hillsborough Advocate* ventured to explain a persistent topic
of speculation for the edification of its readers: "For the benefit of an
inquisitive subscriber the *Advocate* will say that the Santa Fe Ring is an
organization existing under the laws of New Mexico with a capital stock of
$000,000,000 on which dividends amounting to $500,000 are declared annually. Principal place of business, Santa Fe and the towns along the productive valley of the Rio Grande."[1] True enough, the men identified with the
Ring were very much about making money, and they pursued that end
through a variety of enterprises—essentially, anything that might turn a
profit. Friendly governments—territorial and national—were vital accessories to the cause, as they have been since. At the same time, there was something to Franklin Jordan's protestation that those who were denounced as
Ring members also contributed to the stability and progress of the communities in which they lived. The men who organized cattle companies, mining
ventures, banks, and mercantile businesses were, in many cases, the same
ones who led in building schools, churches, civic organizations, and cultural
institutions. The *Advocate*'s beef with Ring men was not that they sought
wealth, but that their gains were so often perceived to have come from legal
trickery and self-serving manipulation of the levers of government.

A diversity of enterprises distinguished the Santa Fe Ring from similar
but more focused combinations. Seeing how matters lay in Lincoln County,
John H. Tunstall marveled that nearly every profitable enterprise was being
worked by a ring. He could discern an Indian ring, an army ring, a political
ring, a legal ring, a Roman Catholic ring, a cattle ring, and a land ring, along
with "half a dozen other rings."[2] Years later, an exasperated governor,
Edmund G. Ross, described a territory awash in "Cattle Rings, Public Land
Stealing Rings, Mining Rings, Treasury Rings, and rings of almost every

description." The result, he said, was that "the affairs of the Territory came to be run almost exclusively in the interest and for the benefit of combinations organized and headed by a few longheaded, ambitious and unscrupulous Americans, attracted hither by the golden opportunities for power and plunder."[3]

What caught the attention of the young Englishman and the battle-weary governor were the exploits of a core group of business and political men whose methods and success had drawn unfavorable notice. At the center of this movement were Elkins and Catron, frequent participants in joint ventures, with each other and with other presumed Ring figures. Their orbit embraced the whole territory and involved diverse pursuits and multiple collaborators.

Foundations of Enterprise

When the originators of New Mexico's dominant economic and political coalition arrived with ambitions in tow, basic structures to support a cash economy were lacking. There was no regular, economical transportation to larger markets, and there were no banks. These were needed for development of the kinds of economic assets the territory offered, including timber, minerals, livestock, and other agricultural products. English-language newspapers, essential to the business infrastructure, cropped up soon after the Occupation, providing for local advertising and promotion of counties and towns to prospective immigrants. Banks and railroads were slower in coming. Men identified with the Ring were involved in organizing all of these, along with related accessories including a bureau of immigration, territorial fairs, and chambers of commerce.

Throughout the 1870s, the railroad was fervently anticipated, but construction stalled in the depth of a financial panic, and recovery sufficient to stimulate capital was painfully slow. But banks were established beginning in 1870, with Elkins, Catron, and other Ring figures taking prominent roles. New Mexico's first bank grew out of Lucien Maxwell's sale of the Maxwell land grant. The First National Bank of Santa Fe was capitalized by Maxwell with $150,000 from proceeds of the sale. Maxwell then became its president. Charles F. Holly, who had been involved in the sale of the grant, and John S. Watts, a director of the new Maxwell Land Grant and Railway Company, were principals in the new bank. Holly was to be its cashier, and both men would sit on the board of directors.[4]

In *Grant of Kingdom*, a novel based on the Maxwell land-grant story, Harvey Fergusson fashioned a paradigm of social and economic change in a frontier society. Maxwell's reign as the owner of an estate first conveyed to Carlos Beaubien and Guadalupe Miranda corresponded to a period characterized by Fergusson as one of "primary pioneering." In keeping with the Maxwell legend, Fergusson's fictional Jean Ballard had the grit and determination to wrest a small empire out of the raw wilderness, and he had a knack for getting along with Indian and Hispanic natives. When the country had been made safe, clever businessmen like the fictional Major Arnold Blore superseded the hardy frontiersmen who had come before them. Maxwell biographer Lawrence R. Murphy suggested that the character of Arnold Blore was based on Stephen B. Elkins.[5] If so, the banking saga bears out Fergusson's larger notion.

Before the new bank could open, Elkins and Catron decided they needed to be in control of any banking business based in Santa Fe. "Apparently irked at Maxwell for not having allotted them shares in the new venture," one narrative goes, "Stephen B. Elkins and Thomas B. Catron, law partners previously retained by Maxwell in many important matters, proceeded to organize their own bank."[6] William Griffin, who had directed the first survey of the Maxwell grant, was also involved. Faced with the prospect of direct competition, Maxwell sold all but ten shares of his bank stock to the new group. By May 17, 1871, Elkins, Catron, and Griffin were in control.

A noticeable alignment of bank principals and presumed Ring figures was evident from the beginning and persisted for several decades. Elkins assumed the office of president, Griffin was cashier, and Catron was a member of the board. Joining them in the enterprise was José Leandro Perea, vice president of the bank and the father of a future bank president, Pedro Perea.[7] Dr. Robert H. Longwill, a political ally in Colfax County, was invited to invest in the bank and was later made a director.[8] Given the supportive roles of Griffin and Longwill in connection with Elkins's interests in Colfax County and as president of the new Maxwell Land Grant and Railway Company, one might wonder whether an object of including them as principals in the banking business may have been to secure their silence concerning past affairs and their loyalty as collaborators well into the future.

Concerning the imminent culmination of efforts to organize the new venture, Elkins told Longwill on May 13, "I finally bought the whole bank and I am sure we will have the Depository quite soon and no opposition. This beyond all peradventure insures our success and handsome profits."[9] As the depository bank, the new institution would hold the territory's public funds and profit from the earnings on them.

Through its first forty-five years, presidents of the bank were Elkins, Griffin, Pedro Perea, and Rufus Palen, the son of Judge Joseph Palen. The bank and its leaders were generally well regarded for soundness of operation, but in 1891, while Perea was its president and Catron vice president, the *Santa Fe Weekly Sun* took out after the bank for what it saw as a Ring-made boondoggle. The *Sun* began by criticizing the territory's financial operations on account of "the accumulation of large sums in the treasury, which are the source of speculation and revenue to a few politicians, commonly known collectively as the Santa Fe ring, through the First National bank of this city which is owned and controlled by those politicians."[10] It was inferred that First National, as the territory's depository bank, benefited from the use of public funds for long periods prior to expenditure, thus providing "a large fund for political manipulation and profit of a few who control the machinery of the territorial government." The paper suggested adjusting the schedule on which taxes were collected or implementing some other remedy, so as to "strike the Santa Fe ring a death blow—by cutting it off at the pockets."

Nothing came of the *Sun*'s rant, but references to the bank as an instrument of the Ring and its leaders surfaced from time to time. In December 1892, the Spanish-language papers *La Union de Albuquerque* and *El Estandarte de Springer* published *La Union*'s analysis of the defeat of Catron and other Republicans in Bernalillo County in the recent election. The paper surmised that one of the party's problems involved "the money that was given by Catron, the [First National] Bank of Santa Fe, and the Perea family," a reported $5,000 contributed by the bank and an additional $1,500 by Catron. The implication was that the bank was using money made on public deposits to advance its directors' political interests. Exclaimed *La Union*, "What kind of infernal ring, other than a knavish one, would sacrifice its party to its own vile interests, while holding funds of the Territory and speculating with them to make money for the bank! We are glad with all our hearts that their silver has helped bring about their defeat."[11]

The most dramatic influence on land values was the availability of transportation for easy access to markets. The arrival of the railroad was anticipated by immigrants and speculators who expected to profit from growth in population and commerce. With the railroad came an influx of farmers, stockmen, and entrepreneurs, along with eastern and foreign capital. Development was pushed by the railroads, by promoters of their securities, and by boosters who advertised land for sale and suggested promising business opportunities for prospective settlers.

Ring figures—and most immigrants who had arrived from the states before 1879—were vitally interested in the coming of the railroad, as were enterprising Hispanics who embraced the emerging market economy. As early as February 1870, Catron, Elkins, Judge Joseph Palen, and Governor William Pile joined General William J. Palmer and others as incorporators of the Rio Grande Rail Road and Telegraph Company, formed for the purpose of extending a proposed north–south line from Colorado through New Mexico to El Paso.[12] Less than a year later, papers reported the organization of the Moreno and Rio Hondo Railroad—a line intended to link the mining districts of the Moreno Valley to the Denver and Rio Grande, affording "a slow but sure mode of travel for all those who wish to visit Mexico or China." Completion was anticipated by June 1, 1871.[13] The counterculture *Thunderbolt* of Elizabethtown was unimpressed and stated, "That pet scheme of certain ward politicians in our midst, and known as the Rio Hondo Railway Company, excites our attention and investigation as journalists, and we propose to smother and expose all such put up jobs whenever the occasion offers."[14] The paper wondered whether locals might be "too free and independent" to endorse such a boondoggle and concluded, "*New Mexican* please answer."

These and other early fits and starts failed to produce the anticipated results, mostly due to the intervention of the Panic of 1873. When construction resumed, there were two major rivals for desirable routes into New Mexico. Ring men hedged their bets, supporting both. A struggle ensued, with legendary tales of desperate horseback rides and midnight grading parties, all for the sake of beating a rival company to the coveted Raton Pass. At the end of 1878, the Atchison, Topeka and Santa Fe (AT&SF) had laid track across the pass into New Mexico, where it would trace the Santa Fe Trail, skirt the Sangre de Cristos, and run to the Rio Grande. The Denver and Rio Grande Western (D&RGW) was preparing to build a line down the Rio Grande drainage to a terminus north of Santa Fe.

Railroad building was generally beyond the means of local investors, including those commonly associated with the Ring. But in 1879, residents of Santa Fe faced the unimaginable prospect that neither the AT&SF nor the D&RGW would reach the capital. A citizens committee including Griffin, William Manderfield, and Antonio Ortiz y Salazar negotiated with the D&RGW concerning a possible extension of its line from Española to the capital, but nothing came of the effort and the link was not completed before 1887.[15] More urgent relief was anticipated with the approach of the AT&SF, which had entered New Mexico in December 1878. When it became known that the line would run south from Las Vegas through Apache Canyon, then turn west without passing through Santa Fe, alarmed local businessmen mobilized.

Railroad executives explained considerations of geography and cost that had determined the intended route. They suggested alternative means by which citizens of Santa Fe could secure a branch line. Their proposal was presented to civic and business leaders in July 1879. Among a score of citizens involved were several who had been linked to the Ring. Ortiz y Salazar, Charles Gildersleeve, William G. Ritch, and Henry L. Waldo represented citizens in initial discussions with the railroad company. These men, with Abraham Staab, William Manderfield, and William Breeden, served on a committee chaired by William W. Griffin. This group was to determine a course of action in response to the AT&SF proposals.[16] In keeping with the committee's recommendation, an election was held and voters approved the issuance of bonds totaling $150,000 as a subsidy to induce construction of a branch line.[17] By February 1880, rails had been laid from the AT&SF station at Lamy, over the mesa and to the capital, and Santa Fe at last had its railroad.

When the AT&SF established a legal department for New Mexico in 1883, Henry Waldo withdrew from a law partnership with William Breeden to become its chief legal counsel. Waldo was a respected attorney and an effective advocate for the company for more than twenty-five years. In making Waldo its solicitor for New Mexico, did railroad executives consider his long-standing relationships with men of power in the combination said to dominate the territory? In the absence of conclusive evidence, it seems plausible that they did.

Throughout the era of railroad building, men identified with the Ring were involved in nearly every major effort and several minor ones. In most cases, they were not pivotal figures in determining corporate plans or raising capital. They provided a semblance of local involvement and an essential liaison with officials whose decisions could make matters easier for the railroad or place obstacles in its path. For native New Mexicans who lived by subsistence farming and stock raising on the common lands of community and tribal grants, the immediate consequences of the railroad and the emergent cash economy may have been more destructive than beneficial.

Figure 19 After stints as chief justice and attorney general in the mid-1870s, Henry Ludlow Waldo settled into a career as solicitor for the Atchison, Topeka and Santa Fe Railway. Photo ca. 1900. Palace of the Governors Photo Archives (NMHM/DCA), No. 13118.

Newspapers provided the primary medium of mass advertising in the territories. They were instruments of political activity and commerce, and they were not given to subtlety. They typically were partisan affairs, inclined to contentious and creative expression of their opinions.

The *Santa Fe New Mexican* was the most durable among a handful of papers published in the territory. By the early 1870s, extending through the joint editorship of William Manderfield and Thomas Tucker, the *New Mexican* was widely regarded as an organ of the Santa Fe Ring. In 1880, the paper's alignment with Ring interests became more explicit when a group composed of Manderfield, Tucker, William Breeden, and William Griffin assumed control of the company. Breeden became its president, Griffin was treasurer, and Manderfield continued as vice president and manager.[18] Beginning in 1883, Max Frost acquired a controlling interest.[19] He took on the editorship in 1889 and was associated with the paper until his death in 1909, ensuring that the *New Mexican* would remain an advocate for the Republican Party, and usually for persons and causes associated with the Santa Fe Ring. The *New Mexican* proclaimed itself the representative of "the progressive, enterprising spirit" that would make the territory a center of mining and agriculture, and affirmed its commitment to promote industry, encourage commerce, support the growth of manufacturing, and cultivate social and cultural amenities for the betterment of the citizenry.[20]

In the 1870s and 1880s, the *New Mexican* and other territorial papers published bilingual editions or at least offered occasional articles in Spanish, but editorial policy and content were generally under the control of Euro-Americans whose values emphasized economic development and progress as defined in the eastern states. New Mexico journalism could trace its origins to the short-lived *El Crepúsculo de la Libertad*, published in Santa Fe in 1834, but papers published in Spanish, edited by Hispanic New Mexicans and representing vital interests of native residents, would not flourish until the early 1890s, when strong editorial voices emerged in reaction to new encroachments on traditional lands and the political dominance of a self-serving elite group.[21]

Room to Graze

The coming of the railroad had an immediate effect on the growth of the western beef industry. In the decade following the arrival of the railroad, cattle companies took advantage of favorable market conditions, free grazing on the public domain, and the availability of accessible transportation to effect a major expansion of the cattle industry. From 137,314 head reported in 1880, just as railroad construction was under way in New Mexico, the number of beef cattle in the territory in 1890 had increased to a reported 554,014—a figure comparable to those reported in the twenty-first century.[22] It took many acres of semiarid grassland to support herds raised on better pasture elsewhere, but with the arrival of the railroad, a region pronounced worthless by early explorers was suddenly of interest. High beef prices in the eastern United States in the years after the Civil War attracted the attention of investors eager to partake in a profitable, growing industry.

Corporate stock-raising enterprises were not unknown before the railroad. The first such organization registered with the territorial secretary could be characterized as a Ring project. The Consolidated Land, Cattle Raising and Wool Growing Company was incorporated in 1872, with offices at Fort Bascom, Santa Fe, and Denver. Incorporators included Surveyor General James K. Proudfit, Governor Marsh Giddings, U.S. Attorney Thomas B. Catron, former U.S. Attorney Stephen B. Elkins, and William W. Griffin.[23] The Pablo Montoya grant and the Baca Number Two in northeastern New Mexico were the major assets conveyed by Wilson Waddingham, who retrained a majority interest. The company was essentially an early iteration of the storied Bell Ranch. The territorial secretary would not register another corporate cattle-raising business until the arrival of the railroad, but thereafter, they proliferated.

Much of the growth in large cattle companies occurred between 1881 and 1885. Some of the new companies were dominated by local men who could provide or raise needed capital, and some were owned by investors who rarely, if ever, laid eyes on their range or cattle. They relied on the ability and integrity of a resident manager—a shaky proposition in some cases. Stockmen in the north were quick to pick up on the trend toward corporate organization. Three companies that registered with the territorial secretary in 1881, the Cimarron Cattle Company, the Maxwell Cattle Company, and the Red River Cattle Company, were in Colfax County. A fourth company, the Waddingham Cattle Association, operated in San Miguel and adjacent counties. Beef-raising enterprises with names like the Akron Live Stock Company, the Dubuque Cattle Company, and the Kentucky Land and Stock Company were indicative of the diversity of new investors attracted to opportunities in the territory. British, Scottish, and Dutch capitalists were also eager investors.

New Mexico saw a dramatic shift in emphasis from sheep raising to speculation in cattle. In February 1884, a reporter for the *St. Louis Globe Democrat* gave readers news of the western territories from an interview with Max Frost, who was passing through the city. Citing costs of $4 per head for production of a three-year-old steer, with an expected return of $30 per head, sold on the hoof straight off the seller's range, the writer declared, "The profits are simply immense."[24] Considering the figures cited, he concluded, "You are bound to make money and grow rich, are you not?" Frost observed that the Prairie Cattle Company was the largest in New Mexico, running some 60,000 head, while the Palo Blanco grazed around 45,000 and the Dubuque about 30,000. Frost allowed that visitors to Lincoln County could see 75,000 head there, with room for at least 200,000 more.

Presumed Ring members were eager to avail themselves of profits in the cattle business. Catron and Surveyor General Atkinson were associated in one of the earlier ventures in corporate cattle raising, the Boston and New Mexico Cattle Company, and later in the American Valley Company and Atkinson's New Mexico Land and Livestock Company. After the Lincoln County War, Catron continued to invest in cattle in the region in partnership with Jimmy Dolan and John Riley, and with sometime business and political ally W. L. Rynerson. By summer 1884, Riley and Rynerson were partners in the Membrillo cattle ranch, and in 1887, Dolan, Numa Reymond, John Lemon, and Rynerson established the Felix Cattle Company in Chaves County. By 1890, Catron, Rynerson, Riley, Albert Christy, and Henry J. Cuniffe had organized the Tularosa Land and Cattle Company.[25]

Investors in cattle lived and died, made money or lost it, stayed in New Mexico or moved on to other pastures. Whatever their fortunes, they were part of a transformation that altered the face of the land forever. This much was clear in 1884, when Max Frost told the *Globe Democrat*, "Large herds of cattle and great corporations are taking the place of sheep and of the poorer Mexicans." Frost explained, "The sheep business had been peculiarly adapted to the habits and necessities of the poorer class of natives of New Mexico. Sheep furnished meat and clothing, and twice a year, after each shearing, the wool would be sold at a fair price and with the money thus obtained debts would be paid and a new supply of necessaries purchased. This is changing."[26] Unprepared for the frenzied competition for wealth, and for the sometimes unscrupulous men who came seeking land and prosperity, natives often came up losers in the clash of values and cultures. Some resisted and some adapted, but for many families that had lived on the land, the pace and direction of change were troubling and traumatic.

Government Contracts

Men identified with the Ring were also interested in the business of selling goods to the government for use on military posts and Indian reservations. Beef, grain, food staples, clothing, and other dry goods were commonly purchased on a contract basis. The business could be lucrative, particularly if the contractor could reduce his costs and maximize profit. This sometimes meant shortchanging the government and the soldiers and Indians for whom goods were purchased. Not all contractors were crooks, but they were all in business to make a profit. Addressing the notion of a "contractors' ring" at work in Lincoln County, an experienced westerner confirmed the basic decency of men who sold to the government. He agreed that such men necessarily tend to look to their own interests, but allowed, "With a somewhat extensive acquaintance among Government Contractors on the frontier, I can truthfully say that I know of no missionaries among them."[27]

The persistence of corrupt practices on the part of some contractors was suspected among informed citizens around the territory. In April 1878, at the height of the chaotic Lincoln County War, Frank Springer, an attorney residing in Cimarron, wrote to Rush Clark, a congressman from his home state of Iowa, to address causes of the chaos. "There is no doubt in my mind," Springer wrote, "from a mass of private information I have received, that the whole power of the territorial government, strengthened by the active aid of the U.S. military forces, has been either intentionally or unintentionally used to protect and assist a small combination of corrupt men—speculators in military and Indian contracts—against the best men in the county."[28] The comment pointed directly to Lawrence G. Murphy, James Dolan, and John Riley, who had dominated business with the Mescalero Apache Indian Agency and Fort Stanton for fully a decade.

A history of difficulties with L. G. Murphy and associates at Mescalero and a handful of current complaints led the Department of the Interior to add Mescalero to Frank Warner Angel's portfolio when Angel was dispatched to investigate corruption and violence in New Mexico in spring 1878. The secretary was concerned about reported irregularities at the Mescalero agency. Angel's report confirmed routine borrowing and unauthorized transfers of goods from the reservation commissary to the Murphy store in Lincoln, leading to dismissal of the Indian agent, Frederick Godfroy. Regardless of the merits of the agent or the situation, when corruption was discovered in Indian country, the agent was apt to take the fall.[29]

In 1892, another Indian agent, Hinman Rhodes, experienced the wrath of Ring men who were associated in the Tularosa ranch—Riley, Rynerson, and Catron. Displeased with the agent, they undertook to flex some political muscle and rid themselves of him. Rhodes's brief tenure was sandwiched between those of two Ring-inspired agents. C. L. Sonnichsen, chronicler of the Mescalero Apaches, described his predecessor, Joseph Bennett, as "seemingly a creature of the notorious 'Santa Fe Ring,'" and his successor as "a political appointee."[30] The phrase carried an implied connotation transcending the simple fact that all Indian agents were political appointees. Through nearly half a century of malign administration, honest and capable agents had been few and far between, and the Mescalero people languished. Rhodes's sins, according to his admirers, included his refusal to pay for cattle already branded as government property or those "too thin to yield anything but hoofs, horns, and hides." He paid for cattle only on the basis of scale weights.[31] These were new and unwelcome practices at the Mescalero agency.

John Riley played a familiar card, complaining to Secretary of War Stephen Elkins. Riley explained the situation: "Col. Rynerson, Mr. Catron and myself own a cattle ranch bordering the Mescalero Reservation and the Indian Agent has been wrongfully annoying us." Confident that the agent's removal would be attended to, Riley expressed his preference and that of Rynerson for a Ring-friendly replacement: Richard Hudson of Grant County, who needed a job due to his recent reversals in the cattle business and the unfortunate loss of his hotel in a fire. Riley further promised to deliver six friendly delegates to be at Elkins's disposal at the upcoming Republican national convention.[32] Hudson assumed the position at Mescalero in July 1892.

If Rhodes was cautious concerning the goods presented by Riley and others in fulfillment of federal contracts, he had good reason to be, for Riley had acquired a reputation for cheating in his transactions with the government. Former governor Miguel A. Otero recalled from hearsay that Riley's mode of operation in fulfilling beef contracts involved a "bait and switch" ploy in which he found the agent at the local saloon, plied him with alcohol, and induced him to sign for four thousand steers without counting them. Riley further reduced the agent's work by providing him with a few fat steers to be weighed. The weights were averaged, the average was multiplied by the number of steers, and payment for the whole shipment was made on this basis. According to Otero, the delivery generally consisted of "scrubby Mexican range cattle, not much larger than a good-sized goat and wild as a March hare."[33] In support of his story, Otero stipulates that it was told in Riley's presence, and that Riley "did not deny the allegation, but merely smiled with self-satisfaction."

Jewish immigrants figured prominently in the growth of the mercantile trade during the territorial period. The stores of the Gusdorf family in Taos, the Herzsteins in Clayton, the Ilfelds of Las Vegas and Albuquerque, the Lindauers of Deming, the Floersheims at Roy, the Bibos at Laguna Pueblo, and the Wertheims in eastern New Mexico were well known. Their proprietors were successful in business and, as a rule, were well-respected members of their communities.

Figure 20 With his brother, Zadoc Staab, Abraham Staab was a successful merchant in Santa Fe and a business associate of Catron and other Ring figures. Photo ca. 1880. Palace of the Governors Photo Archives (NMHM/DCA), No. 11040.

The leading mercantile establishments in Santa Fe during the first half of the territorial period were those of the Staab and Spiegelberg families. In *A History of the Jews in New Mexico*, Henry Tobias anticipates a likely point of curiosity. "Given the power attributed to the Santa Fe Ring and the wealth of the most successful Jewish merchants," he wrote, "the question of their relationship arises."[34] Noting that only Abraham Staab was close enough to Catron and other key figures to warrant consideration as a likely member of the Ring, Tobias reviews the evidence and finds it slight: Staab was said to have purchased military warrants on speculation at the instance of Catron, and he had been named by Colonel Nathan Dudley as one of those contractors associated with the Ring who had provided inferior corn to Fort Stanton.[35] Staab occasionally joined Catron and other presumed Ring members in business ventures, including joint ownership of property. Howard Lamar and William Keleher name Staab as a member of the Ring, but if he was, he was a peripheral figure who stayed safely out of range of the Ring's public critics.

Lincoln County War historian Philip Rasch names Levi Spiegelberg as a member of the Ring. The sole basis for this inclusion, apparently, is that he agreed to represent the Murphy Company in collecting funds owed the company from the estate of Emil Fritz. Spiegelberg was soon released from this obligation in favor of Alexander McSween, but is said to have received $700 for his services.[36] Consignment to Ring membership seems a severe punishment for his limited role in the affair, particularly in view of his having left the territory at the close of the Civil War. Levi backtracked to New York, serving as the company's purchasing agent there until his resignation from the firm in 1884.[37] If any family member merited mention with the Ring, it was Lehman Spiegelberg, the public face of the company in Santa Fe and a regular associate of Ring figures.

Among other Jewish businessmen, William Rosenthal, a cattle broker based in Santa Fe, deserves consideration as a plausible Ring figure. Frederick Nolan characterized Rosenthal as a "paid-up member of the Santa Fe Ring" in connection with his involvement with Rynerson, Riley, and others in supplying beef to the U.S. government in Lincoln County.[38] Rosenthal was also an investor, with alleged Ring figures, in the Maxwell Land Grant and Railway Company.

The Dust within the Rock

The arrival of the railroad also stimulated new activity in mining. New Mexico had long interested prospectors, and there had already been some extraction and use of valuable minerals including gold, silver, copper, turquoise, mica, and coal. Native people had used flint, chert, and other materials since prehistoric times. Mining by the Spanish could be traced to the early years of settlement along the Rio Grande. New Mexico's "Old Placers" and "New Placers," discovered in 1828 and 1839, were among the earliest goldfields in the North American West to attract the attention of commercial miners.[39]

Even before railroads entered the territory, non-Hispanic whites were keenly interested in minerals, prospecting and exploiting discoveries as best they could. By 1857, a mine investor, Juan Eugenio Leitensdorfer, had acquired mining property in Santa Fe County and had installed a steam-powered stamp mill freighted from the states by wagon.[40] A surge in prospecting after the Civil War produced significant discoveries and attracted still more immigrants. Some of the men who found gold in the Moreno Valley of northern New Mexico, at Pinos Altos in the Gila country, in Socorro County, and elsewhere had come to the territory as soldiers.

Rail access to manufacturers and markets changed everything, making it more feasible to build mills and smelters and to transport coal and other minerals to market. Before 1868, mining on a commercial scale was negligible. From 1869 to 1879, corporate filings for mining, milling, and smelting companies ranged from 0 to 4 per year, but the number rose to 37 in 1880 and peaked in 1881, with 94 companies filing to incorporate.[41] Mining activity could be found in all parts of the territory, attracting capital from local investors and from venture capitalists in New York, Illinois, Connecticut, Colorado, and other places. Mining grew steadily in the decade of the 1880s, and by 1889, coal and coke accounted for more than 70 percent of the tonnage hauled from New Mexico by the Southern Pacific and the Atlantic and Pacific Railroads. The territory had been producing an average of more than $5 million in gold and silver annually.[42]

Speculation in mining ventures became a popular, broadly accessible form of investment among business and professional men. Men identified with the Ring eagerly took part in forming new mining companies. In 1877, U.S. Attorney Catron, Surveyor General Henry Atkinson, and Charles Gildersleeve formed the Santa Fe Mica Company. Two years later the Rio Grande Ditch and Placer Company and Corporation was organized by a group that included Catron, Atkinson, William Griffin, William T. Thornton, L. Bradford Prince, Henry Waldo, William Manderfield, and William Breeden. Also named as a director was the new territorial governor, Lew Wallace, whose efforts to suppress the Ring would place him at cross-purposes with the others throughout his tenure. This surprising alliance may have come about as an unsuccessful attempt by the men of Santa Fe to bring the new governor into the orbit of their influence.

One of the more interesting sagas of apparent Ring participation in a mining venture involved a property claimed by the San Pedro and Cañon del Agua Company, a firm whose principal stockholders lived in eastern cities and had access to significant capital for development. As determined by the territorial supreme court in a decision affirmed by the U.S. Supreme Court, the boundaries of the Cañon del Agua grant, awarded to a Mexican citizen in 1844, were fraudulently altered so as to include a feature popularly known as the Big Copper Mine. The grant had been confirmed by Congress in June 1866 under terms of the Treaty of Guadalupe Hidalgo. In August 1866, it was surveyed by William W. Griffin, whose involvements over a quarter century suggest a strong relationship to the Ring. The survey was conducted under the auspices of the surveyor general, preparatory to the filing of an application for a patent that would vest ownership in the claimant. The application included a description of the property as determined by the survey.[43]

This was all according to prescribed procedure. However, there were motives afoot that may not have been apparent to the casual observer. Steps were
being taken by local agents for a group of interested purchasers to ensure that
the Cañon del Agua grant, which did not originally include the Big Copper
Mine, included the mine when surveyed and patented. On May 10, 1866, a
group including representatives of the prospective investors went to look at the
property, with Griffin in tow. They were interested in examining the lay of the
grant, with special reference to its relationship with the Big Copper Mine. They
also contacted the owner of record, José Serafín Ramírez. The group satisfied
itself with respect to questions of geography, and an agreement was concluded
whereby Ramírez sold the claim to investors constituted as Cooley, Kitchen &
Co. In the early months of 1880, a new group of investors led by Boston industrialist George W. Ballou bought the grant, as altered in 1866, and organized
the San Pedro and Cañon del Agua Company.

The Cañon del Agua grant was presented for confirmation by Congress
in 1875. As New Mexico's territorial delegate, Stephen Elkins was said by the
New York World to have "worked a confirmation out of a committee of
Congress, which was agreed to by Congress itself."[44] There remained a potentially thorny problem, however, as the purchasers of the Cañon del Agua
claim should have known. The venerable Otero family, including former territorial delegates Miguel A. Otero and Mariano S. Otero and future governor
Miguel A. Otero II, had held an interest in the property on which the Big
Copper Mine, known also as the Nuestra Señora de los Dolores, was located
as early as 1846—and they had a valid *testimonio* to prove it.

The younger Otero later explained the matter from his perspective. "At
this particular time," he recalled, "New Mexico was dominated by one of the
most corrupt, unscrupulous, and daring organizations ever connected with
its history. Nothing was too rotten for the well known 'Santa Fe Ring' to un-
dertake. This perfectly well greased and smoothly working organization
practically controlled every county in the territory, and the mandate issuing
from headquarters was considered final and had to be obeyed."[45] Miguel
Antonio Otero II—"Gillie"—pressed the family's claim to the mine. In 1883,
he led an armed party in seizing and occupying the mine—presumably to
draw public attention to the issue. Following a standoff at the mine and a
seven-week incarceration for Otero and three associates, courtesy of Judge
Samuel Axtell, Otero and his men surrendered the mine to the court. Told
that Catron, who had interests both as an attorney and as an investor, had
been out to look over the state of affairs at the occupied mine, the *Golden*

Retort was incredulous, telling readers, "Catron would as soon think of jumping into hell naked as to come out here during the present trouble."[46]

If it accomplished nothing else, the disturbance gave added impetus to a lawsuit brought by the U.S. government for the purpose of vacating the patent to the Cañon del Agua grant on account of its fraudulent title. A territorial district court ruled for the company, but on appeal the decision was reversed and the patent was canceled. When the case was reviewed by the territorial supreme court in 1888, the court observed that the boundaries had indeed been altered to satisfy the interests of the original purchasers, and that this fact should have been apparent to subsequent purchasers, including Ballou and his associates. According to Gillie Otero, the grant "was simply turned over" by means of the survey, such that the original eastern boundary became the western boundary.[47] The tract had been extended to include valuable minerals and the homes of residents in a nearby village. Intent to defraud was imputed to the purchasers, but Griffin and New Mexico surveyor general John A. Clark were implicated as well. In the view of the court, as articulated in a lengthy opinion written by Chief Justice Elisha V. Long, all parties to the 1866 and 1880 transactions should have known better.

The legal team for the San Pedro and Cañon del Agua Company reflected a notable Ring presence, with Henry Waldo, William Breeden, and the law firm of Catron, Thornton, and Clancy representing the company. As the case proceeded through the 1880s, judicial outcomes were, as usual, influenced by changes in the federal administration. Two chief justices, L. Bradford Prince and Samuel Axtell, both associated by reputation with the Santa Fe Ring, ruled on some aspects of the case, while Elisha V. Long, an appointee of President Grover Cleveland, presided over the 1888 supreme court review and wrote the controlling opinion.[48] Decisions rendered may simply have reflected the best legal judgment of each jurist, but the rulings were usually consonant with their assumed political allegiances—Axtell dealing severely with Otero's party and Long siding with the majority in canceling the patent held by the San Pedro and Cañon del Agua Company.

Elkins was not a party to the San Pedro and Cañon del Agua case, but Judge Long could not resist speculating as to how the survey lines of the grant came to be so cleverly reconfigured, noting in his written opinion, "It appears that Mr. Elkins had an interest in the Ortiz mine, and that his wife was a stockholder in the San Pedro Company, so it would not be difficult to arrange for a withdrawal of opposition by the Ortiz mine owners; and so by the withdrawal of opposition, by concealments, and *ex parte* affidavits, the action of the commissioner was procured."[49] The Ortiz Mine grant was adjacent to the Cañon del Agua claim at issue.

The U.S. Supreme Court confirmed the territorial court's judgment on appeal in 1892, but the Oteros achieved only a Pyrrhic victory in nullifying the fraudulent patent.[50] According to the ruling, neither party held rights to the contested minerals, because they had not been conveyed in the original grant from Mexico. Catron later came into ownership of the reduced Cañon del Agua grant, sans the coveted mine.

The mining district southwest of Santa Fe had long been of interest to Ring principals and was conveniently located to attract their attention. The area was known to prospectors before the American Occupation and the arrival of fortune-seeking men from the states. Native Americans had mined beds of turquoise on Mount Chalchiuitl, near present-day Cerrillos. The Spanish had also worked the area, producing quantities of lead, silver, and other minerals.[51] A sheepherder's discovery of gold in 1828 brought an influx of miners and prospectors and led to an extended period of productive activity and the designation in 1833 of the Ortiz Mine grant—a property of much interest to the Anglo fortune seekers who were soon to descend on the region.[52]

Elkins readily identified the mineral-rich region of the Ortiz Mountains and Galisteo Creek as one that was ripe for development, particularly in anticipation of the arrival of rail transportation. In 1871 he bought 606 acres on Galisteo Creek, where rails would almost surely be laid to reach the mining district.[53] In 1878, Elkins and Colorado Senator Jerome Chaffee gained control of the New Mexico Mining Company. Incorporated in 1858, the company owned the 69,458-acre Ortiz Mine grant and held other valuable properties.[54] In partnership with Chaffee, Elkins held a controlling interest in the company for most of the next thirty years. Catron became a stockholder in the New Mexico Mining Company, while investing in other mining properties in the area and acting as local agent for Elkins.

The Ortiz Mountains attracted miners and investors eager to extract precious metals, but the area's coal deposits eventually proved to be more than a gold mine for investors. In 1883, Elkins, Catron, and Antonio Ortiz y Salazar formed the Cerrillos Coal Company with Elkins's friend Richard Kerens and New York banker L. M. Lawson. The reorganized Cerrillos Coal and Iron Company, including properties acquired from the New Mexico Mining Company, was sold to the AT&SF in 1891 for bonds and cash reportedly totaling $1 million, but likely yielding less to the sellers.[55] In 1897, Elkins, Kerens, Lawson, and Jerome Chaffee's estate, as stockholders of the New Mexico Mining Company, sold the company and its remaining interest in the Ortiz Mine grant to an American-British syndicate for a reported $1,500,000.[56] Elkins continued to invest, organizing a new company in 1899 to mine gold deposits on leased lands of the Ortiz grant.[57]

Over a period of at least three decades of involvement with mining properties in the Cerrillos region, Elkins, Catron, and associates were able to fend off numerous legal challenges to their claims of ownership. At least three actions resulted favorably for the New Mexico Mining Company.[58] Aside from the trouble of defending itself in court, the company suffered no great damage from legal actions brought during the time of Elkins's involvement.

Elkins and his friends fared less well in the court of public opinion. Under the editorship of R. W. Webb, the *Golden Retort* fired off a steady barrage of broadsides and exposés attacking the Santa Fe Ring, the Cañon del Agua ruse, and perpetrators of fraud in the Ortiz Mountains and elsewhere in New Mexico. The *Las Vegas Gazette* was more direct in its criticism, remarking on the modest provisions made by the Mexican government in ceding land for a mine and declaring, "By some hocus-pocus, the Ortiz grant, when confirmed, is made to consist of 64,000 acres, including the adjacent town, neighboring mines, and the land on which the original grantees only had rights of pasturage in common. It is hard to avoid the conclusion that fraud was used in the obtaining of the confirmation such as would invalidate the title."[59]

The summer of 1884 was a time of discontent in the mining district south of Santa Fe, with multiple controversies dominating public discourse. The writer Charles Fletcher Lummis, a man of opinions and a tireless promoter of Southwest cultures, passed through the mining hotbed of Golden the following December on a tramp across the continent and got an earful concerning the machinations of the Santa Fe Ring. Reporting his observations in a series of letters to readers in Ohio and Los Angeles, he declared Elkins "the boss thief of the lot" and Chief Justice Axtell "his ready tool."[60] Based on hearsay, Lummis awarded a leading role in the manipulation of the Cañon del Agua grant to Elkins and expressed satisfaction that the recent election of Cleveland as president would throttle the Ring's efforts to "steal the whole Territory and carry it off in their vest pockets." So the long-suffering opponents of the Ring could hope.

Commercial and Civic Enterprises

In addition to involvement in the major economic activities of the territory, presumed Ring men engaged in a wide variety of enterprises in business, industry, and politics. They invested in the kinds of innovations that were emergent in western towns of the 1880s and 1890s; these included gas and electric companies, water systems, ice companies, and street railway companies. Men associated with the Ring were nearly always involved in such endeavors in Santa Fe. Albuquerque, Las Vegas, and other communities also had reliable civic and business leaders whose names could be found among the incorporators of such ventures. The Santa Fe Progress and Improvement Company, capitalized at $500,000, functioned as an economic development organization and business lender. Led initially by C. H. Gildersleeve and Abraham Staab, its directors included Catron, Griffin, Lehman Spiegelberg, and William Manderfield.[61] A bureau of immigration and the Santa Fe Hotel and Building Company, both organized in 1880, were typical of local efforts to stimulate economic growth following the arrival of the railroad.

In 1882, Griffin, Atkinson, Prince, Gildersleeve, Robert Longwill, Antonio Ortiz y Salazar, William Breeden, Abraham Staab, and Lehman Spiegelberg joined a long list of Santa Fe men in incorporating the Santa Fe Tertio Millennial Anniversary Association for the purpose of mounting a commemorative exposition. The organizers coined the term "tertio millennial" to denote one-third of a millennium, or 333 years, causing the *New York Times* to falsely inform its readers that the Spanish town of Santa Fe had been founded in 1550.[62] In truth, the year 1883 did not relate precisely to any historic date. It was simply the case that New Mexico had a railroad, and its boosters wanted to promote immigration and investment.

The *Rio Grande Republican* made light of the idea, noting that Santa Fe was trying to raise $200,000 for the event. "We have no objection to their tertio milleniating if they tertio milleniate in the right way," said the *Republican*. "Tertio milleniation is a good thing, if the people are tertio millenianimously inclined."[63] The object was to promote the territory's resources and business opportunities, with emphasis on mining, but dances and art from the pueblos were also featured. At its conclusion, the *New Mexican Review* declared "the Tertio" a success, writing, "It has sent the news far and wide that New Mexico is the most promising country to be found in the west, and the publicity given to the resources and advantages enjoyed here will cause immigration to flow in rapidly and bring capital to seek profitable investment."[64]

Presumed Ring men were also involved in efforts to develop educational, civic, cultural, and religious institutions in the territory. William G. Ritch, Henry Waldo, and William Griffin were among the incorporators of the Santa Fe Academy, and the list of men joining to organize the Educational Association of New Mexico in 1881 included Atkinson, Gildersleeve, Governor Lionel Sheldon, William Breeden, Marshall Breeden, L. Bradford Prince, William Griffin, W. G. Ritch, Thomas B. Catron, Henry Waldo, and Max Frost. The stated object of the association was to establish and manage "an academy or college or university or all." The group also held out the option of organizing kindergarten, primary, and intermediate schools for the city and county of Santa Fe. Efforts to organize a system of public education proceeded slowly and were sometimes opposed by men of the Ring, who presumably were resistant to the associated tax increases. Men identified with the Ring were also prominent in the 1881 reorganization of the Historical Society of New Mexico, and in establishing cemetery associations and Protestant churches.

In the latter half of the nineteenth century, fraternal organizations provided a primary structure for social and civic activity among business and professional men. In the vanguard of these organizations was the Masonic Lodge. Some historians of territorial New Mexico have intimated that Masonry had a major role in facilitating the activities of the Santa Fe Ring. Philip J. Rasch, a student of the troubles in Lincoln County, characterized the Ring as "a predominantly Masonic organization" and held that preferment in the Ring "was restricted almost exclusively to Masons," to the extent that aspiring Ring members might forsake their Catholic heritage to join the Masons.[65] Frederick Nolan, preeminent historian of the Lincoln County War, says that "most of the members of the Ring were Masons," and notes that Catron, L. G. Murphy, James Dolan, and William Brady were involved in the organization of the first Grand Lodge in New Mexico.[66]

The Grand Lodge was organized in August 1877. Murphy, Dolan, and Brady likely were involved as members of one of four constituent lodges forming the Grand Lodge. It is more certain that William Griffin and William L. Rynerson were among eight delegates who served on an organizing committee, and that Catron, Governor Axtell, Henry Waldo, and Thomas Tucker were instrumental in the founding of the Grand Lodge, one of the first acts of which was to raise Max Frost to the degree of Master Mason.[67] Without question, the Ring, as portrayed in contemporary and historical accounts, was well represented in the Masonic Lodge. Those with presumed

Ring connections comprised perhaps a dozen or so among the 165 Masons in the Grand Lodge.

Since there is no objective criterion by which to determine who were "members" of the Santa Fe Ring, it is impossible to say whether "most members of the Ring were Masons," and a distinct link between activities of the Ring and association through the Masonic Lodge has yet to be demonstrated. The Lodge ostensibly provided a structure for constructive fellowship and a source of principles for right living. In a practical sense, the Lodge functioned in its communities as did the Rotary Club of later times—as an informal network of active community members who were usually associated in other contexts. In the absence of evidence to the contrary, it is doubtful that the significance of the Lodge for presumed Ring members went beyond this.

As business and civic leaders, the men designated as Ring members were making the territory over in their own image. It was an image inspired by the Gilded Age ideals that they embodied, reflecting the values and experiences of the politically dominant Euro-Americans. Their ideal society valued progress over tradition, industry over pastoral life, urban development over rural living. For their homes and places of business they preferred bricks and scrolled tin to adobe, Queen Anne and Italianate styles to the Spanish-Pueblo style. Financial success and political efficacy were accepted measures of worth. It was on this basis that like-minded Hispanics were welcomed in the fraternity of the business and political elite. The superiority of Euro-American cultures was implicit, if not overtly expressed, and a hierarchy of classes based on language and economic status was widely assumed, at least among Euro-American members of the elite in the late nineteenth century.

The presence of Native American communities that were stubbornly true to tradition, and of a resilient and resistant native Hispanic population, ensured that Santa Fe would not come to resemble Buffalo or St. Louis, and that New Mexico would retain its diversity of cultures and ideas long after the rise and fall of the territorial ring.

CHAPTER EIGHT

FRACTURE IN THE RANKS

A s the year 1883 drew to a close, the men said to oversee the Santa Fe Ring were riding high and looking to 1884, an election year, with optimism and confidence. The nation was at the midpoint between two crippling financial crises. The Panic of 1873 was a distant memory, and the Panic of 1893 was not yet on the horizon. New Mexico's long wait for railroad access had ended a few years earlier. The territory was enjoying a near boom in the cattle market, an influx of prospectors and mining interests, and an increase in settlers and investors. Earlier in the year, Santa Fe had thrown a month-long exposition, the Tertio Millennial Celebration, to showcase the territory's economic and cultural assets, and to publicize promising opportunities for investors and prospective immigrants.

The territorial administration was familiar and friendly, reflecting mostly harmonious relations with a succession of Republican administrations in Washington extending back to 1869. A Ring favorite, the once-deposed governor Samuel B. Axtell, had recently returned to New Mexico as chief justice of the territorial supreme court. William Breeden had been comfortably ensconced as attorney general since 1872, except for a brief interval in which Henry Waldo held the office, and William G. Ritch had served as territorial secretary nearly as long. As surveyor general, Henry M. Atkinson had been a force for economic progress—especially his own—since 1876. Lew Wallace had departed the territory a frustrated and largely ineffectual reform governor. Though a relative newcomer, Governor Lionel Sheldon had shown that he could be counted on to act in harmony with the established powers in Santa Fe.

Even so, the ground beneath the traditional political and economic powers was shifting. The railroad that provided access to markets and opened the territory to increased investment and settlement had also brought immigrants with a diversity of skills, ideas, and ambitions—potential competitors

in business and politics. As early as 1878, a local merchant noticed a differ-
ence when a party of railroad officials alighted from a coach in front of his
home in the Rio Abajo town of Bernalillo. Motivated by an urgent purpose,
the men hurried into his store. In their leader, about thirty-five years of age,
the merchant recognized a man who was "business from toe to top, quick in
expressing himself and in determining his actions." To the storekeeper, he
was "a true representative of the American man of the world type, full of pep
and energy."[1]

Railroad expansion and increased settlement also had a part in determining and sometimes altering the relative importance of places in the territory. During the era in which the Santa Fe Trail provided the major trade
route between New Mexico and the states, Santa Fe was preeminent as both
the seat of government and the commercial center of the territory, but when
the main line of the Atchison, Topeka and Santa Fe bypassed the city, that
changed. Las Vegas, the base for wholesalers who traded across the eastern
portions of the territory, could for a time claim to be the hub of commerce,
but it was perhaps inevitable that Albuquerque would emerge as the territory's
leading city and commercial center. During the 1870s, the population of Santa
Fe County grew by just 12 percent, from 9,699 in 1870 to 10,867 in 1880. During
the same decade, Santa Fe County was surpassed by Bernalillo, the county in
which Albuquerque was situated, which doubled in size, growing from 7,591
residents in 1870 to 17,225 by 1880.[2]

The relative diminution of Santa Fe and the emergence of Albuquerque
as a rival city—a natural crossroads for commerce and an aspiring center of
political power—brought pressure to bear on old alliances and contributed
to a disruption of the political combination that had worked so well for so
long. This shift in relative importance, accompanied by increasing demands
on the part of Albuquerque leaders for influence commensurate with the
growing city's new status, was at the heart of the first of two acrimonious rifts
that wounded and weakened the Ring in 1884.

A House Divided

A sure and easy way to raise hackles in Santa Fe was to suggest that the capital be moved elsewhere. As Albuquerque overtook Santa Fe in population,
in business activity, and in access to rail transportation—and appeared certain to assume even greater prominence—there were those with the temerity
to suggest that the capital should be located in Albuquerque. With Bernalillo

to the north and Los Lunas to the south, the middle Rio Grande region could already boast a significant and growing population base. With statehood in view, advocates for the rival cities knew what was at stake.

As the legislative session approached in the early weeks of 1884, Albuquerque's aspirations concerning relocation of the capital were well known. Newspaper volleys had been exchanged during the preceding year and battle lines had been drawn. Albuquerque was not alone in advocating the change. The *Las Vegas Gazette* encouraged Albuquerque to move ahead in identifying a site for a capitol building, but the most vociferous calls on Albuquerque's behalf came from Silver City, whose leaders had long resisted domination by Santa Fe and the Ring. Said the *Southwest Sentinel*, "That the change must and will be made sooner or later, there can be no doubt." The *Sentinel* urged the Albuquerque papers to get behind the issue in anticipation of the upcoming legislative session.[3] The *Santa Fe New Mexican and Review* pronounced the notion "sheer nonsense" and concluded, "All attempts to remove the capital from Santa Fe will be futile. It is here and we mean to keep it."[4]

A good deal of forethought apparently was given to the matter, and on the first day of the legislative session, February 18, 1884, the sides came prepared to do battle. Published accounts representing the views of the warring factions were generally consistent concerning the facts, but they varied greatly with respect to legal interpretations.

The council—specifically, the coalition supporting Albuquerque—met in the council chamber of the Old Palace at 11:30 a.m. on the appointed day. J. Francisco Chaves, a member representing Valencia County and a former territorial delegate to Congress, called the meeting to order. Antonio Joseph of Taos was elected temporary chairman, and a committee on credentials was appointed to examine the certificates of election issued by local election boards—essentially boards of county commissioners. Joseph and Chaves had previously been identified with the Ring, or had been sufficiently involved with alleged Ring activities to merit such designation by later historians of the territorial period.[5] Seven men presented certificates of election. Henry Warren of Santa Fe was among those recognized as a council member based on a certificate of election issued by the Board of Commissioners of Santa Fe County. Catron was said to possess a valid credential for the same position. His certificate had been issued by order of Judge Samuel Axtell, the territorial chief justice, who had received Catron's support in the public controversy over his judicial appointment. It is doubtful that Chaves had any intention of recognizing Catron in preference to Henry Warren. Several others thought to hold valid certificates—presumably those partial to the interests of Santa Fe—did not appear in the chamber. Whether they had been informed of the time and place of the meeting is not clear. Chaves was elected president, and the council, so constituted, awaited the arrival of the territorial secretary, William G. Ritch, who, in accordance with custom and protocol, had been invited to swear in the new council members.

Presently the secretary arrived, accompanied by several persons, including the missing members of the council. Ritch declared that he had come "to organize the council," by which he meant to determine the duly elected membership and then to administer the oath of office. To this end, he requested that Chaves step aside, which Chaves declined to do, explaining that the council had already organized itself and that its members were ready to be sworn in. This announcement precipitated a withdrawal of Ritch and his party to the secretary's office, where a rival council comprised of men sympathetic to Santa Fe's interests, including Catron, was organized and sworn in. The group popularly known as the "rump council" or "Chaves council" continued to hold the council chamber. Ritch organized the House in similar fashion. According to Chaves supporters, Ritch had unlawfully recognized as council members three men who failed to receive the majority of votes in their districts.[6]

The Chaves council maintained that each house of the legislature was empowered by law to determine its membership, based on certificates of election. In case of a contest, the council's judgment would determine which applicant should be seated. According to the Chaves faction, the council was not and had not previously been under authority of the territorial secretary for purposes of organizing procedures. Members of this faction cited two previous assemblies in which the bodies had organized themselves, with the secretary then administering the oath of office at the request of each body.[7]

Supporters of the regular council or "Catron council" disputed the notion, insisting that the actions of Chaves and the rump council were illegal, and that the territorial secretary—not local commissioners or members of the legislative body—was legally responsible for determining who had been elected to membership in each house. The Chaves council adopted a memorial praying for relief from Congress, and in response the Catron council issued a "statement of facts" endorsed by numerous territorial officials and members of the regular council and House. It was sent to Congress and published in the *Weekly New Mexican Review*.[8] The document pronounced the memorial "a tissue of falsehoods" and accused the Chaves council of abetting election fraud. Some of those listed as signers of the Catron council statement later claimed that their names had been used without authorization.

The two competing groups, each claiming to constitute the legitimate territorial council, met regularly throughout the session. The house of representatives and Governor Lionel Sheldon recognized the Catron council—the group organized by Ritch—as the "regular council" and maintained channels of communication with its leaders to accomplish the work of the legislature. Four members of the Chaves council acknowledged to have won election to the council were invited to join the regular council. One, Inocencio Valdez, did so, giving the Catron faction a majority. Other members of the Chaves council continued to meet and act in protest of the actions of Catron and Ritch. In essence, Catron and his supporters won the day, and the regular council, or "Catron council," proceeded to draft, debate, and pass legislation.

During the session, Chief Justice Axtell came under scrutiny of the U.S. Department of Justice in relation to charges brought against him to the effect that he was, as summarized by the *New Mexican Review*, "incompetent to discharge properly the duties of his office on account of his ignorance and corruption."[9] The charges apparently were presented by parties to the Cañon del Agua grant controversy, who believed that certain of Axtell's decisions had been arbitrary and extralegal. The justice department dispatched an investigator to examine the charges, collect evidence, and report his findings. Meanwhile, the U.S. House was also looking into the matter.

The New Mexico legislature—that is, the regular council and the House—adopted resolutions in support of Axtell.[10] More unusual was an endorsement from the sitting grand jury of the First Judicial District, for which Axtell was the presiding judge. It is unclear whether the endorsement was initiated by members of the grand jury or orchestrated by friends of Axtell, but it was published on the front page of the *Santa Fe New Mexican Review*.[11] The investigation found no fault with Axtell's integrity, but concluded that he was unsuited for the position of judge. The U.S. House took no further action, but left Axtell's fate in the hands of the Department of Justice.

The plan for securing the capital at Santa Fe included construction of a new capitol building. With the territorial government still housed in a structure built beginning in 1610, derided by Governor Lew Wallace as "a picture of neglect and indifference" and referred to by his wife as "the leaky old Palacio del Gobernador," it could hardly be argued that New Mexico did not need a more spacious and functional edifice for the seat of its territorial government.[12] Planting a substantial new capitol in Santa Fe would go far in quieting the debate on removal. In addition, the legislature proposed construction of a penitentiary, also to be located in Santa Fe. With substantial sums being paid to keep felons out of state, there was again some logic in favor of New Mexico's having its own prison.

Even with legislative opponents neutralized, the path for passage of the capitol and penitentiary bills was not smooth. Charges of corruption flew, and passage of the capitol bill in the House was doubtful. Diego Archuleta, a member from Rio Arriba County, though seriously ill with pneumonia, was carried into the House chamber to cast the deciding vote in favor of the bill. According to Ralph Emerson Twitchell, "The exposure incident to this performance brought about his death a few days later."[13] Bills authorizing construction of the new capitol and a prison won approval and were signed into law.

In its successful management of the legislative session, the pro–Santa Fe faction won the battle and attained at least one enduring result, repelling the most serious in a series of challenges to ensure that Santa Fe would remain the capital. Otherwise, it could be argued that Catron and his allies lost the larger war, for the events of the session produced lasting enmities and led to a persistent condition of disunity among territorial Republicans and the old Ring coalition.

Acknowledging passage of the capitol and penitentiary bills, the *Albuquerque Evening Democrat* declared, "It only remains now for the tertio-millenial bill and the Texas and Northern railroad bill to pass and the main considerations for which a number of the members of the House and Catron council sold out to the ring will have been satisfied and the contract fulfilled."[14] The paper called for a vigorous protest to Congress, complete with evidence of illegal acts committed in the organization of the legislative session. "It should not be forgotten," said the paper, "that over $1,000,000 of appropriations are proposed to be put into the hands of the Santa Fe Ring."

Equally incensed were prominent Republicans of Doña Ana County, which had suffered the loss of a portion of its territory to the creation of the new Sierra County. A mass meeting held on the plaza at Las Cruces attracted "probably the largest gathering of citizens that ever congregated for any purpose."[15] One-time Ring stalwart William L. Rynerson bemoaned the indebtedness with which citizens had been saddled, including $200,000 for the proposed capitol, $150,000 for a penitentiary, and $5,000 for a school—all in Santa Fe—along with pork-barrel expenditures approved in exchange for critical votes. The assembly adopted a resolution drafted by John Riley and others, authorizing a committee to prepare a memorial requesting that Congress order an investigation of the recent session and annul its objectionable acts. This resounding expression of indignation precipitated a second and equally disruptive split among territorial Republicans.

A Political Schism

In a minor setback, at least compared to the drama of the legislative session just past and the Republican Party territorial convention to come, the Republicans lost the territorial delegate seat to Democrat Francisco Manzanares of Las Vegas. In the 1882 election, Tranquilino Luna had been declared the winner on the basis of the vote count. However, voter fraud was suspected in Valencia County, and Manzanares had appealed the outcome to Congress. Extensive evidence revealed a pattern of fraud, and on March 5, 1884, Manzanares was declared the winner and was seated in place of Luna. Since most of the two-year term had expired, there was little at stake. For once, the Republican press and party leaders acquiesced, acknowledging the probability of fraud and blaming it on J. Francisco Chaves.[16] Like Rynerson and Riley in Doña Ana County, Chaves had long been an ally of Catron and the Ring, and would be again, but for the moment he was a convenient scapegoat and pariah. While the party had supported Luna, Catron and his friends had no real problem with Manzanares, a respected businessman who shared many of their interests.

Resentment of the Santa Fe faction of Republicans carried over to the fall election, and at least one man, Albert Jennings Fountain of Doña Ana County, fed up with Santa Fe's monopoly on political offices and territorial expenditures, made it his purpose to ensure that southern New Mexico would not be dismissed or taken for granted. Determined that the established Republican Party leadership would not go unchallenged, he organized Doña Ana Republicans to nominate William L. Rynerson for the office of territorial delegate to Congress. Fountain and Rynerson had feuded over local issues, but in their disgust with recent acts of the legislature and with what they perceived as a sense of entitlement on the part of the Santa Fe leaders, they found common ground. Fountain traveled throughout southern New Mexico to promote Rynerson's candidacy among fellow Republicans in advance of the coming territorial convention.

The convention was preceded by a meeting of the party's Central Executive Committee on August 24, 1884. William Breeden and Catron had dominated the party apparatus for years, and they assumed certain privileges. "As had become traditional," a scholar explains, "the Ring leaders introduced their Congressional candidate, L. Bradford Prince, and asked for unanimous endorsement."[17] Fountain challenged the leadership on this point and over Catron's objection won the right of delegates to offer nominations from the floor of the convention.

Also at issue was the presence of competing delegations from San Miguel County. Party leaders initially agreed to recognize a delegation led by Eugenio Romero, but when it became known that this group would support Rynerson, they reversed course on the opening day of the convention, August 26. A resolution offered with the intent of excluding Romero's group proposed that both delegations purporting to represent San Miguel be excluded from the vote to elect a temporary chairman—an officer whose rulings would influence critical decisions. The exclusion of a contingent already placed on the roll of convention delegates by the Central Executive Committee was highly irregular, but the question was put to a vote, and when it became clear that the old guard would prevail, delegates supporting Rynerson, chiefly those from Doña Ana, Grant, Lincoln, and Luna counties, walked out and organized their own convention.[18]

The "bolters" unanimously elected Rynerson as their nominee for territorial delegate, while "regular Republicans" ratified the choice of Prince as their nominee. When the Democratic Party met and selected Antonio Joseph, the electorate was presented with the spectacle of three candidates running for territorial delegate to Congress, each of whom had been popularly known at some time or other as a member of the Santa Fe Ring.

The vote that triggered the bolt occurred under the administration of William Breeden, who, as chairman of the Republican Party Central Committee, had called the assembly to order and was presiding over the initial phase of organization: the choice of a temporary chair for the convention. Opponents of the dominant Ring faction laid the blame squarely on him. According to the *Rio Grande Republican*, Judge S. B. Newcomb of Doña Ana County challenged Breeden on his ruling to allow such a vote, asking, "Did not the central committee unanimously command you to call the Romero delegates from San Miguel County?" Breeden acknowledged that the Central Committee had so ordered, and when asked why he did not do as instructed, Breeden replied, "Because I don't want to, you can't make me do it, and I won't do it."[19]

Figure 21 Antonio Joseph took advantage of discord in the Republican Party to win the office of territorial delegate, which he held through five successive terms. Photo by Evans Studio, Las Vegas, ca. 1880. Palace of the Governors Photo Archives (NMHM/DCA), No. 9915.

More analytical was the response of S. H. Bogardus, whose letter to the *Albuquerque Morning Journal* characterized Breeden's ruling as a parliamentary blunder, adding that "a boy member of a debating society would have corrected him on that point." The writer argued that a challenge on the basis of credentials could have occurred in due course, but that Breeden's sole duty was to call the meeting to order and to preside over the election of a temporary chairman, entertaining no motion other than one pertaining to the choice of a chairman and accepting the votes of all delegates recognized by the Central Committee. Bogardus acknowledged the very real possibility that the split among Republicans would damage the party's chances in the general election, noting that he personally favored Prince, "yet I do not wish him to gain the nomination through such bare-faced fraud or carelessness, and at the expense of the party at large."[20]

Through the *New Mexican Review*, Breeden broadcast an open letter "To the Republicans of the Third Judicial District."[21] It was self-justifying rather than conciliatory and threatening to the bolters of southern New Mexico in its admonishment that "if they persist in stabbing the party to death, the day will come when they will repent the act." The letter served only to further inflame Rynerson's supporters. In reply, the *Rio Grande Republican* plainly restated the bolters' objection: "What we of Southern New Mexico complain of, is that by the arbitrary ruling of Breeden, as chair of the executive committee at the temporary organization of the convention at Santa Fé, he deprived the legally elected delegates from the county of San Miguel of their seats, and then admitted delegates, fourteen in number, in their places, changing a minority into a majority for Santa Fé."[22]

One of the more bizarre episodes of the election season concerned a letter published in the *Las Vegas Optic* on July 31, 1884, over the pseudonym "Ithurial," that made the Santa Fe Ring an open topic of discussion in the campaign and created a minor commotion by naming its members. Said Ithurial, "The ring proper is accredited with being composed of the following persons: T. B. Catron, S. B. Elkins, W. W. Griffin, H. M. Atkinson, Max Frost, Gov. Sheldon, Gen. Bartlett, W. G. Ritch, Judge Manderfield, Colonel [William] Breeden, Major [Marshall] Breeden, C. B. Hayward, Colonel Fisher, W. H. Bailhache, R. H. Longwill, Judge Axtell, C. M. Phillips, Trinidad Alarid, Antonio Ortiz y Salazar, Ben. M. Read, Colonel Rynerson, of Las Cruces, and quite a following of second fiddlers and henchmen."[23]

The common responses of those accused of membership in the Santa Fe Ring were to either deny its existence or to acknowledge its existence but deny any personal connection with it. Others chose to ignore it altogether. Catron and Elkins preferred the last alternative, seldom if ever allowing the phrase to pass their lips, but Catron was characteristically forthright in an unguarded moment, reportedly telling a writer for the *Las Vegas Daily Optic* that "if there were such an organization as the Santa Fe ring, he certainly belonged to it and was proud of it."[24]

Among those most closely identified with the Santa Fe Ring, William Breeden was the most outspoken in rebutting accusations against the Ring, taking to the pages of the *New Mexican* on multiple occasions to defend his political colleagues. Perhaps in response to the Ithurial letter, the *New Mexican Review* unleashed an unsigned article assailing the demagogues who insisted on perpetuating the myth of a sinister political ring for partisan purposes. There was some truth, however, in the article's assertion that there were other combinations at work in the territory. Of the alleged Santa Fe clique, said the *New Mexican Review*, "Its great shadow obscures the operations of smaller local rings throughout the territory. All the local schemers anywhere in the territory have to do is to shout Santa Fe ring and all eyes are turned away from home affairs. Large objects are always seen first and absorb the greatest attention."[25]

Sometime between July 31 and August 24, when the Republican Central Committee met prior to the nominating convention, someone—probably William Breeden—may have grown leery of a possible Rynerson candidacy and defaulted to the former chief justice, L. Bradford Prince. This result may, in fact, have been an object of the Ithurial letter, which became a matter of discussion among attentive readers. There was considerable speculation concerning the identity of the letter writer, largely dispelled when W. B. Sloan was revealed as the author, with Prince identified as the source of his information concerning identities of Ring figures. A. J. Fountain, as candidate Rynerson's chief sponsor, took delight in exposing this connection.[26]

Once the candidates were in place, the campaign was not particularly acrimonious. In consideration of the Republican cause, Prince courteously passed word through John H. Riley that he would be unable to personally visit many of the mining towns in southern New Mexico. He expressed the hope that Rynerson would campaign in Grant and Lincoln counties rather than cede the votes in those counties to the Democrat, Joseph.[27] The outcome of the election was as might have been expected. The Democratic candidate easily defeated the divided Republicans with vote totals of 12,271 for Joseph, 9,930 for Prince, and 5,192 for Rynerson.

Reversal of Fortune

The loss of Republican Party unity, a challenge to the job security of Chief Justice Axtell, and the loss of the office of territorial delegate to the Democrats must have been disheartening to men accustomed to having their way in territorial politics, but a more serious threat came with a Democratic Party victory in the presidential election of 1884. One of the chief means by which the Santa Fe Ring had been able to maintain its broad influence in territorial affairs was through control of federal appointments. Ring principals worked hard to influence the appointments of governors, judges, U.S. attorneys, surveyors general, land registers, and myriad other offices, down to the postmaster of the smallest village. Catron and his political allies had an effective advocate in Stephen B. Elkins, who, more often than not, could influence a Republican president to good advantage. With the recent passage of the Pendleton Civil Service Reform Act, followed by the defeat of Republican James G. Blaine and the election of Democrat Grover Cleveland as president, it could safely be assumed that the territorial government would undergo an extreme makeover and that it would not be to the liking of the old guard.

New Mexico Republicans and Ring sympathizers had not only to lament changes to come under a Democratic Party administration, but what might have been had Blaine and his running mate, Illinois senator John A. Logan, been elected. Elkins was Blaine's friend, political protégé and confidant, and the manager of his candidacy in the Republican National Convention. Logan was an investor in the American Valley Company. In the event of a Blaine presidency, the *New York Times* had foreseen a golden age of plunder managed by Blaine, Elkins, former Colorado senator Jerome Chaffee, and Jay Gould. As the *Times* saw it, Blaine's election would be "a great victory for the old land ring of Santa Fé," and Stephen Dorsey a beneficiary of greater flexibility in administration of the land laws.[28] Closer to home, the *Golden Retort* invited its readers to consider a government comprised of Elkins as secretary of the interior, his good friend Richard Kerens as land commissioner, Catron as U.S. attorney for New Mexico, A. L. Morrison as U.S. marshal, Antonio Ortiz y Salazar as receiver of public moneys, Max Frost as land register, and Henry Atkinson staying on as surveyor general. "Elect Blaine," said the *Retort*, "and the above is about the size of it so far as this Territory is concerned."[29] The election gave the Democrats a rare victory, but for the old territorial ring, it was Paradise lost.

President Cleveland apparently was well posted concerning alleged irregularities in New Mexico. He began the overhaul of the territorial administration by appointing a new governor, Edmund G. Ross, the former Kansas senator who had sacrificed his political career to block the removal of President Andrew Johnson.[30] George Washington Julian, a party-hopping former congressman, was named surveyor general. The two were appointed with the intent of reforming fraudulent and irregular practices in the disposition of titles to Mexican and Spanish land grants and public lands, and it was understood that a strong political ring would stand in the way of such reforms. If willingness to engage in confrontation was a requisite for the assignments, Cleveland was on the right track with these appointments. Friends who had seen Ross derided for his refusal to cast the Senate vote that would have assured Johnson's removal felt that he had been vindicated with the appointment. One supporter saw "eminent propriety and poetic justice" in the appointment, but neither he nor Ross could anticipate the strife awaiting a new, reform-oriented governor.[31]

The federal administration wasted little time in replacing Samuel Axtell as chief justice, but the appointment of William Vincent to replace him was soon aborted on account of a too-friendly relationship between Vincent and the politically toxic Stephen Dorsey. Elisha V. Long proved a better fit as chief justice. George W. Lane replaced the long-serving William G. Ritch as territorial secretary, and Thomas Smith was made U.S. attorney in place of Sidney M.

Barnes. The sole holdover among key officials was Breeden, a territorial appointee who was protected by a law that precluded his immediate removal; thus he was firmly entrenched as attorney general.

Governor Ross necessarily paid attention to the phenomenon of the Santa Fe Ring and became one of the most astute observers of its methods and activities. A newspaperman by profession and a politician and statesman by experience, he was well equipped to discern the nature of Ring activity and to articulate what he saw. His characterization has probably been the single greatest influence on the myriad historical descriptions of the Ring. In a private letter to a friend in St. Louis, Ross explained, "The ring is composed of Americans possessed of some legal lore with a large amount of cheek and an unusual quantity of low cunning and astuteness that always had an inclination to run in a crooked direction."[32] The core activity of the Ring, as described by Ross, was speculation in Spanish and Mexican land grants, but it was the hub of more specialized rings working a variety of paying enterprises. Elkins and Catron were identified as the Ring's instigators and leading wirepullers. The combination was diversified to include both Republicans and Democrats, and worked to dominate the political and economic affairs of the region, to the manifest benefit of its principal members. According to Ross, "It had the ear of the administration at Washington, and could build up and pull down men at its pleasure." These points have become articles of faith in conventional portrayals of the Santa Fe Ring.

The governor's depiction of affairs as he saw them on March 26, 1887—at the midpoint of his administration—was decidedly gloomy. Ross's outlook doubtless was influenced by the difficult legislative session he had just endured—one in which he was constantly at war with a Republican-dominated assembly that, in his view, contrived to defeat every progressive initiative while pursuing "a mass of special, local and personal schemes, of speculation, plunder and spite."[33] The council's removal of a Democrat previously seated as a duly elected member from Taos County and his replacement with Pedro Sánchez, a reliable ally of Catron and his coalition, was part of an apparent attempt to secure a veto-proof majority in both houses of the legislature.

Ross was frustrated and under siege from presumed Ring men seeking his removal, but he had endured worse in the wake of his vote in the United States Senate sustaining the presidency of Andrew Johnson, and he was by nature an optimist. Ross soldiered on through his term as governor, using his appointment and veto powers to suppress the Ring to the extent possible.

Figure 22 Edmund Gibson Ross fought an uphill battle to curb Ring control of legislation and territorial offices during his tenure as governor, 1885–1889. Barnes Photographic Collection, Georgetown University Library Special Collections Research Center.

Shortly after taking office, he engaged in a messy, ultimately unsuccessful attempt to remove William Breeden as attorney general. Blocked by law from removing an incumbent attorney general for up to two years after he took office, Ross was then sandbagged at the end of his term by a creative piece of new legislation. The office of attorney general was abolished in favor of the new but nearly identical office of solicitor general. Terms of appointment were adjusted in the legislation to prevent Ross's naming an incumbent whose appointment would include the two-year period of protection from executive removal previously accorded new appointees. Ross used the veto in an attempt to extinguish laws that, in his view, were contrary to the public interest, but many of his vetoes were overridden by the legislature. In the first year of his term, the New Mexico Bar Association was organized and reportedly functioned as a Ring-guided screening committee for legislation as it passed through the Republican caucus.[34]

Under Ross, the University of New Mexico, the New Mexico College of Agriculture and Mechanic Arts, and the New Mexico School of Mines were created. Ross was an advocate for the rights of women, and he led in petitioning the federal government for a special court to settle Spanish and Mexican land claims. Still, Ross endured endless frustration and had little success in promoting public education and other progressive measures. The legislative session of 1889, the last of his administration, was even more contentious than that of 1887. Suffice it to say, Ross gave the reform effort his all, but he did not bring the Santa Fe Ring to heel.

An earnest effort on the part of Surveyor General George Julian to redress land-grant abuses and an ongoing federal investigation of public land fraud produced similarly mixed results. While he attacked the Ring and land-grant speculators with a vengeance, the larger grants and those most likely to have been acquired or enlarged by extralegal means had already been titled to their claimants and were beyond his reach. Julian succeeded in limiting the quantity of lands confirmed and patented to private ownership, so that more was preserved in the public domain. At the same time, it is a common judgment that Julian's decisions did considerable harm to the legitimate interests of smaller claimants.

Governor Ross spoke truth when he observed that the territorial electorate was "tending to a reorganization of party lines," owing to the disgust of persons in both the Republican and Democratic parties with the old way of politics.[35] Throughout his tenure, the Santa Fe Ring had successfully resisted his reform efforts and likely caused the governor more grief than he caused them, but the Ring and the Republican Party emerged from the four-year era of Democratic Party governance weaker and more fragmented. This was due in part to the changes in territorial administration and reforms enacted at the national level, but the opponent that the Ring could not permanently defeat or forestall was the tide of change. Increased settlement, increasing economic activity, and the steady push to statehood all led in the direction of a diversified polity that could not easily be dominated by a close group of powerful insiders. Those commonly associated with the Ring could no longer expect to dictate even within the Republican Party. While many of those involved in the legislative and party schisms of 1884 had reconciled and were working amicably, the Ring-dominated faction of the party, sometimes referred to as the "Catron wing," would henceforth face consistent, assertive opposition from within party ranks.

Still, it could not be said that the old Ring was dead, or even on serious life support. As long as Catron remained a fighting force in New Mexico and Elkins had access to power in Washington, much could be accomplished on behalf of their mutual interests and those of their political allies. The old coalition, though increasingly challenged by emergent political forces, remained largely intact. William Breeden, Henry Waldo, Max Frost, Melvin Mills, J. Francisco Chaves, Pedro Sánchez, Stephen Dorsey, William Rynerson, and John Riley were committed to common goals, including New Mexico statehood, and were in at least occasional communication with Catron for years to come. In 1889, Republicans returned to the White House, and the world, as it appeared to men of the old Ring, was at least temporarily restored to its axis. When Stephen Elkins parlayed his national political prominence into a place in President Benjamin Harrison's cabinet in 1891, and then won a seat in the United States Senate representing West Virginia in 1895, at least some continued influence in Washington for Catron and his associates was assured.

A second Grover Cleveland administration, 1893–1897, produced nowhere near the drama of Cleveland's first term. The new Democratic governor, William T. Thornton, had been regarded by some as one of the Ring. Though animosity developed between Catron and the governor, Thornton focused much of his attention on quelling lawlessness and did little that would upset Republicans of the entrepreneurial class. The open split between dissident Republicans and the Catron wing of the party took a respite during this interval of Democratic administration, but would shortly return to stay.

CHAPTER NINE

A TERRITORY OR A STATE?

New Mexico's path to statehood was long and often rocky, made more difficult by the prejudices and political considerations that influenced sitting members of Congress, as well as by differences of opinion among residents of the territory that precluded presentation of a unified appeal for admission. Most of those assumed to be part of the Santa Fe Ring were consistent, strong supporters of statehood, generally for economic and political reasons. In some instances their efforts were public spirited and helpful to the cause, but at times the involvement of Ring figures only served to heighten suspicions among members of Congress that the new state would be dominated by an elite coterie of corporate interests and self-serving political operators.

When a new president, Benjamin Harrison, assumed the federal executive office in the spring of 1889, New Mexico title attorneys and land speculators could rejoice. George Julian, appointed to be a reformer as surveyor general but an abrasive presence to speculators, was suddenly gone, replaced by Edward F. Hobart, a Republican who was more amenable to the entreaties of grant claimants.[1] Edmund G. Ross was also out as governor, but stayed in the territory and resumed his career as a journalist, editor, and printer. He worked briefly for the *New Mexican* in Santa Fe before moving near the border to edit the *Deming Headlight*.

Some of Ross's priorities as governor aligned with those of the Republican governors who preceded him and those who followed, but during his term in office, the muddle resulting from a deeply divided territorial government had stalled progress on major issues. Ross had strongly supported the establishment of a federal land court that could resolve tangled issues of title to Spanish and Mexican land grants. He had also advocated establishment of a strong public school system—a step that many citizens thought was long overdue. The Republican-dominated legislature was of no mind to

accommodate Ross on anything of substance, but with the territorial government in the hands of a Republican executive and with Republican majorities
in the legislature, there was renewed hope for constructive pursuit of these
measures. There was also renewed energy for pursuit of the prize that long
had eluded Ross and other territorial leaders, including enthusiastic supporters identified with the Santa Fe Ring: attainment of statehood.

Resistance to Cultural and Economic Domination

L. Bradford Prince, a native of New York, succeeded Ross as governor, but the
Ring and the Republican Party continued to find the sailing none too
smooth. It fell to Prince to deal with the actions of Las Gorras Blancas, the
White Caps—a popular resistance movement organized in response to controversy over land grants and in rebellion against decades of dominance by
land speculators and political bosses, as well as more recent developments
that threatened the culture and livelihood of rural Hispanics.[2]

Las Gorras Blancas, who were most active and visible in San Miguel
County, embodied the resentment that many of the smaller farmers, stock
raisers, and other residents of ordinary means felt toward the acquisitive
Euro-Americans and aspiring native New Mexicans who had fenced sections
of the range for use in large-scale stock-raising operations.[3] The ranchers
were following a recent trend in organizing large commercial livestock operations, but whether they came as purchasers, lease holders, or claimants by
virtue of inheritance, they were encroaching on lands used by area residents
who had lived there for generations. Most in dispute were properties that
were widely held to be common lands of community grants, including those
of the San Miguel del Bado, Las Vegas, Tecolote, and Anton Chico grants.
Grant boundaries, land titles, and water rights were among the issues contributing to the conflict. In some cases these lands had been appropriated or
diminished through court decisions or willful deceit by shrewd manipulators. Responsibility for alleged abuses was dispersed among individuals, corporations, and government entities, but the Santa Fe Ring and its supposed
leader, Catron, provided accessible objects of hostility for native New
Mexicans who felt themselves dispossessed by the actions of ranchers and
land speculators.

The opinions of Las Gorras Blancas were expressed in an outbreak of
fence cutting—the most direct repudiation of those who were seen as intrud-
ers on the homeland—and in destruction of other property including crops,

Figure 23 LeBaron Bradford Prince was
a consistent champion of New Mexico
statehood and fought eastern bias against
the territory's Hispanic citizens.
Photo by J. M. Crausbay, ca. 1902.
Palace of the Governors Photo Archives
(NMHM/DCA), No. 50446.

homes, and lumber mills.[4] Relatively few participated in these acts of violence, but many residents were at least partly in sympathy with them. Attitudes varied as to whether the acts of the White Caps amounted to wanton lawlessness or righteous resistance.

Prince had come to New Mexico in 1879 to take up an appointment as the territory's chief justice. In the execution of his judicial duties between 1879 and 1882, he had acquired a reputation for rendering decisions friendly to the Ring. In 1884, he was the Ring's ostensible choice for territorial delegate. Despite general agreement with other Republican Party leaders on a variety of issues, Prince was never one of the boys. His aristocratic manner and an independent streak made Catron and others of the Republican inner circle leery of him as an ally. In later years Prince saw himself as an informed observer and critic of the Ring. There were, then, discernible reasons for the ambivalence with which others identified with the Santa Fe Ring appeared to regard him. Prince was by no means a Ring favorite, but he was much preferred over the recently departed Democrat, Ross.

As governor, it was Prince's responsibility to maintain peace and order. During a period of approximately three years between 1889 and 1892, in which Las Gorras Blancas drew public attention through night raids and destruction of fences and other symbols of oppression, he spoke out against violence and urged peaceful resolution of differences. For some citizens, he was slow to act, perhaps reluctant to publicize disorders that might harm the case for statehood. The *Santa Fe Sun* charged that his official response consisted of "firing paper wads at the White Caps, in Spanish and English."[5] At least once he ordered the territorial militia to Las Vegas to forestall or repel a possible assault on the county jail, in which alleged White Cap raiders were being held.[6]

Concurrent with the aggressive activism of Las Gorras Blancas and other manifestations of popular resistance came a proliferation of Spanish-language newspapers advocating interests common to local residents. Between 1888 and 1894, an energized Spanish-language press flourished as an outlet for native perspectives, even as many of the papers struggled financially. Observes Pablo Mitchell, a student of cultural encounter in the borderlands, "Hispano-owned and operated Spanish-language newspapers offered another critical space of resistance, as Hispanos routinely celebrated the endurance of Hispano culture in the face of Anglo incursions."[7]

The vitality of these papers was often due to the presence of articulate and committed editor-entrepreneurs who were willing to hazard the obstacles that came with the work. Referring to these journalists who gave voice to the grievances and aspirations of Hispanic New Mexicans, and to their influence in the turbulent early 1890s, A. Gabriel Meléndez, a scholar and admirer, wrote, "Their work would become an important factor in reinvigorating *Nuevomexicano* cultural identity at a moment of deepening crisis."[8] Intrepid editors such as Felix Martínez, the moving spirit of *La Voz del Pueblo*; Camilo Padilla; and Manuel C. de Baca did not always agree, but together they gave voice to the indignation and aspiration of citizens demanding recognition and justice.

The Ring was a natural object of enmity for a people who felt themselves victimized by unscrupulous land speculators and attorneys. *La Voz del Pueblo* declared that the native people of New Mexico surpassed all nationalities of the world with respect to their devotion to religion, and to one other principle. In questions pertaining to their heritage, the writer said, Hispanic New Mexicans could be counted on to unite to fight enemies of their race. Said *La Voz*, "The New Mexicans know that the race has no enemy more agressive or fierce like Torquemada, than the villainous Santa Fe Ring that has suppressed them through its band of thieves and land sharks. The people have been denied public funds due them, as Ring leaders and their lieutenants speculate on vouchers that were paid to poor people for their services, which the Ring and its associates then purchased at large discounts, to the misery of their owners."[9] The paper extolled the honorable principles of the

New Mexican people and condemned the prejudice heaped on them in Congress and in the eastern press in the context of the statehood debate.

A political movement advocating similar interests achieved notable if short-lived success in San Miguel County, electing a slate of candidates under the banner of El Partido del Pueblo Unido, the "United People's Party." By the end of 1891, the White Cap movement had lost much of its energy, but the grievances that had surfaced concerning use of traditional common lands and associated water sources would remain part of the political discussion for years to come.

Futile Attraction: The Push for Statehood, 1888–1890

Prince, a devoted advocate of statehood, had the misfortune to head the territorial administration through most of the 1888–1890 attempt to attain statehood—an effort that can be characterized as an unmitigated debacle. Prince was not responsible for the defective act that created the 1889 constitutional convention, nor for provisions that caused the resulting document to be labeled a Republican, or Ring, or land-grabber's constitution. Prince unsuccessfully tried to salvage the effort and bring the long quest to fruition. The question of granting statehood to any hopeful territory was politically charged, as leaders in Congress, in considering petitions for statehood, examined the relative strength of parties in the territories and weighed implications for the balance of power in Congress. Concern with party strength had as much to do with the outcome of applications for statehood as did the merits of the territory under consideration.[10]

Political calculations played a role in the ill-fated effort to secure statehood for New Mexico between 1888 and 1890. In March 1888, Illinois congressman William Springer, chairman of the House Committee on the Territories, introduced an omnibus bill seeking admission for Dakota, Montana, Washington, and New Mexico. Similar bills varying in detail were introduced in both houses, but the Springer bill became the focus of debate. While Governor Ross and New Mexico's delegate, Antonio Joseph, were consistent proponents of statehood, Springer's move caught supporters of statehood off guard. Springer, a Democrat, presumably was impressed with the likelihood that New Mexico would add to his party's numbers in Congress. Joseph's success in consecutive elections provided some evidence of such potential.[11]

The bill proceeded through committee hearings, floor votes in both houses, a conference process to resolve differences, final passage, and executive approval. Of territories proposed for statehood, only New Mexico did not receive the votes required for admission. Joseph tried to advance New Mexico's cause in a separate bill, but there were persistent objections that could not be overcome. A petition submitted by dissident residents of the territory gave New Mexico's adversaries in Congress ammunition with which to argue that local citizens were divided on the issue.[12] Among those opposing New Mexico's bid in the House were Congressmen Isaac Struble of Iowa and George Symes of Colorado, who, along with other Republicans, were loath to admit a territory judged likely to send more Democratic legislators to Washington.[13] Racial prejudice was evident as opponents argued that New Mexico lacked a sufficient number of persons well enough educated to take part in democratic processes. Moreover, New Mexico had not taken the critical step of adopting a proposed state constitution.

New Mexico had learned a hard lesson, but proponents emerged with a greater resolve to attain the coveted condition of statehood. In spring 1889, the territorial legislature authorized a convention for the purpose of writing a state constitution, but the process seemed doomed from the beginning. Democratic Party leaders charged that the legislature's Republican majority had favored Republican strongholds in apportioning seats for the upcoming convention. Prince later conceded that "perhaps there was some merit in their objection."[14] Efforts were made to resolve differences, but the result was that all Democrats but one declined to participate. The remaining delegates began the work of forging a state constitution on September 3, 1889. With J. Francisco Chaves presiding, Catron and former territorial secretary William Gillet Ritch taking prominent roles on the Rules Committee, and others including Pedro Perea, Mariano S. Otero, and William L. Rynerson participating as delegates, it is little wonder that the final product was derided as a document by and for "land grabbers."

When the time for public consideration of the proposed constitution came in fall 1890, the *Santa Fe Sun* lamented that, under the new structure, a legislature controlled by landed interests would dictate the selection of judges. "If they do," the *Sun* warned, "God help the thousands of poor settlers whose claims will conflict with that of these land grant thieves and bosses."[15] The *Sun* urged rejection of the document.

Critics complained that land-grant owners were favored in provisions minimizing their exposure to taxation, and Catron was suspected of contriving to discourage legal mining and prospecting on his land through inclusion of a provision that would have taxed the product of unpatented mines.

Debate over the proposed constitution also brought up an old controversy surrounding militia warrants—a form of deferred payment that many recipients had little faith in and were willing to sell at sharply discounted rates. Catron, Mariano Otero, and Abraham Staab were said to have purchased quantities of the warrants on speculation. It was common for new states to assume the indebtedness of their former territorial governments and to pay it off with new tax levies. It was easy for critics of the Ring to discern in the statehood effort a scheme by holders of the warrants to secure a profit on their speculative venture at the taxpayers' expense.

Among ordinary citizens, the statehood question often raised more doubts than hopes. Some resisted the notion of a state government controlled by the territory's Hispanic majority. Others feared that the transition would strengthen the hand of the Ring by placing members of its choosing in both houses of Congress and giving its leaders vast influence over public policy and federal appointments. Many Catholic New Mexicans were apprehensive that pressure to create a system of public schools would threaten the church's primacy in education. Proponents talked up the proposal, but opponents labeled it a "land grabbers'" document. *El Estandarte de Springer*, a Spanish-language edition of the *Springer Banner*, urged readers to defeat the "Constitution of the Ring of Bosses." Advised *El Estandarte*, "I remind the people of their duty. It is to go to the polls in the morning and afternoon, and by your votes defeat this infernal monster."[16] On October 7, 1890, the proposed constitution was resoundingly defeated, with 7,493 citizens voting to approve and 16,180 voters rejecting the document.

In the end, the statehood effort of 1888–1890 came to naught, as opposition on the part of scandalized New Mexico Democrats and other citizens who opposed statehood on terms dictated by the Republicans made the decision of Congress to postpone admission an easy one. Much of the opposition was not so much to statehood as to the defective process that had, in the minds of many citizens, produced a flawed document that best served the interests of the men writing it. Delegates sent to Washington persisted in introducing new statehood bills, but New Mexico's entreaties were repeatedly denied, even as younger and less populous territories were admitted.

A requisite for statehood missing at the time of the 1888–1890 push for admission was a functioning public school system. Low rates of literacy and education, conceded by supporters of statehood, provided a ready stumbling block that was sure to be thrown up by opponents in Congress. It had become clear that no statehood proposal would succeed until proponents could point

to a credible system of public education, a deficiency that was finally addressed in 1891.

In the winter of 1891, during the session of the territorial legislature,
Governor Prince had to deal officially with a sensational crime involving
shots fired through the window of Thomas B. Catron's law office on the eve-
ning of February 5 during a meeting of several legislators. Joseph A. Ancheta,
a member of the council, took a round of buckshot in his neck and shoulder.
Some believed that the shots had been intended for Ancheta, the Grant
County legislator, while others speculated that Catron had been the target.[17]
Prince hired the Pinkerton Detective Agency to investigate, and Charles
Siringo spent some weeks on the job but was unable to identify a perpetrator
or discern a motive.[18] Speculation focused on a school bill then under consideration by the legislature—an essential step in the eyes of statehood advocates, but a matter of deep concern to many Catholics. Ancheta had been
criticized by opponents of public education for his support of the bill.

There was soon good news for the governor. Though the shooting was not
solved, Ancheta recovered from his wounds, and the long-awaited school bill
passed the legislature in 1891 and was signed by Prince. In addition, in 1891
Congress established the Court of Private Land Claims to replace the discredited surveyor-general system. Both actions were praised by ex-governor Ross,
who, from his new place as editor of the *Deming Headlight*, said with reference
to the land-court bill, "From the date of the passage of this act, and contem-
poraneously with it, the passage of a thoroughly American public school bill,
we may safely count upon a revival of the general public interest in New
Mexico—of immigration, of investment, of development, and of all those
incidents which make and mark an era of unparalleled prosperity to all the
economic interests of the territory."[19] These developments also improved the
prospects for statehood.

Catron's image in myth and history is largely that of a land grabber, a
greedy overlord, and a corrupt politician. In fairness, he was both a self-
interested individual and a civic-minded citizen, with near-equal intensity.
In the matter of the public school issue, he faced a quandary of competing
personal interests. On the one hand, he was said by adversaries to be governed
by an aversion to the property taxes that would accompany the adoption of a
public school law. According to the *Santa Fe Sun*, Catron was complicit in "the
murder of the Kistler school bill," a bill introduced in the 1889 legislative session that, according to Howard Lamar, was amended to death.[20] The *Sun*
wrote that Catron was reported to have said that "he did not propose to tax

himself and his friends to educate the damned tramps at Cerrillos."[21] Of the effort to pass a school law two years later, the *Southwest Sentinel* of Silver City recalled that it was common talk that Catron "objected to paying the taxes that the bill imposed on his property for the education of other people's children." Added the *Sentinel*, "He is understood to be abundantly able to send his own children abroad to be educated. Very few other people are able to do that."[22]

Catron was, at least by his own account in 1895, the territory's largest taxpayer.[23] Despite concern for the extent of his tax liability, he was deeply committed to statehood, presumably for the good of the territory as well as for his own welfare. He looked forward to an increase in the value of his land holdings and anticipated increased capital investment in the territory.[24] He also harbored and occasionally expressed an aspiration to represent New Mexico in the United States Senate. In the end, he supported the 1891 legislation creating a modern public school system.

Hispanic New Mexicans, Statehood, and the Ring

In the years following the American Occupation, the regime change experienced by native Hispanics in New Mexico was notable, but perhaps less disruptive than the transitions that occurred elsewhere in the Southwest. Hispanics were in the majority and routinely filled most seats in the territorial assembly. They controlled significant wealth and produced capable leaders in business and politics.[25] At the same time, many Hispanics lost land to lawyers and speculators, and to actions of the U.S. government, as expressed in administrative rulings, legislative acts, and court decisions. All of these have been blamed for the diminution in material and cultural wealth that befell many Hispanic New Mexicans after the Occupation.

For many, loss of land meant loss of a rural culture and of the capacity to support one's self and family. Reliance on hypothetical assumptions makes it nearly impossible to estimate the extent of land losses by Hispanic New Mexicans through fraud, attorneys' fees, and unfavorable resolution of grant claims, but interested observers have tried. Clark S. Knowlton suggested in 1975 that losses totaling more than 2 million acres in private holdings and 1.7 million acres in communal lands had been incurred since 1854.[26] Another source has suggested that by 1900, "four-fifths of the early Spanish and Mexican grants were in Anglo hands."[27] In any event, the losses were severe and had a profound impact on families and communities. Among those affected were female property owners who were also heads of households, for whom ethnicity and gender combined to maximize exposure to injury at the hands of courts, speculators, and self-serving government officials.[28]

The full impact of Euro-American immigration and acquisitiveness was felt after the arrival of the railroad, when waves of cattlemen, farmers, and speculators intensified competition for land. New Mexicans who had become American citizens by virtue of the Treaty of Guadalupe Hidalgo, because they were living in the territory ceded by Mexico, usually were left to defend themselves and their property in unfamiliar political and legal systems, in which business was mostly carried on in English.[29] The effect was staggering in the view of Fray Angélico Chávez, who wrote, "The representative Hispanic leaders of New Mexico, sad to say, were far too few to compete fully with the ever-increasing number of eastern Americans of every description and profession, all wise in the tricks of the modern world of finance especially, which kept on coming every year."[30]

To some extent, the attack on the property, cultural heritage, and self-esteem of Hispanic New Mexicans was attributable to forces beyond their grasp—U.S. policy in implementing the Treaty of Guadalupe Hidalgo, time and change, and a cycle of conquest not unlike the one that had given Spanish colonizers dominion over the Pueblo Indian people and their villages. For many native New Mexicans, the Santa Fe Ring provided a tangible object for the anger they felt at loss of land, culture, and dignity. According to Phillip B. Gonzales, dispossessed heirs of Spanish and Mexican grants "have always reserved a special place of ignominy for the Santa Fe Ring, especially Thomas Catron, nor have they excluded some *comprador* Hispanics, considering them thieves who schemed to steal their land-grant heritage."[31] The Ring was a common topic in the Spanish-language press. Reviewing the fall election in 1888, one article cited Elkins, Catron, and Mariano S. Otero for their involvement in *"el anillo de saqueadores publicos,"* the ring of public looters who had plundered the grants.[32]

Opposition to the Ring was a rallying point for those who resisted loss of land and culture in Colfax County in the 1870s and in San Miguel County in the 1890s. Resentment of old abuses continued to motivate resisters in the twentieth century. Reies López Tijerina's determination to address land issues in Rio Arriba County led to a brief occupation of the courthouse at Tierra Amarilla in 1967. He had organized La Alianza Federal de Mercedes, an alliance of aggrieved land-grant heirs. An inquiry into the region's history led him to stories of Catron's involvement with the Tierra Amarilla grant, and to a more general indictment of the Santa Fe Ring as a leading culprit in the loss of lands once owned by Hispanic settlers.[33] Tijerina blamed courts of law that administered legal processes but that, in his view, did not administer justice. "The judges are the ones who legalized terror," Tijerina wrote. "They are the ones who robbed us of our culture and abused us. They opened the door to Thomas B. Catron and his allies."[34]

The push for statehood surfaced expressions of bias against New Mexico's Mexican American population, and such attributions were used to bludgeon proponents of admission. Bias had been evident from some quarters in New Mexico, Washington, and the national press from the time Congress contemplated the responsibility of governing the territory won from Mexico.[35] A predictable litany of complaints could be expected whenever the statehood question was raised in Congress. New Mexico's Spanish-speaking people, on the whole, were thought to be illiterate, uneducated, and apathetic, lacking sufficient understanding of a republican form of government to render them fit for the duties of citizenship. There were misgivings concerning the likely role of the Catholic Church in a government dominated by native Hispanos.[36] With the exception of a few aristocratic families that held property and sent their children to be educated in the states, the Hispanic people were better suited to be subjects of the territorial government, with limited home rule. Such notions were readily adopted in the eastern states, particularly by those whose political ends were advanced by these depictions. It did not help that purveyors of wild adventure tales of the American West—Mayne Reid, Olivier Gloux, and others—had long popularized a stereotype of Hispanic males as swarthy Mexicans who were lustful, cruel, dishonest, and treacherous.[37]

National policy concerning the territories acquired in the U.S.-Mexican War was complicated by the ongoing tensions over slavery. Senator John C. Calhoun, with an astonishing command of the lore and rhetoric of race, abhorred in 1848 that white citizens should defer in any manner to the "mixed bloods" of Mexico in the new American Southwest. In Calhoun's view of the world, persons of Castilian blood were accorded a certain respect, but mixed bloods of the borderlands were judged impure and "not as good as the Cherokees and Choctaws." In the view of slavery's defender, "the greatest misfortunes of Spanish America are to be traced to the fatal error of placing these colored races on an equality with the white race."[38]

Given the catalog of deficiencies and character flaws attributed to the native Mexican population, why would English-speaking Euro-Americans from established states want to join in a polity on equal footing, or if residents of the area are under discussion, consent to be governed by a majority of such people? Calhoun was offended that native New Mexicans had the temerity to petition for territorial status while asking that the new territory be kept free of the institution of slavery. He was incensed that a conquered people should say to citizens of the victorious nation, thinking particularly of slave states, that they were unwelcome in New Mexico with any manner of property they might own.[39] While the slavery question had been resolved by the time Stephen Elkins sought approval for statehood in 1874 and 1876, some of the pejorative notions expressed by Calhoun and others persisted and were regularly raised as objections.

Years, sometimes decades, passed between major statehood initiatives, but the territorial delegate routinely filed statehood bills in Congress. A bill introduced by Tranquilino Luna and considered in the early months of 1882 drew virulent letters to the *New York Times* from an anonymous writer from Trinidad, Colorado. The *Times* was a reliable opponent of New Mexico statehood, perhaps owing to a presumed dominance of the territory by Republicans. An initial volley from the letter writer was titled "Greasers as Citizens." The writer noted that "about two thirds of the population of the Territory is of the mongrel breed known as Mexicans—a mixture of the blood of Apache, negro, Navajo, white horse thief, Pueblo Indian, and old-time frontiersman with the Mexican stock."[40] The writer charged that local Mexicans were unfit for citizenship by virtue of their ignorance of English and of democratic principles, an implacable hatred of Americans, and subservience to the priesthood. Said the writer, it is plain fact "that in no other part of Christendom are the women of an entire community so generally without a sense of the beauties of virtue and so ready to prove their insensibility for a money consideration."

The letter drew a sharp rejoinder from L. Bradford Prince, then chief justice of the territorial supreme court and a resident since 1879. As to the tone and content of the letter, said Prince, "The motive which could induce any man thus wantonly to slander and vilify over a hundred thousand American citizens seems inexplicable; if not pure malevolence, it must be that strange enjoyment which some persons seem to feel in irresponsible newspaper writing, which they consider spicy and smart in proportion as it is untrue and libelous." He refuted the letter writer's charges of ill will, apathy, and ignorance on the part of native Hispanos. As to the allusion to wholesale prostitution, Prince wrote, "The statement of your correspondent, as relating to the population in general, is a slander so vile, atrocious, and abominable, that words cannot fitly characterize it. The man who would thus wantonly brand with infamy the wives, daughters, and sisters of a whole people is unfit for decent society or the credence of respectable men." In defense of native women, Prince declared, "No more high-bred, noble, and pure-minded women are to be seen on earth than among the Spaniards of New Mexico."[41]

The reference to "the Spaniards of New Mexico" revealed a premise that Prince would reprise repeatedly as he became an ardent champion of statehood and repelled race-based attacks on Hispanic New Mexicans. In place of the mongrel or mixed-blood allusions that critics liked to invoke, Prince emphasized the European origins of New Mexico's Hispanic population. In doing so, he substantially created what Laura Gómez has called the "progressive view of race in New Mexico."[42] He shifted the conversation from race to a broader concern with cultural heritage and emphasized harmonious relations among New Mexico's diverse populations.

Prince was intensely interested in the history and cultures of New Mexico, including the histories of Spanish exploration and settlement and the brief period of Mexican administration. He likely had his own reasons for seeking statehood and for defending Hispanic New Mexicans against the critics, but residents of territorial times and later scholars have had few illusions as to the motives of his associates. "What was the Ring's motivation for statehood?" asks John M. Nieto-Phillips. "What did its members stand to gain from New Mexico's admission into the Union? Ostensibly, statehood was fought on behalf of Nuevomexicanos' right to full participation in national politics, but it was equally a campaign on the part of lawyers, políticos, and ricos to gain greater local control over land, resources, and political offices."[43] If obstacles to statehood were to be cleared, the stereotype of an intellectually and morally inferior race of mixed-blood aliens would have to be effectively countered. Though Prince was commonly identified as a member of the Ring, his impassioned commitment to the statehood battle seems to have come from within.

There is no indication of Ring sponsorship for the ideas promoted by Prince, but others understood his rationale in countering negative stereotypes and stressing the European origins of Hispanic New Mexicans. Catron subscribed to the notion, telling a reporter for the *Indianapolis Journal*, "The Mexicans are not only the most law-abiding citizens in the territory, but in the world." He praised the industry, honesty, and generosity of his Hispanic neighbors, declaring, "The natives will develop with the country, and more rapidly than the country. They have all the elements and only lack the opportunities for greatness. They will become citizens of which the Government will be proud."[44] Catron's words were not all propaganda. Though blamed for land-grant transactions that injured native New Mexicans, Catron was one of a relatively few newcomers who troubled to learn Spanish, and he had an affinity for Nuevomexicanos that some read as genuine. In later years, Catron made a point of promoting Hispanics of his party for public office.

Through stints as chief justice and governor, as a council member in the legislature, and as a private citizen, Prince remained true to the cause of statehood and continued to advocate for Hispanic New Mexicans, emphasizing the settled character of the local population in relation to the transient nature of settlement in much of the West. He touted progress in public education in the territory. Prince argued that, from the time of the American Occupation, New Mexicans had been promised a free government comparable to those found in the states, and that the denial of statehood amounted to denial of full citizenship. He made these points in national publications, in his reports as governor, in testimony before Congress, and in public speeches. He emphasized them in connection with the 1889–1890 statehood bid and the efforts that followed.[45]

Prejudice remained a persistent barrier to admission, evident whenever the issue came up. As territories of lesser merit were welcomed into the Union, one scholar noted, New Mexico was consistently excluded: "Members of Congress did not always say so, but they proved unwilling to accept a prospective state that was dominated numerically and culturally by non-whites."[46] Race and language differences were prominent in the rationale of Senator Albert Beveridge, who as chairman of the Senate Committee on Territories was instrumental in blocking New Mexico's admission through the first decade of the twentieth century. A scheme to admit Arizona and New Mexico as a single state was much discussed between 1904 and 1906, but ultimately failed.

Statehood at Last

There was reluctance among some Euro-American residents to seek statehood until this proportion of the population could grow to approach that of Hispanic New Mexicans. However, those who anticipated the economic and political gains to be realized were all in for statehood. In the view of Robert Larson, "The acquisition of statehood was the project most dear to all Ring members,

Figure 24 As editor and owner of the
Santa Fe New Mexican, Maximilian Frost
was a vocal advocate for New Mexico
statehood. Photo by Rice, ca. 1906.
Palace of the Governors Photo Archives
(NMHM/DCA), No. 9876.

especially Catron, Elkins, and Prince."[47] Max Frost, a tireless advocate as editor of the *Santa Fe New Mexican*, could well be added to this group. They looked forward to an increase in the values of land and mining properties, increased immigration, more capital for investment, and increased transportation and commerce. In short, statehood would be good for business.[48]

The influence of the Santa Fe Ring in territorial New Mexico was something of a two-edged sword. While the men of the Ring usually came to public notice in a negative light, they were also in the vanguard of positive developments, working to bring railroads into the territory, supporting schools and churches, organizing a historical society, and sustaining benevolent and fraternal organizations. As to negative influences of the Ring, Surveyor General George Julian railed, "The influence of these claimants over the fortunes of New Mexico is perfectly notorious. They have hovered over the territory like a pestilence. To a fearful extent they have dominated governors, judges, district attorneys, legislatures, surveyors-general and their deputies, marshals, treasurers, county commissioners, and the controlling business interests of the people. They have confounded political distinctions and subordinated everything to the greed for land."[49]

This contradictory nature of Ring influence is nowhere more apparent than in relation to the pursuit of statehood. Elkins and Catron actively sought admission from the early days of their political lives in New Mexico, and both were still working for the cause when the enabling act was passed in June 1910. They and other Ring figures can be credited with motives that included both the altruistic and the self-serving. Most of the men identified with the Ring were proponents of statehood, but their influence was not always positive, and at times during the long struggle they were their own worst enemies.

There is no better example than that of Elkins, who as New Mexico's territorial delegate strove mightily to have a statehood bill passed and, by most accounts, nearly had it accomplished in 1875. Largely by force of his personality and skillful use of political alliances, he had secured passage by the U.S. House of an enabling bill. The Senate also passed the bill, but with a largely innocuous amendment relating to the timing of a convention to be held in New Mexico for the purpose of crafting a state constitution.[50] Concurrence of the House was widely assumed, but as Elkins had succeeded grandly, he lost New Mexico's main chance through a careless amenity, conspicuously extending a congratulatory handshake to Representative Julius Caesar Burrows, who, during Elkins's absence from the floor, had delivered a stern rebuke to southern members of Congress on the subject of reconstruction and other matters painful to recall. Critical support left the cause and did not return.[51] The incident was infamously remembered as the "Elkins handshake," but statehood advocates could not have imagined that the misstep would conceivably delay New Mexico's admission for some thirty-five years.

Those charged with considering petitions for statehood were apprehensive that, through disproportionate influence in Congress, a small oligarchy in a western territory might come to wield extraordinary power for its own benefit. Members who read the papers—as most surely did—could hardly have missed the reports of "ring rule," land fraud, and political corruption in New Mexico. For some editors and members of Congress, the Santa Fe Ring provided ample reason for caution in dealing with the New Mexico question. With action on the statehood bill approaching in 1876, the *New York Times* had predicted that in the event of admission, "we shall see a couple of rich mining superintendents representing another rotten borough in the Senate, and a knot of crossroads politicians annually dividing among themselves the spoils of office."[52]

Senator Beveridge, New Mexico's chief nemesis in Congress for nearly a decade, was also persuaded that the territory was a sinkhole of corruption controlled by railroads, mining interests, banks, and other self-seeking entities.[53] Even in New Mexico's final, successful effort to secure statehood beginning in 1909, allegations of corruption arose. Beveridge, who had for some time been in a grudging retreat from his implacable position on New Mexico, wanted to put off final consideration of the question. "In the New Mexico land frauds," a student of Beveridge's career states, "he found the excuse he wanted to delay action."[54] Beveridge and fellow senator Knute Nelson brought allegations to the attention of their Senate colleagues. According to the *New York Times*, the Committee on Territories heard charges of corruption, jury bribing, and other offenses attributed to "the gang that is in control of political affairs in New Mexico."[55] At the heart of the allegations was a charge that persons of influence in the territory had attempted to "have agents of the Department of Justice called off when they were investigating land fraud cases." Further investigation failed to reveal a disqualifying condition, and with a helpful shove from President William Howard Taft, Beveridge and the Senate committee allowed the statehood bill to advance.

Likely Ring domination of congressional seats and other elective offices was likewise a concern at home, and accounted for at least some reluctance on the part of Hispanics and other citizens of the territory who were not enthusiasts for statehood. In an informal survey of more than forty local merchants and citizens in 1881, the *Santa Fe Democrat* found more than half opposed or unready to declare for statehood. One respondent wished to remain unnamed for the sake of his business, but said that "the Democratic element was not strong enough yet, and if we were admitted as a Republican state the Santa Fe Ring would have it all their own way."[56]

From Silver City, an outpost of opposition to the Ring, the *Southwest Sentinel* wrote in August 1892, with reference to Catron's candidacy for territorial delegate and continuing efforts to secure admission, "The people of New Mexico are not yet ready to be governed by the Santa Fe ring, nor are they ready to send one of the members of the ring to Washington as a delegate from this Territory in congress. Catron and a Las Cruces colonel would make a fine pair in the United States Senate."[57] The paper did not think it probable that New Mexico would be admitted, declaring, "The democratic members of the House and particularly the majority of the committee on the territories cordially dislike the frowning and unscrupulous land grabbing partner of the smiling and equally unscrupulous Steve Elkins and would find plenty of pretexts to postpone and finally smother a bill that apparently meant his advancement to the United States Senate."[58]

Catron lost his bid to unseat Antonio Joseph as territorial delegate in 1892, but was elected two years later, serving one term before losing to another Democrat, Harvey Fergusson. Fergusson, in turn, was displaced in 1898 by a Republican with strong Ring ties, Pedro Perea, a former president of the First National Bank of Santa Fe. Little direct progress was made in the statehood fight during Perea's brief tenure as delegate, but statehood historian Marion Dargan found value in Perea's service, noting, "There was so much ignorance and prejudice concerning the native people of New Mexico that it must have been significant for the territory to be represented at the national capital by one of the ablest of her native sons."[59]

Catron, Elkins, Prince, and Frost all played key roles in the final attainment of statehood. Frost controlled the *Santa Fe New Mexican* much of the time from 1883 until his death in 1909 and, in the view of Porter Stratton, a historian of the territorial press, he exemplified the best and worst among journalists of his era. A strong partisan with few scruples, he "supported a corrupt clique of politicians who often used their positions for personal advantages." Aside from partisan politics, however, "Frost and the *New Mexican* usually adopted a course that was beneficial to the territory."[60] Frost served as adjutant general of the territorial militia, headed the Bureau of Immigration, and was involved in numerous civic projects. A zealous advocate for the cause of statehood, Frost used the *New Mexican* to help bring it about, and, despite considerable division on the question, "there was not a chance in a thousand that the wily editor would report that the people of New Mexico were indifferent to, or opposed to, statehood."[61]

In addition to using his influence to pursue admission during his term as governor, Prince helped construct and disseminate arguments to answer the most common objections to statehood. As territorial delegate from 1895 to 1896, Catron was intensely focused on the statehood issue, introducing resolutions and scheming to secure a favorable composition of the House Committee on Territories. He was not successful in moving the statehood initiative during his two years as delegate, but he continued to work for the cause, believing that statehood was both inevitable and essential to New Mexico's prosperity. As a senator from West Virginia, Elkins was a reliable ally, lobbying colleagues for favorable final action on the New Mexico petition for statehood.

Catron participated in drafting the 1910 constitution and in the effort to secure voter approval. His account of the drafting convention reflected an aversion to newly popular reforms and his preference for more centralized governance. "We had to agree that the State Officers and Judges should all be elected," Catron told Elkins, expressing his wish that judges of the supreme court might instead have been appointed.[62] In agreeing to the election of judges, Catron noted, Republicans had secured "an agreement that the Initiative, Recall and primary elections should be left out and only a modified referendum, very limited in its scope, was put in."

Following a campaign on the merits of the proposed new constitution, the document won approval of a majority of voters in New Mexico and was approved by Congress and President Taft. The final resolution of Congress approving New Mexico's admission specified that voters should be given the opportunity to approve an easier amendment process than the one initially provided. The "Blue Ballot Amendment," a proposition incorporating this question and printed on a blue-tinted ballot, was submitted to voters in the 1911 general election and was adopted. Taft signed the proclamation granting statehood on January 6, 1912.

It is an irony that, after an interval of some six decades following the first serious effort to secure admission, including approximately forty years in which leading Ring figures were deeply involved, most of those who had expected to benefit financially and politically were not around to enjoy the fruits of success. Elkins had been eminently successful in business, industry, and state and national politics from his adopted base in West Virginia, but his death in January 1911 prevented his witnessing New Mexico's ultimate triumph. Chronic illness had forced William Breeden's retirement and a retreat to his daughter's home in Massachusetts, where he died in January 1913. William Logan Rynerson had passed in 1893, and Max Frost in October 1909. J. Francisco Chaves had been killed by an assailant in 1904. Henry Waldo was nearing the end of a long career, much of it spent in service of the AT&SF Railway Company. He retired in ill health and died in Kansas City in 1915. A politically diminished Catron secured one of New Mexico's United States Senate seats, fulfilling a long-standing aspiration. Catron was among the last senators to be elected by a state legislative body before passage of the Seventeenth Amendment, mandating the direct election of senators. When he stood for election to the seat in 1916, he was defeated. If, as some feared, statehood was to empower a cabal of self-dealing malefactors, that alliance would not be ruled by the old Ring, but by other, younger men representing an emergent generation of leaders.

CHAPTER TEN

THE END OF AN EPOCH

T he end of the Santa Fe Ring was proclaimed repeatedly during the extended period of its dominance in territorial politics and business affairs. Declarations of the Ring's imminent demise were usually premature and grounded more in hope than in fact. An early opponent of the Ring in Colfax County, William R. Morley rejoiced in the removal of Samuel Axtell as governor in 1878, telling his family, "This is the death knell of the Ring."[1] Axtell's removal and Catron's resignation as U.S. attorney proved only a temporary impediment, however, as the Ring retained control of the legislature and eventually regained dominance over critical administrative offices.

In 1880, the short-lived *Era Southwestern* noted the arrival of the railroad, and with it an increase in awareness of the wider world. "Where the 'Ring' at one time was to many a horrible menace," the newspaper said, "it is now only a played out combination; as a power, exciting only derision and contempt."[2] It was not entirely played out, as some Ring-friendly officials held their positions and others who had been removed rose phoenixlike to frustrate their opponents. Henry Atkinson remained as surveyor general, routinely using the office for his own benefit and that of favored allies. William Breeden, who had resigned as attorney general amid turmoil surrounding the Lincoln County War and an investigation of charges against public officials, regained his old place in 1881. Samuel Axtell, deposed as governor in 1878, returned as chief justice in 1882.

In 1884, the *Albuquerque Journal* reported on the reaction of Francisco Perea, a former territorial delegate to Congress, to the end of William G. Ritch's tenure as territorial secretary, telling readers, "He believes that the final wind up of the Santa Fe ring is now near at hand."[3] But it wasn't, and seven years later the *Santa Fe Daily Sun* reported the passage of a school law formerly opposed by Ring men and said, "The Santa Fe Ring—the old Santa

Fe Ring—is about busted."[4] It wasn't quite "busted," but the Elkins-Catron Ring was gradually coming to an end.

The Santa Fe Ring enjoyed its greatest success as a close-knit power elite in an isolated western territory, with close ties to powerful Republican leaders in Washington and advantages that enabled Ring partisans to dominate native populations. The installation of a flawed process for confirmation of land-grant titles and a loosely administered system for distribution of public lands also helped speculators, particularly those who were unburdened by self-imposed ethical restraints. This period ended around 1884, shortly after the arrival of the railroad. The schism in the Republican Party, plainly evident in the 1884 nominating convention, underscored the extent to which the Ring had lost control. For the rest of the territorial period, a weakened Ring faced opposition from Democrats and an emergent group of younger Republicans.

By the early 1890s, a permanent sea change was evident. With Elkins's indulgence, Catron continued in the old manner, but with diminishing returns. Following the Republicans' return to the White House in 1888, Elkins urged that Samuel Axtell be brought back as chief justice, despite his having been twice forced out of office in New Mexico. Elkins probably was humoring Catron and other diehards of the old Ring in pushing for such an unlikely choice. In declining the request, President Harrison stated facts that should have been obvious to all. "As to the New Mexico Judgeship," he wrote, "Mr. Axtell was too old and I found out that he would be attacked in the Committee of the judiciary."[5] Harrison chose James O'Brien, a Minnesota lawyer with a reputation for honesty and no previous connection to New Mexico or its political factions.

Shortly after the election of 1884, New Mexico Republicans and the Ring lost a critical tactical resource, perhaps not fully appreciated, when William Breeden yielded the chairmanship of the Territorial Republican Central Committee. Breeden had led in organizing the party in the territory in 1868, and he had held the chairmanship almost continuously since that time. More to the point, he was an aggressive advocate who stood up for the party against all comers. Breeden was attorney general from 1872 until 1889, except for the two-year period during which Henry Waldo served and disputes delayed the appointment of a successor to Waldo, and he persisted despite the determined efforts of two governors to replace him. Breeden sometimes represented Santa Fe in the council, but whether or not he was a member, he worked to advance his party's legislative interests. Breeden's demeanor could alienate allies, and his personal behavior was occasionally subject to criticism.[6] But he was an effective manager of Republican Party affairs, and his retirement left an unaccustomed void in the party's leadership.

Over the next six years, Breeden was succeeded as party chair by reliable Ring allies: Joseph Dwyer, William Griffin, and briefly the twice-deposed Samuel Axtell. Shorter terms of service became the norm, as Edward L. Bartlett, John S. Clark, Ralph Emerson Twitchell, Frank Hubbell, and other party regulars took turns minding the organizational machinery. Not until the new century did the party find a leader with the vision, energy, and organizational skill to seize and exert persistent, controlling influence from the chair. When such a man came along, he was not a protégé of the old Ring, but the representative of a new generation of Republican leaders. Holm O. Bursum of Socorro was elected chairman in 1904 and served until 1911, when he was an unsuccessful candidate for governor in an election held in anticipation of imminent statehood. In Twitchell's view, the chairmanship was "a position which he filled with great credit, leading his party to victory in every campaign down to and including the election of delegates to the constitutional convention of 1910."[7] After 1890, Catron was generally regarded as the leader of a faction of old-guard Republicans, rather than the undisputed kingpin of his party.

Patronage and the Machine

The political combination built around Thomas Catron used federal jobs to reward party loyalists and to maintain organizational strength. This was fundamental strategy from the beginning of the Ring's emergence, continuing until the machine finally ground to a halt. The practice was by no means peculiar to New Mexico, but was commonplace across the country. Democrats also governed in this manner, in their more limited opportunities to wield the administrative powers.

Party bosses responded to needs of their key supporters, and in turn expected loyalty and hard work in succeeding elections. As New Mexico's territorial delegate, Elkins was accustomed to hearing from party leaders in the territory. In May 1874, William Breeden wrote on behalf of J. Francisco Chaves, a proven force who could mobilize Republican votes in his county. "Col. Chaves is striving very hard to regain his financial footing," Breeden stated. "He says he cannot afford to take an office which would prevent his attending to his business—He could hold an Indian agency anywhere west of the Rio Grande or a Post Tradership."[8] Chaves was a sheepman by family inheritance and an attorney by profession. A political appointment did not immediately materialize, but upon the death of Ben Stevens in 1878, Governor Axtell appointed Chaves district attorney for the Second Judicial District. Through much of the territorial period, presidents tended to appoint from outside New Mexico, perhaps mindful that citizens in the territories did not vote in presidential elections. Catron increasingly pressed for appointment of residents of the territory to offices. In his mind, an appointment was wasted if not used to strengthen the party.

Disloyalty on the part of political appointees invited punishment. Max Frost complained to Judge A. L. Morrison in 1892 concerning the postmasters at Folsom, Lordsburg, and Springer, who were newspaper editors and who were not supporting Republicans in the fall election. Frost had already asked Governor L. Bradford Prince to identify federal officials who "were not doing their duty," meaning their political duty. Suggested Frost, "I think Twitchell should as chairman write a letter to the president about every federal office holder who does not support the ticket; the president should know what his appointees are doing out here; supposing they do not like the ticket, the party has put them into power and they certainly should stand by its nominees when they have fat offices."[9]

The combination of newspaper editor and postmaster was commonplace in the 1890s, as editors sought to replace reduced commercial revenue with government business.[10] At least eight New Mexico papers of the nineties were published by men who were also postmasters. Once taken for granted, this form of patronage was closely scrutinized as the Progressive movement gained momentum. In 1892, the *Civil Service Record* cited some 64,371 offices that were subject to patronage appointment and opined, "It seems high time that something should be done to take them out of politics."[11] Fourth-class post offices—the smallest offices—were placed under Civil Service by the president in 1911, but the following year a progressive Republican congressman, George Norris, advocated for more sweeping reform. "I consider the Post Office Department an enormous political machine," Norris declared, but it was not until the post office was privatized that all such appointments were divorced from politics.[12]

Delegate Catron

Catron scored a significant victory in 1894, unseating the incumbent territorial delegate, Antonio Joseph, who had held the office for five terms. A

Democrat except where Ring interests were concerned, Jimmy Dolan wrote from Lincoln County in the midst of the fall campaign to advise Catron that "Mr. Curry"—presumably George Curry—had "offered before a large crowd" to wager $5,000 against $2,500 that Catron would be defeated and Joseph reelected. Francisco Manzanares, the Las Vegas wholesale merchant, was identified as having furnished the money.[13] The offer apparently was not accepted, but Catron prevailed in the November election.

Once seated as New Mexico's delegate in the new session of Congress, Catron threw himself into the struggle for statehood, but the political climate was not favorable, and he did little otherwise to distinguish himself in Washington. He did, however, have the satisfaction of serving with Elkins, who was in his first term as United States senator from West Virginia.

A reputation for political shenanigans preceded both men in the capital, and at least one joint venture reinforced this impression. Under the headline "A Political Job Spoiled," the *New York Times*, then as later a journal favoring Democrats, detailed an effort to gain a partisan political advantage in New Mexico by changing the dates for the coming legislative session. In anticipation of a Republican victory in the presidential election of 1896, Catron and Elkins proposed to change the opening of the legislative assembly from the traditional December date to May. The new president could then appoint a Republican governor to work with a Republican legislature and could place party members in key territorial offices. The change was to be accomplished by means of a rider to the bill appropriating funds for operation of the national government. The gambit was noticed and publicized by a senator from New York who declared that the provision had been "sneaked in," a characterization verbally resented by Elkins. Catron joined Elkins at his senate desk to witness the final debate and action on the matter. The offending provision was stricken, the bill was passed, and Catron, the *Times* reported, exited the senate chamber "wearing a look which showed that he was afflicted with a 'tired feeling.'"[14]

Catron subscribed to the principle that political spoils are earned and should be used and enjoyed to the fullest. He believed that appointive offices should go to members of the victorious party, particularly when it was his party, and that supporters should be rewarded for their loyalty. An extension of this attitude to other privileges of his office led to further unwelcome notoriety during Catron's one term in Congress. Declaring Catron "a genius in the line of self-seeking," the *New York Times* reported in September 1896, "Congressional Delegate Thomas B. Catron of New-Mexico, having two sons, has with great thriftiness appointed one a cadet in the Military Academy at

West Point and the other as a naval cadet at Annapolis, and, that there may
be less danger of his plans miscarrying, has made each a substitute candidate
for the other, so that if one fails in the examination at either institution the
other may stand ready to take the place."[15] Catron was thinking of the two
oldest of his four sons, John and Charles. Having contracted malaria, Charles
was unable to take advantage of the appointment. John entered the Naval
Academy in 1896 and attended West Point in 1897, but did not persist at either
place. A third son, Thom, later enrolled at West Point and graduated.[16]

During his term as delegate, Catron was forced to deal with a significant
distraction when he was charged with witness tampering in a highly publicized murder case, in which he defended four men who were charged with
capital murder. A panel of attorneys appointed to examine the charges found
cause to move for his disbarment. The matter was heard by the territorial
supreme court in a trial that consumed most of the month of October 1895.
There were strong political overtones surrounding the murder of Francisco
Chavez of Santa Fe, a popular Democratic Party activist. Some believed that
the charges against Catron also stemmed from political motives, and cir-
cumstances seemed to support this notion.[17] Four reputable attorneys—
Frank Springer, Frank Clancy, Neill B. Field, and Albert B. Fall—came to
Catron's aid and put on a spirited defense. The charges were dismissed, and
Catron was immediately elected president of the New Mexico Bar Association.
Even so, the incident inflicted further damage on his checkered reputation.

Whatever the impact of the disbarment suit and Catron's acquittal, the
political winds had shifted. Longtime allies were finding it easier to declare
their independence. When party leaders organized in anticipation of the
1896 Republican National Convention, T. D. Burns, previously a reliable political operative and business associate in Rio Arriba County, felt at liberty
to support Solomon Luna to replace Catron as New Mexico's national com-
mitteeman.[18] Despite a welcome Republican victory in the 1896 presidential
election, Catron was unable to hold onto the office of territorial delegate and
was defeated by the Democratic candidate, Harvey B. Fergusson.

During the December lame duck session of Congress following the fall
election, Catron worked to secure one more piece of legislation that appeared
to tilt toward his personal interests. In this instance, he hoped to amend an
1887 law prohibiting foreign ownership of real property in the territories. In
the view of statehood scholar Robert W. Larson, "Catron opposed the act
because he had large tracts of land to sell and could make more money selling them undivided to wealthy foreigners."[19] Catron was not successful in

Figure 25 The son of a pioneer merchant
and an early territorial delegate,
Miguel Antonio Otero II was governor
for nine years and had more success in
curbing the power of the Ring coalition
than any of his predecessors.
Palace of the Governors Photo Archives
(NMHM/DCA), No. 9915.

effecting the changes he proposed, despite support for his ideas in the western territories—at least from speculators in land and minerals.

A New Day

Catron's loss of the delegate seat aside, he and others of the old Ring must have been exultant over the return of a Republican to the White House in 1896. Indeed, Catron was soon busy laying plans for the new territorial administration, pushing Pedro Perea for appointment to the office of governor. Doubtless he had nominees in mind for most appointive positions. In fact, Catron wished to return to the office of U.S. attorney for the Territory of New Mexico.

Catron's favor had long been advantageous to men seeking public office in New Mexico. In anticipation of William McKinley's inauguration and the inevitable makeover of territorial and federal administrations, hopeful office seekers sought his support. Among these was Miguel A. Otero II of Las Vegas, scion of a prominent family and a rising Republican functionary. His father had been a partner in the prerailroad mercantile firm of Otero and Sellar, a three-term territorial delegate, and an original director of the Maxwell Land Grant and Railway Company. Otero, the son, asked Catron's help in securing an appointment as U.S. marshal. He was thirty-nine years of age and had been engaged in banking and related business activities in Las Vegas.

Catron was favorably disposed to Otero's request and appears to have considered himself something of a mentor to the younger man, who had been educated in the states at the University of Notre Dame. They had corresponded on political and business matters, Catron addressing the younger Otero with the familiar "Dear Gillie" used by personal friends. In the glow of his victory in the 1894 delegate race, Catron had written to thank Gillie for his "efficient and splendid work" in turning out the Republican vote in San Miguel County. He invited Otero to "command" him if Catron could somehow repay the favor.[20] With Otero's request in hand, Catron, now a lame duck as delegate, responded in a manner that was cordial but noncommittal. He explained that there were many applicants for the office of marshal, and that some had strong political connections. Catron could not say what the extent of his influence with the incoming president might be.[21]

The selection of a new territorial governor proved a dilemma for McKinley, who desired a consensus among New Mexico Republicans, but was instead faced with multiple competing applicants, including former governor Prince. Few appeared willing to forego candidacy for the position.[22] Forced to make a choice after fruitless attempts to have influential Republicans come to a meeting of the minds, the president ignored the announced candidates and surprised nearly everyone by naming Miguel Otero governor on June 2, 1897.

A friend and political ally, John S. Clark, reported to Otero that Catron was "very sore" about the appointment, but if so, Catron recovered quickly. His affinity for the Spanish-speaking people of New Mexico was widely acknowledged, and in later years he increasingly felt that capable Republicans who were Hispanic should share in holding responsible political offices. With his own suggestion of Pedro Perea rejected, he found enthusiasm for Otero as governor, praising the choice in letters to Elkins in October and November 1897.[23]

Catron was discovering that his opinions did not count for much with the new president. With his own aspiration for appointment as U.S. attorney in abeyance, he grumbled to Elkins, "The appointments already made (except that of Mr. Otero, which is really an excellent one), have done a great deal of injury to the party, as neither Mr. [George H.] Wallace, [Quinby] Vance, [Creighton] Foraker, nor [Edward F.] Hobart have any political influence or standing with the voters of the party, and the people think that the hard workers, those who go out and take off their coats to support the ticket, ought to be rewarded."[24] Catron later itemized his complaints with the men appointed as territorial secretary, surveyor general, U.S. marshal, and land office receiver, and stated, "We ought to have received two of these offices for the Mexican people."[25] Along with Pedro Perea, his choice for governor, Catron likely was thinking of Solomon Luna, his choice for U.S. marshal in preference to Otero.

Catron, Perea, and Luna provided $500 to support Miguel Otero's travel to Washington to consult with the president on appointments—those of federal judges and others, including the office of U.S. attorney. Throughout the new governor's month-long trip to New York and the capital, Catron remained anxious about his own prospects, finally concluding that Otero was not advocating on his behalf. He continued pressing his case with Elkins, but concluded, "The fact is that Otero is an ingrate and when he left here I raised the money for him to pay his expenses, on a positive promise that he would support me."[26] McKinley apparently was averse to appointing Catron under any circumstances. Opposition from citizens in the territory and from former governor Lew Wallace likely reinforced his doubts. In the end, he left the incumbent, William B. Childers, in place. Catron still hoped to secure the position, but when Childers was reappointed to serve in McKinley's second term, the fate of his ambition was clear to Catron, as it had been to others.

Otero proved a capable governor and more than capable as a politician. He gained the support of a strong coalition, and the Republican Party became accustomed to dealing with the competing preferences of the "Otero wing," representing the new guard, and the "Catron wing," anchored by more traditional party leaders. Not all members of the old Ring coalition remained loyal to Catron. The once and future attorney general, Edward L. Bartlett, and Max Frost, still owner and editor of the *New Mexican*, were among those who moved to support Otero.

The split between Otero and Catron widened rapidly, fueled by pride and mistrust, and by Otero's determination to pursue an independent course. As the end of Otero's term approached, Catron was determined that he should not be reappointed. As usual, Elkins was the instrument by which he hoped to work the levers of official Washington. In April 1901, Catron wrote to advise of the proximate expiration of the governor's term, complaining to Elkins, "Our people have grown tired of having this irresponsible upstart ruling over us, and throwing slime and mud upon us. He is not true to any one or anything, except himself," Catron grumbled.[27] Well satisfied with Otero's service as governor, McKinley reappointed him for a second term.

Theodore Roosevelt's succession to the presidency following the terrible assassination of William McKinley gave Catron hope that something could yet be done about the governor. On November 11, 1901, following the September assassination, Catron assailed Elkins with a new diatribe, complaining of Governor Otero, "If we are to have him for another four years I will sell my property for what I can get and leave the town, and I know of many others who will do the same. I mean business by this letter, and I wish you, if you have any regard for me or any friendship for me, to take this letter in the most serious way and to do what you can to help this Territory, and help its people, and help me also."[28] It is not clear that Elkins did much in response to Catron's harangue, or that it would have been to his political advantage to do so. Disagreements between Otero and the new president concerning political appointments and the statehood issue presaged a change in territorial administration. It became clear that Otero would not be reappointed at the expiration of his second full term as governor. He left office on January 22, 1906.

Despite mounting obstacles, Catron did not retreat from political combat during the Otero years. On the contrary, he was elected to the territorial council in 1898 and 1904, and was defeated in 1900 and 1906, but won election as Santa Fe's mayor in 1906. Catron also succeeded in sandbagging Otero in his second term, agitating for replacement of officials of the governor's choosing with men who were friendlier to the Catron faction.[29] Otero missed the warmth of his friendship with President McKinley, finding Roosevelt cool to him, perhaps more attuned to the men he had led as Rough Riders fighting the Spanish in Cuba. After the abortive tenure of Herbert Hagerman, who had followed Otero as governor, Roosevelt appointed George Curry a member of the regiment of Rough Riders.

Catron remained optimistic, combative, and insistent with those upon whom he relied for support. His attention was fixed on long-standing objectives of personal political and financial success, Republican domination of territorial politics, and New Mexico statehood. But the tides had changed in New Mexico politics, and for Catron. As described by Twitchell, "Until the year 1896 he was recognized as the leader of the republican party, framed its policies, wrote its platforms, controlled its conventions, represented the party in national conventions, and was a member of the republican national committee. With the administration of Governor Miguel A. Otero, aided by the executive, a powerful party machine was erected and Mr. Catron was compelled to divide the leadership with younger men anxious for political preferment and recognition in the party councils."[30] By the time Otero left office, Catron had endured nearly a decade of contention with a younger

Figure 26 Stephen Benton Elkins represented West Virginia in the United States Senate from 1895 until his death in 1911. Photo ca. 1908. Harris and Ewing Collection, Library of Congress, No. LC-DIG-hec-15111.

governor who refused to be bossed and had encountered increasing opposition within his own party. The prospect of a new territorial administration not including Otero must have come as a relief to Catron and the remnants of his coalition, but there would be no return to the Ring rule of former times, for too many other things had changed.

An End and a Beginning

By the mid-1890s, the Santa Fe Ring of Elkins and Catron was largely forgotten, but not gone. Diminished in numbers and influence, it was no longer the dominant force of territorial politics or the object of regular newspaper screeds. The ranks of the old Ring had begun to thin, but some important associations continued. Elkins rose in the Republican hierarchy, attaining national visibility and, in some cases, notoriety. He had been a valuable contact in Washington, and his ascendancy to the United States Senate in 1895 made him an even more powerful ally.

When Elkins won the Senate seat, he assumed a position of primacy in the Republican Party in West Virginia and directed a political machine of legendary efficiency. Serving between 1897 and 1913, George Atkinson, Albert White, William Dawson, and William Glasscock came to be known as the "Elkins governors," having attained the office with his support.[31] Given Senator Elkins's responsibility to his constituents in West Virginia, Catron's concerns and New Mexico's interests were relegated to a secondary position. Despite long absence from the territory, Elkins continued to hear from political friends and business associates, including Abraham Staab, with whom he owned property; Henry Waldo, who looked up public records at Elkins's request; Max Frost, who sought help in advancing resolutions adopted by the New Mexico Republican Party; and William Breeden, who wrote asking assistance in securing a pension for a military veteran.[32]

Catron did his best to direct a diminished remnant of the old Ring. In Breeden's absence, he took on more of the work of prompting local party leaders to organize, raise campaign funds, and get out the Republican vote. Between 1890 and 1912, when the Ring was supposed by many to be a dead issue, Catron carried on a steady correspondence with presumed Ring men of former times. In addition to Elkins, these included J. Francisco Chaves, Stephen W. Dorsey, Max Frost, Charles Gildersleeve, Antonio Joseph, Melvin Mills, Mariano Otero, Pedro Perea, L. Bradford Prince, John Riley, Pedro Sánchez, Lehman Spiegelberg, Abraham Staab, William Thornton, and Henry Waldo. Most of these were Republicans who continued to support the Catron faction.

Their mutual concerns included both political and business matters. Catron complained to Lehman Spiegelberg concerning the treatment he received as a borrower at the Second National Bank in Santa Fe. He plied Robert Longwill, a director of the First National Bank of Santa Fe, with requests related to an urgent need for cash, imploring Longwill to help in securing approval of a loan. In the midst of their contentious election battles, Catron and Antonio Joseph still took care of business, keeping up essential correspondence concerning properties in which they were jointly interested. Catron regularly exchanged letters with John Riley concerning ranching business in Lincoln County.

Catron prodded Melvin Mills of Colfax and Pedro Sánchez of Taos to carry their counties for the Republican ticket. Encouraged to run again as a candidate for territorial delegate, he sought the counsel of two old confidants, Mills and Stephen Dorsey. He coached Pedro Perea on strategy for manipulating his adversaries in an upcoming party convention. He conferred with Prince concerning the ongoing quest for statehood and sought Henry Waldo's assistance in lobbying for favorable judicial appointees, characterizing the incumbent district judge as "a contemptible little ignoramous."[33] He dispensed advice on use of the *New Mexican* to refute charges in the heat of a political campaign, telling Max Frost, "I think it best to wait until a few days before the election and then publish a general manifesto to the entire people of the territory, refuting all these matters at once, and send it out too late for them to tell any additional lies or make any additional statements."[34] Catron was often frustrated in efforts to exercise the influence imputed to him in former times—the power to command governors, judges, surveyors, and attorneys general—but he remained the focal point of a considerable network of associates, and he continued pulling the wires and working the levers of an increasingly balky political machine.

As New Mexico neared the promised land of statehood, speculation concerning likely candidates for the coveted Senate seats intensified. Catron had long aspired to represent New Mexico in the Senate. With Elkins in the hunt to fill a Senate seat representing West Virginia in 1894 and New Mexico still chasing the elusive goal of statehood, Catron mused, "If we can get the New Mexico bill through I hope I may be able to meet you in the Senate, both at the same time."[35] He would have been discouraged to know how far in the future his goal lay, but Catron did not surrender his ambition, and when the goal appeared in reach, he remained hopeful.

By 1909, when statehood appeared imminent, Catron had plenty of competition in his own party, but retained his usual self-confidence. Of W. H. "Bull" Andrews, a rising power in the party, the current territorial delegate and a logical candidate for a Senate seat, Catron told Elkins, "Andrews has not the ghost of a show to be elected Senator, but I am sure, if we can get the statehood bill this session, that I will be elected one of the Senators without opposition."[36]

Elkins evidently suggested that Henry Waldo run for the other Senate seat, a move that could potentially have placed the three men from western Missouri—friends since the 1860s—in the United States Senate together. Waldo's disavowal of interest put an end to that fleeting notion.[37] In proposing Waldo, a Democrat, was Elkins just indulging a kindly sentiment for two old friends, or was he covering bets in the manner of the old Ring, trying to ensure some access to the inner sanctums of power in the event of a shift in party influence in Congress or the White House? Probably the former, but Elkins was capable of such foresight in planning for contingencies.

With the passage of the statehood bill and the certainty that the legislature would be electing two senators, rumors flew. One of these had Catron and Andrews combining forces to seek the two seats in tandem, a report that was without foundation and that was denied by both men, who were nonetheless on friendly terms.[38] Of greater concern was the rising popularity of

Figure 27 Albert Bacon Fall represented a rising generation of Republican leaders whose ambitions would supersede those of Thomas B. Catron and the old Ring coalition. Photo ca. 1912. George Grantham Bain Collection, Library of Congress, No. LC-B2-1398-6.

Albert Bacon Fall, a Democrat until 1900 but an immediate and formidable force in the territorial Republican Party following his conversion. Fall had attracted Catron's notice by 1893, when Catron complained of Fall's nomination for appointment to the territorial supreme court, telling Elkins, "He is the most offensive man in the whole Territory and the most venal."[39] Catron may have revised his appraisal when Fall came to his aid in the disbarment case. Fall was confirmed as an associate justice and twice served as attorney general. A member of the council in 1891, he championed and passed a public school bill initially opposed by Catron.[40] Relations between the men were nominally cordial, but they represented different eras and different interests.

When members of the legislature convened for the purpose of electing United States senators, they had an even dozen candidates to consider—ten Republicans and two Democrats, including four Hispanic men. Frenzied jockeying ensued through seven ballots, with weaker candidates, including Bull Andrews and William J. Mills, falling by the wayside. Catron came nowhere near winning a seat "without opposition" as he had so confidently predicted, and was fortunate to be elected with Fall in the eighth round of balloting.[41]

Time and Change

By the time the statehood had been attained, the Santa Fe Ring of Elkins and Catron was spent. Most of those regularly identified with the Ring were dead or infirm. Some were inactive, living with grown children in distant states. Within a few years, nearly all remaining vestiges of the Ring had vanished. It is ironic that deferral of statehood sustained the motives and conditions that enabled the Ring to exist, but ultimately denied many of those who had sought admission the satisfaction of realizing the anticipated benefits, including higher property values, new business prospects, and opportunities for political influence at the federal level.

Catron, leader of the alliance since Elkins's departure from the territory, was literally the last man standing in a combination that had exerted forceful if not dominating influence for more than four decades. Widowed, bereft of his lifelong friend and ally with Elkins's death in 1911, dismissed without fanfare at the end of his Senate term in 1916 by a younger set of Republican leaders, Catron was unbowed, hoping at age seventy-five to be named as U.S. ambassador to Chile.[42] That call never came. Catron died in Santa Fe on May 15, 1921.

The Santa Fe Ring and other self-serving local combinations were products of the Gilded Age—of a permissive regulatory environment and attitudes that endorsed the unhindered pursuit of personal wealth. Political power, more easily harnessed in the western territories than in the states, helped sustain the quest. With the arrival of railroads, the quickening pace of commerce, the more direct democratic processes that accompanied statehood, and an increasingly punitive and determined Progressive reaction to Gilded Age excess, the old Ring did not prosper.

With the railroad came increased settlement and access to markets, and a closer link with Washington. These things were mostly good for business, but statehood and modern modes of transportation and communication also brought increased political and business competition and more attentive federal oversight. When the Court of Private Land Claims was established in 1891, an easily manipulated system for confirmation of land-grant claims was replaced with a tribunal that operated for thirteen years in relative stability and competence. Though the court has been criticized for legal interpretations that were seen as overly restrictive and unfair to some claimants, its integrity was not seriously challenged. The Pendleton Civil Service Reform Act of 1883 had little impact in New Mexico, but statehood had a major impact, converting numerous offices from patronage appointments to officials chosen by direct election. Such changes worked against the Ring. Progressive reforms continued to chip away at conditions that allowed corrupt alliances to dominate in the western territories.

The decline of the old Ring did not signify the extinction of official corruption or shrill political rhetoric, and over the years observers have detected vestiges of a dominant political elite still at work, perhaps evolving from the Ring of Elkins and Catron. Howard Lamar saw the Elkins-Catron combination superseded by a "new Santa Fe Ring" headed by Holm Bursum, who chaired the Republican Central Committee from 1904 to 1911.[43] Lamar did not identify others in the new group, but it may have included men named by statehood historian David V. Holtby as belonging to an emergent group of leaders who, in his view, dominated the Santa Fe Ring in the years just before and after the turn of the twentieth century.[44] These included Albert Bacon Fall, Bursum, Charles Spiess, Charles Springer, and the still influential Catron.

Malcolm Ebright has identified three attorneys of the same era as "members of the Santa Fe Ring." Charles Catron, Alonzo B. McMillan, and Alois B. Renehan represented claimants to the Las Trampas grant in legal proceedings between 1900 and 1914. In Ebright's estimation, the lawyers failed to properly represent their clients, opting instead to profit at their expense.[45]

None of the three had any notable involvement in the old Ring save for Charles Catron, who inherited some of his father's grant-related legal and financial problems, but their methods and the values that they reflected were reminiscent of those associated with the Ring of former times.

Having observed the heavy-handed management style of the Bursum organization in the final territorial Republican Party convention in 1911, the *Albuquerque Morning Journal* expressed dismay, recalling an era better left behind. The writer enumerated changes that had come to the territory, including an increase in rail and motor transportation, the proliferation of "unmuzzled newspapers," and introduction of safeguards against election fraud that rendered the old way of politics obsolete. Concluded the paper, "The machine forgets in short that the people of New Mexico are not having as much of their thinking done by proxy as in former years." In the editorialist's view, it was time for a new age of openness and integrity in party affairs, and for recognition of the empowerment that statehood would soon confer on citizens.[46]

A century has passed since the combination known as the Santa Fe Ring receded and vanished from the political stage. Amorphous by nature, its very existence subject to dispute, the fabled Santa Fe Ring remains a notion in cherished western myth, an indelible remembrance of unbridled greed and grievous loss. Whatever the lessons or legends of the Ring, it symbolizes the economic and social encounters that have been, as surely as soaring mountains and living deserts and the people and cultures that inhabit them, essential elements of New Mexico's long history of enchantment and conflict.

CHAPTER ELEVEN

THE MYTH OF THE RING

I n September 1878, the *Santa Fe Weekly New Mexican* addressed recent criticism of the territory's political elite, commenting, "We have had a surfeit of howling about a mythical ring and of vague and uncertain general charges of fraud, robbery, oppression and wrong."[1] The *New Mexican* went on to launch a spirited defense of the much maligned political elite that detractors insisted on calling the "Santa Fe Ring." The paper disputed the very existence of such an entity. The term *mythical* was used to indicate something imaginary—fabricated, fictitious, conjured up out of thin air—which is what the writer thought of the allusions he was complaining about.

Another common usage for the word *myth* has more to do with the legend or narrative growing up around a person, event, or phenomenon that may have some accepted factual basis. The existence of Stephen Elkins, Thomas Catron, Max Frost, and other familiar individuals as figures of importance in the public life of the territory was not disputed. Whether they comprised an alliance of men deliberately pursuing purposes inimical to the public interest was a matter of interpretation. Newspaper critics and political opponents, with later historians, fiction writers, film makers, and tellers of village and family tradition, have contributed to the construction of a narrative, simplified for ease in retelling, concerning a powerful elite group and its impact on the economic and political life of the territory. This is the other myth of the Santa Fe Ring.

It could be said with some justification that the Santa Fe Ring is mostly or entirely myth. In the absence of artifacts confirming the existence of an organized conspiracy and identifying its participants, even serious historical works refer to the Ring in terms better suited for a discussion of traditional interpretive stories than for a clinical description of social and political phenomena. Scholars who are normally meticulous in researching and documenting assertions may fall prey to the myth, foregoing some of the usual

Figure 28 "Santa Fe Ring," cartoon in *Thirty-Four,* October 27, 1880. From early declarations of its existence to the present, the Santa Fe Ring has been an iconic symbol of corrupt power and a target of derision for its detractors. Image from Archives and Special Collections, New Mexico State University Library.

rigor in research and documentation, and referring to the Ring as though its existence, nature, and impact were common knowledge.

One of the first clues to the mythic character of the Santa Fe Ring, as revealed in various literary and historical references, is found in the language used to describe it. References to the Ring commonly imply structure and official character that did not exist. The well-respected Hal K. Rothman referred to Catron and Prince as "charter members of the Santa Fe Ring," although there were no members other than by inference, and there was no charter.[2] It is not unusual to see someone referred to as a "paid-up member of the Santa Fe Ring," a "card-carrying member of the Ring," or "a peripheral member." In a literal sense, there were none of these. Howard Roberts Lamar writes that Charles Gildersleeve, a lawyer and Democratic Party leader, was "a land-grant speculator and unofficially a member of the ring."[3] Were there, then, official members, and if so, who were they and what made them official?

Based on an informal survey of nonfiction works referring to the Santa Fe Ring, the most common adjectives used in introducing the notion to readers are *notorious* and *infamous*. Other common descriptors are *ruthless*, *shadowy*, *nefarious*, and the more clinical and less emotionally charged *corrupt* and *powerful*. A more creative writer styled the Ring *malodorous*. Sometimes the writer goes on to explain who has done what to merit such a judgment. Often he or she does not. Without elaboration, such depictions contribute more to the myth than to an understanding of the history associated with the phenomenon known as the "Santa Fe Ring."

Narratives that have the Santa Fe Ring generating collective decisions and acting as an entity have no documentary basis in history. Statements to the effect that "the Santa Fe Ring had lobbied the Department of Interior," or that the Ring "arranged for Marshal Sherman to appoint Peppin an acting deputy U.S. marshal" or "levied exorbitant taxes on grant and settler property" contribute to a persistent myth of the Ring as an organized body, unified in purpose, deliberate in its decisions, and more directed in its actions than was the case.[4] Someone, or some combination of individuals, may have done these things, but who?

As subjects of fiction and film, Catron and the Ring have scored only minor appearances. Fiction thrives on a conflict of wills and values, so the men of the Ring are conveniently cast as conspirators who hold the town or the territory in their evil grasp, pending the arrival of a worthy protagonist. The mythic Ring is ideally suited for mass-market western fiction, which eschews subtlety. When a cover blurb proclaims, "A great new western hero rips open a Santa Fe Ring of cutthroat killers," the book's plot is effectively revealed.[5] As fiction tends to magnify virtue and vice for dramatic effect, the incorrigible reprobates of the Ring are predictably greedy, menacing, corrupt, and more than willing to engage in violence. Those familiar with treatments of the Ring in credible histories may find such references amusing, but taking a cue from Henry Nash Smith and others concerning the impact of popular fiction on perception of actual persons and events, one has to wonder what effect fabricated or exaggerated accounts have in shaping the collective memory of Elkins, Catron, and associates, and of their deeds and their times.[6]

Those who tell and perpetuate traditional stories also contribute to the myth of the Ring. Especially powerful, at least in the experience of those who hear them, are tales of family lands lost to lawyer tricks, a relative's farm foreclosed, common lands given to *la floresta*—the Forest Service, and the deeds of *el anillo de saqueadores publicos*—the ring of public looters.

Early Narratives

The Ring may first have come to the notice of readers in memoirs and popular historical narratives concerning Billy the Kid and the Lincoln County War. The most popular of these, by far, were Pat Garrett's *The Authentic Life of Billy the Kid* and Walter Noble Burns's *The Saga of Billy the Kid*, each of which has appeared in editions issued by more than a dozen publishers. Originally published in Santa Fe in 1882, Garrett's book received wider notice beginning in 1927, when the Macmillan Company published an edition annotated by the Lincoln County War authority Maurice Garland Fulton. Garrett's brief mention linking Catron to the Murphy-Dolan faction was not especially pejorative, but Fulton deemed it "courageous" that Garrett, writing in 1882, had dared to identify Catron by name. In a note, Fulton elaborated on Catron's activities and added, "Besides all this he was a powerful member of the clique of politicians and business men called in those days the 'Santa Fe Ring,' which largely controlled the Territory of New Mexico."[7] Fulton tamped down some of the embellishments introduced by Garrett's imaginative personal editor, Marshall Ashman Upson, and provided a leavening dose of historical accuracy.

Neither the Garrett book nor Burns's *Saga*, a narrative posing as history but viewed by many skeptics as containing a large dose of fiction, directly address the Ring, but both portray figures commonly associated with the Ring: Governor Samuel Axtell, Catron, and Judge Warren Bristol among them, along with the Lincoln County trio of Lawrence Murphy, James Dolan, and John Riley. Burns reinforces the notion of Murphy and his associates as men who profit from stolen cattle, defraud the government, and use hired guns to enforce their will. Whatever its value as history, Burns's book undoubtedly had an impact on the popular persona of William Bonney and probably on perceptions of nineteenth-century New Mexico as a debauched wasteland. The book inspired feature films titled *Billy the Kid*, produced in 1930 and 1941, with Johnny Mack Brown and Robert Taylor each starring in the title role.

A third narrative that attained some exposure on a national scale was George Coe's autobiography, *Frontier Fighter*, published by Houghton Mifflin in 1934. Coe refers to the Santa Fe Ring as a subject of apprehension among citizens of the 1870s and 1880s. Coe and his family had pioneered in Colfax County during the struggle over the Maxwell land grant, moving south in time to witness and take part in the Lincoln County War. Coe family members knew many of those involved in the conflicts and were privy to talk of Ring influence. Evidence of involvement of the Santa Fe Ring in incidents cited by Coe was scant, but where manipulation of money and politics was apparent, suspicion often fell on assumed Ring men.

More strident in his criticism was the former territorial governor Miguel Otero, whose four volumes of memoirs spanning the years between 1864 and 1906 provided ample space for expression of his views. In *The Real Billy the Kid, with New Light on the Lincoln County War,* published in 1936, Otero described the Santa Fe Ring as the "political power-house of New Mexico and the most lawless machine in that territory's history," and characterized Catron as the "ruthless overlord of all Southwest racket interests."[8] Concerning the Ring's alliance with the Murphy-Dolan faction in Lincoln County, Otero said, "As this crowd felt themselves protected by the powerful influences in the old Santa Fé Ring, they scrupled at nothing. No one will ever know the many horrible crimes which were committed, particularly in Lincoln and Socorro Counties that must be laid at the door of this group of villains."[9]

Another former governor who later served as state historian and curator at the historic courthouse in Lincoln came to Catron's defense. Of speculation that the Santa Fe Ring had been involved in a plot to murder John Tunstall, George Curry wrote in his autobiography, "Knowing the late Thomas Benton Catron, as I knew him over many years, I view the charge that he was party to a 'ring' which plotted against Tunstall and connived at his death as ridiculous."[10]

The early accounts stoked public curiosity concerning Billy the Kid, the Lincoln County War, and, to a lesser extent, the Santa Fe Ring. Their authors could hardly have guessed that the subject of the Kid, at least, would prove inexhaustible, inspiring new works of history, fiction, and film in the twenty-first century.

Gene Rhodes and the Santa Fe Ring

It is hard to imagine a writer better suited to evoke the myth of the Ring in fiction than Eugene Manlove Rhodes, who grew up in southern New Mexico in the fleeting days of the open range. Rhodes was personally acquainted with men who did the Ring's bidding in Lincoln and Doña Ana counties. His family suffered injury at their hands. Rhodes became a fine writer of literary western novels and could deliver a satirical haymaker as well as anyone. He was a close observer of social phenomena, and a shrewd and opinionated follower of political affairs. Rhodes's stories of cowboys, miners, and maidens, and of corrupt officials and corpulent capitalists, were influenced by his experience with Ring men, but when he imagined a conspiracy, it had no such colorful title as the "Santa Fe Ring," and he didn't use actual names. Rhodes readily confessed that he was "telling as fiction what I could not repeat as fact."[11]

Rhodes's knowledge of the Ring began with his father's experience of being let go as Indian agent on the Mescalero reservation as a result of political influence. Of the cooperation expected of the Indian agent by Ring-connected neighbors like John Riley and W. L. Rynerson, a resident of the region told a Washington official, "They generally saddle the Indian Agent before he gets into office and then they ride him."[12] Said Rhodes scholar William Hutchinson, "Events on the Mescalero Reservation dominated the life of Rhodes's family upon his return from college. They played an immediate part in his own life and, for an opinion, played a considerable part in shaping his philosophy of life for all time."[13]

Rhodes later encountered Ring influence in a confrontation with the former territorial secretary William G. Ritch, who owned land in the San Andres region near the Rhodes family homestead. Looking to expand his holdings, Ritch reportedly contested Hinman Rhodes's claim, brought about its cancellation, and gained ownership of the property for himself. Rhodes again found himself opposed to the Santa Fe Ring in the prosecution of his friend Oliver Lee, who stood trial for the murder of Albert Jennings Fountain and Fountain's young son, Henry, in 1899. To some, Catron's involvement as a special prosecutor signaled the Ring's apparent interest in the case. Lee was acquitted, but Rhodes was again impressed with the power and reach of the Ring.

The general theme of corruption on the part of powerful business and political interests is pervasive in Rhodes's western fiction, but Hutchinson cites examples in which references to Ring figures are more explicit and specific. According to Hutchinson, the antagonists in Rhodes's first novel, *Good Men and True* (1910), were drawn from his experience with Ring figures, including Riley, Ritch, and Rynerson.[14] Similarly, a prologue to the novel *Bransford in Arcadia* (1914) is said to be "based very definitely on the feud between the Rhodeses and the William G. Ritch family over the latter's contesting and eventual acquisition of the original Rhodes homestead in the San Andrés Mountains."[15] Rhodes's 1934 novel *Beyond the Desert* includes allusions to the trouble at Mescalero with Ring figures including Riley, Rynerson, and James Dolan, "whose control of the country is fictionally told in the acquisition of the *Catorce/Dorayme* country."[16]

In an early novel, *West Is West*, Rhodes satirizes "Johnny-the-Slick," the "Easy Boss" of the territory. The model for Rhodes's character is not identified, but his persona is reminiscent of the popular image of "Smooth Steve" Elkins. The boss is "an upstanding, broad-shouldered muscular man of forty, with a shrewd face and keen though furtive eyes, and with a square chin said by its possessors to indicate determination."[17] Notable were the boss's political instincts, a facade of congeniality that seemed to mask something sneaky, and a natural inclination to look out for his own interests: "A born wire-puller, of cool temper and a plausible tongue, a reader of motives, a generous divider, and—to give everybody his due—unquestionably a good friend to his friends, The Boss was a natural leader of any body of men—that could not go without a leader." The hero of Rhodes's story, Steve "Wildcat" Thompson, has the rare pleasure of prevailing over the powerful corruptionists—a feat more easily accomplished in fiction than in life.

In response to an inquiry from Maurice Garland Fulton concerning his open embrace of the Tunstall-McSween faction in the Lincoln County trouble, Rhodes offered his most explicit comment on the Ring. "During the Eighties and Nineties," he explained, "my father and myself saw the people who had backed Murphy-Dolan-Riley and found them detestable." Based on the bitter taste left by the experience, Rhodes concluded, "the combination of public office with private gain is what caused the Lincoln County War—it would make trouble in Hell—or to be plain, the Elkins-Catron-Riley succession; the sheriff–post office–land register–Indian contracts–Federal appointments–arrest or suppress anyone who doesn't acquiesce-in-your-domination."[18]

The Ring in Historical Fiction

Of Arizona and its "Tucson Ring," C. L. Sonnichsen observes, "The myth of the Tucson Ring is so commonly accepted that many a popular novelist would have trouble plotting his stories if he were deprived of the wicked ring as a whipping boy."[19] That is not quite the case for New Mexico authors and the Santa Fe Ring, but the Ring makes occasional appearances in works of historical fiction as well as adventure western novels. The role of a ring is much the same for New Mexico–based fiction as it is for Arizona: it serves as

Figure 29 Book jacket, 1920 reprint of Eugene Manlove Rhodes's 1910 novel *Good Men and True*. Antagonists in this and other Rhodes novels were likely inspired by Ring figures known to Rhodes in southern New Mexico. Cover art by H. T. Dunn. New York: Grosset and Dunlap. Collection of the author.

a menacing antagonist and emphasizes the extent of the collective power arrayed against the people and the protagonist.

One of the better fictional renderings of the Lincoln County War is Amelia Bean's *Time for Outrage*, published in 1967. The author follows accepted historical accounts of the conflict and makes frequent use of the Santa Fe Ring as villain. Powerful, greedy, and ruthless, the Ring has its agents in every village and town throughout the territory. The book ends with the burning of the McSween home in Lincoln and leaves many questions unanswered. It is not conclusive as to the fate of the Ring, but a rising tide of public opinion condemning official actions in Lincoln County portends a change in the political climate, delivering "a jolting shock" to Judge Bristol and District Attorney Rynerson, "along with all adherents of the Santa Fe Ring."[20]

Elizabeth Fackler's *Billy the Kid: The Legend of El Chivato* (1995) can also be considered as a work of historical fiction, with acknowledged debts to Maurice Garland Fulton, William Keleher, Frederick Nolan, and other historians of the Lincoln County War. The book is frankly partisan, opening with a dedication to several of the Regulators and concluding with an author's note in which Fackler contends that "folk heroes do not attain public adulation without cause." William Bonney is portrayed as a folk hero who was destroyed because he opposed the established order. "As such," Fackler states, "he was a freedom fighter on the western frontier, and the Lincoln County War was a battle for individual rights against the machine of big business."[21]

Fackler's framing of the conflict as a morality play leads to a casting of the Santa Fe Ring as a collective antagonist. When the news of Alexander McSween's arrest in Las Vegas reaches Tunstall and Rob Widenmann in Lincoln County, Widenmann is led to exclaim, "Damn that Dolan! The Santa Fe Ring's behind this." With this news, it dawns on Tunstall that the Ring must have the courts within its power, a revelation that bodes ill for McSween's safety and his own.[22]

When McSween is returned to southern New Mexico and held by order of Judge Warren Bristol in lieu of an unreasonably high cash bond, Tunstall's suspicions are confirmed. After his store in Lincoln is falsely attached to satisfy McSween's alleged debt to the heirs of Emil Fritz, Tunstall spurns a suggestion that he appeal to a higher court. "I wouldn't get justice there either," he responds. "The judiciary are the most despicable of all the pawns of the Santa Fe Ring."[23]

Fackler's conclusion is intentionally pessimistic, ending with Bonney's death at the hands of Pat Garrett. In the moments just after the shooting,

Garrett reflects on his first impression of the Kid as "simply a rambunctious youth" caught up in the circumstances of a political feud. In Fackler's view, "The Lincoln County War was a battle for individual rights against the machine of big business. The war was lost, and is continuing to be lost in America today."²⁴

The Ring again is cast as the heavy in Johnny D. Boggs's fictionalized account of the trial of Billy Bonney for the murder of "Buckshot" Roberts at the Battle of Blazer's Mill. In *Law of the Land: The Trial of Billy the Kid* (2004), Boggs weaves a tale embracing events before and after the trial, showing a persistent pattern of collusion among those identified as participants in the Ring: Catron, William Rynerson, Judge Warren Bristol, U.S. attorney Sidney Barnes, Jimmy Dolan, Simon Newcomb, William G. Ritch, and others. Ring men are portrayed as being mostly Irish, false Republicans, and members of the Masonic Lodge. Some of their scheming is done at the Lodge hall at Las Cruces.

Boggs follows the story to Bonney's death on July 14, 1881, at Peter Maxwell's home at old Fort Sumner. An epilogue reveals that, in the wake of the turbulence, two Ring men have died by suicide and others have succumbed to illness, leaving Catron a lone survivor, prosperous and powerful in the early years of a new century. The two suicides may have been contrived for literary effect, without basis in history. At least one Ring figure, Robert H. Longwill, died in an apparent suicide, but long after the dust had settled in Lincoln County.

A work dealing with a later time period is Daniel Aragón y Ulibarrí's *Devil's Hatband* or *Centillo del Diablo* (1999), a novel of Las Vegas during the turbulent years of struggle between Anglo land-grant speculators and native Hispanics determined to maintain control of their lands. The period of interest is around 1890, when the Gorras Blancas or White Caps organized to cut fences and make mischief for outsiders attempting to fence the land and use it to build personal fortunes. The White Caps were believed to be related to the broader movement of the Knights of Labor, and many of their interests were aligned with those of the KOL. In New Mexico, their views brought them into conflict with Thomas Benton Catron and others of the Santa Fe Ring.

When Catron visits Las Vegas for the purpose of propping up his local political machine, Aragón y Ulibarrí takes the opportunity to render an unflattering portrayal—one of several found in works of fiction. "Catron had an air of conceit about him as any man would with his wealth and holdings," the author writes. Further, the Catron character is possessed of a quick temper and browbeats local operatives while reminding them of their debts to him. Failing to get satisfaction from his local henchmen, Catron mobilizes the Ring and its Washington friends to come down on the White Caps. Catron continues with business as usual, defending accused murderers and taking his pay in land. By 1895 the Mexicano resistance has dissipated. Some local Hispanics leave their fortunes to the mercy of the new regime, and others join the power faction.

Catron is again in for some rough treatment in Mike Blakely's *Spanish Blood* (1996). Bart Young, a Texan, heads for the Territory in 1870 with dreams of empire in his head. He has heard that old Spanish land grants are ripe for picking, and he starts by aligning himself with the most knowledgeable man on the subject, Santa Fe attorney Vernon Regis. Blakely's portrayal of Regis evokes the popular image of Catron: "He stood and unbuttoned his vest to give his gut some room. He was a large man, poorly built. He had narrow shoulders and hips, a large head, a bulging stomach, and tremendous feet. His hands were soft, pale, and thin-skinned, with fingers like pitchfork tines."[25] Regis is also corrupt, humorless, and easily angered when opposed.

Regis controls the secretary of the territorial archives and enjoys a mutually beneficial relationship with the surveyor general. He gets Bart a job in the archives, where he can learn the finer points of the business of land-grant speculation. Drawn into an abyss of corruption, Bart pursues his own ambition and eventually opposes his mentor in the struggle over a vast grant in the Sacramento Mountains. Justice is served when, driven by greed, both men die in the quest, victims of misplaced ambition.

Paperback Plotters

It is dangerous to generalize about mass-market Westerns, because the genre that brought readers Longarm, Slocum, Long Rider, Skye Fargo, Edge, and Bolt—sensational and sometimes vulgar heroes—has published real and respected writers like Louis L'Amour, Theodore Olsen, and Frank O'Rourke. Series books that are produced by multiple writers and published under a "house name" afford anonymity that writers may appreciate, as long as they are paid for their work. Following the lead of dime novels produced in the nineteenth century, these books hew to commercially driven formulas. Essential ingredients include a conflict, a hero, a villain, and a desirable woman. Sex and violence are not unexpected.

Matt Braun's *Jury of Six* (1980) reflects more than passing familiarity with Ring lore. Caught in a firestorm of controversy in Lincoln County, range detective Luke Starbuck realizes that William Bonney—Billy the Kid—is just a tool of more clever men who must be stopped. When the smoke has cleared in Lincoln, many evildoers and quite a few good men lie dead, but the corrupt power behind the violence seems to have survived intact. John Chisum explains it to Starbuck like this: "The true-blue scoundrels hardly ever get caught in the ringer. I'm talkin' about the men behind the scenes—the ones with the *real* power—like that bunch in Santa Fe. One way or another, they usually manage to slip loose. It's the kings and conquerors that get their heads lopped off. The men pullin' their strings are goddam near invisible—and untouchable."[26]

Frederic Bean takes the Lincoln County War and spreads it over the eastern half of New Mexico in *Santa Fe Showdown* (1993). All along the Pecos Valley and up to the capital of Santa Fe, Jimmy Dolan and John Chisum are locked in a cattle war with outsized profits and economic dominance at stake. Also at risk are the property and dignity of the small ranchers, who are under pressure to sell their cattle to the Dolan firm, at Dolan's price. The treachery is traced to Thomas Catron, boss of the Ring in Santa Fe. Among those threatened by the greed of the Ring is Porfirio Valdez, who runs cattle on his ranch near Santa Fe.

En route to Santa Fe, Bean's hero, Trey Marsh, finds himself in the middle of the local trouble and meets the Valdez daughter, Maria, at Fort Sumner. He takes on the job of escorting her to the family ranch, learns plenty about the range war, and falls in love with Maria. Once in Santa Fe, Marsh confronts Tom Catron. Having warned Frank Taggart, one of Dolan's men, that harassment of the Valdez family would bring dire consequences, Marsh seeks Catron to deliver the same message. Forcing his way in, he tells Catron to rein in Dolan and Taggart, warning, "Make sure they understand that if anyone shows up at the Valdez Ranch with a threat about selling his calves to you, I'll kill both of them, and then I'm coming to Santa Fe to kill you. Make no mistake about my intentions, Catron. I'll splatter your brains all over this office wall if just one more gunman shows up at that ranch."[27] Bean's Catron wisely cowers and backpedals.

These books and those below them in the literary pecking order essentially appropriate characters from history and make caricatures. Honed to serve the author's dramatic purpose, the Ring and its personifications, including Catron, are shorn of subtlety. They are one-dimensional entities whose function is to bully, dominate, and threaten until driven to defeat by the hero.

Screen Shots

Hollywood has found only limited use for a collective antagonist composed of men who spend their time chasing federal supply contracts, making backroom deals with the land office, and pulling strings in the legislature to advance their schemes. Such pursuits might pay in life, but they don't pay in the film business. The Western typically craves kinetic and visual appeal, danger and daring that viewers can see and hear. Allusions to the Santa Fe Ring in cinema owe their appeal to an enduring fascination with a certifiable icon of western myth: Billy the Kid. References to the Ring are generally scant and passing, but they are there to make a point.

In the Sam Peckinpah film *Pat Garrett and Billy the Kid* (1973), Garrett and Bonney are on familiar if not friendly terms. Upon learning that Garrett has been appointed sheriff and given orders to get Billy out of the country, the Kid needles Pat, saying, "Ol' Pat . . . Sheriff Pat Garrett. Sold out to the Santa Fe Ring. How does it feel?" Garrett says, "It feels like times have changed." The response sounds a familiar refrain in works about the fleeting nature of the romantic West. The inference is that settlement and progress are inexorably transforming the wide open, largely self-regulated spaces that Billy and others have inhabited, bringing order and ending the time in which freedom and outlawry could flourish.

In the 1988 film *Young Guns*, forces of the Ring are arrayed against John Tunstall, the Kid, and a scrappy band of Regulators. The evil associated with the Ring is vested in the Lincoln County business sharp and manipulator L. G. Murphy. In a confrontation with Tunstall over the pending award of a contract for supply of beef to the government, Murphy makes it clear that he has the law behind him, including Sheriff William Brady, whose life savings are at stake in the deal. Murphy advises that his powerful supporters include not only the sheriff, but "the territorial district attorney, the chief justice, the U.S. district attorney, and the Santa Fe Ring."

The film follows usual accounts of the Lincoln County War, culminating in the torching of the McSween home and the routing of the Regulators. Viewers are advised that following the conflagration, the Murphy-Dolan forces and the Santa Fe Ring collapsed. This is not quite true, since Ring influence was evident into the late 1890s and beyond, and Dolan and friends returned to prominence in stock raising and contracting.

Remembering the Ring

In a biography of the famed frontiersman and land-grant owner of the Cimarron, author Lawrence R. Murphy concludes by considering two distinct images of Lucien Maxwell. One is a historic figure whose story is supported by documentary evidence and contemporary accounts, the other a myth created by "generations of amateur writers, novelists, and historians."[28] As it turns out, the historic Maxwell struggles to compete with the legend in the hearts and minds of readers. The historic figure is simply overwhelmed by the circulation attained by popular fiction, compared to that of the carefully researched, painstakingly footnoted, scholarly monograph. Of a major source of the myth, Harvey Fergusson's 1950 novel *Grant of Kingdom*, Murphy says, "It was aggressively promoted by Fergusson's publisher, William Morrow; it was certainly read by more people throughout the United States than all other books about Maxwell combined."[29]

Something similar happens with pretty much any historic figure who attracts the attention of novelists and screenwriters, and of the editors and business people who hone their products to maximize appeal to the consuming public. Exposure matters, and maximum exposure signifies a disproportionate influence on perceptions of the subject—the Ring, for instance. As to members of the general public in the 1980s and 1990s, who did more of them pay attention to: young guns like Emilio Estevez, Kiefer Sutherland, Lou Diamond Phillips, and Charlie Sheen, or a senior scholar who emerges from the archives to offer conclusions on political phenomena of the Gilded Age? While the body of novels and motion pictures dealing with the Santa Fe Ring is modest, it seems likely that film and fiction have reached many more people than have historical narratives, and with a simpler message: there was a political clique in New Mexico the late 1800s known as the Santa Fe Ring, and it was corrupt, ruthless, and very bad.

In the twenty-first century, the Santa Fe Ring endures as a symbol of conflict in the borderlands—a shorthand for conquest, exploitation, dispossession, and cynical uses of economic and political power. In *Desert America* (2012), a contemporary memoir of struggle in the high desert, Rubén

Martínez examines a region of abundant but degraded natural beauty; a land once largely rural and agricultural, since overtaken by forces of technology and urbanization. He points to a pattern of dysfunction and to stark contrasts in the lives of people who inhabit the region. The Ring is named as one in a succession of forces contributing to the involuntary alienation of native New Mexicans from the land.[30] The Santa Fe Ring is not made to bear all blame for poverty, drug abuse, and environmental degradation, but its name is understood to evoke a syndrome of ills and aggressions that helped shape the present. Rooted in the past, the myth helps Martínez and his friends on the upper Rio Grande make sense of the present as they contemplate the future with equal measures of trepidation and hope.

CHAPTER TWELVE

CONQUEST AND CONSEQUENCE

Reflections on the Ring

In 1884, the *Boston Herald* passed this intelligence from the Southwest: "Few people not directly interested in the affairs of the Territory have any conception of the power and extent of the land ring that owns and governs New Mexico. It is an association unorganized, but with a perfect system and unity of purpose, composed of Territorial officers, United States Senators and Representatives concerned in the great land and cattle companies, and certain speculators and capitalists, American and foreign. This combination, which is known as the New Mexican Land ring, or, locally, as the Santa Fé ring, shapes Territorial legislation both in New Mexico and Washington, controls the courts, and has for the last twenty years been all-powerful in securing the appointment to Federal offices within the Territory of men pledged to its purposes."[1]

This article appeared as federal investigators were examining allegations of land fraud in the Territory of New Mexico and uncovering a mass of details related to the scandal. Its premises have been widely accepted among historians interested in the region, and little has emerged to alter these perceptions. The Ring and equivalent coalitions in other western territories are among the manifestations of a conquest described by Patricia Nelson Limerick, a historian whose focus on economic and cultural differences in the West invites readers to view traditional accounts of expansion and settlement in a different light.[2] In territorial times, the notion of a "Santa Fe Ring" composed of influential insiders gave disgusted citizens of varied origins and values a name for the powerful elite that appeared to dominate political and business affairs.

A century has passed since Elkins, Catron, and the combination known to adversaries as the Santa Fe Ring passed from the economic and political stage in New Mexico. A longer period has elapsed since the power of its leaders was sufficient to inspire admiration, servility, defiance, grudging respect, fear, and loathing. These responses to the Ring varied based on the individual's place in a culturally and economically diverse society at the convergence of three frontiers, including those of Native American peoples, northern Mexico, and westward Euro-American expansion.

But what was the Santa Fe Ring, or was it anything? Referring to popular ideas that have defined the Ring, Robert M. Utley notes, "No one has documented its membership, organization, techniques, and purposes to show that it existed as an entity rather than simply as a group of men individually pursuing similar ends in similar ways."[3] There is still little evidence to indicate that the Ring was, in any ordinary sense, an "entity." There was no formal structure or designation of membership, and beyond a small core, there was little agreement as to who its members were.

The Ring referred to in contemporary and historical accounts was, however, something more than a collection of individuals "pursuing similar ends in similar ways." Cooperation was a central feature of Ring activity, occurring in multiple contexts including business relationships, political party affairs, and the organization and operation of the legislature. Collaboration among alleged Ring members involved use of official powers for personal benefit, as when surveyors general took part in decisions that advanced their interests as speculators or investors in stock-raising operations, and when prosecutors targeted their political enemies. Governors, territorial delegates to Congress, and U.S. land registers were also alleged to have acted in ways that benefited their own interests. The impression that judicial prejudice favored Ring men dates from the acquittals of William Breeden and William L. Rynerson in the late 1860s, when it appeared to some that a partisan judge intervened to ensure positive outcomes for the defendants.

What attracted and held the attention of critics was the persistence of an influential group of men, variable in composition, in which economic and political ambitions were evident, and in which participants appeared to collaborate with the expectation that each of them would benefit personally. Despite the structures established to ensure democratic processes, presumption of due process and an impartial judiciary, and all the high principles upon which the government of the United States was established, people on the wrong side of the elite could not get around the idea that the territory was being run by a clique of like-minded men who took care of themselves first.

Who Was in the Santa Fe Ring?

The Santa Fe Ring was not a formal organization, and those said to be members did not acknowledge involvement. Most did not agree that such a combination existed, though critics of the Ring insisted that it did. Those who endorse the notion of a territorial ring can only postulate its membership on the basis of such indicators as identification by contemporaries, the judgments of historians, observed business and political alliances and activities, and associations with other assumed Ring members. The designations derived from such data are largely subjective and are inherently debatable. The potential for guilt by association is significant.

Appendices A and B offer a tentative and unscientific guide to participation in the Ring. Appendix A provides a tabulated summary compiled from published views of some who have ventured to identify Ring members, including contemporary detractors, historical figures who witnessed apparent Ring activity, historians, and writers of popular nonfiction. Sources include personal narratives, newspaper articles, correspondence, and government reports. These accounts may refer to persons as Ring members, but were not intended as systematic efforts to identify all who may have been associated with the Ring. Writers sometimes draw distinctions between a "Ring member" and one who is "influenced by the Ring," is a "tool" or "friend" of the Ring, or has "close ties to the Santa Fe Ring." Appendix B provides a brief profile description of each of those named in appendix A, with brief comments concerning alleged Ring connections.

Conventional descriptions of the Santa Fe Ring indicate that it was dominated by non-Hispanic white men who were members of the Republican Party, but that influential Democrats and Hispanics were included as a way of extending Ring influence and ensuring access to both Republican and Democratic administrations. Hispanic men aligned with the Ring played critical roles in mobilizing a large segment of potential voters. Democrats and Hispanics were involved, but not necessarily on an equitable basis with the Ring's Euro American leadership. Democrats identified with the Ring helped their Republican colleagues defeat unwanted legislation during the administration of Governor Edmund G. Ross, and Democrats such as Antonio Joseph and Charles Gildersleeve regularly engaged in land speculation and other business ventures with presumed Ring members. But party allegiances intervened at times, taking precedence and placing Joseph, Gildersleeve, and others in direct opposition to the Republican leadership of the Ring. Two other notable Democrats, William T. Thornton and Henry Waldo, were associated with the Ring in a friendly way, but maintained a large degree of independence. Hispanics associated with the Ring also were subject to conflicting allegiances concerning the relative desirability of statehood and of public schools that would inevitably compete with the influence of Catholic schools. Usually a Catron ally, always a stalwart among Republican leaders, J. Francisco Chaves did not hesitate to go his own way when his political interests collided with those of the Catron-led Ring faction.

Some accounts have suggested that the Ring was closely aligned with other associations of the territorial period. The Masonic Lodge is often named as an organization having a parallel membership, perhaps providing a structure for coordination of Ring activities behind a ritualistic veil of secrecy. There is little or no evidence to indicate that the Lodge played a critical role in the Ring's business. Membership in the Masonic Lodge was so general among men of ambition that assignment of such significance to Lodge membership is hardly justified. A large proportion of supposed Ring members were Masons, but so were many other business and professional men. Accounts naming the New Mexico Bar Association as a surrogate for the Ring during the Ross administration are more persuasive, at least in the context of that era when, according to Ross, a Ring-dominated group in the local bar screened all proposed legislation.

A business whose leadership structure overlapped with that of the Ring on a consistent basis was the First National Bank of Santa Fe, whose presidents between 1871 and 1894 were Elkins, William Griffin, and Pedro Perea. Rufus Palen, the son of Judge Joseph Palen, followed Perea, but was rarely if ever named as a Ring member. Bank directors included Catron, Robert Longwill, Abraham Staab, Henry Waldo, and Louis Sulzbacher, a sometime friend of the Ring. Though officially serving as cashier in the early years, Griffin was the executive officer in practice virtually from the time the bank opened in 1871, with the mostly absent Elkins holding the office of president. Despite his early reputation as a generous and perhaps biased surveyor, Griffin steered a steady course, nurturing the bank's financial success and "taking the lead in Santa Fe's civic affairs, as well as in territorial and Masonic events."[4]

When individuals were identified with the Ring by editors, business competitors, or political rivals, the connotation was generally pejorative.

However, the reputations of individuals commonly associated with the Ring varied, and many, like Griffin, were leaders in civic, cultural, and benevolent activities as well as partisan political matters and business affairs.

Did the Ring Sponsor Violence?

The men to whom Ring membership is imputed were not gunslingers or highway robbers. Most were educated men who applied their advantages, worked the margins of ethical and legal behavior, and used their collective resources to their mutual benefit. Pursuit of wealth and power involved them in competitive activities and regularly brought them into conflict, much of which played out in the political arena and in the courts. Some contemporaries described the Ring as "ruthless" and intimated that its members would stop at nothing to accomplish their selfish ends.

At the same time, Ring men of the late nineteenth century were operating in an environment in which lawlessness and violence were common. Many of those associated with the Ring were veterans of the Civil War. Most knew how to employ violent means and some had done so. William L. Rynerson had shot and killed the chief justice over a personal offense in 1867. James J. Dolan drank to excess and more than once settled business or personal differences by shooting his rival. Rightly or wrongly, a number of violent incidents provoked speculation concerning possible Ring involvement. Whether or not there was fire, an abundance of smoke begs the question: Did men prominently identified with the Ring instigate, procure, condone, or otherwise sponsor violence against their rivals? Regardless of the culpability of alleged Ring figures, the incidents were widely publicized and helped focus attention on charges that an insidious combination was at work in the territory.

Violence in Colfax and Lincoln counties helped bring the notion of a menacing ring in New Mexico to the attention of local residents and a national audience. These well-publicized conflicts erupted in similar fashion, with the murder of a sympathetic figure, polarization of local opinion, and a series of violent recriminations. In both cases, economic interests of the Ring were at stake. Speculation concerning conspiracies to eliminate F. J. Tolby in Colfax County and John Tunstall in Lincoln County traced back to men commonly identified with the Ring, but the allegations were not proven.

In Colfax County, at least eight men died violently, and Henry Waldo put the total nearer sixteen or eighteen.[5] In July 1879, the *Santa Fe Weekly*

Figure 30 Thomas B. Catron remained a force to be reckoned with in New Mexico well into the twentieth century and maintained correspondence with surviving members of the old Ring coalition. Clara Olson Photograph Collection, New Mexico State Records Center and Archives, No. 22592.

New Mexican reported that forty-two violent deaths had occurred in Lincoln County "out of a voting population of one hundred and sixty." Historian John P. Wilson cited an estimate of fifty deaths over the course of the con-flict.[6] The foremost authority on the Lincoln County War, Frederick Nolan, says only that the number killed is "as impossible to quantify as it is to define what they died for."[7]

Some of the deaths in Lincoln County had economic and political im-plications, but none of the killings appears to have been plotted by leaders of the Ring. Chronic lawlessness, personal animosity, hot tempers, and alcohol were likely contributors. It is tempting to hypothesize that in Colfax and Lincoln counties, a surplus of testosterone, rather than a Ring conspiracy, was at least partly to blame for the violence. Of thirteen counties surveyed in the censuses of 1870 and 1880, only Grant County, with a military post and a large mining industry, had higher proportions of male residents. In 1870, 65 percent of those counted in Colfax County were male, as were 59 percent in Lincoln County. By 1880, when the railroad had reached the northern counties, the proportion of males in Colfax County had moderated to 58 percent, but in Lincoln County, men accounted for 62 percent of residents.

Catron was accused, usually by innuendo, in several instances of violence. These charges seemingly had more to do with his penchant for offending people and feuding with political and business associates, and less to do with facts, but they fed the perception of Catron as a ruthless competitor and likely damaged his candidacy for political office at least once. He was accused of paying a livery bill for horses used in carrying out the American Valley murders, and of plotting to poison political enemies; these accusations were fraudulent and were exposed as such. Catron was also accused of complicity in the murder of Santa Fe sheriff Frank Chavez and of scheming to have Albert Jennings Fountain "put away," but no evidence was offered, and the charges were not taken seriously.[8] Still, they added luster to Catron's reputation as a good man to leave alone. In 1884, when Oliver M. Lee settled in southern New Mexico, memories of the Lincoln County War were still fresh and painful, and "there was talk of the 'Santa Fe Ring,' of its ability to first threaten and frighten people and then to act, perhaps with violence, always with serious results."[9]

Catron was a lightning rod for criticism, and in Victor Westphall's estimation, "a ruthless frontier politician, lawyer, and businessman who used his power and guile and who would run roughshod over opponents to fight fire with fire."[10] Catron is, however, an unlikely candidate for a planner or procurer of murder. Violence ill suited his purposes. Catron and his allies could do more damage and risk fewer negative repercussions by manipulating political and legal systems, but at times they relied on men who were not averse to trouble. Acts of violence in Lincoln and Colfax counties and elsewhere were often spontaneous and personal, sometimes aggravated or induced by alcohol. Some violent acts likely were undertaken at the initiative of the perpetrator with the intent of advancing the employer's interests. With the possible exception of the Tolby murder in 1875, pre-sumed Ring figures do not appear to have been directly responsible for acts of violence. A further question is, did they foster or condone a climate in which it was invited?

Can New Mexico's Historians Improve Their Discipline?

Norman Cleaveland, a devoted student of the Colfax County War, posed this question with reference to historical treatments of the decade between 1875 and 1885, one of the most turbulent in New Mexico's history.[11] In his view, some hard realities had been ignored, if not explicitly covered up. He be-lieved that Frank Warner Angel's reports exposing the corruption of territo-rial officials had been a deliberate blind spot for generations of historians. He criticized William G. Ritch, L. Bradford Prince, and Ralph Emerson Twitchell, successive presidents of the Historical Society of New Mexico, each of whom added to the historical record with published materials and personal papers. These men were involved in political and governmental af-fairs, and had been named as likely Ring members. It is little wonder that they may have been less than interested in accusing contemporaries or in drawing attention to allegations for which they did not wish to be remem-bered. The writer's criticism also extended to later historians such as Lawrence R. Murphy, the biographer of Lucien Maxwell and one of several chroniclers of the Colfax County War, who, in Cleaveland's estimation, had perpetuated a "cover-up" of Ring iniquities.[12]

In answer to Cleaveland's question—yes, New Mexico's historians can improve their discipline where the Santa Fe Ring is concerned. John Porter Bloom had a point when, speaking to an audience heavily populated with historians, he professed dissatisfaction with most references to the Ring in histories of New Mexico. Having perused a good many narratives touching on the Ring, and having given the matter serious thought, he had concluded that their common faults, and the source of his discomfort, were their per-sistent qualities of "vagueness" and "exaggeration."[13]

To address this criticism and elevate understanding of the phenomenon known as the Santa Fe Ring, historians and writers of nonfiction narratives can avoid referring to the Ring as a rational entity capable of thoughts and actions representing the diverse collection of individuals to whom member-ship has been imputed. Insofar as possible, they can attribute motive and action to individuals, rather than to an indeterminate body. They can itemize or at least give examples of allegations that may justify the use of adjectives like *notorious, infamous,* and *ruthless* in characterizations of the Ring. They can shun the conventional wisdom that depicts the Ring as a solid conspiracy of evildoers, and instead acknowledge the contradictory motives and deeds that animated those identified with the Ring. Historians can eschew the simpler conventions of the prevailing myth in favor of more complicated ambiguities that emerge from the historical record.

Meanwhile, there is work to be done in the direction suggested by Robert M. Utley: documenting the specific activities that can be fairly attributed to the much-discussed coalition of the territorial period, detailing, to the extent possible, its "membership, organization, techniques, and purposes." The present volume relies on documentary evidence and existing scholarship in western and social history, but also on newspaper rhetoric, unsubstantiated allegations, and hearsay. When one considers the burden of proof that prosecutors face in trying to substantiate even one charge of corruption or illegal activity comparable to those attributed to Ring figures, along with the fact that such accusations against members of the Elkins-Catron Santa Fe Ring represent the coldest of cases, the task of bringing the Ring into sharper focus is daunting.

Legend or Legacy?

Did the territorial experience with the Ring give rise to a culture of corruption? Can the Santa Fe Ring be blamed for twenty-first-century corruption, as its contemporary defenders once complained that the Ring was denounced as the cause of wind storms, crop failures, dust, bad water, and the low price of wool? Probably not, but studies of public corruption provide food for thought respecting a possible "western tradition" of malfeasance in government, perhaps derived from the governance traditions of multiple cultures, Gilded Age ideas of success and progress as adopted by fortune-seeking Euro-Americans, and a condition of protracted territorial status.

In a 2012 study of government transparency, accountability, and anticorruption policies, former western territories did not fare well. In a comparison of state policies, the bottom quartile included Utah, New Mexico, Idaho, Nevada, North Dakota, Wyoming, and South Dakota. These are the former homes of the reputed Santa Fe Ring, Boise Ring, Elko Gem Ring, Cheyenne

Ring, and Yankton Ring, and of Brigham Young, who is said by Howard Lamar to have functioned as "a one man 'Santa Fé Ring.'"[14] Of western states, only Washington, Nebraska, and Hawaii made the top half of states. Noting the less-than-stellar showing of sparsely peopled western states, an accompanying article suggests that libertarian ideas, a neighborly approach to governance, and the comforting sense that "everybody knows everybody" contribute to some public apathy regarding protections against official corruption.[15] Similar ideas, involving freedom from regulation and friendly and familiar relations with helpful public officials, were integral to the Ring's formula for success.

As to the influence of the Elkins-Catron Ring, surely it was profound in its day, but it can be exaggerated. Roxanne Dunbar-Ortiz is no fan of Catron, but in considering the history of land tenure in New Mexico, she declines to demonize him as many have done, noting, "Catron could not have turned his initial $10,000 into two million acres of land without the help of federal land policies."[16] Predating and supporting his remarkable feats of accumulation were early actions that led to the "capitalization" of land, reducing it to the status of a commodity in trade, which in turn accelerated the process by which New Mexicans who worked the land to support themselves and their families became landless. It would be a mistake, she tells readers, to let the exploits of a highly visible opportunist obscure the greater evil of public policy that invites self-serving manipulation of people, communities, and resources.

The end of the Elkins-Catron Ring did not write an end to the machinations of individuals and combinations in New Mexico, any more than did the passing of similar cabals rid other state governments of corruption. Nor was mischief confined to the Wild West. In addition to conditions fostering corruption that have already been mentioned—the political environment, cultural values, and public policy—there was another force at work: for lack of a better name, the impulse of self-seeking. An editor for the *Grant County Herald*, writing in September 1878, implied as much in remarks on frustrations with the reviled Santa Fe Ring. Musing on the possibility of a political plate shift, the writer asked, "Does anyone doubt that, in case the Democratic party were to triumph in the next national contest, a new set of cormorants would be foisted on our people, and that a new ring would be organized in Santa Fé? Does anyone believe that such a ring would hold the welfare of the people in higher esteem than the gratification of their own selfish ends?"[17]

In fact, there were other, mostly local circles of friendly business associates and political movers and shakers, but one such combination stood apart by virtue of its scope, its longevity, and its efficacy. Through most of the territorial period, this oligarchy of ambitious newcomers and native collaborators labored to harness the territory's resources and work the machinery of government to their own benefit, and in the context of their values, perhaps, to the benefit of the territory. "Known as the Santa Fé Ring," says Howard Lamar, "its members have been damned for their iniquities or grudgingly admired for their Machiavellian cleverness." For good or for ill, these men applied their energy and Machiavellian cleverness to the pursuit of prosperity and influence, attempting to impose Gilded Age notions of personal ambition and economic progress on diverse populations with profoundly varying world views.

The men of the Ring, those who opposed them, and those whose lives were impacted by their actions met in a vast land of contradictions—a borderland of deserts and mountains, and of extremes in climate and culture. Writing of New Mexico from the perspective of an outsider who came with low expectations but was enough enthralled to make it his home, the novelist Oliver La Farge observed, "It is primitive, underdeveloped, overused, new, raw, rich with tradition, old and mellow. It is a land full of the essence of peace, although its history is one of invasions and conflicts."[18] New Mexicans of the territorial period lived through intense economic and political conflicts in their time and region, and in doing so wrote one of the more interesting and vexing chapters in New Mexico's history.

APPENDIX A

Who Was in the Santa Fe Ring?

The following table displays a tabulation of persons identified in association with the Santa Fe Ring from a perusal of thirty sources, including contemporaneous and historical accounts. In few cases were the writers who named Ring members doing so in a comprehensive way. Those named were mentioned in the context of the writer's subject. The point of reference for some accounts is specific: an episode such as the Lincoln County War, for example, or a study of land grants.

Some of those named in source documents are identified as "members" or principals who initiated or participated in activities attributed to the Ring, and who may have hoped to benefit personally. Individuals are sometimes referred to as agents, operatives, allies, tools, functionaries, or friends of the Ring. The inclusion of names in this compilation involves some judgment, for which the author is responsible.

This compilation includes those most commonly named in association with the Santa Fe Ring, as well as some persons who are named only occasionally. It does not include every person who has been identified with the Ring in a newspaper, in correspondence, or by later historians.

Names of individuals presumed to have been part of the Santa Fe Ring are from the following sources. Full citations are in the bibliography. The numbers in this list refer to the heading numbers in the table.

1. Angel, Frank Warner. In Lee Scott Theisen, "Frank Warner Angel's Notes on New Mexico Territory, 1878" (1976). Also, Angel's *Report and Testimony in the Matter of Charges Against Samuel B. Axtell* (1878). Angel's brief comments are open to interpretation. The frequent mention of individuals as being "tools of" or "influenced by" Catron and Elkins in Angel's notes is indicative of their primacy in the Ring, as Angel had heard or read in the course of his investigation.
2. Ball, Larry D. *The United States Marshals of New Mexico and Arizona Territories, 1846–1912* (1978). Ball's study of law enforcers unearthed information on territorial

politics not seen elsewhere. He makes a good case for John Pratt, U.S. marshal from 1866 to 1876, as a member of the Ring.

3. Cleaveland, Norman. *The Morleys* (1971); *Colfax County's Chronic Murder Mystery* (1977); *Comments to Huntington Westerners* (1987); *Can New Mexico's Historians Improve Their Discipline?* (1982). Cleaveland's forebears opposed perceived Ring attempts to dominate Colfax County.

4. Corbet, Sam. Corbet to Tunstall, September 23, 1878, reproduced in Frederick Nolan, *The Lincoln County War* (1992). Corbet was an eyewitness to events of the Lincoln County War and a participant on the Tunstall-McSween side.

5. Dunham, Harold H. *Government Handout* (1941). As the title intimates, Dunham's is a mostly critical study of federal administration of public lands.

6. Ebright, Malcolm. *Land Grants and Lawsuits in Northern New Mexico* (1994). Ebright provides an overview of the origin and treatment of Spanish and Mexican land grants with case studies of several notable grants.

7. Gómez, Laura E. "Race, Colonialism, and Criminal Law: Mexicans and the American Criminal Justice System in Territorial New Mexico" (2000). Gómez focuses on the experience of Hispanos in New Mexico, including the impact of U.S. political and legal systems on their interests.

8. Kaye, E. Donald. *Nathan Augustus Monroe Dudley* (2007). This biography of a controversial figure examines his involvement in the Lincoln County War.

9. Keleher, William A. *The Fabulous Frontier* (1945). Keleher was an Albuquerque attorney who wrote extensively on the territorial period in New Mexico.

10. Lamar, Howard Roberts. *The Far Southwest, 1846–1912* (1966). This work includes arguably the most authoritative scholarly treatment of the Santa Fe Ring.

11. Larson, Robert W. *New Mexico's Quest for Statehood, 1846–1912* (1968); *New Mexico Populism* (1974); "Territorial Politics and Cultural Impact" (1985). Larson emphasizes the role of Ring figures in the struggle for statehood.

12. Lowry, Sharon K. "Mirrors and Blue Smoke: Stephen Dorsey and the Santa Fe Ring in the 1880s," *New Mexico Historical Review* (1984). This is an account of Dorsey's activities and relationships with the Elkins-Catron combination.

13. Meyer, Doris. *Speaking for Themselves* (1996). Meyer encounters the Ring in the course of her study of the Spanish-language press in New Mexico.

14. Montoya, María E. *Translating Property* (2002). Montoya considers Ring activity and impact in relation to the Maxwell land grant saga.

15. Newman, Simeon H., III. "The Santa Fe Ring: A Letter to the *New York Sun*," *Arizona and the West* (Autumn 1970). Newman contextualizes an exposé sent to the Sun by his grandfather, Simeon Harrison Newman.

16. Nieto-Phillips, John. *The Language of Blood* (2004). The author studies the evolution of Hispano identity in New Mexico under U.S. administration.

17. Nolan, Frederick. *The Lincoln County War: A Documentary History* (1992). This is probably the most comprehensive study of the Lincoln County War.

18. Otero, Miguel Antonio, II. *The Real Billy the Kid* (1936); *My Life on the Frontier*, vol. 2: *1882–1897* (1939). Otero's lifelong exposure to and involvement in New Mexico politics provide a wealth of remembered incidents and impressions.

19. Prince, L. Bradford, and W. B. Sloan. "Ithurial" letter to the *Las Vegas Optic*, July 31, 1884. Some of those named in this odd exposé lived in New Mexico only briefly and their connections with the Ring were tenuous.

20. Rasch, Philip J. "The People of the Territory of New Mexico vs. the Santa Fe Ring" (1972); *Gunsmoke in Lincoln County* (1997). Rasch researched and wrote extensively on the Lincoln County War and related subjects.

21. Roberts, Gary L. *Death Comes for the Chief Justice* (1990). Roberts's study is one of the few to focus on the formative period of the Ring, in the late 1860s.

22. Ross, Edmund G. Edmund G. Ross to John O'Grady, March 26, 1887, EGR/CSWR. Ross's experience as governor provides the context for this highly opinionated analysis of the Ring and its methods.

23. Springer, Frank. Deposition of Frank Springer, in Angel, *Report and Testimony in the Matter of Charges Against Samuel B. Axtell*. Springer was an enemy of the Santa Fe Ring in Colfax County and Maxwell land-grant affairs. His testimony likely contributed to the removal or resignation of several officials.

24. Stratton, Porter A. *The Territorial Press of New Mexico, 1834–1912* (1969). This study of the territorial press includes discussion of editors with Ring connections.

25. Tapia y Anaya, Santiago. "The Great Land Robbery," in *Poverty, Equal Opportunity, and Full Employment* (1975). The author was testifying before Congress on land grants as president of the Alianza Federal de Mercedes.

26. Taylor, Morris F. *O. P. McMains and the Maxwell Land Grant Conflict* (1979); "Stephen W. Dorsey: Speculator-Cattleman" (1974). The context for Taylor's observations is the Maxwell land-grant controversy.

27. Twitchell, Ralph Emerson. *Old Santa Fe: The Story of New Mexico's Ancient Capital* (1925). Twitchell was a long time mentioning the Santa Fe Ring in his extensive historical writings. When he did, he handled the subject gingerly, frequently using a more benign term, "Santa Fe group."

28. Wallace, Lew. Wallace to A. H. Markland, November 14, 1878; Wallace to Carl Schurz, February 16, 1880, Lew Wallace Collection, Indiana Historical Society. Wallace was well acquainted with the combination that seemed to thwart his every attempt to reform territorial politics and administration.

29. Wallis, Michael. *Billy the Kid: The Endless Ride* (2007). Wallis provides a general survey of the Lincoln County War, including alliances of local merchants and officials with Samuel Axtell, Thomas B. Catron, and other reputed Ring figures.

30. Westphall, Victor. *The Public Domain in New Mexico, 1854–1891* (1965). Westphall speaks more freely of the Ring in this book than elsewhere in his writings.

WHO WAS IN THE SANTA FE RING?
Men Named in Association with the Ring as Compiled from Selected Sources

Name	1	2	3	4	5	6	7	8	9	10	11	12	13	14	15	16	17	18	19	20	21	22	23	24	25	26	27	28	29	30	Total
Abeytia, Aniceto																		•													1
Alarid, Trinidad																			•												1
Atkinson, Henry M.		•	•			•													•								•			•	6
Axtell, Samuel B.	•	•	•	•		•	•			•	•			•	•			•	•										•		12
Bailhache, W. H.																		•	•					•							2
Barela, Mariano	•																														1
Bartlett, Edward L.																			•												1
Bernstein, Morris J.																				•											1
Brady, William																	•		•	•											3
Breeden, Marshall A.							•												•												2
Breeden, William		•	•				•			•					•				•		•		•			•	•	•			11
Bristol, Warren				•				•																							2
Burns, Thomas D.																									•						1
Catron, Charles						•																									1
Catron, Thomas B.	•	•	•	•	•	•	•	•	•	•	•	•	•	•	•	•	•	•	•	•	•	•	•	•	•	•	•	•	•	•	30
Chaffee, Jerome B.														•																	1
Chaves, J. Francisco	•										•										•			•							4
Dolan, James J.	•	•						•									•	•		•					•						7
Dorsey, Stephen W.												•														•		•		•	4
Dudley, Nathan A. M.																				•											1
Elkins, John	•																														1
Elkins, Stephen B.	•	•	•			•				•	•	•			•				•	•	•	•	•		•	•	•	•	•	•	24
Fisher, Silas W.																				•											1
Fritz, Emil										•	•																				2
Frost, Max										•	•								•			•		•			•		•		7
Giddings, Marsh		•																													1
Gildersleeve, Charles H.											•	•							•								•				4
Godfroy, Frederick			•																												1
Griffin, William					•													•	•												4
Hayward, C. B.													•																		1
Joseph, Antonio						•				•		•							•					•		•					6
Kinney, John													•																		1
Longwill, Robert	•	•	•			•			•		•			•					•	•			•			•	•			•	12
Luna, Tranquilino																								•							1

Name	Count
McMillan, Alonzo B.	1
Mills, Melvin	5
Morrison, A. L.	1
Murphy, Lawrence G.	7
Ortiz y Salazar, Antonio	2
Otero, Mariano S.	3
Otero, Don Miguel A.	1
Palen, Joseph G.	8
Perea, Pedro	2
Phillips, C. M.	1
Pile, William	3
Pratt, John	1
Prince, L. Bradford	9
Proudfit, James K.	3
Read, Benjamin M.	1
Renehan, Alois B.	1
Riley, John H.	5
Ritch, William G.	3
Rosenthal, William	1
Rynerson, William L.	9
Sánchez, Pedro	3
Sheldon, Lionel	3
Sherman, John T.	1
Spencer, T. Rush	3
Spiegelberg, Lehman	2
Spiegelberg, Levi	1
Springer, Frank	2
Staab, Abraham	4
Thornton, William T.	3
Tucker, Thomas S.	4
Twitchell, R. E.	2
Waldo, Henry M.	10
Watts, John S.	1

APPENDIX B

Profiles of Alleged Ring Participants

The following profiles provide vital facts and a brief indication of the rationale for a person's having been identified as being a part of, or closely associated with, the Santa Fe Ring. This summary of core, secondary, and peripheral or doubtful participants includes persons named by the thirty sources cited in appendix A. Additional names may be found in other sources, but this list includes all of those who are mentioned generally or frequently, and others whose credentials for Ring designation are slight.

Core Participants

These men were associated with others in the group over an extended period, mainly during the most active phase of Ring activity, 1872–1884.

Henry Martyn Atkinson (b. 1838 VA; to NM 1876; d. 1886 NM). Republican. As surveyor general (1876–1884) Atkinson was involved with Thomas Benton Catron in the Anton Chico grant and the American Valley Company. Both affairs attracted allegations that he was using his office for personal gain. In the 1882–1885 Department of the Interior investigation of land fraud in New Mexico, Atkinson was accused of knowingly dealing in fraudulent homestead entries; his death in 1886 may have precluded likely legal sanctions. Frank Warner Angel, in notes prepared for Governor Lew Wallace, described him as "Honest and very reliable—only official who courted investigation."

Samuel Beach Axtell (b. 1819 OH; to NM 1875; d. 1891 NJ). Republican. As governor (1875–1878) Axtell walked into political turmoil in Colfax and Lincoln counties and was judged by investigator Frank Warner Angel to have aggravated both situations as a result of his partisan alignment with Catron and other presumed Ring members. As chief justice (1882–1885) he was again criticized for partisanship in the execution of his judicial duties. Axtell served a brief term as chairman of the territorial Republican Central Committee before his death in 1891.

William Breeden (b. 1841 KY; to NM 1864; d. 1913 MA). Republican. Breeden organized the New Mexico Republican Party in 1868 and was its Central Committee chair almost continuously until 1884. Critics styled Breeden the "newspaper apologist for the Ring" for his aggressive defense of political allies who were accused of Ring activity. Breeden held the territorial office of attorney general (1872–1878 and 1882–1889), and successfully resisted the efforts of two reform governors, Lew Wallace and Edmund G. Ross, to deny him the office.

Thomas Benton Catron (b. 1840 MO; to NM 1866; d. 1921 NM). Republican. Catron was active in land-grant speculation, mining, cattle raising, banking, and other ventures, and was widely regarded as the leader of the Santa Fe Ring after Stephen Elkins left the territory. Catron was accused of abuse of his office as U.S. attorney. He was accused of inciting political violence on several occasions, but some charges were proven baseless and none resulted in an indictment. Catron's involvement in affairs of the Maxwell land grant and the American Valley Company, and with the Tierra Amarilla, Mora, and Anton Chico grants drew various accusations and criticisms.

José Francisco Chaves (b. 1833 NM; d. 1904 NM). Republican. Chaves was a longtime Republican party boss in Valencia County and a longtime leader in the territorial legislature, helping pass legislation favored by presumed Ring colleagues. Chaves was accused of manipulating vote counts in Valencia County. He was a leader in the 1884 revolt of dissident Republicans against Catron, Breeden, and the traditional party leadership, but he reconciled with the Catron faction and was a strong ally until his assassination by unknown parties in 1904.

Stephen Benton Elkins (b. 1841 OH; to NM 1863; d. 1911 WV). Republican. Elkins was widely recognized as the original leader of the combination that he and Catron dominated. He was involved in land speculation and mining, and was president of the First National Bank of Santa Fe (1871–1884). Relocated in the eastern United States by 1877, he was a power in the Republican Party and in Washington, serving as secretary of war and as United States senator from West Virginia, and providing political support to New Mexico friends. Elkins married into a powerful West Virginia family, and built and led a strong political coalition in that state. Charges of corruption dogged Elkins throughout his political career but never resulted in legal sanctions.

Maximilian Eugene Frost (b. 1852 LA; to NM 1876; d. 1909 NM). Republican. Frost exercised editorial control over the *Santa Fe New Mexican* from 1883 until his death in 1909 and supported Republican causes and candidates. As U.S. land register (1881–1886) he was charged with fraud and official misconduct. He was convicted on some counts, but the conviction was overturned on appeal. Frost was represented in the matter by Henry L. Waldo. Letters in Frost's support signed by numerous Ring figures were included in the Department of the Interior report issued in 1885.

William W. Griffin (b. 1830 VA; to NM 1860; d. 1889 NM). Republican. Early in his career, Griffin worked as a U.S. deputy surveyor under contract with the surveyor general. At least two surveys, of the Cañon del Agua grant and the Maxwell grant, were criticized because they appeared to deliberately favor speculators. Perhaps growing out of his work on the Maxwell survey, Griffin was named cashier for the First National Bank of Santa Fe and was its president from 1884 to 1889. He served as chairman of the Republican Central Committee from 1887 to 1889. Frank W. Angel described Griffin as "reliable and honest," though influenced by Stephen Elkins.

Robert Hamilton Longwill (b. 1840 VA; to NM 1867; d. 1895 PA). Republican. In the 1870s, Longwill was recognized by some as the Ring's agent in Colfax County. While probate judge, he was suspected of arranging the death of Reverend F. J. Tolby in 1875, an event that led to an outbreak of violence and inspired local resistance to the Ring. W. R. Morley later inferred that Longwill may have engaged in other acts of political violence. Relocated in Santa Fe, Longwill was part of the Republican inner circle and was a director of the First National Bank of Santa Fe.

Melvin Whitson Mills (b. 1845 Canada; to NM ca. 1868; d. 1925 NM). Republican. Mills, an attorney in Colfax County, was also suspected of involvement in the Tolby assassination. He was arrested and examined, but was not brought to trial. In 1876, he acted as agent for Catron in purchasing the Maxwell land grant at a foreclosure sale. The claim was conveyed to Catron, but the company regained ownership. Mills was elected to the territorial assembly in 1873 and 1875, representing Colfax County. He was an organizer for Catron and the Republican Party in Colfax County and was still a political confidant when Catron sought a seat in the United States Senate in 1912.

Joseph G. Palen (b. 1812 NY; to NM 1869; d. 1875 NM). Republican. Palen was named chief justice for New Mexico by President Grant in 1869 and served until his death in December 1875. His performance won him both admirers and detractors. He was accused of colluding with Catron and Elkins, deciding cases in their favor for mutual benefit. Some Colfax County citizens regarded Palen as a "Ring judge." Enemies tried but failed to have Palen moved to the southern judicial district. While in New Mexico, he was a member of the National Republican Committee.

LeBaron Bradford Prince (b. 1840 NY; to NM 1879; d. 1922 NY). Republican. Prince was named chief justice of the territorial supreme court in 1878 and was perceived by some as a Ring-friendly judge. He was appointed governor during the Benjamin Harrison administration, serving from 1889 to 1893. Prince was a persistent advocate of statehood. In later years he posed as a critic and opponent of the Ring.

William Logan Rynerson (b. 1828 KY; to NM 1862; d. 1893 NM). Republican. Rynerson was thought by some to have benefited from political intervention to secure acquittal when he was accused of murdering Chief Justice John Slough in 1867. As district attorney for the Third Judicial District, he was accused of partisanship on behalf of the Murphy-Dolan-Riley faction in Lincoln County. At the urging of southern New Mexico Republicans who resented Santa Fe's domination of territorial affairs, Rynerson ran unsuccessfully for delegate in 1884. With T. B. Catron and John Riley, he engaged in stock raising in Lincoln County in the 1880s.

Henry Ludlow Waldo (b. 1844 MO; to NM 1873; d. 1915 MO). Democrat. Waldo was a boyhood friend of Stephen Elkins in Missouri and got on well with Elkins and Catron. He held the office of chief justice (1876–1878) and served as attorney general (1878–1880). Waldo was a law partner of William Breeden (1879–1883) and then became chief solicitor for the AT&SF Railway in New Mexico. Waldo was a Democrat, but sided with Republicans on matters of mutual interest. Associations with Elkins and Catron likely caused others to consider Waldo a Ring member, but political involvements with them were infrequent after 1883.

Secondary Participants

These individuals were involved in affairs attributed to the Ring on a limited or inconsistent basis, sometimes in the context of a specific episode or activity.

Edward Leland Bartlett (b. 1847 ME; to NM 1880; d. 1904 NM). Republican. Bartlett was solicitor general from 1889 to 1895 and 1897 to 1904. He was chairman of the territorial Republican Central Committee from 1894 to 1895. Bartlett was named as a Ring member in a letter that reportedly was inspired by L. Bradford Prince, published in the *Las Vegas Daily Optic* of July 31, 1884. From its inception until his death, Bartlett was secretary of the New Mexico Bar Association, a group that reportedly screened legislation on behalf of the Ring during the Ross administration.

William Brady (b. 1829 Ireland; to NM 1862; d. 1878 NM). Democrat. Association with fellow Irishmen L. G. Murphy, James Dolan, and John Riley in Lincoln County helps explain Brady's supposed affiliation with the Santa Fe Ring. His attachment of the property of Alexander McSween and John Tunstall pursuant to a court order targeting McSween was judged illegal by some. Said Robert Utley, Brady "had a commitment to the public welfare that set him apart from most of his associates." He was killed in Lincoln by allies of Tunstall and McSween.

Marshall A. Breeden (b. 1848 KY; to NM 1872; d. 1916 CA). Republican. "Major" Breeden followed his brother, William Breeden, to New Mexico and was appointed postmaster, a position he held from 1873 to 1884. A later appointment to the office of assistant attorney general was explained by the *Las Vegas Optic* in July 1884. According to the *Optic*, the appointment was made "so that the Major could resign the post office in favor of Mr. Hayward, another of the ring!" Frank Warner Angel termed Breeden a "weak ring man." Relocated in Utah, he served two terms as attorney general.

Warren Henry Bristol (b. 1823 NY; to NM 1872; d. 1890 NM). Republican. Bristol earned his Ring designation largely in connection with judicial decisions rendered in the course of the Lincoln County War, including the trial of William Bonney for murder. In instructions to the jury and other actions, Bristol appeared to demonstrate prejudice in favor of the Dolan-Riley side and against Alexander McSween. Bristol was a polarizing figure in his tenure on the bench in southern New Mexico, earning accolades from some citizens and contempt from others. In his notes for Lew Wallace, Angel judged Bristol "honest and reliable outside of Lincoln troubles."

Thomas D. Burns (b. 1844 Ireland; to NM ca. 1866; d. 1916 NM). Republican. Burns settled in Rio Arriba County in about 1866 and was a merchant and sheep raiser. He was an early buyer of claims on the Tierra Amarilla grant and was involved with Catron in business. He was a Republican organizer in Rio Arriba County and worked with Catron to mobilize voters for territorial elections, but he sometimes opposed Catron in politics. Burns served several terms in the legislature and was a member of the New Mexico Republican Central Committee.

James Joseph Dolan (b. 1848 Ireland; to NM 1869; d. 1898 NM). Democrat. A partner with L. G. Murphy and John Riley in Lincoln, Dolan was involved in supply of goods to the Mescalero Apache Indian Agency and Fort Stanton. The firm was accused of irregularities in relations with the fort and Indian agency. The men allegedly were allied with the Ring and Catron, who aided them in a dispute with John Tunstall and Alexander McSween, arranging a dubious arrest of McSween in Las Vegas. Accused of murdering Huston Chapman in 1879, Dolan was represented by Catron and W. T. Thornton, who were able to secure a dismissal of the charges. Dolan was later involved in ranching ventures with Catron and William L. Rynerson.

Stephen W. Dorsey (b. 1842 VT; to NM 1876; d. 1916 CA). Republican. As a senator from Arkansas, Dorsey was indicted in the Star Route mail fraud scandal. He later went to New Mexico and looked into acquiring the Uña de Gato grant, but the grant was exposed as a fraud. Dorsey was later accused of benefiting from illegal entries on the public domain and engaging in illegal fencing on public lands. He was a sometime political ally and confidant of Catron, but did not hold a significant elective or appointive office in New Mexico.

Marsh Giddings (b. 1816 CT; to NM 1871; d. 1875 NM). Republican. According to Howard Lamar, Giddings was a weak governor, described by the *Borderer* of

Las Cruces as a tool of Elkins. Giddings sided with presumed Ring interests in 1872, vetoing a bill that would have transferred Chief Justice Palen from the First Judicial District to the Third at the behest of Ring opponents. At about the same time, Giddings came to Catron's aid, rejecting accusations that Catron had sought to buy legislative votes and was unfit to hold public office.

Charles H. Gildersleeve (b. 1848 NM; to NM ca. 1876; d. 1909 NY). Democrat. An early law partner of Catron, Gildersleeve engaged in transactions with Catron and others concerning the Anton Chico, San Cristóbal, and other grants, prompting Surveyor General Julian to declare party labels meaningless for men like Catron and Gildersleeve. In a July 1887 article in the *North American Review*, Julian wrote, "They have a diversity of gifts, but the same spirit. They are politicians 'for revenue only,' and have a formidable following." Gildersleeve helped the Ring defeat reforms proposed by Democratic governor Ross.

Antonio Joseph (b. 1846 NM; d. 1910 NM). Democrat. Along with many Republicans associated with the Ring, Joseph was interested in land speculation, but his purchases of tracts in the Taos Pueblo grant, in apparent violation of federal law, brought him into conflict with U.S. Attorney Catron in 1873. The two were often at political loggerheads thereafter. Although a Democrat, he was not an enthusiastic supporter of Governor Edmund G. Ross. In 1892 Joseph defeated Catron for territorial delegate, but Catron prevailed in 1894, ending Joseph's ten-year tenure. Joseph was not an early supporter of statehood, but efforts in his last three terms brought the territory closer to admission.

William Henry Manderfield (b. 1841 PA; to NM 1863; d. 1888 NM). Republican. According to Porter A. Stratton, Manderfield came to the territory as a "practical printer," but adapted to the politically charged environment of the capital, editing and publishing the *Santa Fe New Mexican* with his partner, Thomas Tucker. Manderfield and Tucker became associated with the Ring, supporting its men and positions through the *New Mexican*. Alignment with the Ring was also beneficial in business, providing access to highly valued government printing contracts.

Alexander L. Morrison Sr. (b. 1831 Ireland; to NM 1881; d. 1917 AZ). Republican. Morrison was a strong Republican with influential connections, including Senator John A. Logan of Illinois and presidents Garfield, Arthur, and McKinley. Morrison was appointed U.S. marshal for New Mexico by Arthur in 1882 and served until replaced by a Democrat following the election of Grover Cleveland in 1884. He was appointed collector of internal revenue during the administration of President McKinley. With Max Frost, Ralph Emerson Twitchell, and others, Morrison worked to animate the party machinery and elect Republican candidates in the 1890s.

Lawrence Gustave Murphy (b. 1831 Ireland; to NM 1861; d. 1878 NM). Democrat. With Dolan and Riley, Murphy has been considered an ally of the Ring in Lincoln County, doing business with Catron and the First National Bank of Santa Fe, and relying on territorial and federal officials for support. As de facto post trader at Fort Stanton and Indian agent for the Mescaleros, Murphy clashed with army officers and was banished from the fort in 1873. As explained by Frederick Nolan, Murphy was accused of dishonesty in his handling of business transactions with the Mescalero agency.

Antonio Ortiz y Salazar (b. 1830 NM; d. 1907 NM). Republican. Ortiz y Salazar was a longtime member of the Catron-led faction of Republicans and a partner in business ventures with Ring figures. He held the offices of probate clerk, county commissioner, probate judge, and sheriff, and was several times elected to the territorial assembly. He held the appointive position of territorial treasurer for New Mexico for a total of eighteen years. Ortiz y Salazar was accused by the *Albuquerque Democrat* of using the office to serve the interests of the Santa Fe Ring.

Pedro José Aniceto Perea (b. 1852 NM; d. 1906 NM). Republican. A native of the community of Bernalillo, Perea was a Catron political organizer in Bernalillo County prior to the creation of Sandoval County. He was one of a succession of presidents of the First National Bank of Santa Fe reputed to have a Ring connection. Perea was a council member in 1889, 1891, and 1895, and served as territorial delegate from 1899 to 1901.

William Anderson Pile (b. 1829 IN; to NM 1869; d. 1889 CA). Republican. Pile was governor of New Mexico from 1869 to 1871, and an original director of the Maxwell Land Grant and Railway Company. His inclusion was meant to add prestige to the board and to advance the plans of presumed Ring members including Elkins and Catron. Pile joined Joseph Palen, Elkins, and

Catron as incorporators of William J. Palmer's Rio Grande Railroad and Telegraph Company in 1870, for which Howard Roberts Lamar labeled him a "restless seconder of grand schemes."

John Pratt (b. 1840 MA; to NM ca. 1866; d. 1902 NY). Republican. Larry D. Ball (1978) may be the only historian to name Pratt as a Ring member, but he makes a strong case. As U.S. marshal in New Mexico (1866-1882) Pratt formed a close relationship with S. B. Elkins and joined him on the boards of the Maxwell Land Grant and Railway Company and the First National Bank of Santa Fe. His identification with the Ring was reinforced by his actions in the Colfax County War, including protection of Robert Longwill when Longwill stood accused in the Tolby murder.

James Kerr Proudfit (b. 1832 NY; to NM 1872; d. 1917 MO). Republican. Proudfit, who served as surveyor general for New Mexico from 1872 to 1876, was characterized by Malcolm Ebright as a "blatant speculator." Victor Westphall notes that Proudfit tended to favor large grants over smaller claims in priority for confirmation. He maintained close relations with presumed Ring members, joining with Elkins, Governor Marsh Giddings, Catron, and William Griffin to form the Consolidated Land, Cattle Raising and Wool Growing Company just three weeks after taking office.

John Henry Riley (b. 1850 Ireland; to NM 1874; d. 1916 CO). Republican. A partner with Murphy and Dolan, Riley was involved in affairs of the Lincoln County War, including collaboration with friendly Ring contacts. He unintentionally leaked documents concerning local Ring alliances: a strident letter from District Attorney Rynerson urging a hard line against the McSween faction and a notebook giving code names for Catron and other key figures. A young Riley reportedly shot Juan Patron after a heated row and engaged in deception in selling cattle to the Indian agency. After the turmoil ended, he had ranching interests with Catron and Rynerson.

William Gillet Ritch (b. 1830 NY; to NM 1873; d. 1904 NM). Republican. Ritch served as territorial secretary from 1873 to 1884. He held office at the pleasure of Republican presidents and was predictably partisan in support of territorial officials. When push came to shove, as it did in organizing the legislature in 1884, he could shove with the best, helping a "regular council" of Catron allies maintain dominance while repelling the efforts of a dissident "rump council." Ritch supported presumed Ring men, writing letters or articles on behalf of those who came under fire.

William Rosenthal (date and place of birth unknown; to NM ca. 1867; d. 1880 NM). Party affiliation unknown. Rosenthal was, at various times, an army quartermaster, a deputy U.S. marshal, and an assistant revenue collector. His link with the Ring was as a beef contractor supplying to forts and Indian agencies. According to Frederick Nolan, he was "a paid-up member of the Santa Fe Ring." In concert with Dolan, Riley, and Rynerson, Rosenthal sold beef to the Mescalero agency. In Lincoln County, his interests aligned with those of Catron and the Ring—and against John Chisum, a competing beef supplier. He was an early stockholder in the Maxwell Land Grant and Railway Company, along with other named Ring figures.

Pedro Sánchez (b. 1831 NM; d. 1904 NM). Republican. Sánchez was a reliable Catron ally in Taos County. When Colfax and Taos counties were joined for judicial purposes in 1876, Sánchez was said to control the selection of jurors, ensuring favorable verdicts for the Ring. He was a reliable vote in the legislature and a party organizer in Taos. Sánchez was Indian agent for the Pueblo people in Santa Fe from 1880 to 1884. When the Department of the Interior examined land-fraud charges in the mid-1880s, Sánchez was accused in relation to illegal homestead entries, but was not convicted.

Lionel Allen Sheldon (b. 1831 NY; to NM 1881; d. 1917 CA). Republican. A former congressman representing Louisiana, Sheldon was a friend of President James A. Garfield when appointed governor in 1881. For the Ring, Sheldon was a relief from the tenure of the Democrat Edmund G. Ross. By his own account, Sheldon accomplished much, putting down Indian unrest, imprisoning or running off outlaws, improving medical practice, and instituting a public-school law. Howard R. Lamar remarked that Sheldon "found that the territory ran itself and willingly let a member of the Ring, Attorney General Breeden, virtually assume all gubernatorial duties."

Thomas Rush Spencer (b. 1818 NY; to NM 1869; d. 1872 NM). Republican. Spencer, a physician, was surveyor general for New Mexico from 1869 until his death in 1872. With Governor William Pile and former chief justice John Watts, he fronted for English buyers organizing the Maxwell Land Grant and Railway Company. He was criticized for approving the suspect Griffin survey of the Maxwell land grant. In his brief tenure, Spencer quickened the pace of reviews for confirmation, but according to Victor Westphall, he favored the claims of speculators over those of residents claiming smaller parcels. He was a partner in the Mora grant with Catron and Elkins.

Lehman Spiegelberg (b. 1842 Germany; to NM 1857; d. 1904 NY). Republican. The "Spiegelberg Brothers" are sometimes named in connection with the Ring. Lehman Spiegelberg had the most extensive involvements in New Mexico among the brothers, including association with alleged Ring men in the Santa Fe and Denver Railroad Company, the Santa Fe Gas Company, and other ventures. The family business involved mercantile, banking, mining, and contracting enterprises. Lehman's brother Levi Spiegelberg left New Mexico after the Civil War, serving the firm in New York until 1884. It is doubtful that he had any substantial involvement with the Ring.

Abraham Staab (b. 1839 Germany; to NM 1857; d. 1913 NM). Republican. Abraham and Zadoc Staab carried on a mercantile business in Santa Fe beginning in 1858. Zadoc Staab died in 1884, but his brother was involved in a diverse array of business pursuits in Santa Fe for the rest of his life. These included ill-advised speculation in military warrants and investments in land with Catron and Elkins. Staab was vice president of the Santa Fe Progress and Improvement Company, in association with Charles Gildersleeve, Lehman Spiegelberg, William Manderfield, and Catron. The Staabs were enthusiastic contractors to Indian agencies and military posts.

William Taylor Thornton (b. 1843 MO; to NM 1877; d. 1916 NM). Democrat. Thornton was from the same west-central Missouri region as Catron, Elkins, and Waldo, and was Catron's law partner from 1877 to 1883. He represented Catron's interests in Lincoln County in the early stages of the violence there. During Thornton's tenure as governor, he and Catron had a heated falling-out from which the relationship never recovered. He was associated with alleged Ring members including Catron, William Griffin, Henry Atkinson, L. Bradford Prince, William Manderfield, Henry Waldo, and William Breeden in mining and other business ventures.

Thomas Sheridan Tucker (b. 1837 PA; to NM 1861; d. 1886 NM). Republican. Tucker served as adjutant general for the Territory of New Mexico (1873–1880) but his connection with the Ring is attributable to his involvement as longtime copublisher and editor of the *Santa Fe New Mexican*, along with his partner, William Manderfield. Manderfield started earlier with the paper and stayed a few months longer, but the familiar "Manderfield and Tucker" editorial credit line appeared at the top of the paper from 1864 until 1880.

Peripheral or Doubtful Participants

Numerous individuals, including some not named by any of the thirty sources summarized in appendix A, have been mentioned by just one or two observers, usually on the basis of a brief association, an isolated incident, or a limited role. Only those cited in appendix A are profiled here.

Aniceto Abeytia (b. 1856 NM; d. 1930 NM). Republican. In Las Vegas, from 1885 to 1896, Abeytia was school superintendent and tax assessor. In Socorro, from 1896 to 1930, he served as mayor, as a regent for the New Mexico School of Mines, and in the New Mexico state senate. Miguel Otero II wrote in his autobiography that Abeytia was "notoriously a *Catronista* and a servant of the 'Santa Fe Ring.'" As a juror, Abeytia reportedly had initially voted to convict Otero in the occupation of the Nuestra Señora de los Dolores mine, but he joined in the verdict of acquittal.

Trinidad Alarid (b. 1841 NM; d. 1919 NM). Republican. Alarid was territorial auditor from 1872 to 1891 and was influential in the 1884 legislative effort to secure funds for a new capitol at Santa Fe. He was named a Ring member in the "Ithurial" letter attributed to L. Bradford Prince and W. B. Sloan, published in the *Las Vegas Optic* of July 31, 1884. A charge that Alarid and Catron tried to bribe the clerk of the Chaves council in the 1884 legislative session was unsubstantiated and largely discredited, but may have prompted Alarid's designation as a Ring member.

William Henry Bailhache (b. 1827 OH; to NM 1881; d. 1905 CA). Republican. In 1881, Bailhache moved to New Mexico and took charge of the *Albuquerque Daily Journal*. He was appointed receiver in the land office at Santa Fe, working with Max Frost, with whom he also published the *Santa Fe New Mexican Review* for a time. Bailhache was subject to scrutiny in the 1882–1885 investigation of land fraud in New Mexico, but was not convicted. By 1886, he had departed for California.

Mariano Barela (b. 1844 NM; d. 1892 NM). Democrat, later Republican. Barela was a Doña Ana County commissioner and receiver in the land office at Las Cruces. He was sheriff of Doña Ana County for fifteen years. In notes for Lew Wallace, Frank Warner Angel called Barela a "ring tool." According to Larry D. Ball (1982), Barela, while a deputy marshal, purchased jury and witness vouchers at a discount, for redemption at full value. He used the certificates as surety when borrowing money with Catron's help, possibly incurring both political and financial debts.

Morris J. Bernstein (b. 1856 England; to NM 1873; d. 1878 NM). Party affiliation unknown. Bernstein was clerk at the Mescalero Apache Indian Agency under supervision of the agent, Frederick Godfroy. He had formerly kept books for the Spiegelberg brothers in Santa Fe. According to Frederick Nolan, Bernstein's allegiances in Lincoln County were not entirely clear. Philip Rasch, however, names Bernstein as a Ring member on the basis of his association with the Dolan-Riley faction and his affiliation with other alleged Ring members in the Masonic Lodge.

Charles Christopher Catron (b. 1879 CT; to NM 1879; d. 1951 NM). Republican. Charles Catron joined his father in law practice in 1904. He was involved in adjudication of claims to common lands of the Las Trampas grant. In the view of Malcolm Ebright, he failed to properly represent his clients and contributed to an injustice suffered by descendants of original settlers of the Las Trampas grant. A House member in the first state legislature, Charles helped bring about his father's election as United States senator. Charles arrived too late to be part of the Ring's heyday, and he did not inherit his father's role as land baron and political boss.

Jerome Bunty Chaffee (b. 1825 NY; d. 1886 NY). Republican. A Colorado speculator, businessman, and political figure, Chaffee was not a New Mexico resident, but orchestrated the purchase and sale of the Maxwell land grant in 1870. As a territorial delegate to Congress and a United States senator, he was a reliable political ally for Stephen B. Elkins, with whom he acquired the New Mexico Mining Company in 1878. María E. Montoya names Chaffee as member of the Santa Fe Ring. Others have acknowledged his ties to the Ring through business relationships and political alliances in Congress.

Nathan Augustus Monroe Dudley (b. 1825 MA; to NM 1876; d. 1910 MA). Party affiliation unknown. As post commander at Fort Stanton during the Lincoln County War, Dudley appeared to favor the Dolan-Riley faction. His permissive use of military force helped their cause, notably in the assault and burning of Alexander McSween's home and the killing of McSween. Dudley's credentials as a Ring man are otherwise doubtful. A relationship with Catron had soured, and he had no lasting political or financial stake in the territory. When his career ended, he retired to Massachusetts.

John T. Elkins (b. 1843 OH; to NM ca. 1875; d. 1886 CO). Republican. Stephen Elkins's brother lived a few years in New Mexico before locating in Colorado, where he was involved in mining and was elected a state senator. As a deputy surveyor, he and Robert Marmon contracted with Surveyor General Atkinson to survey land claims, including large grants. They surveyed the Maxwell grant, in which Stephen Elkins was interested, and the Anton Chico grant, which Henry Atkinson was angling to purchase. To detractors it appeared that the surveys were "made to order" for the benefit of alleged Ring members. A third brother, Samuel Elkins, lived in New Mexico for a time and was involved in mining ventures.

Silas W. Fisher (b. 1824 PA; to NM 1883; d. 1897 WA). Republican. Fisher was briefly a resident of Santa Fe, serving as collector of internal revenue for New Mexico and Arizona. The *Las Vegas Optic* criticized him for the hiring of a deputy revenue collector in Las Vegas. The *Santa Fe New Mexican* defended Fisher, explaining that the official referred to was not a regular employee, but someone appointed locally to serve the needs of local merchants. This may have been Fisher's only stumble into territorial politics, and it hardly merits a place in the Ring, though he was named in the 1884 "Ithurial" letter, for which L. Bradford Prince supposedly furnished identities of Ring participants.

Emil Christian Adolf Fritz (b. 1832 Germany; to NM 1861; d. 1874 Germany). Democrat. Fritz arrived in New Mexico in 1861 as captain of a cavalry unit with Carleton's California Column. He settled in New Mexico and went into business with Lawrence G. Murphy, bidding on federal supply contracts in southern New Mexico. Fritz died in June 1874, before the rival Tunstall-McSween and Murphy-Dolan-Riley factions had formed.

Frederick Charles Godfroy (b. 1827 MI; to NM 1876; d. 1885 NY). Party affiliation unknown. Godfroy's work as Indian agent at the Mescalero agency (1876–1878) was the subject of an inquiry conducted by Frank Warner Angel in 1878. It was alleged that Godfroy permitted agents of Dolan and Riley to take goods from the agency to be sold at their store in Lincoln and to replace the goods with inferior stock or none at all. Godfroy is also said to have authorized payments to contractors based on inaccurate counts of inhabitants fed and supplied. Godfroy was dismissed on the basis of Angel's report.

Charles Bingley Hayward (b. 1843 IN; to NM 1883; d. 1919 IL). Republican. Hayward was a printer and newspaperman who moved to Santa Fe in 1883 and edited the *Santa Fe New Mexican Review* until 1886. Illinois Senator John A. Logan may have helped secure Hayward's appointment as postmaster at Santa Fe in 1884, but the change to a Democratic administration caused his resignation in 1886, and he returned to Illinois. Hayward's mention as a Ring member in the "Ithurial" letter of L. Bradford Prince and W. B. Sloan is scant evidence of a Ring affiliation.

John Kinney (b. 1853 MA; to NM ca. 1873; d. 1919 AZ). Party affiliation unknown. Kinney entered the cattle business after the Civil War, but much of his business was extralegal. Established in southern New Mexico, says Frederick Nolan, he built "arguably the largest horse- and cattle-rustling operation in the Territory." During the Lincoln County War, Kinney led a band of ruffians known as "the boys," who served the Murphy-Dolan-Riley faction and were responsible for several violent deaths resulting from the conflict.

Tranquilino Luna (b. 1847 NM; d. 1892 NM). Republican. Luna was born to a landed sheep-raising family in Valencia County. He won election as New Mexico's territorial delegate to Congress in 1880. When Luna sought reelection in 1882, according to Porter Stratton, "Only with unfair methods were Ring members able to get the nomination for Luna" over his opponent, L. Bradford Prince. Luna initially won reelection, but the vote was contested on grounds of fraud, and in March 1884, the seat was awarded to Francisco Manzanares.

Jacob Basil Mathews (b. 1847 TN; to NM 1867; d. 1904 NM). Republican. J. B. "Billy" Mathews was a business partner of James Dolan in Lincoln

County and a strong ally in affairs of the Lincoln County War. As chief deputy sheriff for Lincoln County, Mathews was in charge of the posse whose execution of a writ of attachment precipitated the violent death of John Tunstall. He continued in occasional business associations with Dolan into the 1880s and 1890s, and had at least limited financial transactions with Catron involving transfer of property to satisfy a debt.

Alonzo B. McMillan (b. 1861 OH; to NM 1895; d. 1927 NM). Democrat. McMillan represented an heir to the Las Trampas grant in a suit to partition the grant's common lands, sell the land, and distribute shares of the proceeds to the legal heirs. In the view of Malcolm Ebright, McMillan failed to adequately notify all heirs of the suit. He received one-fourth of net proceeds from the sale and bought additional shares. His actions and those of two other attorneys involved displayed questionable ethics and were reminiscent of the storied "land ring" of former times.

Mariano Sabino Otero (b. 1844 NM; d. 1904 NM). Republican. Otero was New Mexico's territorial delegate to Congress in the 1879–1880 session. He was descended from one of the older and more prosperous families of the territory, whose leading members tended to identify with the business values of the non-Hispanic Republican newcomers. In pursuit of statehood, Otero was willing to oppose the Catholic archbishop, Jean-Baptiste Salpointe, in deliberations of the 1889 constitutional convention, advocating for establishment of a strong public school system.

Don Miguel Antonio Otero (b. 1829 NM; d. 1882 NM). Republican. Don Miguel, father of Miguel Antonio Otero II, served as territorial delegate to Congress between 1855 and 1860. He served briefly as territorial secretary in 1861 and was a member of the dominant faction of the Republican Party. His occasional identification as a Ring member relates most directly to his involvement, along with Elkins, Governor William Pile, and John S. Watts, as an original director of the Maxwell Land Grant and Railway Company.

Charles M. Phillips (b. 1849 MI; to NM 1883; d. unknown). Republican. Phillips was clerk of the territorial supreme court from 1883 to 1885. He was appointed to the position by his father-in-law, Chief Justice Samuel B. Axtell. When Grover Cleveland was elected president in 1884, the offices of Axtell and

Phillips were in jeopardy, and both were eventually displaced. William Breeden and Catron resisted efforts of the new administration to replace Phillips, but in the end, Phillips yielded the office and left the territory. The "Ithurial" letter may be the only source identifying Phillips as a Ring member.

Benjamin Maurice Read (b. 1853 NM; d. 1927 NM). Republican. Read was elected to the territorial legislature several times and served as speaker of the House in 1901. The list of presumed Ring members published in the *Las Vegas Daily Optic* in July 1884, attributed to L. Bradford Prince, includes some puzzling names, including Read. In making the list, Prince seems to have been strongly influenced by events of the moment, as reflected in the inclusion of a few men who, though Republicans with offices, were short-term residents of New Mexico.

Alois Bernard Renehan (b. 1869 VA; to NM 1892; d. 1928 OH). Democrat. Renehan, a lawyer, served in the territorial council, and as a state representative and senator. He was classified as a Ring member by Malcolm Ebright for his less-than-stellar representation of claimants to the Las Trampas grant. Apparently Renehan did not fully reveal to the heirs terms that made the property attractive to the buyer, while enhancing his own position and damaging the interests of the heirs. The episode played out between 1900 and 1914, and involved methods similar to those of the old "New Mexican Land Ring," but otherwise had little relation to the Ring of Elkins and Catron.

John Sherman Jr. (b. OH 1854; to NM 1876; d. D.C. 1890). Republican. Sherman was appointed U.S. marshal for New Mexico in 1876, and was soon caught up in the Lincoln County War. Accounts of his activities and Ring connection vary. Some believed him to be controlled by the Ring, and others complained of incompetence and drunkenness. Frank Warner Angel's notes describe Sherman as "reliable" if lacking in fortitude. He remained as U.S. marshal until 1882.

Frank Springer (b. 1848 IA; to NM 1873; d. 1927 PA). Republican. Springer was local attorney for and later president of the Maxwell Land Grant Company for some fifty-four years. He opposed the Santa Fe Ring during the Colfax County War, but later reconciled with Catron. When Catron faced possible disbarment in 1895, Springer was one of four leading attorneys who conducted his defense. Springer had little association with presumed Ring members in business or politics. His business ventures occurred mainly in the context of enterprises related to the Maxwell grant.

Ralph Emerson Twitchell (b. 1859 MI; to NM 1882; d. 1925 CA). Republican. Upon graduation from law school, Twitchell located in Santa Fe to assist Henry Waldo in representing the Atchison, Topeka and Santa Fe Railway. He was active in Republican Party politics, serving as chairman of the territorial Central Committee from 1902 to 1903. A prolific chronicler of New Mexico history, Twitchell is sometimes criticized for his silence on the Ring. He acknowledged a "Santa Fe Group" or "clique" or "ring" in the 1925 book *Old Santa Fe*, naming names, but not his own.

John Sebrie Watts (b. 1816 KY; to NM 1851; d. 1876 IN). Whig, later Republican. Watts was appointed to the territorial supreme court by President Millard Fillmore in 1851. He was elected to the office of territorial delegate in 1861 and served briefly as chief justice from 1868 to 1869. As a practicing attorney, Watts represented numerous land-grant claimants. His occasional mention in connection with the Ring is also attributable to his involvement as an original incorporator of the Maxwell Land Grant and Railway Company.

NOTES

Abbreviations

EGR/CSWR	Edmund G. Ross Papers, Center for Southwest Research, University of New Mexico, Albuquerque
EGR/KSHS	Edmund G. Ross Papers, Kansas State Historical Society, Topeka
FS/CS	Frank Springer Papers, CS Cattle Company, Cimarron, NM
FS/NMNH	Frank Springer Papers, National Museum of Natural History, Washington, D.C.
HBW/RGHC	Herman B. Weisner Papers, Rio Grande Historical Collections, New Mexico State University, Las Cruces
LBP/NMRCA	L. Bradford Prince Papers, New Mexico Records Center and Archives, Santa Fe
LW/FACHL	Lew Wallace Collection, Fray Angélico Chávez History Library, Palace of the Governors, Santa Fe, NM
LW/IHS	Lew Wallace Collection, Indiana Historical Society, Indianapolis
MDP/CSWR	Marion Dargan Papers, Center for Southwest Research, University of New Mexico, Albuquerque
MLG/CSWR	Maxwell Land Grant Collection, Center for Southwest Research, University of New Mexico, Albuquerque
NARA	National Archives and Records Administration, Washington, D.C.
RG	Record Group
RNM/HML	Robert N. Mullin Collection, Haley Memorial Library and History Center, Midland, TX
SBE/WVU	Stephen B. Elkins Papers, West Virginia Collection, West Virginia University, Morgantown. Papers are arranged in several series. "A&M No." refers to a series number in Archives and Manuscripts.
TANM	Territorial Archives of New Mexico, New Mexico State Records Center and Archives, Santa Fe

TBC/CSWR   Thomas Benton Catron Papers, Center for Southwest
                                Research, University of New Mexico, Albuquerque
WGR/HL   Papers of William Gillet Ritch, Huntington Library, San
                                Marino, CA

Introduction

1. Deposition of Frank Springer, August 9, 1878, in *Report and Testimony in the Matter of Charges Against Samuel B. Axtell, Governor of New Mexico*, by Frank Warner Angel, October 3, 1878, Records of the Office of the Secretary of the Interior, NARA, RG 48.
2. *Albuquerque Review*, January 26, 1878.
3. *Herald and Southwest*, September 18, 1880.
4. *Santa Fe Weekly New Mexican*, September 14, 1878.
5. Victor Westphall, *Thomas Benton Catron and His Era* (Albuquerque: University of New Mexico Press, 1973), 98.
6. W. B. Matchett and Mary E. McPherson to President Rutherford B. Hayes, April 1877; Matchett and McPherson to Secretary of the Interior Carl Schurz, May 5, 1877; Angel, *Report and Testimony in the Matter of Charges Against Samuel B. Axtell*.
7. For an account of Susan McSween's involvement, see Kathleen P. Chamberlain, *In the Shadow of Billy the Kid: Susan McSween and the Lincoln County War* (Albuquerque: University of New Mexico Press, 2013).
8. *Santa Fe Weekly New Mexican Review*, March 8, 1894.
9. *Colorado Daily Chieftain*, May 11, 1872.

Chapter One

1. Mark Twain and Charles Dudley Warner, *The Gilded Age: A Tale of To-day* (Hartford, CT: American Publishing Co., 1873), 243.
2. Rebecca Edwards, *New Spirits: Americans in the Gilded Age, 1865–1905* (New York: Oxford University Press, 2006), 13.
3. Sean Dennis Cashman, *America in the Gilded Age: From the Death of Lincoln to the Rise of Theodore Roosevelt* (New York: New York University Press, 1984), 13.
4. Edward C. Kirkland, *Industry Comes of Age: Business, Labor, and Public Policy, 1860–1897* (New York: Holt, Rinehart, and Winston, 1961), 400.
5. Richard A. Bartlett, ed., *The Gilded Age in America, 1865–1900* (Reading, MA: Addison-Wesley, 1969), 5.
6. For an extended discussion of the impact of the American Occupation and the Mexican Cession on Spanish-speaking New Mexicans, see Laura E. Gómez, *Manifest Destinies: The Making of the Mexican American Race* (New York: New York University Press, 2007).

7. Bartlett, *The Gilded Age in America*, 1.

8. Eugene Manlove Rhodes, *West Is West* (New York: H. K. Fly Co., 1917), 122.

9. "Farming Lands Under Irrigation; Colfax County, New Mexico" (Raton, NM: Maxwell Land Grant Company, n.d.).

10. Gene M. Gressley, *West by East: The American West in the Gilded Age* (Provo, UT: Brigham Young University Press, 1972), 37.

11. Cashman, *America in the Gilded Age*, 125.

12. See Alexander B. Callow Jr., *The Tweed Ring* (New York: Oxford University Press, 1966).

13. Cashman, *America in the Gilded Age*, 126–27.

14. Leo Marx, *The Machine in the Garden: Technology and the Pastoral Ideal in America* (New York: Oxford University Press, 1964).

15. Frank Springer to Charles Wachsmuth, April 5, 1881, FS/NMNH.

16. Kenneth N. Owens, "Pattern and Structure in Western Territorial Politics," *Western Historical Quarterly* 1:4 (October 1970): 375.

17. Earl S. Pomeroy, *The Territories and the United States, 1861–1890: Studies in Colonial Administration* (Philadelphia: University of Pennsylvania Press, 1947), 19.

18. *Denver Mirror*, February 1, 1874.

19. *Colorado Transcript*, April 24, 1872.

20. *Denver Mirror*, February 1, 1874.

21. *Colorado Daily Chieftain*, October 6, 1875.

22. Howard Roberts Lamar, *The Far Southwest, 1846–1912: A Territorial History* (New Haven: Yale University Press, 1966), 262.

23. Odie B. Faulk, *Crimson Desert: Indian Wars of the American Southwest* (New York: Oxford University Press, 1974), 167–68.

24. Jay J. Wagoner, *Arizona Territory, 1863–1912: A Political History* (Tucson: University of Arizona Press, 1970), 144.

25. Richard N. Ellis, "The Humanitarian Generals," *Western Historical Quarterly* 3:2 (April 1972): 171–73.

26. John Gregory Bourke, *On the Border with Crook* (New York: Charles Scribner's Sons, 1891), 437.

27. Angie Debo, *Geronimo: The Man, His Time, His Place* (Norman: University of Oklahoma Press, 1976), 264.

28. Lamar, *The Far Southwest*, 459.

29. Ibid., 458–59.

Chapter Two

1. Joel Jacobsen, *Such Men as Billy the Kid: The Lincoln County War Reconsidered* (Lincoln: University of Nebraska Press, 1994), 45.

2. G. Emlen Hall, *Four Leagues of Pecos: A Legal History of the Pecos Grant, 1800–1933* (Albuquerque: University of New Mexico Press, 1984), xi.

3. Ibid., 147–48.

4. Victor Westphall, *Mercedes Reales: Hispanic Land Grants of the Upper Rio Grande Region* (Albuquerque: University of New Mexico Press, 1983), 50–51.

5. See R. L. Duffus, *The Santa Fe Trail* (New York: Longmans, Green and Co., 1930), 67–84. Duffus notes that most of the great trading routes and emigrant trails were in use before the coming of westering Americans. General use of the route from Missouri, according to Duffus, is associated with the year 1821 and with Captain William Becknell, the "Father of the Santa Fe Trail," mainly because his party was the first to make the journey using wagons and because "after he opened the Trail, it stayed open."

6. Breeden was born on February 18, 1840; Catron on October 6, 1840; Elkins on September 26, 1841. The small size of the Masonic College—a total of 124 students reported in 1855—suggests that Breeden, Catron, and Elkins would have known each other well. *Western Journal and Civilian* n.s., 7 (St. Louis: M. Tarver and H. Cobb, 1855).

7. Oscar Doane Lambert, *Stephen Benton Elkins: American Foursquare* (Pittsburgh, PA: University of Pittsburgh Press, 1955), 21–26. According to Lambert, Elkins's decision to migrate to the Southwest was influenced through conversations with Henry Connelly, territorial governor of New Mexico, and Richard McCormick, secretary-designate of the new Territory of Arizona.

8. Ibid., 29.

9. Westphall, *Thomas Benton Catron*, 14–22.

10. Ibid., 26.

11. H. L. Waldo to S. B. Elkins, February 18, 1866; May 9, 1866; September 8, 1866. Waldo addresses Elkins variously as "My most loved friend" and "My Dear Steve." SBE/WVU, A&M No. 0053.

12. See Darlis A. Miller, *The California Column in New Mexico* (Albuquerque: University of New Mexico Press, 1982).

13. Ibid., 68–69.

14. Herbert Bartlett Holt, "Biographical Sketches of Prominent Pioneer Members of Aztec Lodge No. 3, A.F.&A.M. of New Mexico: Colonel William L. Rynerson," RNM/HML.

15. Darlis A. Miller, "William Logan Rynerson in New Mexico, 1862–1893," *New Mexico Historical Review* 48:2 (Spring 1973): 112–13.

16. Ralph Emerson Twitchell, *The Leading Facts in New Mexican History*, vol. 2 (Cedar Rapids, IA: Torch Press, 1912), 397–98.

17. *Santa Fe Daily New Mexican*, December 22, 1875.

18. Twitchell, *Leading Facts*, 2:398.

19. *New York Sun*, July 5, 1875.

20. Lamar, *The Far Southwest*, 181.

21. Westphall, *Thomas Benton Catron*, 24. See also, for example, references to the "Chaves Party" in the *Santa Fe Daily New Mexican*, August 22, 1868.

22. *Thirty-Four*, August 18, 1880.

23. *Papers and Testimony in the Contested-Election Case of F. A. Manzanares vs. T. Luna* (Washington, D.C.: U.S. House of Representatives, 48th Cong., 1st Sess. Miscellaneous Document No. 17, 1884), 225–27. Chaves had previously been the accuser in a fraud case arising from the 1867 election for territorial delegate. Charles P. Clever had been declared the winner, but Chaves, his opponent, contested the outcome and was declared the victor.

24. Westphall, *Thomas Benton Catron*, 24.

25. *Santa Fe Weekly Gazette*, January 25, 1868.

26. George W. Coe, *Frontier Fighter: The Autobiography of George W. Coe* (Boston: Houghton Mifflin, 1934), 10.

27. See Ovando James Hollister, *History of the First Regiment of Colorado Volunteers*, republished as *Colorado Volunteers in New Mexico, 1862* (Chicago: R. R. Donnelley and Sons, 1962).

28. Gary L. Roberts, *Death Comes for the Chief Justice: The Slough-Rynerson Quarrel and Political Violence in New Mexico* (Niwot: University Press of Colorado, 1990), 53–56.

29. Ibid., 54–65.

30. *Santa Fe Weekly Gazette*, February 15, 1868.

31. Roberts, *Death Comes for the Chief Justice*, 108.

32. *Santa Fe Weekly Gazette*, April 18, 1868.

33. Roberts, *Death Comes for the Chief Justice*, 129–57.

34. The history of this incident can be read in documents in the file, "Records Concerning Charges Against William Breeden, 1865–1868," NARA, RG 48, Records of the Office of the Secretary of the Interior, MLR Entry A1-738.

35. William Breeden to "Dear Col.," October 10, 1868. The addressee may have been Hawkins Taylor, an apparent confidant and ally in the affair. "Records Concerning Charges Against William Breeden."

36. Comments on file in "Records Concerning Charges Against William Breeden."

37. *Santa Fe Daily New Mexican*, October 22, 1868.

38. J. L. Collins to O. H. Browning, October 24, 1868. "Records Concerning Charges Against William Breeden."

39. Calvin Horn, *New Mexico's Troubled Years: The Story of the Early Territorial Governors* (Albuquerque: Horn and Wallace, 1963), 136–37.

40. See Ibid., 115–33. Mitchell was absent from the territory for extended periods of time during his tenure as governor (1866–1869) and quarreled almost constantly with the legislature and two different territorial secretaries, spawning factional conflict and fiscal chaos in the territory.

41. *Santa Fe Daily New Mexican*, October 30, 1869; December 15, 1869; December 17, 1869.

42. *Santa Fe Daily New Mexican*, February 4, 1870.

43. *Borderer*, December 20, 1871.

44. *Republican Review*, August 26, 1873. The *Review*, published in Albuquerque, attributed the article cited to the *Cimarron News and Press*.

45. "A Most Audacious Ring," letter from S. H. Newman. *New York Sun*, August 16, 1875. Formerly editor of newspapers in Las Vegas and Las Cruces, New Mexico, Newman was living in West Las Animas, Colorado, at the time of his letter to the *Sun*. Newman's letter was dated July 31, 1875.

46. The *Herald and Southwest*, Grant County, New Mexico, October 9, 1880. Otero, a Democrat, lost the election to the Republican candidate, Tranquilino Luna.

47. "A Most Audacious Ring," *New York Sun*, August 16, 1875.

48. Affidavit of W. R. Morley, June 15, 1878, FS/CS. Copy in files of the author. The date of this affidavit indicates that it may have been prepared in support of charges made against the territorial governor, Samuel B. Axtell, and investigated by Frank Warner Angel in summer and fall 1878.

49. *Las Vegas Daily Optic*, September 2, 1884.

50. *Moore v. Huntington*, 84 U.S. 417 (1873).

51. Arie W. Poldervaart, *Black-Robed Justice* (Santa Fe: Historical Society of New Mexico, 1948), 87–88.

52. *Borderer*, January 10, 1872.

53. *Colorado Daily Chieftain*, May 11, 1872.

54. *Borderer*, February 28, 1872. Rubén Sálaz Márquez, *The Santa Fe Ring: Land Grant History in American New Mexico* (Albuquerque: Cosmic House, 2008), 2, 47–50. In a work focusing on land-grant history, Márquez cites a reference to Samuel Ellison as the Ring's "mouthpiece." Though Ellison is seldom named as a Ring member, his mention with Elkins and Catron in the Kirchner matter is indicative of some involvement.

55. Simeon H. Newman III, "The Santa Fe Ring: A Letter to the *New York Sun*," *Arizona and the West* 12:3 (Autumn 1970): 274.

56. See Pomeroy, *The Territories and the United States*, 80–89. Pomeroy writes, "General interest in elections for delegate probably attests to the influence and importance of the post as well as to the pleasures of life in Washington."

57. Deposition of John L. Taylor, August 6, 1877, *Report and Testimony in the Matter of the Charges Against Samuel B. Axtell, Governor of New Mexico*, October 3, 1878, NARA, RG 48, Records of the Office of the Secretary of the Interior, 1826–1981, National Archives at College Park, MD.

58. *New York Sun*, July 5, 1875.

59. Deposition of Frank Springer, August 9, 1878, in Angel, *Report and Testimony in the Matter of Charges Against Samuel B. Axtell*.

60. Ibid. Springer identifies Griego's friend only as "C. Lara." See also James S. Peters, *Robert Clay Allison: Requiescat in Pace* (Santa Fe: Sunstone Press, 2008). In this undocumented narrative account, this person is identified as Cipriano Lara. Lara, a resident of Colfax County, was referred to on December 10, 1875, by the Ring-friendly *Santa Fe Daily New Mexican* as "nuestro amigo," or "our friend Don Cipriano Lara."

61. Horn, *New Mexico's Troubled Years*, 174–75. Axtell had become embroiled in a controversy between Mormon and anti-Mormon political factions in Utah. He sought and obtained a new appointment from President Grant.

62. *Santa Fe Daily New Mexican*, August 18, 1875.

63. *Borderer*, February 28, 1872.

Chapter Three

1. Tom Hilton, *Nevermore, Cimarron, Nevermore* (Fort Worth, TX: Western Heritage Press, 1970), 116.

2. Agnes Morley Cleaveland, *Satan's Paradise: From Lucien Maxwell to Fred Lambert* (Boston: Houghton Mifflin, 1952).

3. *Santa Fe Daily New Mexican*, October 28, 1870.

4. *Arizona Citizen*, May 6, 1871.

5. James Stephen Peters et al., *Mace Bowman: Texas Feudist, Western Lawman* (Yorktown, TX: Hartmann Heritage Productions, 1996), 73.

6. Concerning Elkins's role, see Lawrence R. Murphy, *Philmont: A History of New Mexico's Cimarron Country* (Albuquerque: University of New Mexico Press, 1972), 105; and Lambert, *Stephen Benton Elkins*, 31.

7. See, for example, María E. Montoya, *Translating Property: The Maxwell Land Grant and the Conflict over Land in the American West, 1840–1900* (Berkeley: University of California Press, 2002), 108–17.

8. Abstract of Stock Ledger, Maxwell Land Grant and Railway Company, August 31, 1870, MLG/CSWR.

9. *Colorado Daily Chieftain*, October 19, 1873.

10. Norman Cleaveland, *The Morleys: Young Upstarts on the Southwest Frontier* (Albuquerque: Calvin Horn, 1971), 87.

11. Affidavit of Asa F. Middaugh, March 31, 1876. Copy included in the deposition of Frank Springer, August 9, 1878, in Angel, *Report and Testimony in the Matter of Charges Against Samuel B. Axtell*.

12. Thomas Harwood, *History of New Mexico Spanish and English Missions of the Methodist Episcopal Church from 1850 to 1910*, vol. 1 (Albuquerque: El Abogodo Press, 1908), 262.

13. *New York Sun*, July 5, 1875.

14. M. W. Mills to C. N. Blackwell, February 13, 1924. Collection of the Old Mill Museum, Cimarron, NM.

15. Harwood, *History of New Mexico Spanish and English Missions*, 1:266.

16. Morris F. Taylor, *O. P. McMains and the Maxwell Land Grant Conflict* (Tucson: University of Arizona Press, 1979), 50.

17. According to the *Santa Fe Daily New Mexican*, November 11, 1875, Cárdenas was killed on the night of November 10, 1875. Frank Springer's deposition of August 9, 1878, indicating that the murder occurred on November 11, appears to be in error on this point.

18. Lamar, *The Far Southwest*, 154.

19. *Santa Fe Weekly New Mexican*, November 16, 1875.

20. Deposition of Frank Springer, in Angel, *Report and Testimony in the Matter of Charges Against Samuel B. Axtell.*

21. Ibid.

22. Ibid.

23. Cleaveland, *The Morleys*, 120.

24. *Colorado Daily Chieftain*, May 10, 1877.

25. *Colorado Daily Chieftain*, April 11, 1878.

26. Jim Berry Pearson, *The Maxwell Land Grant* (Norman: University of Oklahoma Press, 1961), 49–50.

27. Lambert, *Stephen Benton Elkins*, 31.

28. Lawrence R. Murphy, *Lucien Bonaparte Maxwell: Napoleon of the Southwest* (Norman: University of Oklahoma Press, 1983), 182.

29. Twitchell, *Leading Facts*, 2:351–52. Twitchell also notes that Griffin was a leading member of the Masonic Lodge and "chairman of the republican committee for several years."

30. J. A. Williamson to Henry M. Atkinson, June 28, 1877, MLG/CSWR.

31. Pearson, *Maxwell Land Grant*, 76.

32. Stephen B. Elkins to W. R. Morley, March 17, 1874, FS/CS. Copy in the files of the author.

33. Ibid.

34. William A. Keleher, *The Fabulous Frontier: Twelve New Mexico Items* (Albuquerque: University of New Mexico Press, 1945), 104.

35. Stephen B. Elkins to Frank Springer, February 9, 1886, FS/CS.

36. Mary E. McPherson to Alphonso Taft, February 7, 1877, NARA, RG 60; W. B. Matchett and Mary E. McPherson to Rutherford B. Hayes, April 1877; and Matchett and McPherson to Carl Schurz, May 5, 1877, in Angel, *Report and Testimony in the Matter of Charges Against Samuel B. Axtell.* The printed document summarizing the charges alleged by McPherson and Matchett was *In the Matter of the Charges vs. Gov. S. B. Axtell and Other New Mexican Officials*, privately printed, August 1877.

37. Letters from William R. Morley and Ada McPherson Morley to Mary E. McPherson, dated March 6 and March 7, 1877, are quoted at length in Cleaveland, *The Morleys*, 127–32.

38. Concerning final stages in the shift of control in Maxwell grant affairs, see David L. Caffey, *Frank Springer and New Mexico: From the Colfax County War to the Emergence of Modern Santa Fe* (College Station: Texas A&M University Press, 2006), 89–97.

39. The major source concerning this incident is Conrad K. Naegle, "The Rebellion of Grant County, New Mexico in 1876," *Arizona and the West* 10:3 (Autumn 1968): 225–40.

40. Ibid., 229.

41. *Grant County Herald*, September 16, 1876.

42. *Colorado Daily Chieftain*, October 12, 1876.

43. *Inventory of the County Archives of New Mexico, No. 9: Grant County*, 9–10, New Mexico Historical Records Survey, U.S. Work Projects Administration, 1941, NARA, RG 69.

44. Naegle, "Rebellion of Grant County," 235–36.

45. Ibid., 237.

46. See Porter A. Stratton, *The Territorial Press of New Mexico, 1834–1912* (Albuquerque: University of New Mexico Press, 1969), 251–95, for an extensive index to territorial newspapers. See also Pearce S. Grove, Becky J. Barnett, and Sandra J. Hansen, eds., *New Mexico Newspapers: A Comprehensive Guide to Bibliographical Entries and Locations* (Albuquerque: University of New Mexico Press, 1975).

47. *Colorado Daily Chieftain*, May 20, 1876.

48. *Santa Fe Weekly New Mexican*, October 17, 1876; *Santa Fe Weekly New Mexican*, September 14, 1878; *Santa Fe Daily New Mexican*, October 7, 1880.

49. *Grant County Herald*, September 21, 1878.

Chapter Four

1. Frederick Nolan, *The Lincoln County War: A Documentary History* (Norman: University of Oklahoma Press, 1992), 32–55.

2. Data on the origins of these principal figures is from Nolan, *Lincoln County War*.

3. Deposition of James J. Dolan, June 25, 1878, in Frank Warner Angel, *Report as to the Death of John H. Tunstall, and Relative to Troubles in Lincoln County, New Mexico*. NARA, RG 60.

4. Wayne L. Mauzy, *A Century in Santa Fe: The Story of the First National Bank of Santa Fe* (Santa Fe: First National Bank of Santa Fe, 1970).

5. Deposition of James J. Dolan, June 25, 1878.

6. Nolan, *Lincoln County War*, 149, 506–7.

7. See, for example, the deposition of George Vansickle, June 12, 1878; and that of John Newcomb, June 8, 1878, in Angel, *Report as to the Death of John H. Tunstall*.

8. Deposition of Alexander A. McSween, June 6, 1878, in Angel, *Report as to the Death of John H. Tunstall*.

9. Nolan, *Lincoln County War*, 178.

10. Ibid., 185–86. According to Nolan, "McSween was subjected to harsh and partisan questioning by both District Attorney Rynerson and Bristol himself." Further, though bail was set at $8,000, the district attorney refused to accept "any and all" bondsmen proposed by McSween.

11. Deposition of Adolph P. Barrier, June 11, 1878, in Angel, *Report as to the Death of John H. Tunstall*.

12. *Grant County Herald*, January 30, 1876.

13. *Grant County Herald*, February 6, 1876.

14. Deposition of Adolph P. Barrier, June 11, 1878.

15. E. Donald Kaye, *Nathan Augustus Monroe Dudley* (Parker, CO: Outskirts Press, 2007), 47.

16. Deposition of Alexander A. McSween, June 6, 1878.

17. Nolan, *Lincoln County War*, 188.

18. John H. Tunstall to John P. Tunstall, April 27–28, 1877, quoted in Frederick W. Nolan, *The Life and Death of John Henry Tunstall* (Albuquerque: University of New Mexico Press, 1965), 213.

19. Deposition of James J. Longwell, May 14, 1878, in Angel, *Report as to the Death of John H. Tunstall*. See also Nolan, *Life and Death of John Henry Tunstall*, 269. The writ of attachment was issued on February 7 and the sheriff's office had begun its execution on February 8, ten days before Tunstall's death.

20. Deposition of Alexander A. McSween, June 6, 1878.

21. Montague R. Leverson to Sir Edward Thornton, March 21, 1878, transcript copy in RNM/HML; Leverson to Thornton, March 16, 1878, reproduced in Nolan, *Life and Death of John Henry Tunstall*, 292–95.

22. Robert Widenmann to R. Guy McClellan, February 26, 1878; *Santa Fe Daily New Mexican*, March 23, 1878.

23. William Keleher, *Violence in Lincoln County, 1869–1881* (Albuquerque: University of New Mexico Press, 1957), 30n3.

24. Twitchell, *Leading Facts*, 2:418n345.

25. Frederick Nolan's extensive and highly regarded work on the Lincoln County War is the source concerning many of the events related here. See *Lincoln County War*, especially Nolan's detailed chronology, 494–520.

26. W. L. Rynerson to S. B. Axtell, February 24, 1878, copy in HBW/RGHC.

27. S. B. Axtell to Edward Hatch, February 15, 1878, copy in HBW/RGHC.

28. Nolan, *Lincoln County War*, 223.

29. Ibid., 225.

30. Thomas B. Catron to S. B. Axtell, May 30, 1878, copy in HBW/RGHC.

31. Axtell to Edward Hatch, May 30, 1878, copy in HBW/RGHC.

32. Coe, *Frontier Fighter*, 71. In his report on charges against S. B. Axtell, Frank Warner Angel examined the accusation that Axtell knowingly appointed "bad men" to office. Angel found the charge sustained with respect to the appointment of Peppin as sheriff, but not sustained with respect to the appointment of J. Francisco Chaves as district attorney for the Second Judicial District.

33. *Santa Fe Daily New Mexican*, March 23, 1878.

34. R. A. Widenmann to J. P. Tunstall, February 23, 1878, reproduced in Nolan, *Lincoln County War*, 208–11; R. A. Widenmann to R. Guy McClellan, February 26, 1878, published in the *Santa Fe Daily New Mexican*, March 23, 1878.

35. Montague R. Leverson to Sir Edward Thornton, March 16, 1878, reproduced in Nolan, *Life and Death of John Henry Tunstall*, 292–95; Leverson to Thornton,

March 21, 1878, transcript in RNM/HML; Leverson to John Sherman, March 20, 1878, NARA, RG 60; Leverson to Carl Schurz, April 1, 1878, NARA, RG 60; Leverson to Rutherford B. Hayes, April 1, 1878, and April 2, 1878, NARA, RG 60.

36. Montague R. Leverson to Rutherford B. Hayes, March 16, 1878; Angel, *Report and Testimony in the Matter of Charges Against Samuel B. Axtell*.

37. Carl Schurz to Frank W. Angel, April 16, 1878, NARA, RG 48.

38. Angel's commission from the War Department is reported by the *Santa Fe Daily New Mexican*, August 17, 1878.

39. Carl Schurz to Lew Wallace, September 4, 1878, LW/IHS.

40. *Denver Daily Tribune*, September 4, 1878.

41. Charles Devens to Stephen B. Elkins, September 16, 1878, NARA, RG 60.

42. W. G. Ritch to Charles Devens, September 13, 1878, NARA, RG 60.

43. T. B. Catron to Charles Devens, October 10, 1878, NARA, RG 60.

44. R. B. Hayes to Frederick Godfroy, August 2, 1878, NARA, RG 75.

45. Westphall, *Thomas Benton Catron*, 128.

46. 1878 notebook prepared by Frank Warner Angel for Lew Wallace, LW/IHS.

47. Patricia Nelson Limerick, *The Legacy of Conquest: The Unbroken Past of the American West* (New York: W. W. Norton and Co., 1987), 80.

48. Lew Wallace to Susan Wallace, October 8, 1878, LW/IHS.

49. Lew Wallace to Carl Schurz, October 1, 1878, LW/IHS.

50. Wallace to Schurz, October 5, 1878, LW/IHS.

51. Rutherford B. Hayes, "By the President of the United States of America: A Proclamation," October 7, 1878, LW/IHS.

52. Lewis Wallace, "Proclamation by the Governor," November 13, 1878, LW/IHS.

53. For information about Dudley's life and military career, see Kaye, *Nathan Augustus Monroe Dudley*.

54. Wallace to A. H. Markland, November 14, 1878, LW/IHS.

55. *Washington Sunday Herald*, November 3, 1878, as quoted in the *Rocky Mountain Sentinel*, November 14, 1878.

56. *Rocky Mountain Sentinel*, December 19, 1878.

57. Wallace to W. M. Evarts, November 18, 1878, LW/IHS.

58. H. I. Chapman to Wallace, November 29, 1878, LW/IHS.

59. Wallace to Capt. Henry Carroll, March 11, 1878, LW/IHS.

60. Nolan, *Lincoln County War*, 383.

61. Ira Leonard to Wallace, April 25, 1879; Leonard to Wallace, May 20, 1879, LW/IHS.

62. W. R. Morley to Wallace, May 5, 1879, LW/IHS.

63. Lew Wallace to Henry Wallace, March 19, 1881, LW/IHS.

64. Wallace to Susan Elston Wallace, April 29, 1881, LW/IHS.

65. *Cimarron News and Press*, April 18, 1878.

66. Wallace to Schurz, February 16, 1880, LW/IHS.

67. Ibid.

68. Wallace to Eugene Fiske, April 21, 1882, LW/FACHL.

Chapter Five

1. *New York Sun*, July 5, 1875. The dateline of the article is June 2, 1875.
2. Charles Fletcher Lummis, *Letters from the Southwest: September 20, 1884 to March 14, 1885*. Edited by James W. Byrkit (Tucson: University of Arizona Press, 1989), 168; E. G. Ross to John O'Grady, March 26, 1887, EGR/CSWR.
3. Robert W. Larson, *New Mexico Populism* (Boulder: Colorado Associated University Press, 1974), 25. Larson says that Elkins and Catron "had the dubious distinction of being the organizers of the Santa Fe Ring." Montoya, *Translating Property*, 109; Montoya writes that Elkins and Catron were key members of the Ring and that their office "often served as the informal headquarters of the Ring's activities." Robert M. Utley, *High Noon in Lincoln County: Violence on the Western Frontier* (Albuquerque: University of New Mexico Press, 1987), 25; Utley says of Elkins and Catron, "Nearly everyone credited the two with founding the Santa Fe Ring."
4. Westphall, *Thomas Benton Catron*, 39–40.
5. Herbert O. Brayer, *William Blackmore*, vol. 1: *The Spanish-Mexican Land Grants of New Mexico and Colorado, 1863–1878* (Denver: Bradford-Robinson, 1949), 163–67.
6. Robert D. Shadow and Marie Rodriguez Shadow, "A History of the Mora Land Grant, 1835–1916," New Mexico Digital History Project, Office of the State Historian, New Mexico State Records Center and Archives, 2004–2010.
7. Mauzy, *Century in Santa Fe*.
8. Edgar Walz to Catron, June 8, 1897, TBC/CSWR.
9. Mauzy, *Century in Santa Fe*.
10. Lambert, *Stephen Benton Elkins*, 10–22.
11. Frank W. Clancy, "Reminiscences of Territorial Days," *Minutes of the New Mexico Bar Association, Thirty-Third Annual Session* (Santa Fe: New Mexico Bar Association, 1919), 51–52.
12. *Chicago Tribune*, January 3, 1895.
13. *New York Times*, April 25, 1881.
14. One of several references to Elkins's possible culpability in the Star Route scandal appears in an article critical of him in the *New York World*, January 6, 1895. The article states, "Elkins's connection with the star-route thievery was notorious at the time," and says of the outcome, "His prosecution was not reached because of political influence and the purchased failure of the Dorsey trial."
15. See, for example, "It Looks Like Elkins," *New York World*, November 23, 1894.
16. Edward D. Bartlett et al. to *Wheeling Intelligencer*, January 3, 1895, copy in MDP/CSWR.
17. L. Bradford Prince to S. B. Elkins, January 3, 1895, SBE/WVU, A&M No. 0053.

18. *Las Vegas Daily Optic*, April 22, 1892.
19. *Las Vegas Daily Optic*, November 5, 1896.
20. See Viola Clark Hefferan, "Thomas Benton Catron" (MA thesis, University of New Mexico, 1940), 17.
21. Ibid., 19.
22. George W. Prichard, "Eulogy on the Life and Character of Hon. Thomas Benton Catron," May 17, 1921, TBC/CSWR.
23. Keleher, *Fabulous Frontier*, 110.
24. Ibid., 110.
25. Catron to John H. Riley, August 7, 1892, transcript in MDP/CSWR.
26. James Garland to John H. Knabel, January 16, 1889; Catron to James Garland, January 23, 1889, transcripts in MDP/CSWR.
27. Catron to Elkins, April 4, 1901, transcript in MDP/CSWR.
28. Miguel Antonio Otero, *My Nine Years as Governor of the Territory of New Mexico, 1897–1906* (Albuquerque: University of New Mexico Press, 1940), 196.
29. Catron to Elkins, April 9, 1893, transcript in MDP/CSWR.
30. Benjamin Butler to Elkins, August 23, 1887, SBE/WVU, A&M No. 1794.
31. Catron to Sánchez, October 27, 1888, transcript in MDP/CSWR.
32. Catron to Burns, April 12, 1895, TBC/CSWR.
33. Robert W. Larson, "Territorial Politics and Cultural Impact," *New Mexico Historical Review* 60:3 (July 1985): 260–61.
34. Wallace to Eugene A. Fiske, November 6, 1897, LW/FACHL.
35. *El Defensor del Pueblo*, August 22, 1891. In the original Spanish, the passage quoted reads, "Denunciamos al mundo entéro, y en particular al Territorio de N. M. al Tomas B. Catron (presidente de la junta de indignacion tenida en Santa Fé) como fraudista de terranos y mercedes de este Territorio, y segun nuestro concurso, el hombre mas perjuicioso politicalmente, usurpador de la libertad de los Neo Mejicanos; Jefe del Anillo Inquisistorial en contra de nuestra raza de los denominados Republicanos."
36. Catron to Pedro Perea, November 11, 1894, TBC/CSWR.
37. Catron to Pedro Sánchez, November 22, 1896, TBC/CSWR.
38. Catron to Elkins, September 26, 1892, TBC/CSWR.
39. Catron to Elkins, February 5, 1893, TBC/CSWR. Whatever the disposition of Catron's request, four reports prepared by Frank Warner Angel remain on file in the U.S. National Archives in the twenty-first century, in records of the U.S. Department of the Interior, the Justice Department, and the Bureau of Indian Affairs. Multiple scholars have speculated that a report addressing charges against Catron is, in fact, missing from the files of the Department of Justice. It is also possible that no such report was prepared or submitted.
40. Catron to J. Francisco Chaves, March 21, 1892, TBC/CSWR.
41. Catron to Elkins, November 18, 1893, TBC/CSWR.
42. Elkins to Catron, August 15, 1879, copy in SBE/WVU, A&M No. 0053.
43. Elkins to Catron, October 5, 1888, TBC/CSWR.

44. Catron to Elkins, November 8, 1888, transcript in MDP/CSWR.
45. Catron to Elkins, January 23, 1894, TBC/CSWR.
46. Ibid.
47. Elkins to Catron, February 1, 1895; Kerens to Catron, February 4, 1895, TBC/CSWR.
48. Catron to Elkins, February 15, 1895, TBC/CSWR.
49. Marion Dargan, "New Mexico's Fight for Statehood, 1895–1912, Part I: The Political Leaders of the Latter Half of the 1890s and Statehood," *New Mexico Historical Review* 14:1 (January 1939): 29.
50. Catron to Elkins, April 4, 1901, transcript in MDP/CSWR.
51. Catron to Elkins, November 29, 1889, transcript in MDP/CSWR.
52. Robert W. Larson, *New Mexico's Quest for Statehood, 1846–1912* (Albuquerque: University of New Mexico Press, 1968), 271.
53. Catron to Elkins, December 21, 1910, SBE/WVU, A&M No. 0053.
54. Catron to Hallie Elkins, March 28, 1912, TBC/CSWR.

Chapter Six

1. *Raton Guard*, April 14, 1882.
2. Frank Springer, "Land Titles in New Mexico," annual address of the retiring president of the New Mexico Bar Association, January 7, 1890 (Santa Fe: New Mexican Printing, 1890).
3. Corruption was notable during the Mexican period and in the administration of Governor Manuel Armijo, who was a vested partner in some of the grants that he approved. See White, Koch, Kelley, and McCarthy, Attorneys at Law, *Land Title Study* (Santa Fe: New Mexico State Planning Office, 1971), 19–20.
4. See Malcolm Ebright, *Land Grants and Lawsuits in Northern New Mexico* (Albuquerque: University of New Mexico Press, 1994), 23–25.
5. G. Emlen Hall, "Juan Estevan Pino, 'Se Los Coma': New Mexico Land Speculation in the 1820s," *New Mexico Historical Review* 57:1 (January 1982): 37.
6. G. Emlen Hall, "Giant Before the Surveyor-General: The Land Career of Donaciano Vigil," in *Spanish and Mexican Land Grants in New Mexico and Colorado*, ed. John R. Van Ness and Christine Van Ness (Manhattan, KS: Sunflower University Press, 1980), 64–73.
7. Harold H. Dunham, "Discussion of Howard R. Lamar, 'Land Policy in the Spanish Southwest, 1846–1891: A Study in Contrasts,'" *Journal of Economic History* 22:4 (December 1962): 519–20.
8. Marianne L. Stoller, "Grants of Desperation, Lands of Speculation: Mexican Period Land Grants in Colorado," in Van Ness and Van Ness, *Spanish and Mexican Land Grants*, 34–35.
9. Howard R. Lamar, "Land Policy in the Spanish Southwest, 1846–1891: A Study in Contrasts," *Journal of Economic History* 22:4 (December 1962): 501.

10. Westphall, *Mercedes Reales*, 282–83. The tally of claimants represented is according to figures compiled by Westphall and does not include cases in which they represented clients in collaboration with other attorneys.

11. Ebright, *Land Grants and Lawsuits in Northern New Mexico*, 38; J. J. Bowden, "Private Land Claims in the Southwest," vol. 1 (MA thesis, Southern Methodist University, 1969), 182–83.

12. For extensive discussion of this issue with specific reference to the Beaubien and Miranda or Maxwell grant, see Montoya, *Translating Property*.

13. See *Tameling v. United States Freehold and Emigration Company*, 93 U.S. 644 (1877).

14. Ebright, *Land Grants and Lawsuits in Northern New Mexico*, 44.

15. Mark Schiller, "Surveyor General George W. Julian: Reformer or Colonial Bureaucrat?" *La Jicarita News* 15:4 (April 2010).

16. Richard Wells Bradfute, *The Court of Private Land Claims: The Adjudication of Spanish and Mexican Land Grant Titles, 1891–1904* (Albuquerque: University of New Mexico Press, 1975), 220.

17. R. C. Kerens to S. B. Elkins, February 5, 1892, SBE/WVU, A&M No. 0053.

18. Westphall, *Mercedes Reales*, 254. On the basis of examination of claims presented for confirmation and several hypothetical calculations, Westphall estimates that between Congress and the Court of Private Land Claims, some "eight or nine million more acres of land" should have been confirmed.

19. *New York Times*, May 18, 1884.

20. Ebright, *Land Grants and Lawsuits in Northern New Mexico*, 52.

21. Clark S. Knowlton, "The Mora Land Grant: A New Mexican Tragedy," in *Spanish and Mexican Land Grants and the Law*, ed. Malcolm Ebright (Manhattan, KS: Sunflower University Press, 1989), 65.

22. For one discussion of the Mora land grant, see Westphall, *Thomas Benton Catron*, 39–46.

23. Robert D. Shadow and María Rodriguez Shadow, "From *Repartición* to Partition: A History of the Mora Land Grant, 1835–1916," *New Mexico Historical Review* 70:3 (July 1995): 277–78.

24. Ibid., 267–69.

25. Ibid., 279–84.

26. Westphall, *Thomas Benton Catron*, 71.

27. *Chicago Herald*, March 12, 1892.

28. Westphall, *Mercedes Reales*, 156–58.

29. Ibid., 99.

30. Ebright, *Land Grants and Lawsuits in Northern New Mexico*, 41.

31. For an account of the Anton Chico grant saga, see Michael J. Rock, "Anton Chico and Its Patent," in Van Ness and Van Ness, *Spanish and Mexican Land Grants in New Mexico and Colorado*, 86–91.

32. Ibid., 89. Sulzbacher merits consideration as at least a friend of the Santa Fe Ring. In addition to his involvement in the Anton Chico matter, he was associated with

presumed Ring members in the Grand Consolidated New Mexico Mining Company, and at times he held claims to the Pecos Pueblo and Las Vegas grants. Sulzbacher was appointed administrator of Robert Longwill's estate in 1895. He served on the supreme court of Puerto Rico, and with the support of Senator Stephen B. Elkins was appointed judge for the western district of the Indian Territory, serving from 1904 to 1907. See also Oscar Kraines, "Louis Sulzbacher: Justice of the Supreme Court of Puerto Rico, 1900–1904," *Jewish Social Studies* 13:2 (April 1951): 127–32.

33. Rock, "Anton Chico and Its Patent," 89.

34. Ibid., 90.

35. For an interpretive account of injustice with regard to this property, see Malcolm Ebright, *The Tierra Amarilla Grant: A History of Chicanery* (Santa Fe: Center for Land Grant Studies, 1980).

36. Ibid., 21–22.

37. Ibid., 25–26.

38. See David Correia, *Properties of Violence: Law and Land Grant Struggle in Northern New Mexico* (Athens: University of Georgia Press, 2013), 30–37.

39. Westphall, *Mercedes Reales*, 228.

40. Westphall, *Thomas Benton Catron*, 47; *Mercedes Reales*, 224–26. Elkins refers to his effort with regard to the Tierra Amarilla patent in the course of a testy exchange of letters with Catron. S. B. Elkins to Thomas B. Catron, October 5, 1888, TBC/CSWR.

41. Requirements for notice in such suits were changed by rulings in two New Mexico supreme court cases. In *Priest v. Town of Las Vegas*, 16 N.M. 692 (1911), the court decreed that potential claimants must be named and served, and that newspaper notice was insufficient. In *Rodriguez v. La Cueva Ranch Co.*, 17 N.M. 246 (1912), the court made more explicit that persons in possession of property that was the subject of a partition or quiet title suit must be personally served, and that notice could not be served by publication. Malcolm Ebright, "The Humphries Wildlife Management Area: History of Title and History of the Tierra Amarilla Grant," submitted to the Commission for Public Records pursuant to Contract #09-36099-008720 (Santa Fe, CPR, 2009), 7.

42. Michael J. Rock, "Catron's Quiet Title Suit," paper in files of the Center for Land Grant Studies, Guadalupe, NM, n.d.

43. Council Journal, 22nd Legislative Assembly, Territory of New Mexico, TANM. The journal is handwritten and contains errors requiring interpretation. At one point the partition act is referred to as "H.B. 86," but there was no House Bill 86. The entry apparently refers to C.B. 86, the partition act. The wording of the title varies in the Council Journal, but the bill is referred to in the House Journal by its correct title, as recorded in the published session laws.

44. House Journal, 22nd Legislative Assembly, Territory of New Mexico, TANM.

45. *Acts of the Legislative Assembly of the Territory of New Mexico, Twenty-Second Session,* 1876.

46. David Benavides and Ryan Golten, "Report to the New Mexico Attorney General—A Response to the GAO's 2004 Report, 'Treaty of Guadalupe Hidalgo: Findings and Possible Options Regarding Longstanding Community Land Grant Claims in New Mexico,'" *Natural Resources Journal* 48 (Fall 2008): 23.

47. Benavides and Golten, "Report to the New Mexico Attorney General," 28; Westphall, *Mercedes Reales,* 233.

48. David Benavides, "Lawyer-Induced Partitioning of New Mexican Land Grants: An Ethical Travesty," *Research Papers of the Center for Land Grant Studies* (Santa Fe: Center for Land Grant Studies, 2005), 11.

49. Clark S. Knowlton, "'Poverty, Equal Opportunity and Full Employment,' Hearings Before the Subcommittee on Equal Opportunities of the Committee on Education and Labor," House of Representatives, 94th Congress, 1st Sess., May 1975, 65. The *Santa Fe New Mexican* is cited as the source of figures for Catron's land holdings.

50. Ibid., 71.

51. Lionel Allen Sheldon, *Report of the Governor of New Mexico to the Secretary of the Interior for the Year 1883* (Washington, D.C.: U.S. Government Printing Office, 1883).

52. George Washington Julian, "Land-Stealing in New Mexico," *North American Review* 145:368 (July 1887):18–24.

53. The most extensive source on activities of the American Valley Company is an undated, unpublished manuscript, "The American Valley Murders," by Victor Westphall, used by permission of Walter Westphall. A related article appeared in *Ayer y Hoy en Taos: Yesterday and Today in Taos County and Northern New Mexico* 9 (Fall 1989).

54. Westphall, "American Valley Murders" (unpublished manuscript), 17.

55. Westphall, *Thomas Benton Catron,* 151.

56. Westphall, "American Valley Murders," 19.

57. See Westphall, "American Valley Murders."

58. Affidavit of Edward McGinty, June 4, 1884, *Fraudulent Acquisition of Titles to Lands in New Mexico,* Senate Executive Document No. 106, 48th Congress, 2nd Sess., March 3, 1885, 339. Hereafter referred to by the short title *Titles to Lands in New Mexico.*

59. Affidavit of Richard F. Mitchell, June 3, 1884, *Titles to Lands in New Mexico,* 340.

60. Affidavit of Daniel H. McAllister, June 5, 1884, *Titles to Lands in New Mexico,* 342.

61. T. B. Catron to S. B. Elkins, December 16, 1905, SBE/WVU, A&M No. 1794. Elkins's interest in the American Valley Company may have had to do with his involvement with other nearby grants, specifically the Bosque del Apache and

Antonio Sandoval grants. Administrative disposition of these claims is detailed in "New Mexico Land Grant Records, Surveyor General," microfilm ed., New Mexico State Records Center and Archives, Santa Fe.

62. Westphall, *Thomas Benton Catron*, 182.

63. See Morris F. Taylor, "Stephen W. Dorsey, Speculator-Cattleman," *New Mexico Historical Review* 49:1 (1974).

64. *Santa Fe New Mexican Review*, August 2, 1883.

65. Taylor, "Stephen W. Dorsey, Speculator-Cattleman," 41.

66. Sharon K. Lowry, "Mirrors and Blue Smoke: Stephen Dorsey and the Santa Fe Ring in the 1880s," *New Mexico Historical Review* 59:4 (1984): 399-400.

67. Frank D. Hobbs to N. C. McFarland, June 21, 1884. *Titles to Lands in New Mexico*, 310-15.

68. Frank D. Hobbs to N. C. McFarland, July 17, 1884. *Titles to Lands in New Mexico*, 321.

69. Julian, "Land-Stealing in New Mexico," 27.

70. Stephen W. Dorsey, "Land Stealing in New Mexico: A Rejoinder," *North American Review* 145:371 (October 1887): 403.

71. See Thomas J. Caperton, *Rogue! Being an Account of the Life and High Times of Stephen W. Dorsey, United States Senator and New Mexico Cattle Baron* (Santa Fe: Museum of New Mexico Press, 1978), 36-38.

72. Grover Cleveland, "First Inaugural Address, March 4, 1885," in *Inaugural Addresses of the Presidents of the United States*, ed. John Vance Cheney (Chicago: R. R. Donnelley and Sons, 1905).

73. Elias Brevoort to N. C. McFarland, Dec. 5, 1881, *Titles to Lands in New Mexico*, 19-20.

74. See *Titles to Lands in New Mexico*.

75. Ibid., 327, 340-42. "Catron" is misspelled as "Cobron" in the investigator's cover letter on page 327, but the name is spelled correctly in the supporting witness testimony.

76. *Santa Fe Weekly New Mexican*, December 23, 1886.

77. *New York Times*, December 24, 1886.

78. *Titles to Lands in New Mexico*, 393.

79. See Victor Westphall, *The Public Domain in New Mexico, 1854-1891* (Albuquerque: University of New Mexico Press, 1965), 102-3, 151-52.

80. *Santa Fe Herald*, February 11, 1888.

81. Westphall, *Public Domain in New Mexico*, 110.

82. Dorsey, "Land Stealing in New Mexico: A Rejoinder," 401.

83. Twitchell, *Leading Facts*, 2:498.

84. Affidavit of Franklin Jordan, *Titles to Lands in New Mexico*, 396-98.

85. Ibid., 396.

86. *In Re Renehan* (19 N.M. 640).

87. Rudolfo Anaya, *Heart of Aztlan* (Berkeley: Justa Publications, 1976), 105-6.

88. Correia, *Properties of Violence*, 48.

Chapter Seven

1. *Hillsborough Advocate*, November 25, 1891.
2. John H. Tunstall to John Partridge Tunstall, April 27–28, 1877; *Life and Death of John Henry Tunstall*, 213.
3. E. G. Ross to John O'Grady, March 26, 1887, EGR/CSWR.
4. Paul A. F. Walter, *Banking in New Mexico Before the Railroad Came* (New York: Newcomen Society in North America, 1955), 11.
5. Murphy, *Lucien Bonaparte Maxwell*, 224.
6. Mauzy, *Century in Santa Fe*. Catron and Elkins were law partners between 1874 and 1876. They were not in joint practice at the time they became involved with the First National Bank of Santa Fe.
7. See Walter, *Banking in New Mexico*, 9–20.
8. Elkins to "Dear Doctor," May 13, 1871, holographic copy in FS/CS, copy in files of the author. Elkins prompts Longwill to forward $5,000—apparently Longwill's contribution to the capital of the new bank. Elkins adds, "Your certificate will be sent direct to you. Send me your proxy."
9. Ibid.
10. *Santa Fe Weekly Sun*, December 26, 1891.
11. *La Union*'s analysis, as reported in *El Estandarte de Springer*, December 1, 1892. The original passage reads: "La 4ta fue la plata que gasto Catron, el Banco de Santa Fe, y la familia de los Pereas; pues se díce, que el banco dio $5,000, y Catron $1,500. Sera verdad? Que tal porta-estandarte del partido republicano! Que anillo infernal no sota aquel, cuando a sacrificado su partido por el vil ínteres de quedarse todavia con el el dinero del Territorio, y especular con el en Banco! Mas nos alegramos de todo corazon, que su plata ha servido para su propia derrota." Almost certainly, "el Banco de Santa Fe" refers to the First National Bank, of which Pedro Perea was president and Catron a director.
12. Articles of Incorporation, Rio Grande Rail Road and Telegraph Company, February 1, 1870, Records of the Territorial Secretary, 1851–1911, TANM. See also Herbert O. Brayer, *William Blackmore*, vol. 2: *Early Financing of the Denver and Rio Grande Railway* (Denver: Bradford-Robinson, 1949), 19–30.
13. *Santa Fe Weekly New Mexican*, January 31, 1871.
14. *Thunderbolt*, February 20, 1871.
15. David F. Myrick, *New Mexico's Railroads: An Historical Survey* (Golden, CO: Colorado Railroad Museum, 1970), 95–103.
16. *Rocky Mountain Sentinel*, July 24, 1879.
17. Ralph Emerson Twitchell, *Old Santa Fe: The Story of New Mexico's Ancient Capital* (Santa Fe: Santa Fe New Mexican Publishing Corp., 1925), 400. Twitchell

notes that courts ruled the issuance of the bonds to be beyond the authority of the city or county, but that they were later validated by action of Congress.

18. Certificate of Incorporation, New Mexican Printing and Publishing Company, February 14, 1880, Records of the Territorial Secretary, TANM.

19. See Stratton, *Territorial Press of New Mexico*, 27.

20. W. G. Ritch, "New Mexico: A Sketch of Its History and Review of Its Resources," appended to *The Legislative Blue Book of the Territory of New Mexico* (Santa Fe: Charles W. Greene, Public Printer, 1882), 38.

21. Fray Angélico Chávez, *But Time and Chance: The Story of Padre Martínez of Taos, 1793–1867* (Santa Fe: Sunstone Press, 1981), 49. According to Fray Chávez, the 1834 iteration of *El Crepúsculo* was not published by Padre Martínez as popularly supposed, but by don Antonio Barreiro.

22. *Census of Agriculture* (Washington, D.C.: U.S. Department of Agriculture, 1880, 1890). Numbers cited are totals for "Neat Cattle," exclusive of milch cows and oxen.

23. See Frank D. Reeve, *History of New Mexico*, vol. 2 (New York: Lewis Historical Publishing Co., 1961), 211; and David Remley, *Bell Ranch: Cattle Ranching in the Southwest, 1824–1947* (Albuquerque: University of New Mexico Press, 1993), 69.

24. The *St. Louis Globe Democrat* report of an interview with Max Frost is reproduced in the *Santa Fe New Mexican Review*, February 22, 1884.

25. With reference to Rynerson's involvement in the cattle business, see Miller, "William L. Rynerson in New Mexico," 117–24.

26. *Santa Fe New Mexican Review*, February 22, 1884.

27. L. W. Haskell to Charles Devens, May 13, 1878, NARA, RG 60.

28. Frank Springer to Hon. Rush Clark, April 9, 1878, Records of the War Department, NARA, RG 165. Copy in Chase Ranch Records, RGHC.

29. See Hana Samek, "No 'Bed of Roses': The Careers of Four Mescalero Indian Agents, 1871–1878," *New Mexico Historical Review* 57:2 (1982): 149–51.

30. C. L. Sonnichsen, *The Mescalero Apaches* (Norman: University of Oklahoma Press, 1958), 218–20.

31. W. H. Hutchinson, ed., *A Bar Cross Man: The Life and Personal Writings of Eugene Manlove Rhodes* (Norman: University of Oklahoma Press, 1956), 39. Hinman Rhodes was the father of the novelist Eugene Manlove Rhodes.

32. John H. Riley to S. B. Elkins, March 8, 1892, letter reproduced in Hutchinson, *A Bar Cross Man*, 41–42.

33. Miguel Antonio Otero, *The Real Billy the Kid, with New Light on the Lincoln County War* (New York: Rufus Rockwell Wilson, 1936), 34–38. Otero's story seems the likely source for a similar but unattributed reference in Westphall, *Thomas Benton Catron*, 76–77. Westphall stipulates that, while Riley condoned dishonest trading practices, he refused to deal in stolen cattle.

34. Henry J. Tobias, *A History of the Jews in New Mexico* (Albuquerque: University of New Mexico Press, 1990), 84–85.

35. Regarding the military warrant issue, see Floyd Fierman, "The Staabs of Santa Fe," *Rio Grande History* 13 (1983): 9.

36. Philip Rasch, *Gunsmoke in Lincoln County* (Laramie: National Association for Outlaw and Lawman History, 1997), 17.

37. Floyd S. Fierman, *The Spiegelbergs of New Mexico* (El Paso: Texas Western College Press, 1964), 41.

38. Nolan, *Lincoln County War*, 47.

39. Rodman Wilson Paul, *Mining Frontiers of the Far West, 1848–1880* (New York: Holt, Rinehart and Winston, 1963), 156.

40. William Baxter, *The Gold of the Ortiz Mountains: A Story of New Mexico and the West's First Major Gold Rush* (Santa Fe: Lone Butte Press, 2004), 70–72.

41. Records of the Territorial Secretary, TANM.

42. L. Bradford Prince, *Report of the Governor of New Mexico to the Secretary of the Interior* (Washington, D.C.: U.S. Government Printing Office, 1890).

43. For a general history of the Cañon del Agua Grant, see J. J. Bowden, *Private Land Claims in the Southwest*, vol. 2, chap. 6 (Master of Laws thesis, Southern Methodist University, 1969), 472–84.

44. *New York World*, January 6, 1895.

45. Miguel Antonio Otero, *My Life on the Frontier*, vol. 2: *1882–1897* (Albuquerque: University of New Mexico Press, 1939), 83.

46. *Golden Retort*, May 25, 1883.

47. Otero, *My Life on the Frontier*, 2:83–84.

48. *United States v. San Pedro and Cañon del Agua Co.*, 17 Pac. 337 (1888).

49. Ibid.

50. *San Pedro and Cañon del Agua Co. v. United States*, 146 U.S. 120 (1892).

51. Paige W. Christiansen, *The Story of Mining in New Mexico* (Socorro: New Mexico Bureau of Mines and Mineral Resources, 1974), 17–18.

52. Ibid., 24–25.

53. T. B. Catron to S. B. Elkins, December 26, 1889, SBE/WVU, A&M No. 1794.

54. Baxter, *Gold of the Ortiz Mountains*, 64–80, 102–16.

55. Ibid.

56. *New York Times*, September 13, 1897.

57. *Santa Fe New Mexican*, October 3, 1899.

58. *Las Vegas Daily Optic*, May 18, 1897. See also White, Koch, Kelley and McCarthy, Attorneys at Law, *Land Title Study*, 230.

59. *Las Vegas Gazette*, August 5, 1880. As patented, the grant contained 69,458, rather than the 64,000 cited.

60. Lummis, *Letters from the Southwest*, 146.

61. Ritch, "New Mexico: A Sketch of Its History and Review of Its Resources," 28.

62. *New York Times*, June 14, 1883.

63. *Rio Grande Republican*, January 20, 1883.

64. *Santa Fe New Mexican Review*, August 16, 1883.

65. Rasch, *Gunsmoke in Lincoln County*, 42, 60.

66. Nolan, *Lincoln County War*, 47.

67. LaMoine Langston, *A History of Masonry in New Mexico* (Roswell, NM: Hall-Poorbaugh Press, 1977), 1–5.

Chapter Eight

1. Nathan Bibo Sr., "The 'Making' of Albuquerque," *Santa Fe Magazine* 17:2 (January 1923): 55.
2. Francis A. Walker, *Compendium of the Ninth Census*, 1870 (Washington, D.C.: U.S. Government Printing Office, 1872); Walker, *Compendium of the Tenth Census*, 1880 (Washington, D.C.: U.S. Government Printing Office, 1883).
3. As reported in the *Albuquerque Morning Journal*, June 5, 1883.
4. *Santa Fe New Mexican and Review*, June 7, 1883.
5. Chaves was identified as a Ring member by Frank Warner Angel as quoted in Lee Scott Theisen, "Frank Warner Angel's Notes on New Mexico Territory, 1878," *Arizona and the West* 18:4 (1976): 346; by Larson, *New Mexico Populism*, 25; and by Roberts, *Death Comes for the Chief Justice*, 120–22. Antonio Joseph was named as a member of the Ring, primarily for his activity in land grant speculation, by Larson, *New Mexico's Quest for Statehood*, 144, 163; and by Ebright, *Land Grants and Lawsuits in Northern New Mexico*, 43.
6. This account is primarily as presented in a memorial to Congress, composed and adopted by the Chaves council, as published in the *Albuquerque Evening Democrat*, March 13, 1884.
7. Ibid.
8. *Santa Fe Weekly New Mexican Review*, March 13, 1884.
9. *Santa Fe New Mexican Review*, February 16, 1884.
10. *Santa Fe New Mexican Review*, April 5, 1884.
11. *Santa Fe New Mexican Review*, February 29, 1884.
12. Lew Wallace to Susan Wallace, October 8, 1878, IHS; Susan E. Wallace, *The Land of the Pueblos* (New York: John B. Alden, 1889), 15.
13. Twitchell, *Leading Facts*, 2:493–94.
14. *Albuquerque Evening Democrat*, March 27, 1884. The Tertio Millennial Celebration had occurred in 1883. The bill referred to was for payment of outstanding obligations incurred in connection with the exposition.
15. *Rio Grande Republican*, April 12, 1884.
16. *Santa Fe New Mexican Review*, March 6, 1884.
17. Gordon R. Owen, *The Two Alberts: Fountain and Fall* (Las Cruces, NM: Yucca Tree Press, 1996), 159.
18. *Rio Grande Republican*, August 30, 1884.
19. *Rio Grande Republican*, September 13, 1884.
20. *Albuquerque Morning Journal*, August 30, 1884.
21. *Santa Fe New Mexican Review*, September 3, 1884.
22. *Rio Grande Republican*, September 6, 1884.
23. *Las Vegas Daily Optic*, July 31, 1884. According to the memorandum upon which the letter is supposedly based, the Elkins mentioned is Samuel Elkins, who was managing his brother's mining interests in Santa Fe County. As to the pseudonym of the writer, "Ithurial" (more commonly spelled "Ithuriel") refers to a

cherub or angel in John Milton's *Paradise Lost*. Ithuriel had been sent by Gabriel to locate Satan, whose identity was concealed as he moved at large in Paradise. The touch of Ithuriel's spear was said to expose deceit.

24. *Las Vegas Daily Optic*, March 7, 1884.

25. *Santa Fe New Mexican Review*, August 14, 1884.

26. *Rio Grande Republican*, September 27, 1884. A note listing the names appearing in the published Ithurial letter is on file in the Catron Papers (TBC/CSWR), series 401. A note signed "WBS" reads, "This is the original memorandum made by me as Prince talked, which forms part of the Ithurial letter of the 31st July."

27. L. Bradford Prince to John H. Riley, October 22, 1884, copy in LBP/NMRCA.

28. *New York Times*, November 1, 1884.

29. *Golden Retort*, August 22, 1884.

30. For detailed information on Ross's life and times, see Richard A. Ruddy, *Edmund G. Ross: Soldier, Senator, Abolitionist* (Albuquerque: University of New Mexico Press, 2013).

31. William W. Warden to President Grover Cleveland, June 12, 1885, EGR/KSHS.

32. Edmund G. Ross to John O'Grady, March 26, 1887, copy in EGR/CSWR.

33. Ibid.

34. Twitchell, *Leading Facts*, 2:501. In the John O'Grady letter of March 26, 1887, Ross says only that decisions on pending legislative matters were "well known to be dictated by conspicuous members of the Ring outside the membership of the body."

35. Ross to John O'Grady, March 26, 1887.

Chapter Nine

1. See Ebright, *Land Grants and Lawsuits in Northern New Mexico*, 216. According to Ebright, Hobart advocated for issuance of a patent that would designate the common lands of the Las Vegas grant as private property, even as he claimed an interest in the same property.

2. See Anselmo Arellano, "The People's Movement: Las Gorras Blancas," in *The Contested Homeland: A Chicano History of New Mexico*, ed. Erlinda Gonzales-Berry and David R. Maciel (Albuquerque: University of New Mexico Press, 2000), 59–82.

3. See Robert J. Rosenbaum and Robert W. Larson, "Mexicano Resistance to the Expropriation of Grant Lands in New Mexico," in *Land, Water, and Culture: New Perspectives on Hispanic Land Grants*, ed. Charles L. Briggs and John R. Van Ness (Albuquerque: University of New Mexico Press, 1987), 88–90. For a more elaborate narrative on the White Caps, see Robert J. Rosenbaum, *Mexicano Resistance in the Southwest: The Sacred Right of Self-Preservation* (Austin: University of Texas Press, 1981), 99–124.

4. Rosenbaum, *Mexicano Resistance in the Southwest*, 99.

5. *Santa Fe Sun*, August 9, 1890.

6. Arellano, "The People's Movement: Las Gorras Blancas," 65.

7. Pablo Mitchell, *Coyote Nation: Sexuality, Race, and Conquest in Modernizing New Mexico, 1880–1920* (Chicago: University of Chicago Press, 2005), 18.

8. A. Gabriel Meléndez, *Spanish-Language Newspapers in New Mexico, 1834–1958* (Tucson: University of Arizona Press, 2005), 66.

9. Article attributed to *La Voz del Pueblo*, reprinted in *El Estandarte de Springer*, October 13, 1892. In original Spanish, the passage reads, "El otro es que en cuestiones que atenen á su sangre directamente, con rarísimas excepciones, todos son unos para combatir al enemigo de su raza. Los Neo-Mexicanos saben que no tiene su raza enemigo mas agresivo o feroz que Torquemada del anillo de Santa Fé; que los a reducido con su gavilla de ladrones y terrenos, y con negar los fondes públicos, para que pueden él y sus tenientes especular con los bonos que se le pagan al pobre pueblo por sus servicios, comprandóselos con descuento á las mas grande y ruin miseria."

10. For an in-depth study of the road to statehood, the most current and comprehensive at this writing, see David V. Holtby, *Forty-Seventh Star: New Mexico's Struggle for Statehood* (Norman: University of Oklahoma Press, 2012).

11. See Larson, *New Mexico's Quest for Statehood*, 147–68.

12. Ibid., 151–52. According to Larson, signers of the petition were mostly "prominent commercial people, of whom approximately half were Jewish businessmen from Albuquerque." Some had influential connections in Washington.

13. Ibid., 149–54.

14. L. Bradford Prince, *New Mexico's Struggle for Statehood: Sixty Years of Effort to Obtain Self Government* (Santa Fe: New Mexican Printing Co., 1910), 48.

15. *Santa Fe Sun*, October 4, 1890.

16. *El Estandarte de Springer*, September 25, 1890. The original Spanish reads, "El pueblo debe recordárse que en el día 7 de Octubre próimo [próximo] el documento llamado la 'constitutión del Anillo de Amos' sera sometida al pueblo á según un decreto de la finada trasera. Recuerdo el pueblo cual es su deber. Es este, de ír á las urnas electorales de mañana y tarde y ayudar por sus votos al aborto infernal."

17. Twitchell, *Leading Facts*, 2:509–10.

18. Howard R. Lamar, *Charlie Siringo's West: An Interpretive Biography* (Albuquerque: University of New Mexico Press, 2005), 158–59.

19. *Deming Headlight*, March 14, 1891.

20. *Santa Fe Sun*, September 27, 1890; Lamar, *The Far Southwest*, 187. Lamar notes that Catron worked closely with Pedro Perea, a reliable Republican ally, to fight the school bill.

21. *Santa Fe Sun*, September 27, 1890. According to Victor Westphall, Catron vehemently denied any hostility to the Kistler bill and claimed to have offered

amendments to turn an impractical and unfair result into a workable act. *Thomas Benton Catron*, 206.

22. *Southwest Sentinel*, September 27, 1892.

23. Larson, *New Mexico's Quest for Statehood*, 170.

24. Ibid., 145.

25. See John R. Chávez, *The Lost Land: The Chicano Image of the Southwest* (Albuquerque: University of New Mexico Press, 1984), 43–62, for a discussion of differences in California, Texas, and New Mexico following transitions to U.S. administration.

26. Clark S. Knowlton, "Land-Grant Problems Among the State's Spanish-Americans," in *Poverty, Equal Opportunity and Full Employment, Hearings Before the Subcommittee on Equal Opportunities, Committee on Education and Labor*, U.S. House of Representatives, 94th Congress (1975).

27. Chávez, *Lost Land*, 55.

28. See Deena J. González, *Refusing the Favor: The Spanish-Mexican Women of Santa Fe, 1820–1880* (New York: Oxford University Press, 1999), 79–106.

29. Ibid. While citizenship was accorded to Hispanic residents of New Mexico following the American Occupation and as a provision of the Treaty of Guadalupe Hidalgo, Native American residents were not initially designated as full citizens of the United States.

30. Fray Angélico Chávez, *My Penitente Land: Reflections on Spanish New Mexico* (Albuquerque: University of New Mexico Press, 1974), 253.

31. Phillip B. Gonzales, "Struggle for Survival: The Hispanic Land Grants of New Mexico, 1848–2001," *Agricultural History* 77:2 (Spring 2003): 304.

32. *Santa Fe Herald*, November 5, 1888.

33. See multiple references to Catron and the Ring in Reies López Tijerina, *They Called Me "King Tiger"* (Houston, TX: Arte Público Press, 2000).

34. Ibid., 58.

35. For an analysis of the role of Hispanic ethnic identity in the quest for statehood, see John Nieto-Phillips, "Spanish American Ethnic Identity and New Mexico's Statehood Struggle," in Gonzales-Berry and Maciel, *The Contested Homeland*, 97–142.

36. See Larson, *New Mexico's Quest for Statehood*, 70–71, concerning a dispute between political factions in 1852.

37. For a discussion of the stereotyping of Hispanics and the "Black Legend of Spain," see C. L. Sonnichsen, *From Hopalong to Hud: Thoughts on Western Fiction* (College Station: Texas A&M University Press, 1978), 83–102.

38. John C. Calhoun, *Congressional Globe*, 30th Congress, 1st Sess., new series No. 7 (January 6, 1848), 98–99.

39. John C. Calhoun, *Congressional Globe*, 30th Congress, 2nd Sess., new series No. 3 (December 19, 1848), 33.

40. *New York Times*, February 6, 1882.

41. *New York Times*, February 28, 1882.

42. Gómez, *Manifest Destinies*, 47–79.

43. John M. Nieto-Phillips, *The Language of Blood: The Making of Spanish-American Identity in New Mexico, 1880s-1930s* (Albuquerque: University of New Mexico Press, 2004), 60.

44. *New York Times*, August 23, 1881. The item referenced is reprinted from the *Indianapolis Journal*.

45. See, for example, L. Bradford Prince, "Claims to Statehood," in *North American Review* 156:436 (March 1893): 346–54. Prince also presented resolutions of the Trans-Mississippi Commercial Congress, adopted November 21, 1907, to the House Committee on Territories on January 29, 1908. See *Official Proceedings, Trans-Mississippi Commercial Congress*, 18th Sess., Muskogee, Oklahoma (November 19–22, 1907), 82–84.

46. Charles Montgomery, *The Spanish Redemption: Heritage, Power, and Loss on New Mexico's Upper Rio Grande* (Berkeley: University of California Press, 2002), 73.

47. Larson, *New Mexico's Quest for Statehood*, 144.

48. See Dargan, "New Mexico's Fight for Statehood, 1895–1912, Part 1," 28.

49. George W. Julian, "Land-Stealing in New Mexico," *North American Review* 145:368 (July 1887): 28.

50. See "The New-Mexico Job," *New York Times*, May 24, 1876. The *Times* found it "amazing" that the House should have taken so irresponsible an action as to pass a statehood bill for New Mexico "to oblige Elkins."

51. Larson, *New Mexico's Quest for Statehood*, 116–34.

52. *New York Times*, March 11, 1876.

53. David Townsend, *The 47th Star: New Mexico's Struggle for Statehood* (Alamogordo, NM: Alamogordo Statehood Centennial Committee, 2012), 24–25.

54. John Braeman, "Albert J. Beveridge and Statehood for the Southwest," *Arizona and the West* 10:4 (Winter 1968): 337.

55. *New York Times*, February 28, 1909.

56. *Santa Fe Democrat*, December 15, 1881.

57. *Southwest Sentinel*, August 2, 1892. As to the "Las Cruces Colonel" suggested as Catron's colleague in the Senate, the *Sentinel* was likely referring to William Logan Rynerson or possibly Albert Jennings Fountain. The *Sentinel*'s suggestions for United States senator were purely tongue-in-cheek. The paper generally preferred Democratic candidates.

58. *Southwest Sentinel*, October 11, 1892.

59. Dargan, "New Mexico's Fight for Statehood, 1895–1912, Part 1," 31–32.

60. Stratton, *Territorial Press of New Mexico*, 202.

61. Marion Dargan, "New Mexico's Fight for Statehood, 1895–1912, Part 3: The Opposition Within the Territory (1888–1890)," *New Mexico Historical Review* 15:1 (January 1940): 133–87.

62. T. B. Catron to S. B. Elkins, December 21, 1910, SBE/WVU, A&M No. 0053.

Chapter Ten

1. William R. Morley to Ada McPherson Morley, September 8, 1878, quoted in Cleaveland, *The Morleys*, 158.
2. *Era Southwestern*, March 4, 1880.
3. *Albuquerque Daily Journal*, June 28, 1884. The quote is attributed to "J. Francisco Perea." Reference to Perea's place of residence as Jemez Springs indicates that the person referred to was Francisco Perea, who was elected territorial delegate in 1863 and served one term in Congress.
4. *Santa Fe Daily Sun*, February 8, 1891.
5. Benjamin Harrison to Elkins, January 23, 1890, SBE/WVU, A&M No. 0053.
6. "A Drunken Atty. Gen. with an Important Criminal Case pending," holographic note, n.d., WGR/HL. William G. Ritch describes indiscretions of the attorney general during the fall 1875 court term at Mora. Governor E. G. Ross told Breeden in a published letter dated November 24, 1885, that he was removed for "drunkenness, licentiousness, gambling," and other failings. A clipping containing the letter is in the Ritch scrapbooks, WGR/HL. Some newspapers referred to Ross's letter but declined to print it. Breeden fought removal and retained the office of attorney general.
7. Twitchell, *Leading Facts*, 2:552.
8. Breeden to Elkins, May 31, 1874, SBE/WVU, A&M No. 0053.
9. Frost to Judge A. L. Morrison, September 26, 1892, TBC/CSWR.
10. Stratton, *Territorial Press of New Mexico*, 34.
11. *Civil Service Record* 11:7 (January 1892).
12. *New York Times*, January 5, 1912.
13. James J. Dolan to Catron, October 6, 1894, TBC/CSWR.
14. *New York Times*, March 28, 1896.
15. *New York Times*, September 14, 1896.
16. Westphall, *Thomas Benton Catron*, 142–48.
17. Ibid., 230–68.
18. Robert J. Torrez, "'El Bornes': La Tierra Amarilla and T. D. Burns," *New Mexico Historical Review* 56:2 (April 1981): 171.
19. Larson, *New Mexico's Quest for Statehood*, 191.
20. T. B. Catron to M. A. Otero, November 9, 1884, TBC/CSWR.
21. T. B. Catron to M. A. Otero, December 14, 1896, TBC/CSWR.
22. Westphall, *Thomas Benton Catron*. Westphall details events leading to the choice of Otero as governor, 270–75.
23. Catron to Elkins, October 4, 1897, and November 18, 1897, TBC/CSWR.
24. Catron to Elkins, October 4, 1897, TBC/CSWR.
25. Catron to Elkins, November 18, 1897, TBC/CSWR.

26. Catron to Elkins, April 19, 1898, TBC/CSWR.

27. Catron to Elkins, April 4, 1901, TBC/CSWR.

28. Catron to Elkins, November 11, 1901, SBE/WVU, A&M No. 0053.

29. Miguel Antonio Otero, *My Nine Years as Governor of the Territory of New Mexico, 1897–1906* (Albuquerque: University of New Mexico Press, 1940), 329–30.

30. Twitchell, *Leading Facts*, 2:520.

31. Otis K. Rice, *West Virginia: A History* (Lexington: University Press of Kentucky, 1985), 208–9.

32. Elkins to A. Staab, May 12, 1896; H. L. Waldo to Elkins, February 18, 1900; Max Frost to Elkins, March 21, 1900; William Breeden to Elkins, February 1900, SBE/WVU, A&M No. 0053.

33. Catron to Waldo, March 20, 1893, TBC/CSWR. The object of Catron's wrath presumably was James O'Brien, who had been sent from Minnesota to serve as a federal judge in New Mexico. O'Brien had angered Catron with words of sympathy for the White Caps of San Miguel County.

34. Catron to Frost, October 16, 1892, TBC/CSWR.

35. Catron to Elkins, July 18, 1894, TBC/CSWR.

36. Catron to Elkins, February 6, 1909, TBC/CSWR.

37. Catron to Elkins, September 19, 1910, TBC/CSWR. Catron tells Elkins, "After coming from Washington, I talked to Henry and told him what you said, and asked him, rather urged him, to go into the campaign with me and make a fight for the senatorship. He answered very positively that he did not want it and that he had made up his mind to not have anything to do with it." In view of the close personal relationship among the three men, it seems likely that "Henry" was Henry Waldo, who was active in Santa Fe as solicitor for the AT&SF Railway at the time.

38. W. H. Andrews to T. B. Catron, August 16, 1910, TBC/CSWR.

39. Catron to Elkins, April 9, 1893, transcript in MDP/CSWR.

40. See David H. Stratton, ed., *The Memoirs of Albert B. Fall*, monograph No. 15 (El Paso: Texas Western Press, 1966), 49–50.

41. Westphall, *Thomas Benton Catron*, 348–56.

42. C. C. Catron to John W. Catron, March 14, 1921, TBC/CSWR.

43. Lamar, *Far Southwest*, 496. For a summary of Bursum's political career, see Ron Hamm, *The Bursums of New Mexico: Four Generations of Leadership and Service* (Socorro: Manzanares Street Publishing, 2012).

44. Holtby, *Forty-Seventh Star*, 247. The identification of Santa Fe Ring leaders is attributed to Dorothy I. Cline, *New Mexico's 1910 Constitution: A 19th Century Product* (Santa Fe: The Lightning Tree, 1985); and Jack E. Holmes, *Politics in New Mexico* (Albuquerque: University of New Mexico Press, 1967). There is little consistency in persons named as newer Ring members after the decline of the Elkins-Catron group starting around 1890. Of those named by Holtby and Cline based on Holmes's analysis, Fall, Spiess, and Charles Springer are outliers, identified as Ring members in few, if any, other sources.

45. Ebright, *Land Grants and Lawsuits in Northern New Mexico*, 145–68.

46. *Albuquerque Morning Journal*, September 29, 1911.

Chapter Eleven

1. *Santa Fe Weekly New Mexican*, September 9, 1878.

2. Hal K. Rothman, *On Rims and Ridges: The Los Alamos Area Since 1880* (Lincoln: University of Nebraska Press, 1992), 34.

3. Lamar, *The Far Southwest*, 164.

4. Montoya, *Translating Property*, 115; Rasch, *Gunsmoke in Lincoln County*, 101; Rosenbaum, *Mexicano Resistance in the Southwest*, 76.

5. Jon Sharpe, *Canyon O'Grady #10: The Great Land Swindle* (New York: Signet, 1990).

6. Concerning actual and potential influence of fiction works on historical perception, see, for example, Henry Nash Smith, *Virgin Land: The American West as Symbol and Myth* (Cambridge, MA: Harvard University Press, 1950); C. L. Sonnichsen, *From Hopalong to Hud* (College Station: Texas A&M University Press, 1978); and David L. Caffey, Land of Enchantment, Land of Conflict: New Mexico in English-Language Fiction (College Station: Texas A&M University Press, 1999).

7. Pat F. Garrett, *The Authentic Life of Billy the Kid*, new edition annotated by Maurice Garland Fulton (1882; New York: Macmillan Co., 1927), 52–59.

8. Otero, *The Real Billy the Kid*, 54.

9. Ibid., 122.

10. H. B. Henning, ed., *George Curry, 1861–1947: An Autobiography* (Albuquerque: University of New Mexico Press, 1958), 29.

11. W. H. Hutchinson, *A Bar Cross Liar* (Stillwater, OK: Redlands Press, 1959), 54.

12. Quoted in W. H. Hutchinson, *A Bar Cross Man: The Life and Personal Writings of Eugene Manlove Rhodes* (Norman: University of Oklahoma Press, 1956), 38.

13. Ibid., 36–37.

14. Hutchinson, *A Bar Cross Liar*, 24.

15. Ibid., 26.

16. Ibid., 40.

17. Rhodes, *West Is West*, 138–39.

18. Hutchinson, *A Bar Cross Man*, 261–62.

19. C. L. Sonnichsen, *Tucson: The Life and Times of an American City* (Norman: University of Oklahoma Press, 1982), 72.

20. Amelia Bean, *Time for Outrage* (Garden City, NY: Doubleday, 1967), 289.

21. Elizabeth Fackler, *Billy the Kid: The Legend of El Chivato* (New York: Forge, 1995), 511–12.

22. Ibid., 154.

23. Ibid., 169.

24. Ibid., 512.

25. Mike Blakely, *Spanish Blood* (New York: Forge, 1996), 57.
26. Matt Braun, *Jury of Six* (New York: St. Martin's Press, 1980), 229–30.
27. Frederic Bean, *Santa Fe Showdown* (New York: Zebra Books, 1993), 251.
28. Murphy, *Philmont: A History of New Mexico's Cimarron Country*, 210.
29. Ibid., 224.
30. Rubén Martínez, *Desert America: Boom and Bust in the New Old West* (New York: Metropolitan Books, 2012).

Chapter Twelve

1. *Boston Herald*, May 23, 1884.
2. See Limerick, *Legacy of Conquest*.
3. Utley, *High Noon in Lincoln County*, 188.
4. Walter, *Banking in New Mexico*, 20.
5. See Cleaveland, *The Morleys*, 123.
6. *Santa Fe Weekly New Mexican*, July 12, 1879; John P. Wilson, *Merchants, Guns and Money: The Story of Lincoln County and Its Wars* (Santa Fe: Museum of New Mexico Press, 1987), 125.
7. Nolan, *Lincoln County War*, 440–41.
8. Hearsay concerning Catron's possible involvement in the murder of Albert Jennings Fountain and the poisoning of rivals at a dinner at the territorial penitentiary is reported in a letter to the *Syracuse Post-Standard*, July 2, 1899. The allegation that Catron and former sheriff Charles Conklin arranged the murder of Frank Chavez is referenced in a letter from Max Frost to Judge A. L. Morrison, September 26, 1896, TBC/CSWR. Several accusations referenced in this section are discussed in Westphall, *Thomas Benton Catron*.
9. Keleher, *Fabulous Frontier*, 212.
10. Victor Westphall, "Thomas Benton Catron: A Historical Defense," *New Mexico Historical Review* 63:1 (January 1988): 57. Westphall speaks in Catron's defense regarding several of the common charges of complicity in violent acts.
11. Norman Cleaveland, *Can New Mexico's Historians Improve Their Discipline?* (privately published with *The Great Santa Fe Coverup*, 1982).
12. Norman Cleaveland, *A Synopsis of the Great New Mexico Cover-Up* (privately published, 1989), 10–11.
13. John Porter Bloom, "The Santa Fe Ring: Toward a Definition," prepared for presentation at the annual conference of the Historical Society of New Mexico, 1993.
14. Howard R. Lamar, "Political Patterns in New Mexico and Utah Territories, 1850–1900," *Utah Historical Quarterly* 28:4 (October 1960): 377.

15. Caitlin Ginley, *Grading the Nation: How Accountable Is Your State?* Center for Public Integrity, March 19, 2012. www.publicintegrity.org.

16. Roxanne Dunbar-Ortiz, *Roots of Resistance: A History of Land Tenure in New Mexico*, 2nd ed. (Norman: University of Oklahoma Press, 2007), 104.

17. *Grant County Herald*, September 21, 1878.

18. Oliver La Farge, "New Mexico," *Holiday* 11:2 (February 1952): 46.

BIBLIOGRAPHY

Archival and Manuscript Sources

Chase Ranch Records. Rio Grande Historical Collections, New Mexico State University, Las Cruces.

Collection of the Old Mill Museum. Cimarron, NM.

Edmund G. Ross Papers. Center for Southwest Research, University of New Mexico, Albuquerque.

Edmund G. Ross Papers. Kansas State Historical Society, Topeka.

Frank Springer Papers. CS Cattle Company, Cimarron, NM.

Frank Springer Papers. National Museum of Natural History, Department of Paleobiology, Smithsonian Institution, Washington, D.C.

Herman B. Weisner Papers. Rio Grande Historical Collections, New Mexico State University, Las Cruces.

L. Bradford Prince Papers. New Mexico State Records Center and Archives, Santa Fe.

Lew Wallace Collection. Fray Angélico Chávez History Library, Museum of New Mexico, Santa Fe.

Lew Wallace Collection. Indiana Historical Society, Indianapolis.

Marion Dargan Papers. Center for Southwest Research, University of New Mexico, Albuquerque.

Maxwell Land Grant Collection. Center for Southwest Research, University of New Mexico, Albuquerque.

Papers of William Gillet Ritch. Huntington Library, San Marino, CA.

Records of the Bureau of Indian Affairs. RG 75, NARA, Washington, D.C.

Records of the Department of Justice. RG 60, NARA, College Park, MD.

Records of the Office of the Secretary of the Interior. RG 48, NARA, College Park, MD.

Records of the War Department. RG 165, NARA, College Park, MD.

Records of the Work Projects Administration. RG 69, NARA, College Park, MD.

Robert N. Mullin Collection. Haley Memorial Library and History Center, Midland, TX.

Stephen B. Elkins Papers. West Virginia Collection, West Virginia University, Morgantown.

Territorial Archives of New Mexico, 1846–1912. Microfilm edition, New Mexico State Records Center and Archives, Santa Fe.

Thomas Benton Catron Papers. Center for Southwest Research, University of New Mexico, Albuquerque.

Print Materials

Anaya, Rudolfo A. *Heart of Aztlan*. Berkeley, CA: Justa Publications, 1976.

Aragón y Ulibarrí, Daniel. *Devil's Hatband/Centillo del Diablo: A Story About a People's Struggle Against Land Theft and Racism*. Santa Fe: Sunstone Press, 1999.

Ball, Larry D. *The United States Marshals of New Mexico and Arizona Territories, 1846–1912*. Albuquerque: University of New Mexico Press, 1982.

Bartlett, Richard A., ed. *The Gilded Age in America, 1865–1900*. Reading, MA: Addison-Wesley, 1969.

Baxter, William. *The Gold of the Ortiz Mountains: A Story of New Mexico and the West's First Major Gold Rush*. Santa Fe: Lone Butte Press, 2004.

Bean, Amelia. *Time for Outrage*. Garden City, NY: Doubleday, 1967.

Bean, Frederic. *Santa Fe Showdown*. New York: Zebra Books, 1993.

Benavides, David. "Lawyer-Induced Partitioning of New Mexican Land Grants: An Ethical Travesty." Research Paper of the Center for Land Grant Studies, Guadalupita, NM, 2005.

Bibo, Nathan, Sr. "The 'Making' of Albuquerque." *Santa Fe Magazine* 17:2 (January 1923): 55–56.

Blakely, Mike. *Spanish Blood*. New York: Forge, 1996.

Bloom, John Porter. "The Santa Fe Ring: Toward a Definition." Paper prepared for presentation at the annual conference of the Historical Society of New Mexico, Albuquerque, April 22–24, 1993.

Bourke, John G. *On the Border with Crook*. New York: Charles Scribner's Sons, 1891.

Bowden, J. J. "Private Land Claims in the Southwest." Vols. 1–6. Master of Laws thesis, Southern Methodist University, 1969.

Bradfute, Richard Wells. *The Court of Private Land Claims: The Adjudication of Spanish and Mexican Land Grant Titles, 1891–1904*. Albuquerque: University of New Mexico Press, 1975.

Braeman, John. "Albert J. Beveridge and Statehood for the Southwest." *Arizona and the West* 10:4 (Winter 1968): 313–42.

Braun, Matt. *Jury of Six*. New York: St. Martin's Press, 1980.

Brayer, Herbert O. *William Blackmore*. Vol. 1: *The Spanish-Mexican Land Grants of New Mexico and Colorado, 1863–1878*. Denver: Bradford-Robinson, 1949.

———. *William Blackmore*. Vol. 2: *Early Financing of the Denver and Rio Grande Railway*. Denver: Bradford-Robinson, 1949.

Caffey, David L. *Frank Springer and New Mexico: From the Colfax County War to the Emergence of Modern Santa Fe*. College Station: Texas A&M University Press, 2006.

——. *Land of Enchantment, Land of Conflict: New Mexico in English-Language Fiction.* College Station: Texas A&M University Press, 1999.

Callow, Alexander B., Jr. *The Tweed Ring.* New York: Oxford University Press, 1966.

Caperton, Thomas J. *Rogue! Being an Account of the Life and High Times of Stephen W. Dorsey, United States Senator and New Mexico Cattle Baron.* Santa Fe: Museum of New Mexico Press, 1978.

Carter, Clarence E. "Colonialism in Continental United States." *South Atlantic Quarterly* 47:1 (January 1948): 17–28.

Cashman, Sean Dennis. *America in the Gilded Age: From the Death of Lincoln to the Rise of Theodore Roosevelt.* New York: New York University Press, 1984.

Chamberlain, Kathleen P. *In the Shadow of Billy the Kid: Susan McSween and the Lincoln County War.* Albuquerque: University of New Mexico Press, 2013.

Chávez, Fray Angélico. *But Time and Chance: The Story of Padre Martínez of Taos, 1793–1867.* Santa Fe: Sunstone Press, 1981.

——. *My Penitente Land: Reflections on Spanish New Mexico.* Albuquerque: University of New Mexico Press, 1974.

Chávez, John R. *The Lost Land: The Chicano Image of the Southwest.* Albuquerque: University of New Mexico Press, 1984.

Chávez, Thomas E. *New Mexico Past and Future.* Albuquerque: University of New Mexico Press, 2006.

Christiansen, Paige W. *The Story of Mining in New Mexico.* Socorro: New Mexico Bureau of Mines and Mineral Resources, 1974.

Clancy, Frank W. "Reminiscences of Territorial Days." In *Minutes of the New Mexico Bar Association, Thirty-Third Annual Session,* 47–60. Santa Fe: New Mexico Bar Association, 1919.

Cleaveland, Agnes Morley. *Satan's Paradise: From Lucien Maxwell to Fred Lambert.* Boston: Houghton Mifflin, 1952.

Cleaveland, Norman. *Can New Mexico's Historians Improve Their Discipline?* and *The Great Santa Fe Coverup.* Privately published, 1982.

——. *Colfax County's Chronic Murder Mystery.* Santa Fe: Rydal Press, 1977.

——. *Comments Made to the Huntington Westerners in San Marino, California, on September 19, 1987.* Privately published, 1987.

——. *A Synopsis of the Great New Mexico Cover-Up.* Privately published, 1989.

——— with George Fitzpatrick. *The Morleys: Young Upstarts on the Southwest Frontier.* Albuquerque: Calvin Horn, 1971.

Cleveland, Grover. "First Inaugural Address, March 4, 1885." In *Inaugural Addresses of the Presidents of the United States,* edited by John Vance Cheney. Chicago: R. R. Donnelley and Sons, 1905.

Cline, Dorothy I. *New Mexico's 1910 Constitution: A 19th Century Product.* Santa Fe: Lightning Tree, 1985.

Clum, Woodworth. *Apache Agent: The Story of John P. Clum.* Boston: Houghton Mifflin, 1936.

Coe, George W. *Frontier Fighter: The Autobiography of George W. Coe.* Boston: Houghton Mifflin, 1934.

Congressional Globe. Debates of the 30th Congress, 1st and 2nd Sess., 1847–1849.

Correia, David. *Properties of Violence: Law and Land Grant Struggle in Northern New Mexico.* Athens: University of Georgia Press, 2013.

Dargan, Marion. "New Mexico's Fight for Statehood, 1895–1912. Part 1: The Political Leaders of the Latter Half of the 1890s and Statehood." *New Mexico Historical Review* 14:1 (January 1939): 1–33.

———. "New Mexico's Fight for Statehood, 1895–1912. Part 3: The Opposition Within the Territory (1888–1890)." *New Mexico Historical Review* 15:1 (January 1940): 133–87.

Debo, Angie. *Geronimo: The Man, His Time, His Place.* Norman: University of Oklahoma Press, 1976.

Dorsey, Stephen W. "Land Stealing in New Mexico: A Rejoinder." *North American Review* 145:371 (October 1887): 17–31.

Duffus, R. L. *The Santa Fe Trail.* New York: Longmans, Green and Co., 1930.

Dunbar-Ortiz, Roxanne. *Roots of Resistance: A History of Land Tenure in New Mexico.* 2nd ed. Norman: University of Oklahoma Press, 2007.

Dunham, Harold H. "Discussion of Howard R. Lamar, 'Land Policy in the Spanish Southwest, 1846–1891: A Study in Contrasts.'" *Journal of Economic History* 22:4 (December 1962): 519–22.

———. *Government Handout: A Study in the Administration of Public Lands, 1875–1891.* Ann Arbor, MI: Edwards Brothers, 1941.

Ebright, Malcolm. "The Humphries Wildlife Management Area: History of Title and History of the Tierra Amarilla Grant." Prepared for the New Mexico Commission of Public Records, Santa Fe, 2009.

———. *Land Grants and Lawsuits in Northern New Mexico.* Albuquerque: University of New Mexico Press, 1994.

———, ed. *Spanish and Mexican Land Grants and the Law.* Manhattan, KS: Sunflower University Press, 1989.

———. *The Tierra Amarilla Grant: A History of Chicanery.* Santa Fe: Center for Land Grant Studies, 1980.

Edwards, Rebecca. *New Spirits: Americans in the Gilded Age, 1865–1905.* New York: Oxford University Press, 2006.

Ellis, Richard N. "The Humanitarian Generals." *Western Historical Quarterly* 3:2 (April 1972): 162–78.

Fackler, Elizabeth. *Billy the Kid: The Legend of El Chivato.* New York: Forge, 1995.

Faulk, Odie B. *Crimson Desert: Indian Wars of the American Southwest.* New York: Oxford University Press, 1974.

Fierman, Floyd S. *The Spiegelbergs of New Mexico.* El Paso: Texas Western College Press, 1964.

———. "The Staabs of Santa Fe." *Rio Grande History* 13 (1983): 2–23.

Fulton, Maurice Garland. *History of the Lincoln County War.* Edited by Robert N. Mullin. Tucson: University of Arizona Press, 1968.

Garrett, Pat F. *The Authentic Life of Billy the Kid.* Santa Fe: New Mexican Printing and Publishing Co., 1882. New edition annotated by Maurice Garland Fulton, *Pat F. Garrett's Authentic Life of Billy the Kid.* New York: Macmillan Co., 1927.

Gibson, A. M. *The Life and Death of Colonel Albert Jennings Fountain.* Norman: University of Oklahoma Press, 1965.

Gómez, Laura. *Manifest Destinies: The Making of the Mexican American Race.* New York: New York University Press, 2007.

———. "Race, Colonialism, and Criminal Law: Mexicans and the American Criminal Justice System in Territorial New Mexico." *Law and Society Review* 34:4 (2000): 1129–1201.

Gonzales, Phillip B. "Struggle for Survival: The Hispanic Land Grants of New Mexico, 1848–2001." *Agricultural History* 77:2 (Spring 2003): 293–323.

Gonzales-Berry, Erlinda, and David R. Maciel. *The Contested Homeland: A Chicano History of New Mexico.* Albuquerque: University of New Mexico Press, 2000.

González, Deena J. *Refusing the Favor: The Spanish-Mexican Women of Santa Fe, 1820–1880.* New York: Oxford University Press, 1999.

Gressley, Gene M. *West by East: The American West in the Gilded Age.* Charles Redd Monographs in Western History No. 1. Provo, UT: Brigham Young University Press, 1972.

Grove, Pearce S., Becky J. Barnett, and Sandra J. Hansen, eds. *New Mexico Newspapers: A Comprehensive Guide to Bibliographical Entries and Locations.* Albuquerque: University of New Mexico Press, 1975.

Hall, G. Emlen. *Four Leagues of Pecos: A Legal History of the Pecos Grant, 1800–1933.* Albuquerque: University of New Mexico Press, 1984.

———. "Juan Estevan Pino, 'Se Los Coma': New Mexico Land Speculation in the 1820s." *New Mexico Historical Review* 57:1 (January 1982): 27–42.

Hamm, Ron. *The Bursums of New Mexico: Four Generations of Leadership and Service.* Socorro, NM: Manzanares Street Publishing, 2012.

Harwood, Thomas. *History of New Mexico Spanish and English Missions of the Methodist Episcopal Church from 1850 to 1910.* 2 vols. Albuquerque: El Abogado Press, 1908, 1910.

Hefferan, Viola Clark. "Thomas Benton Catron." MA thesis, University of New Mexico, 1940.

Henning, H. G., ed. *George Curry, 1861–1947: An Autobiography.* Albuquerque: University of New Mexico Press, 1958.

Hilton, Tom. *Nevermore, Cimarron, Nevermore.* Fort Worth, TX: Western Heritage Press, 1970.

Hollister, Ovando J. *Colorado Volunteers in New Mexico, 1862.* Lakeside Press edition. Chicago: R. R. Donnelley and Sons, 1962. Originally published in 1863 as *History of the First Regiment of Colorado Volunteers.*

Holmes, Jack E. *Politics in New Mexico*. Albuquerque: University of New Mexico Press, 1967.

Holt, Herbert Bartlett. "Biographical Sketches of Prominent Pioneer Members of Aztec Lodge No. 3, A.F.&A.M. of New Mexico: Colonel William L. Rynerson." Typed transcription in Robert N. Mullin Collection, Haley Memorial Library and History Center, Midland, TX, n.d.

Holtby, David V. *Forty-Seventh Star: New Mexico's Struggle for Statehood*. Norman: University of Oklahoma Press, 2012.

Horn, Calvin. *New Mexico's Troubled Years: The Story of the Early Territorial Governors*. Albuquerque: Horn and Wallace, 1963.

Hutchinson, W. H. *A Bar Cross Liar*. Stillwater, OK: Redlands Press, 1959.

——, ed. *A Bar Cross Man: The Life and Personal Writings of Eugene Manlove Rhodes*. Norman: University of Oklahoma Press, 1956.

Jacobsen, Joel. *Such Men as Billy the Kid: The Lincoln County War Reconsidered*. Lincoln: University of Nebraska Press, 1994.

Julian, George W. "Land-Stealing in New Mexico." *North American Review* 145:368 (July 1887): 17–31.

Kaye, E. Donald. *Nathan Augustus Monroe Dudley*. Parker, CO: Outskirts Press, 2007.

Keleher, William A. *The Fabulous Frontier: Twelve New Mexico Items*. Albuquerque: University of New Mexico Press, 1945.

——. *Violence in Lincoln County, 1869–1881*. Albuquerque: University of New Mexico Press, 1957.

Kirkland, Edward C. *Industry Comes of Age: Business, Labor, and Public Policy, 1860–1897*. New York: Holt, Rinehart, and Winston, 1961.

Kraines, Oscar. "Louis Sulzbacher: Justice of the Supreme Court of Puerto Rico, 1900–1904." *Jewish Social Studies* 13:2 (April 1951): 127–32.

La Farge, Oliver. "New Mexico." *Holiday* 11:2 (February 1952): 34–47.

Lamar, Howard R. *Charlie Siringo's West: An Interpretive Biography*. Albuquerque: University of New Mexico Press, 2005.

——. *The Far Southwest, 1846–1912: A Territorial History*. New Haven: Yale University Press, 1966.

——. "Land Policy in the Spanish Southwest, 1846–1891: A Study in Contrasts." *Journal of Economic History* 22:4 (December 1962): 498–515.

——. "Political Patterns in New Mexico and Utah Territories, 1850–1900." *Utah Historical Quarterly* 28:4 (October 1960): 362–87.

Lambert, Oscar Doane. *Stephen Benton Elkins: American Foursquare*. Pittsburgh, PA: University of Pittsburgh Press, 1955.

Langston, LaMoine. *A History of Masonry in New Mexico*. Roswell, NM: Hall-Poorbaugh Press, 1977.

Larson, Robert W. *New Mexico Populism*. Boulder: Colorado Associated University Press, 1974.

———. *New Mexico's Quest for Statehood, 1846–1912.* Albuquerque: University of New Mexico Press, 1968.

———. "Territorial Politics and Cultural Impact." *New Mexico Historical Review* 60:3 (July 1985): 249–69.

Limerick, Patricia Nelson. *The Legacy of Conquest: The Unbroken Past of the American West.* New York: W. W. Norton and Co., 1987.

Lowry, Sharon K. "Mirrors and Blue Smoke: Stephen Dorsey and the Santa Fe Ring in the 1880s." *New Mexico Historical Review* 59:4 (1984): 395–409.

Lummis, Charles. *Letters from the Southwest: September 20, 1884 to March 14, 1885.* Edited by James W. Byrkit. Tucson: University of Arizona Press, 1989.

Martínez, Rubén. *Desert America: Boom and Bust in the New Old West.* New York: Metropolitan Books, 2012.

Marx, Leo. *The Machine in the Garden: Technology and the Pastoral Ideal in America.* New York: Oxford University Press, 1964.

Mauzy, Wayne L. *A Century in Santa Fe: The Story of the First National Bank of Santa Fe.* Santa Fe: First National Bank of Santa Fe, 1970.

Maxwell Land Grant Company. "Farming Lands Under Irrigation; Colfax County, New Mexico." Raton, NM: Maxwell Land Grant Company, n.d.

McPherson, M. E., and W. B. Matchett. *In the Matter of the Charges vs. Gov. S.B. Axtell and Other New Mexican Officials.* Privately printed, August 1877.

Meléndez, A. Gabriel. *Spanish-Language Newspapers in New Mexico, 1834–1958.* Tucson: University of Arizona Press, 2005.

Meyer, Doris. *Speaking for Themselves: Neomexicano Cultural Identity and the Spanish-Language Press.* Albuquerque: University of New Mexico Press, 1996.

Miller, Darlis A. *The California Column in New Mexico.* Albuquerque: University of New Mexico Press, 1982.

———. *Soldiers and Settlers: Military Supply in the Southwest, 1861–1885.* Albuquerque: University of New Mexico Press, 1989.

———. "William Logan Rynerson in New Mexico, 1862–1893." *New Mexico Historical Review* 48:2 (Spring 1973): 101–31.

Mitchell, Pablo. *Coyote Nation: Sexuality, Race, and Conquest in Modernizing New Mexico, 1880–1920.* Chicago: University of Chicago Press, 2005.

Montgomery, Charles. *The Spanish Redemption: Heritage, Power, and Loss on New Mexico's Upper Rio Grande.* Berkeley: University of California Press, 2002.

Montoya, María E. *Translating Property: The Maxwell Land Grant and the Conflict over Land in the American West, 1840–1900.* Berkeley: University of California Press, 2002.

Murphy, Lawrence R. *Lucien Bonaparte Maxwell: Napoleon of the Southwest.* Norman: University of Oklahoma Press, 1983.

———. *Philmont: A History of New Mexico's Cimarron Country.* Albuquerque: University of New Mexico Press, 1972.

Myrick, David F. *New Mexico's Railroads: An Historical Survey.* Golden: Colorado Railroad Museum, 1970.

Naegle, Conrad K. "The Rebellion in Grant County, New Mexico in 1876." *Arizona and the West* 10:3 (Autumn 1968): 225–40.

Newman, Simeon H., III. "The Santa Fe Ring: A Letter to the *New York Sun*." *Arizona and the West* 12:3 (Autumn 1970): 269–88.

Nieto-Phillips, John M. *The Language of Blood: The Making of Spanish-American Identity in New Mexico, 1880s–1930s.* Albuquerque: University of New Mexico Press, 2004.

Nolan, Frederick W. *The Life and Death of John Henry Tunstall.* Albuquerque: University of New Mexico Press, 1965.

———. *The Lincoln County War: A Documentary History.* Norman: University of Oklahoma Press, 1992.

Otero, Miguel Antonio. *My Life on the Frontier: 1882–1897.* Vol. 2 of Otero's personal memoir. Albuquerque: University of New Mexico Press, 1939.

———. *My Nine Years as Governor of the Territory of New Mexico, 1897–1906.* Albuquerque: University of New Mexico Press, 1940.

———. *The Real Billy the Kid, with New Light on the Lincoln County War.* New York: Rufus Rockwell Wilson, 1936.

Owen, Gordon R. *The Two Alberts: Fountain and Fall.* Las Cruces, NM: Yucca Tree Press, 1996.

Owens, Kenneth N. "Pattern and Structure in Western Territorial Politics." *Western Historical Quarterly* 1:4 (October 1970): 373–92.

Parsons, Chuck. *Clay Allison: Portrait of a Shootist.* Seagraves, TX: Pioneer Book Publishers, 1983.

Paul, Rodman Wilson. *Mining Frontiers of the Far West, 1848–1880.* New York: Holt, Rinehart and Winston, 1963.

Pearson, Jim Berry. *The Maxwell Land Grant.* Norman: University of Oklahoma Press, 1961.

Peters, James Stephen, Charles Norman Parsons, and Marianne Elizabeth Hall-Little. *Mace Bowman: Texas Feudist, Western Lawman.* Yorktown, TX: Hartmann Heritage Productions, 1996.

———. *Robert Clay Allison: Requiescat in Pace.* Santa Fe: Sunstone Press, 2008.

Poldervaart, Arie W. *Black-Robed Justice.* Santa Fe: Historical Society of New Mexico, 1948.

Pomeroy, Earl S. *The Territories and the United States, 1861–1890: Studies in Colonial Administration.* Philadelphia: University of Pennsylvania Press, 1947.

Prince, L. Bradford. "Claims to Statehood." *North American Review* 156:436 (March 1893): 346–54.

———. *New Mexico's Struggle for Statehood: Sixty Years of Effort to Obtain Self Government.* Santa Fe: New Mexican Printing Co., 1910.

Rasch, Philip J. *Gunsmoke in Lincoln County.* Laramie, WY: National Association for Outlaw and Lawman History, 1997.

———. "The People of the Territory of New Mexico vs. the Santa Fe Ring." *New Mexico Historical Review* 57:2 (1972): 185–202.

Reeve, Frank D. *History of New Mexico.* 3 vols. New York: Lewis Historical Publishing Co., 1961.

Remley, David. *Bell Ranch: Cattle Ranching in the Southwest, 1824–1947.* Albuquerque: University of New Mexico Press, 1993.

Rhodes, Eugene Manlove. *Beyond the Desert.* Boston: Houghton Mifflin Co., 1934.

———. *Bransford in Arcadia; Or, The Little Eohippus.* New York: Henry Holt and Co., 1914.

———. *Good Men and True.* New York: Henry Holt and Co., 1910.

———. *West Is West.* New York: H. K. Fly Co., 1917.

Rice, Otis K. *West Virginia: A History.* Lexington: University Press of Kentucky, 1985.

Ritch, W. G., ed. *The Legislative Blue Book of the Territory of New Mexico.* Santa Fe: Charles W. Greene, Public Printer, 1882.

Roberts, Gary L. *Death Comes for the Chief Justice: The Slough-Rynerson Quarrel and Political Violence in New Mexico.* Niwot: University Press of Colorado, 1990.

Rock, Michael J. "Anton Chico and Its Patent." In *Spanish and Mexican Land Grants in New Mexico and Colorado,* edited by John R. Van Ness and Christine M. Van Ness. Manhattan, KS: Sunflower University Press, 1980.

———. "Catron's Quiet Title Suit." Paper in files of the Center for Land Grant Studies, Guadalupita, NM, n.d.

Rosenbaum, Robert J. *Mexicano Resistance in the Southwest: "The Sacred Right of Self-Preservation."* Austin: University of Texas Press, 1981.

Rosenbaum, Robert J., and Robert W. Larson. "Mexicano Resistance to the Expropriation of Grant Lands in New Mexico." In *Land, Water, and Culture: New Perspectives on Hispanic Land Grants,* edited by Charles L. Briggs and John R. Van Ness, 269–310. Albuquerque: University of New Mexico Press, 1987.

Rothman, Hal K. *On Rims and Ridges: The Los Alamos Area Since 1880.* Lincoln: University of Nebraska Press, 1992.

Ruddy, Richard A. *Edmund G. Ross: Soldier, Senator, Abolitionist.* Albuquerque: University of New Mexico Press, 2013.

Samek, Hana. "No 'Bed of Roses': The Careers of Four Mescalero Indian Agents, 1871–1878." *New Mexico Historical Review* 57:2 (April 1982): 138–57.

Schiller, Mark. "Surveyor General George W. Julian: Reformer or Colonial Bureaucrat?" *La Jicarita News* 15:4 (April 2010).

Shadow, Robert D., and María Rodríguez Shadow. "From *Repartición* to Partition: A History of the Mora Land Grant, 1835–1916." *New Mexico Historical Review* 70:3 (July 1995): 257–98.

Sharpe, Jon. *Canyon O'Grady #10: The Great Land Swindle.* New York: Signet, 1990.

Sheldon, Lionel Allen. "Lionel A. Sheldon Biographical Material and Essay." Typescript autobiographical statement in the Bancroft Library, University of California, 1888.

Smith, Henry Nash. *Virgin Land: The American West as Symbol and Myth.* Cambridge, MA: Harvard University Press, 1950.

Sonnichsen, C. L. *From Hopalong to Hud: Thoughts on Western Fiction.* College Station: Texas A&M University Press, 1978.

———. *The Mescalero Apaches.* Norman: University of Oklahoma Press, 1958.

———. *Tucson: The Life and Times of an American City.* Norman: University of Oklahoma Press, 1982.

Springer, Frank. "Land Titles in New Mexico." Annual address of the retiring president of the New Mexico Bar Association, January 7, 1890. Santa Fe: New Mexican Printing, n.d.

Stanley, F. [Stanley Francis Louis Crocchiola]. *Ciudad Santa Fe: Territorial Days, 1846–1912.* Pampa, TX: Pampa Print Shop, 1965.

Stratton, David H. *The Memoirs of Albert B. Fall.* Monograph No. 15. El Paso: Texas Western Press, 1966.

Stratton, Porter A. *The Territorial Press of New Mexico, 1834–1912.* Albuquerque: University of New Mexico Press, 1969.

Taylor, Morris F. *O. P. McMains and the Maxwell Land Grant Conflict.* Tucson: University of Arizona Press, 1979.

———. "Stephen W. Dorsey, Speculator-Cattleman." *New Mexico Historical Review* 49:1 (January 1974): 27–48.

Theisen, Lee Scott. "Frank Warner Angel's Notes on New Mexico Territory, 1878." *Arizona and the West* 18:4 (Winter 1976): 333–70.

Tijerina, Reies López. *They Called Me "King Tiger."* Translated and edited by José Angel Gutiérrez. Houston: Arte Público Press, 2000.

Tobias, Henry J. *A History of the Jews in New Mexico.* Albuquerque: University of New Mexico Press, 1990.

Torrez, Robert J. "'El Bornes': La Tierra Amarilla and T. D. Burns." *New Mexico Historical Review* 56:2 (April 1981).

Townsend, David. *The 47th Star: New Mexico's Struggle for Statehood.* Alamogordo, NM: Alamogordo Statehood Centennial Committee, 2012.

Twain, Mark, and Charles Dudley Warner. *The Gilded Age: A Tale of To-day.* Hartford, CT: American Publishing Co., 1873.

Twitchell, Ralph Emerson. *The Leading Facts of New Mexican History.* Vols. 1–5. Cedar Rapids, IA: Torch Press, 1912–1917.

———. *Old Santa Fe: The Story of New Mexico's Ancient Capital.* Santa Fe: Santa Fe New Mexican Publishing Corp., 1925.

Utley, Robert M. *Billy the Kid: A Short and Violent Life.* Lincoln: University of Nebraska Press, 1989.

———. *High Noon in Lincoln County: Violence on the Western Frontier.* Albuquerque: University of New Mexico Press, 1987.

Van Ness, John R., and Christine M. Van Ness, eds. *Spanish and Mexican Land Grants in New Mexico and Colorado.* Manhattan, KS: Sunflower University Press, 1980.

Wagoner, Jay J. *Arizona Territory, 1863–1912: A Political History.* Tucson: University of Arizona Press, 1970.

Wallace, Susan E. *The Land of the Pueblos.* New York: John B. Alden, 1889.

Walter, Paul A. F. *Banking in New Mexico Before the Railroad Came.* New York: Newcomen Society in North America, 1955.

Waters, L. L. *Steel Trails to Santa Fe.* Lawrence: University of Kansas Press, 1950.

Western Journal and Civilian. Vol. 7, new series. St. Louis: M. Tarver and H. Cobb, 1855.

Westphall, Victor. "The American Valley Murders." *Ayer y Hoy en Taos* 9 (Fall 1989): 3–8.

———. "The American Valley Murders." Unpublished manuscript, n.d., courtesy of Walter Westphall. Copy in files of the author.

———. *Mercedes Reales: Hispanic Land Grants of the Upper Rio Grande Region.* Albuquerque: University of New Mexico Press, 1983.

———. *The Public Domain in New Mexico, 1854–1891.* Albuquerque: University of New Mexico Press, 1965.

———. "Thomas Benton Catron: A Historical Defense." *New Mexico Historical Review* 63:1 (January 1988): 43–57.

———. *Thomas Benton Catron and His Era.* Tucson: University of Arizona Press, 1973.

Williams, Jerry L. *New Mexico in Maps.* 2nd ed. Albuquerque: University of New Mexico Press, 1986.

Wilson, John P. *Merchants, Guns and Money: The Story of Lincoln County and Its Wars.* Santa Fe: Museum of New Mexico Press, 1987.

Government Documents

Acts of the Legislative Assembly of the Territory of New Mexico, Twenty-Second Session. Santa Fe: Manderfield and Tucker, Public Printers, 1876.

Angel, Frank Warner. *In the Matter of the Examination of the Charges Against C. F. Godfroy, U.S. Indian Agent, Mescalero Apaches, N.M.* October 2, 1878. Records of the U.S. Bureau of Indian Affairs, NARA, RG 75.

———. *Report and Testimony in the Matter of Charges Against Samuel B. Axtell, Governor of New Mexico.* October 3, 1878. Records of the Office of the Secretary of the Interior, NARA, RG 48.

———. *Report as to the Death of John H. Tunstall, and Relative to Troubles in Lincoln County, New Mexico.* October 7, 1878. Records of the U.S. Department of Justice, NARA, RG 60.

Benavides, David, and Ryan Golten. "Report to the New Mexico Attorney General—A Response to the GAO's 2004 Report, *Treaty of Guadalupe Hidalgo: Findings and Possible Options Regarding Longstanding Community Land Grant Claims in New Mexico*. Office of the Attorney General of New Mexico, August 14, 2008.

Census of Agriculture. Washington, D.C.: U.S. Department of Agriculture, 1880, 1890.

Council Journal, 22nd Legislative Assembly, Territory of New Mexico, Territorial Archives of New Mexico, New Mexico State Records Center and Archives, Santa Fe, 1875–1876.

Effect of Federal Programs on Rural America. Hearings Before the Subcommittee on Rural Development of the Committee on Agriculture, House of Representatives, 90th Congress, 1st Sess., June–July, 1967. Washington, D.C.: U.S. Government Printing Office, 1967.

Fraudulent Acquisition to Titles of Lands in New Mexico (Letter from the Secretary of the Interior, Transmitting Copies of Reports upon the Subject of). Senate Executive Document No. 106, 48th Congress, 2nd Sess., March 3, 1885.

General Accounting Office. *Treaty of Guadalupe Hidalgo: Findings and Possible Options Regarding Longstanding Community Land Grant Claims in New Mexico*. Washington, D.C.: GAO, 2004.

House Journal, 22nd Legislative Assembly, Territory of New Mexico, Territorial Archives of New Mexico, New Mexico State Records Center and Archives, Santa Fe, 1875–1876.

Inventory of the County Archives of New Mexico. No. 9: *Grant County*. Albuquerque: New Mexico Historical Records Survey, 1941.

Official Proceedings, Trans-Mississippi Commercial Congress. 18th Sess., November 19–22, 1907, Muskogee, OK. N.p.: Phoenix Printing Co., 1907.

Papers and Testimony in the Contested-Election Case of F. A. Manzanares vs. T. Luna, from the Territory of New Mexico. Washington, D.C.: U.S. House of Representatives, 48th Congress, 1st Sess. Miscellaneous Document No. 17, 1884.

Poverty, Equal Opportunity and Full Employment. Hearings Before the Subcommittee on Equal Opportunities, Committee on Education and Labor, House of Representatives, 94th Congress, 1st Sess., May 1975. Washington, D.C.: U.S. Government Printing Office, 1975.

Prince, L. Bradford. *Report of the Governor of New Mexico to the Secretary of the Interior*. Washington, D.C.: U.S. Government Printing Office, 1890.

Pueblo de Cochiti Lands Bill. Hearing Before the Select Committee on Indian Affairs, United States Senate, 98th Congress, 2nd Sess., March 1984. Washington, D.C.: U.S. Government Printing Office, 1984.

Sheldon, Lionel Allen. *Report of the Governor of New Mexico to the Secretary of the Interior for the Year 1883*. Washington, D.C.: U.S. Government Printing Office, 1883.

Status of Community Land Grants in Northern New Mexico. Oversight Hearing Before the Subcommittee on General Oversight and Investigations of the Committee on Interior and Insular Affairs, House of Representatives, 100th Congress, 2nd Sess., October 1988. Washington, D.C.: U.S. Government Printing Office, 1989.

Walker, Francis A. *A Compendium of the Ninth Census, June 1, 1870*. Washington, D.C.: U.S. Government Printing Office, 1872.

———. *A Compendium of the Tenth Census, June 1, 1880*. Washington, D.C.: U.S. Government Printing Office, 1883.

White, Koch, Kelley, and McCarthy, Attorneys at Law. *Land Title Study*. Santa Fe: New Mexico State Planning Office, 1971.

Zuni Land Claims; and 1937 Housing Act. Hearing Before the Select Committee on Indian Affairs, United States Senate, 101st Congress, 2nd Sess., May 1990. Washington, D.C.: U.S. Government Printing Office, 1990.

Newspapers and Newsletters

Albuquerque Daily Journal (Albuquerque, NM), 1884.
Albuquerque Evening Democrat (Albuquerque, NM), 1884.
Albuquerque Morning Journal (Albuquerque, NM), 1883–1911.
Albuquerque Review (Albuquerque, NM), 1878.
Arizona Citizen (Tucson, AZ), 1871.
Borderer (Las Cruces, NM), 1871–1872.
Boston Herald (Boston, MA), 1883–1884.
Chicago Herald (Chicago, IL), 1892.
Chicago Tribune (Chicago, IL), 1895.
Cimarron News and Press, (Cimarron, NM) 1878.
Civil Service Record (Boston, MA), 1892.
Colorado Daily Chieftain (Pueblo, CO), 1872–1875.
Colorado Transcript (Golden, CO), 1872.
Defensor del Pueblo, El (Albuquerque, NM), 1891.
Deming Headlight (Deming, NM), 1891.
Denver Daily Tribune (Denver, CO), 1878.
Denver Mirror (Denver, CO), 1874.
Era Southwestern (Santa Fe, NM), 1880.
Gallup Independent (Gallup, NM), 1972.
Golden Retort (Golden, NM), 1883–1884.
Grant County Herald (Silver City, NM), 1876–1878.
Herald and Southwest (Silver City, NM), 1880.
Hillsborough Advocate (Hillsboro, NM), 1891.
La Jicarita News (Chamisal, NM), 2010.
Las Vegas Daily Optic (Las Vegas, NM), 1884–1897.
Las Vegas Gazette (Las Vegas, NM), 1880.
Las Vegas Weekly Mail (Las Vegas, NM), 1872.

Mesilla Valley Independent (Mesilla, NM), 1877–1878.
New York Sun (New York, NY), 1875–1876.
New York Times (New York, NY), 1876–1909.
New York World (New York, NY), 1893–1895.
Raton Guard (Raton, NM), 1882.
Republican Review (Albuquerque, NM), 1873.
Rio Grande Republican (Las Cruces, NM), 1883–1885.
Rocky Mountain Sentinel (Santa Fe, NM), 1878–1879.
Santa Fe Daily New Mexican (Santa Fe, NM), 1868–1921.
Santa Fe Daily Sun (Santa Fe, NM), 1891.
Santa Fe Democrat (Santa Fe, NM), 1881.
Santa Fe Herald (Santa Fe, NM), 1888.
Santa Fe New Mexican (Santa Fe, NM), 1899.
Santa Fe New Mexican and Review (Santa Fe, NM), 1883.
Santa Fe New Mexican Review (Santa Fe, NM), 1883–1894.
Santa Fe Sun (Santa Fe, NM), 1890.
Santa Fe Weekly Gazette (Santa Fe, NM), 1868.
Santa Fe Weekly New Mexican (Santa Fe, NM), 1871–1886.
Southwest Sentinel (Silver City, NM), 1892.
St. Louis Globe-Democrat (St. Louis, MO), 1884.
Syracuse Post-Standard (Syracuse, NY), 1899.
Thirty-Four (Las Cruces, NM), 1880.
Thunderbolt (Elizabethtown, NM), 1871.
Wheeling Intelligencer (Wheeling, WV), 1895.

Motion Pictures

Pat Garrett and Billy the Kid. 1973, Metro-Goldwyn-Mayer. Director: Sam Peckinpah.
Young Guns. 1988, Morgan Creek Productions/Twentieth Century-Fox. Director: Christopher Cain.

Court Decisions

Farish et al. v. New Mexico Mining Company, 21 Pac. 654 (1889).
In Re Renehan, 19 N.M. 640 (1914).
Moore v. Huntington, 84 U.S. 417 (1873).
United States v. San Pedro and Cañon del Agua Co., 17 Pac. 337 (1888).
San Pedro and Cañon del Agua Co. v. United States, 146 U.S. 120 (1892).
Priest v. Town of Las Vegas, 16 N.M. 692 (1911).
Rodriguez v. La Cueva Ranch Co., 17 N.M. 246 (1912).
Tameling v. United States Freehold and Emigration Company, 93 U.S. 644 (1877).

Digital Resources

Ginley, Caitlin. *Grading the Nation: How Accountable Is Your State?* State Integrity Investigation, Center for Public Integrity, March 19, 2012. www.publicintegrity. org.

Shadow, Robert D., and Marie Rodriguez Shadow. "A History of the Mora Land Grant, 1835–1916." New Mexico Digital History Project, Office of the State Historian, New Mexico State Records Center and Archives, 2004–2010. http://www .newmexicohistory.org/filedetails_docs.php?fileID=22561.

INDEX

Page numbers in italic text indicate illustrations.